Grades 9 10 11 12

Teacher's Guide

Great Source Education Group
a Houghton Mifflin Company
Wilmington, Massachusetts

www.greatsource.com

AUTHORS

Jim Burke
Author
Burlingame High School, Burlingame, California
Jim Burke, author of *Reading Reminders: Tools, Tips, and Techniques* and *The English Teacher's Companion,* has taught high school English for 13 years. His most recent books, *Tools for Thought* and *Illuminating Texts: How to Teach Students to Read the World,* further explore reading and those strategies that can help all students succeed in high school. He was the recipient of the California Reading Association's Hall of Fame Award in 2001 and the Conference on English Leadership's Exemplary English Leadership Award in 2000. He currently serves on the National Board of Professional Teaching Standards for English Language Arts.

Ron Klemp
Contributing Author
Los Angeles Unified School District, Los Angeles, California
Ron Klemp is the Coordinator of Reading for the Los Angeles Unified School District. He has taught Reading, English, and Social Studies and was a middle school Dean of Discipline. He is also a coordinator/facilitator at the Secondary Practitioner Center, a professional development program in the Los Angeles Unified School District. He has been teaching at California State University, Cal Lutheran University, and National University.

Wendell Schwartz
Contributing Author
Adlai Stevenson High School, Lincolnshire, Illinois
Wendell Schwartz has been a teacher of English for 36 years. For the last 24 years he also has served as the Director of Communication Arts at Adlai Stevenson High School. He has taught gifted middle school students for the last 12 years and graduate-level courses for National Louis University in Evanston, Illinois.

Editorial: Developed by Nieman Inc. with Phil LaLeike

Design: Ronan Design: Christine Ronan, Sean O'Neill, Maria Mariottini, and Victoria Mullins

Illustrations: Mike McConnell

Printed in the United States of America
International Standard Book Number: 0-669-49500-X
1 2 3 4 5 6 7 8 9—VHG—08 07 06 05 04 03 02

READERS AND REVIEWERS

Dr. Leslie Adams
Division of Language Arts and Reading
Miami, FL

Ceci Aguilar
Telles Academy
El Paso, TX

Lynn Beale
Irvin High School
El Paso, TX

Jeannie Bosley
West Education
San Francisco, CA

John Brassil
Mt. Ararat High School
Topsham, ME

Doug Buehl
Madison East High School
Madison, WI

Maria Bunge
Austin High School
El Paso, TX

Roseanne Comfort
Westview High School
Portland, OR

Paula Congdon
Rockwood School District
Eureka, MO

Bonnie Davis
Education Park
St. Louis, MO

Lela DeToye
Southern Illinois University
Edwardsville, IL

Kathy Dorholt
New York Mills High School
New York Mills, MN

Steve Edwards
Central High School
Clearwater, FL

Lyla Fox
Loy Norrix High School
Kalamazoo, MI

Jodi Gardner
Assata High School
Milwaukee, WI

Karen Gibson
Appleton North High School
Appleton, WI

Laura Griffo
Jefferson Co. International
Irondale, AL

Carol Hallman
Ross Local School District
Hamilton, OH

Kerry Hansen
Dominican High School
Whitefish Bay, WI

Carol Sue Harless
DeKalb County School System
Stone Mountain, GA

Rebecca Hartman
Penn-Harris High School
Mishawaka, IN

Christine Heerlein
Rockwood Summit High School
Fenton, MO

Vicky Hoag
Fresno Co. Office of Education
Fresno, CA

Jack Hobbs
San Marcos High School
Santa Barbara, CA

Eileen Johnson
Edina Public Schools
Edina, MN

Laurel Key
Central High School
West Allis, WI

Michelle Knotts
Sinagua High School
Flagstaff, AZ

Kathleen Lask
Pattonville Senior High School
Maryland Heights, MO

Jean Lawson
Coronado High School
El Paso, TX

Jean Lifford
Dedham High School
Dedham, MA

Tom Lueschow
University of WI–Whitewater
Whitewater, WI

Maria Manning
Dade County Public Schools
Miami, FL

Jean-Marie Marlin
Mountain Brook High School
Birmingham, AL

Karen McMillan
Miami-Dade County Schools
Miami, FL

Judith Lynn Momirov
Buckeye Trail High School
Lore City, OH

Lisa Muller
Castle High School
Newburgh, IN

David P. Noskin
Adlai E. Stevenson High School
Lincolnshire, IL

Cheryl Nuciforo
Enlarged City School District of Troy
Troy, NY

Carolyn Novy
Chicago, IL

Rebecca Romine
Traverse City Central High School
Kewadin, MI

Jeannie Scott
Colorado Springs Dist. 11
Colorado Springs, CO

Susie Schneider
El Paso School District
El Paso, TX

Cathleen Search
Traverse City West High School
Traverse City, MI

Judy Smith
Rockwood School District
Eureka, MO

Leslie Somers
Miami-Dade Public Schools
Miami, FL

Sharon Straub
Joel E. Ferris High School
Spokane, WA

Michael Thompson
Minnesota Dept. of Children, Families, and Learning
Roseville, MN

Mary Ann Warnoff
Eureka High School
Glendale, MO

Mary Weber
Waterford Kettering High School
Waterford, MI

Nancy Wilson
Gladstone High School
Gladstone, OR

Susan Wilson
South Orange Middle School
South Orange, NJ

Sandy Wojcik
Downers Grove High School South
Downers Grove, IL

Fred Wolff
Educational Consultant
Lee, NH

Table of Contents

Lessons

THEME

DIRECTOR
Understanding
Theme

MORE
LOOK
BUY
SALE!
MORE IN STOCK
WEEKEND WOW
YOU!
You've WON
Last chance!
NEW

Guide to the Program

Teach with the *Reader's Handbook* program in three easy steps. First, use the *Teacher's Guide* to plan how to teach the lessons in the handbook. Then, teach the lesson using other teaching resources, such as the *Lesson Plan Books*, *Overhead Transparencies*, *Content Area Guides*, or the website, to supplement the lesson. Then, practice with the *Student Applications Books*, *Content Area Packages*, website, or through independent practice using your own texts.

Program Components

The *Reader's Handbook* program includes the following materials in addition to the handbook:

Teacher's Guide

grades 9–12

Lesson Plan Books

grade 9

grade 10

grade 11

grade 12

Test Book

grades 9–12

Student Applications Books

Teacher's Editions available

grade 9

grade 10

grade 11

grade 12

Overhead Transparencies

grades 9–12

Content Area Packages

grades 9–12

Website

www.greatsource.com/rehand/

Teacher's Guide

The *Teacher's Guide* walks through each lesson in the *Reader's Handbook,* highlights what to teach, and suggests ways to extend lessons.

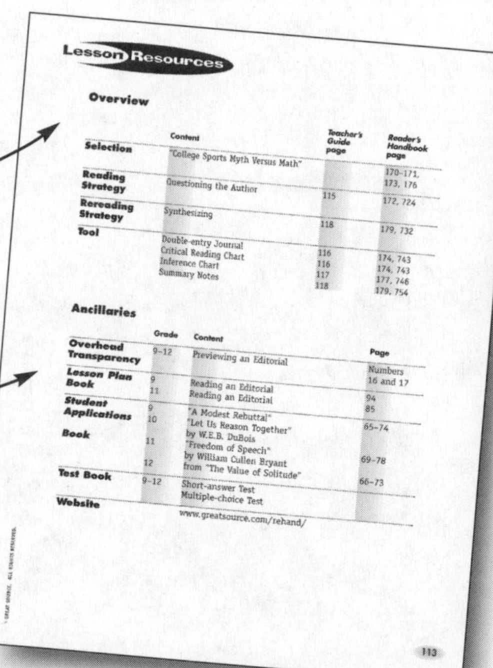

Lesson Resources

Overview

	Content	Teacher's Guide page	Reader's Handbook page
Selection	"College Sports Myth Versus Math"		170–171, 173, 176
Reading Strategy	Questioning the Author	115	172, 724
Rereading Strategy	Synthesizing	118	179, 732
Tool	Double-entry Journal Critical Reading Chart Inference Chart Summary Notes	116 116 117 118	174, 743 174, 743 177, 746 179, 754

Ancillaries

	Grade	Content	Page
Overhead Transparency	9–12	Previewing an Editorial	Numbers 16 and 17
Lesson Plan Book	9 11	Reading an Editorial Reading an Editorial	94 85
Student Applications Book	9 10 11 12	"A Modest Rebuttal" "Let Us Reason Together" by W.E.B. DuBois "Freedom of Speech" by William Cullen Bryant from "The Value of Solitude"	65–74 69–78 66–73
Test Book	9–12	Short-answer Test Multiple-choice Test	
Website		www.greatsource.com/rehand/	

113

The **Overview** chart lists the literature, strategies, and tools taught in each lesson.

The **Ancillaries** chart shows where to find additional materials to supplement the lesson.

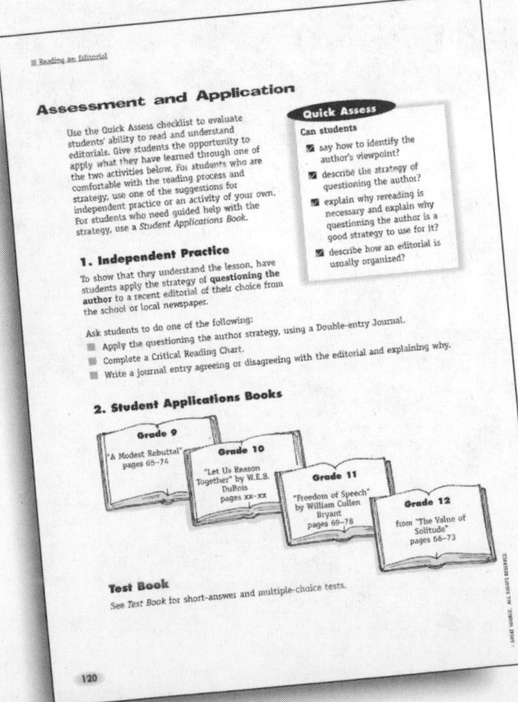

Reading an Editorial

Assessment and Application

Use the Quick Assess checklist to evaluate students' ability to read and understand editorials. Give students the opportunity to apply what they have learned through one of the two activities below. For students who are comfortable with the reading process and strategy, use one of the suggestions for independent practice or an activity of your own. For students who need guided help with the strategy, use a *Student Applications Book.*

Quick Assess

Can students

- say how to identify the author's viewpoint?
- describe the strategy of questioning the author?
- explain why rereading is necessary and explain why questioning the author is a good strategy to use for it?
- describe how an editorial is usually organized?

1. Independent Practice

To show that they understand the lesson, have students apply the strategy of **questioning the author** to a recent editorial of their choice from the school or local newspaper.

Ask students to do one of the following:

- Apply the questioning the author strategy, using a Double-entry Journal.
- Complete a Critical Reading Chart.
- Write a journal entry agreeing or disagreeing with the editorial and explaining why.

2. Student Applications Books

Test Book

See *Test Book* for short-answer and multiple-choice tests.

120

At the end of each lesson, you assess and then have students apply the strategies either a) independently or b) in guided practice in the *Student Applications Books*.

Lesson Plan Book

The *Lesson Plan Book* (one per grade level) gives day-by-day and week-by-week lesson plans. These books show how to use the *Reader's Handbook* to set up a complete reading curriculum in high schools.

The curriculum plan suggests the year-long plan for teaching reading at each grade level.

Individual lesson plans outline weekly and daily lessons.

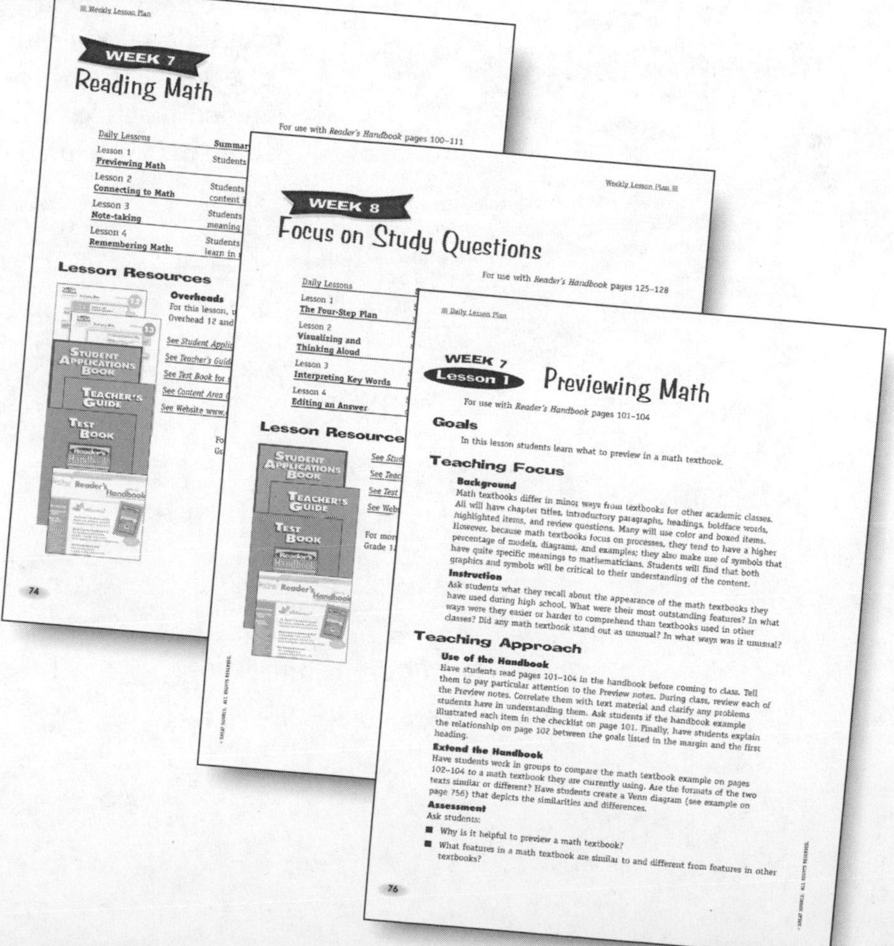

Weekly Lesson Plan

WEEK 7

Reading Math

For use with *Reader's Handbook* pages 100–111

Weekly Lesson Plan

WEEK 8

Focus on Study Questions

For use with *Reader's Handbook* pages 125–128

Daily Lesson Plan

WEEK 7 Lesson 1

Previewing Math

For use with *Reader's Handbook* pages 101–104

Goals

In this lesson students learn what to preview in a math textbook.

Teaching Focus

Background

Math textbooks differ in minor ways from textbooks for other academic classes. All will have chapter titles, introductory paragraphs, headings, boldface words, highlighted items, and review questions. Many will use color and boxed items. However, because math textbooks focus on processes, they tend to have a higher percentage of models, diagrams, and examples; they also make use of symbols that have quite specific meanings to mathematicians. Students will find that both graphics and symbols will be critical to their understanding of the content.

Instruction

Ask students what they recall about the appearance of the math textbooks they have used during high school. What were their most outstanding features? In what ways were they easier or harder to comprehend than textbooks used in other classes? Did any math textbook stand out as unusual? In what ways was it unusual?

Teaching Approach

Use of the Handbook

Have students read pages 101–104 in the handbook before coming to class. Tell them to pay particular attention to the Preview notes. During class, review each of the Preview notes. Correlate them with text material and clarify any problems students have in understanding them. Ask students if the handbook example illustrated each item in the checklist on page 101. Finally, have students explain the relationship on page 102 between the goals listed in the margin and the first heading.

Extend the Handbook

Have students work in groups to compare the math textbook example on pages 102–104 to a math textbook they are currently using. Are the formats of the two texts similar or different? Have students create a Venn diagram (see example on page 756) that depicts the similarities and differences.

Assessment

Ask students:

- Why is it helpful to preview a math textbook?
- What features in a math textbook are similar to and different from features in other textbooks?

76

Student Applications Book

The *Student Applications Book* (one per grade level) extends the lessons with a new selection for students to work through.

NAME

FOR USE WITH PAGES 210–224

Reading a Memoir

In a memoir, a writer describes some important events from his or her life. The writer reflects on the meaning of those events and their influence.

Before Reading

Here, you'll use the reading process and the strategy of synthesizing to help you read an excerpt from Harriet Jacobs's memoir, *Incidents in the Life of a Slave Girl.*

A Set a Purpose

Your purpose in reading a memoir is twofold. First, you need to understand the life experiences the writer describes. Second, you need to form your own impression of the writer and the people, places, times, and events described.

- **To set your purpose, ask two questions about the writer of the memoir.**

Directions: Ask two questions about Harriet Jacobs or her memoir.

Purpose question #1

Purpose question #2

B Preview

After you set your purpose, begin your preview of the memoir. Look carefully at the front and back covers of the book. What information can you find that helps you meet your purpose?

Directions: Preview the front and back covers of *Incidents in the Life of a Slave Girl* on the next page. Make notes on the stickies.

94

Lessons let students apply the reading strategies and tools to a new selection, give them guided practice, and help you to assess their understanding.

The *Student Applications Book Teacher's Edition* includes suggested answers.

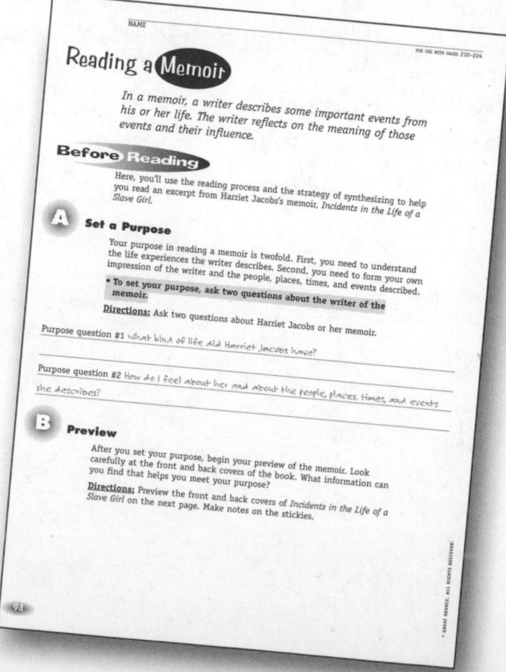

NAME

FOR USE WITH PAGES 210–224

Reading a Memoir

In a memoir, a writer describes some important events from his or her life. The writer reflects on the meaning of those events and their influence.

Before Reading

Here, you'll use the reading process and the strategy of synthesizing to help you read an excerpt from Harriet Jacobs's memoir, *Incidents in the Life of a Slave Girl.*

A Set a Purpose

Your purpose in reading a memoir is twofold. First, you need to understand the life experiences the writer describes. Second, you need to form your own impression of the writer and the people, places, times, and events described.

- **To set your purpose, ask two questions about the writer of the memoir.**

Directions: Ask two questions about Harriet Jacobs or her memoir.

Purpose question #1 What kind of life did Harriet Jacobs have?

Purpose question #2 How do I feel about her and about the people, places, times, and events she describes?

B Preview

After you set your purpose, begin your preview of the memoir. Look carefully at the front and back covers of the book. What information can you find that helps you meet your purpose?

Directions: Preview the front and back covers of *Incidents in the Life of a Slave Girl* on the next page. Make notes on the stickies.

94

Overhead Transparencies

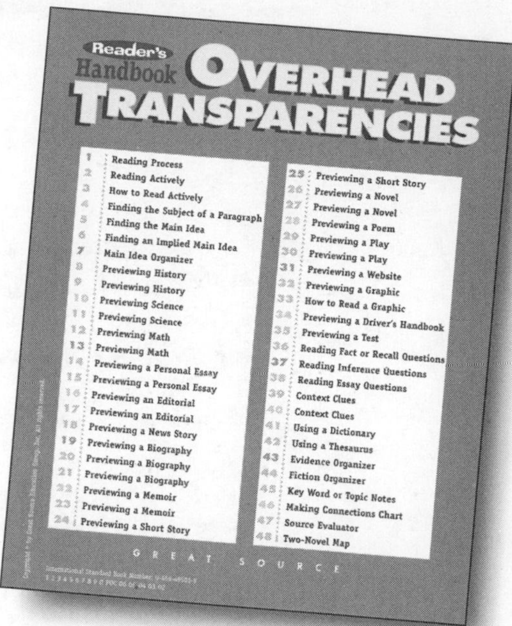

The *Overhead Transparencies* display key parts of the handbook to help in-class teaching of important concepts, such as the reading process and previewing different kinds of reading.

Test Book

The *Test Book* contains two kinds of tests for each lesson in the *Reader's Handbook*.

Short-Answer Test

NAME

The Reading Process

1. What are the three main stages of the reading process?

NAME Multiple-choice

The Reading Process

1. Which item below is not a main stage of the reading process?
   a. Set a Purpose
   b. Preview
   c. Draft
   d. Connect

2. What is a characteristic of previewing?
   a. Reading the supporting details
   b. Browsing the index
   c. Underlining and highlighting
   d. Quickly skimming the material

3. What step have you applied when you compare a reading to your own life?
   a. Connect
   b. Preview
   c. Reflect
   d. Reread

4. What is a characteristic of rereading?
   a. Rereading clarifies confusing parts of the reading.
   b. Rereading requires a new reading purpose.
   c. Rereading involves memorizing key passages.
   d. Rereading is often a lengthy process.

5. What is an effective way to remember the material you have read?
   a. Read the material only once.
   b. Read in a noisy environment.
   c. Personalize the material and make it your own.
   d. Reread all of the material word for word.

Assess students' understanding of the handbook lessons through short-answer tests and multiple-choice quizzes.

Content Area Packages

Each package contains the following:

- A *Content Area Guide*
- Overhead Transparencies
- A *Reader's Handbook*

The *Content Area Guides* contain lesson plans and activities designed to build reading skills in science, math, and social studies.

Website

The *Reader's Handbook* website contains a preview of the *Reader's Handbook* program as well as numerous resources both for teachers and students.

The *Teacher Center* has a lesson plan library, information on how to apply for grants, a reading bibliography, and web resources.

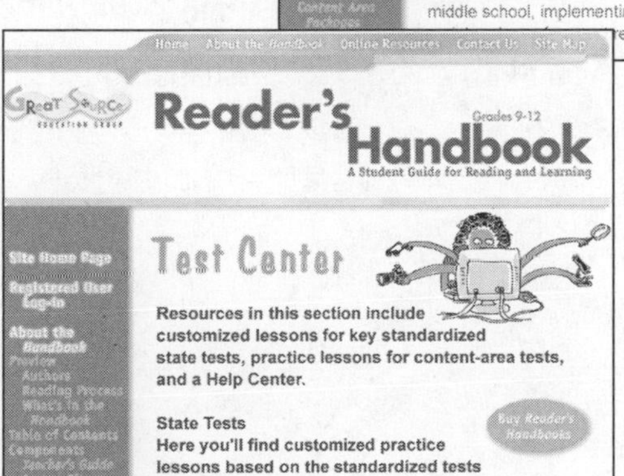

The *Test Center* has state-specific lessons to help prepare for standardized tests.

Reading Strategies Overview

Handbook Lesson	Selection	Reading Strategy	Rereading Strategy
Reading History	"The Rise of Islam"	Note-taking	Using Graphic Organizers
Reading Science	"Biology in Your World"	Outlining	Note-taking
Reading Math	"Numbers and Number Operations"	Visualizing and Thinking Aloud	Note-taking
Reading a Personal Essay	"The Indian Dog" by N. Scott Momaday	Outlining	Questioning the Author
Reading an Editorial	"College Sports Myth Versus Math"	Questioning the Author	Synthesizing
Reading a News Story	"Violent Images May Alter Kids' Brain Activity"	Reading Critically	Summarizing
Reading a Biography	*Rickey & Robinson* by John C. Chalberg	Looking for Cause and Effect	Outlining
Reading a Memoir	*Out of Africa* by Isak Dinesen	Synthesizing	Visualizing and Thinking Aloud
Reading a Short Story	"Powder" by Tobias Wolff	Synthesizing	Close Reading
Reading a Novel	*All Quiet on the Western Front* by Erich Maria Remarque	Using Graphic Organizers	Synthesizing
Reading a Poem	"Sonnet 43" by Elizabeth Barrett Browning	Close Reading	Paraphrasing
Reading a Play	*The Miracle Worker* by William Gibson	Summarizing	Visualizing and Thinking Aloud
Reading a Website	Google search engine and "National Gallery of Art" site	Reading Critically	Skimming
Reading a Graphic	"Digital Kids"	Paraphrasing	Reading Critically
Reading a Driver's Handbook	from *Rules of the Road*	Skimming	Visualizing and Thinking Aloud
Reading Tests	"The Laugher" by Heinrich Böll	Skimming	Visualizing and Thinking Aloud

Focus Lesson	Selection	Reading Strategy/Tools
Focus on Foreign Language	"Vocabulario y gramática"	Note-taking
Focus on Science Concepts	"The Scientific Process"	Outlining
Focus on Study Questions	Sample Study Questions	Visualizing and Thinking Aloud
Focus on Word Problems	Sample Problem	Visualizing and Thinking Aloud
Focus on Persuasive Writing	"Appearances Are Destructive"	Reading Critically
Focus on Speeches	"Blood, Toil, Tears, and Sweat" by Winston Churchill	Reading Critically
Focus on Plot	from "Blues Ain't No Mockinbird" by Toni Cade Bambara	Using Graphic Organizers
Focus on Setting	from *Cry, the Beloved Country* by Alan Paton	Close Reading
Focus on Characters	from "The Necklace" by Guy de Maupassant	Using Graphic Organizers
Focus on Theme	*Jasmine* by Bharati Mukherjee	Using Graphic Organizers
Focus on Dialogue	from "Blues Ain't No Mockinbird"	Close Reading
Focus on Comparing and Contrasting	*David Copperfield* and *Great Expectations* by Charles Dickens	Using Graphic Organizers
Focus on Language	"Identity" by Julio Noboa Polanco	Close Reading
Focus on Meaning	"Ex-Basketball Player" by John Updike	Close Reading
Focus on Sound and Structure	"Suicide in the Trenches" by Siegfried Sassoon	Close Reading
Focus on Language	from *The Miracle Worker* by William Gibson	Inference Chart
Focus on Theme	from *The Miracle Worker*	Topic and Theme Organizer
Focus on Shakespeare	from *Romeo and Juliet* by William Shakespeare	Using Graphic Organizers
Focus on Reading Instructions	Cell Phone Instructions DVD Player Instructions	Close Reading
Focus on Reading for Work	Memo on Workplace Safety Job Description Work Schedule	Skimming
Focus on English Tests	*A Tale of Two Cities* by Charles Dickens	Skimming
Focus on Writing Tests	Sample Writing Test	Main Idea Organizer
Focus on Standardized Tests	Sample Questions	Think Aloud
Focus on History Tests	Sample History Test	Think Aloud
Focus on Math Tests	Sample Math Test	Visualizing and Thinking Aloud
Focus on Science Tests	Sample Science Test	Visualizing and Thinking Aloud

How to Use a

Teacher's Guide Lesson

Begin by reading the **Goals** for the lesson to the class or by asking a student to read them.

A **Background** section helps you connect the lesson to students' own knowledge.

Introduce the lesson with an **Opening Activity**.

Reading History

Getting Ready

Goals

Here students read a selection called "The Rise of Islam." This lesson will help them to learn to:

- read history
- use the strategy of note-taking
- see the way history textbooks are often organized

Background

Help students connect this lesson with their existing knowledge by asking them to:

- talk about how reading history is different from reading science books, math books, and literature
- name some special characteristics of history textbooks, including the different parts of these books
- discuss why reading a history textbook is sometimes difficult or uninteresting
- say what they like about reading history

Opening Activity

Using an example of a current history textbook, show students the different features of the book. Emphasize that a good history book not only tells *what* happened, *when* and *where* it happened, and *who* was involved, but *why* something happened. Also emphasize that looking for the 5 W's and the H (*who, what, when, where, why,* and *how*) while reading a history textbook can help students read faster and with better comprehension.

45

The **Overview** chart lists the content, strategies, and tools in the lesson.

The **Ancillaries** chart lists all supplementary materials available for the lesson.

Reading History

Lesson Resources

Overview

	Content	Teacher's Guide page	Reader's Handbook page
Selection	"The Rise of Islam"		75–79, 83, 84
Reading Strategy	Note-taking	48	80, 81, 718
Rereading Strategy	Using Graphic Organizers	51	85, 86, 734
Tool	5 W's and H Organizer Key Word or Topic Notes Web	48 48 51	80, 82, 745 81, 82, 746 86, 757

Ancillaries

	Grade	Content	Page
Overhead Transparency	9–12	Previewing History	Numbers 8 and 9
Lesson Plan Book	9 10 11 12	Reading History Reading History Reading History Reading History	64 64 55 55
Student Applications Book	9 10 11 12	"The Supreme Court" "Mesoamerican Civilization: The Olmec" "World War I Begins: The First Three Years" "The Cold War Begins"	20–30 21–31 22–32
Test Book	9–12	Short-answer Test Multiple-choice Test	
Website		www.greatsource.com/rehand/	
Content Area Guide		This lesson appears in the *Content Area Guide: Social Studies.*	

46

Before Reading

Use the questions in the **Setting a Purpose** section to give students a clear purpose for their reading.

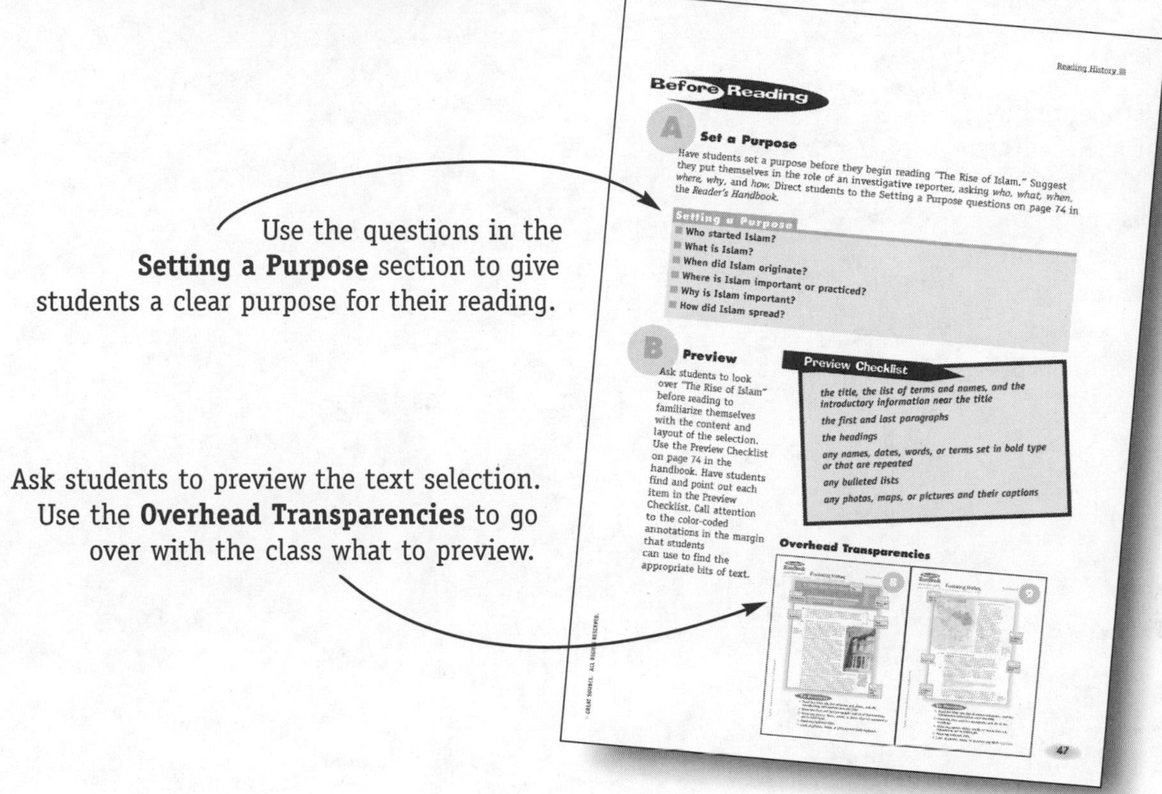

Reading History

Before Reading

A Set a Purpose

Have students set a purpose before they begin reading "The Rise of Islam." Suggest they put themselves in the role of an investigative reporter, asking *who, what, when, where, why,* and *how.* Direct students to the Setting a Purpose questions on page 74 in the *Reader's Handbook.*

Setting a Purpose

- **Who started Islam?**
- **What is Islam?**
- **When did Islam originate?**
- **Where is Islam important or practiced?**
- **Why is Islam important?**
- **How did Islam spread?**

B Preview

Ask students to look over "The Rise of Islam" before reading to familiarize themselves with the content and layout of the selection. Use the Preview Checklist on page 74 in the handbook. Have students find and point out each item in the Preview Checklist. Call attention to the color-coded annotations in the margin that students can use to find the appropriate bits of text.

Preview Checklist

the title, the list of terms and names, and the introductory information near the title

the first and last paragraphs

the headings

any names, dates, words, or terms set in bold type or that are repeated

any bulleted lists

any photos, maps, or pictures and their captions

Overhead Transparencies

47

Ask students to preview the text selection. Use the **Overhead Transparencies** to go over with the class what to preview.

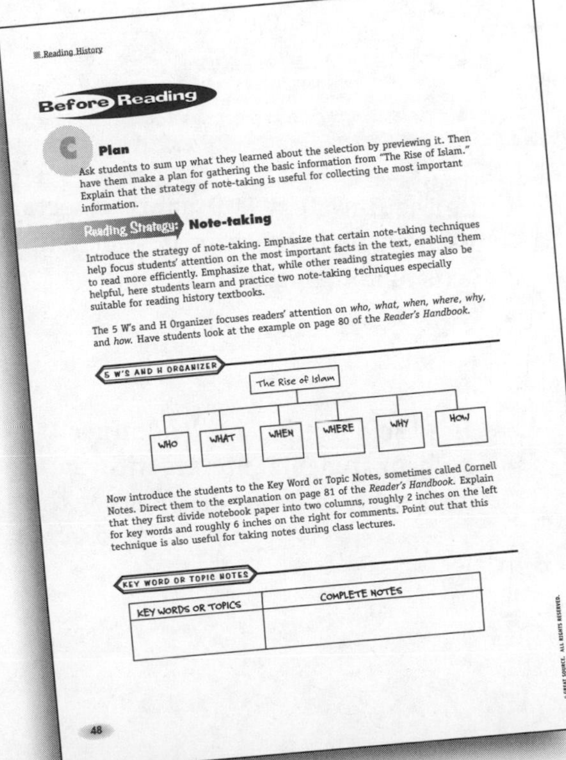

Reading History

Before Reading

C Plan

Ask students to sum up what they learned about the selection by previewing it. Then have them make a plan for gathering the basic information from "The Rise of Islam." Explain that the strategy of note-taking is useful for collecting the most important information.

Reading Strategy: Note-taking

Introduce the strategy of note-taking. Emphasize that certain note-taking techniques help focus students' attention on the most important facts in the text, enabling them to read more efficiently. Emphasize that, while other reading strategies may also be helpful, here students learn and practice two note-taking techniques especially suitable for reading history textbooks.

The 5 W's and H Organizer focuses readers' attention on *who, what, when, where, why,* and *how.* Have students look at the example on page 80 of the *Reader's Handbook.*

Now introduce the students to the Key Word or Topic Notes, sometimes called Cornell Notes. Direct them to the explanation on page 81 of the *Reader's Handbook.* Explain that they first divide notebook paper into two columns, roughly 2 inches on the left for key words and roughly 6 inches on the right for comments. Point out that this technique is also useful for taking notes during class lectures.

KEY WORD OR TOPIC NOTES

KEY WORDS OR TOPICS	COMPLETE NOTES

48

After previewing, help students **Plan** which Reading Tool to use. Point out how the reading purpose and type of reading affect which strategy to use.

During Reading

Next, show students how to implement the reading strategy by using the Reading Tools suggested in the lesson.

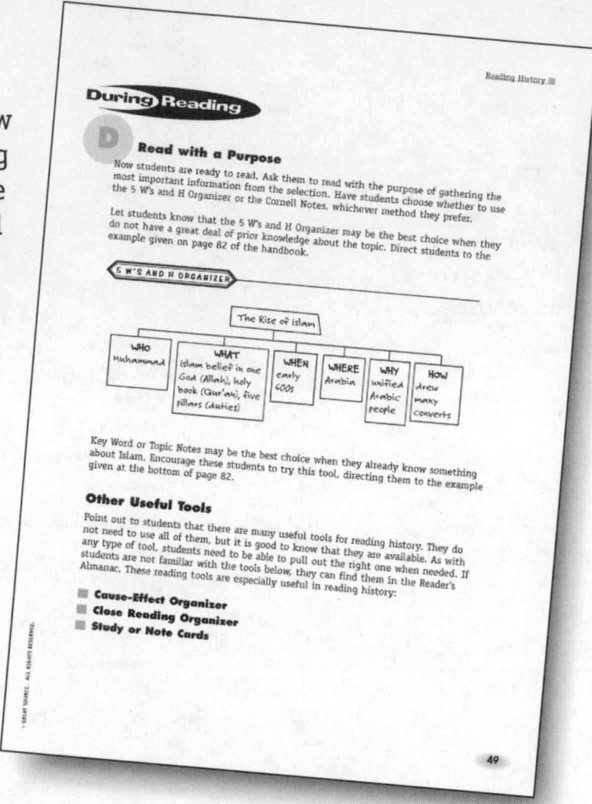

Reading History

During Reading

D

Read with a Purpose

Now students are ready to read. Ask them to read with the purpose of gathering the most important information from the selection. Have students choose whether to use the 5 W's and H Organizer or the Cornell Notes, whichever method they prefer.

Let students know that the 5 W's and H Organizer may be the best choice when they do not have a great deal of prior knowledge about the topic. Direct students to the example given on page 82 of the handbook.

5 W'S AND H ORGANIZER

Key Word or Topic Notes may be the best choice when they already know something about Islam. Encourage these students to try this tool, directing them to the example given at the bottom of page 82.

Other Useful Tools

Point out to students that there are many useful tools for reading history. They do not need to use all of them, but it is good to know that they are available. As with any type of tool, students need to be able to pull out the right one when needed. If students are not familiar with the tools below, they can find them in the Reader's Almanac. These reading tools are especially useful in reading history:

- **Cause-Effect Organizer**
- **Close Reading Organizer**
- **Study or Note Cards**

© GREAT SOURCE. ALL RIGHTS RESERVED.

49

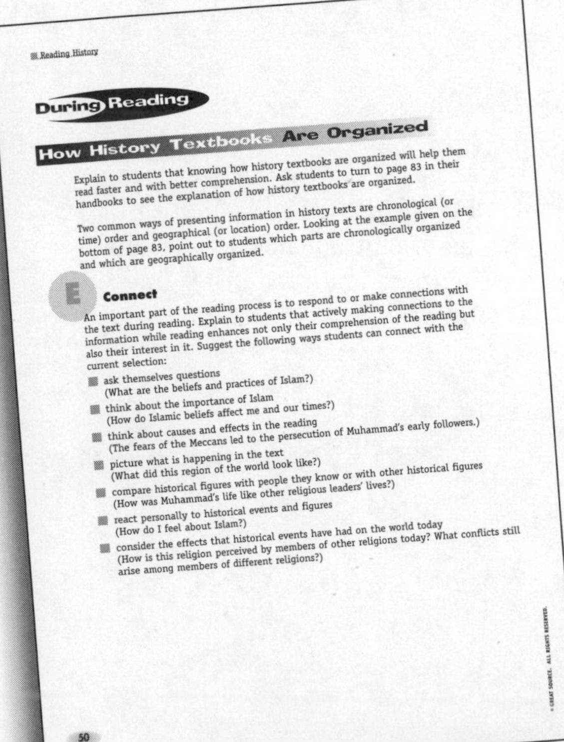

Reading History

During Reading

How History Textbooks Are Organized

Explain to students that knowing how history textbooks are organized will help them read faster and with better comprehension. Ask students to turn to page 83 in their handbooks to see the explanation of how history textbooks are organized.

Two common ways of presenting information in history texts are chronological (or time) order and geographical (or location) order. Looking at the example given on the bottom of page 83, point out to students which parts are chronologically organized and which are geographically organized.

E

Connect

An important part of the reading process is to respond to or make connections with the text during reading. Explain to students that actively making connections to the information while reading enhances not only their comprehension of the reading but also their interest in it. Suggest the following ways students can connect with the current selection:

- ask themselves questions (What are the beliefs and practices of Islam?)
- think about the importance of Islam (How do Islamic beliefs affect me and our times?)
- think about causes and effects in the reading (The fears of the Meccans led to the persecution of Muhammad's early followers.)
- picture what is happening in the text (What did this region of the world look like?)
- compare historical figures with people they know or with other historical figures (How was Muhammad's life like other religious leaders' lives?)
- react personally to historical events and figures (How do I feel about Islam?)
- consider the effects that historical events have had on the world today (How is this religion perceived by members of other religions today? What conflicts still arise among members of different religions?)

© GREAT SOURCE. ALL RIGHTS RESERVED.

50

Use the **How Text Is Organized** section to teach students the ways in which different texts are organized.

Use the questions in the **Connect** section to help students interact with the reading and see how it has meaning for them.

After Reading

After reading, ask students to reflect on whether they have met their reading purpose.

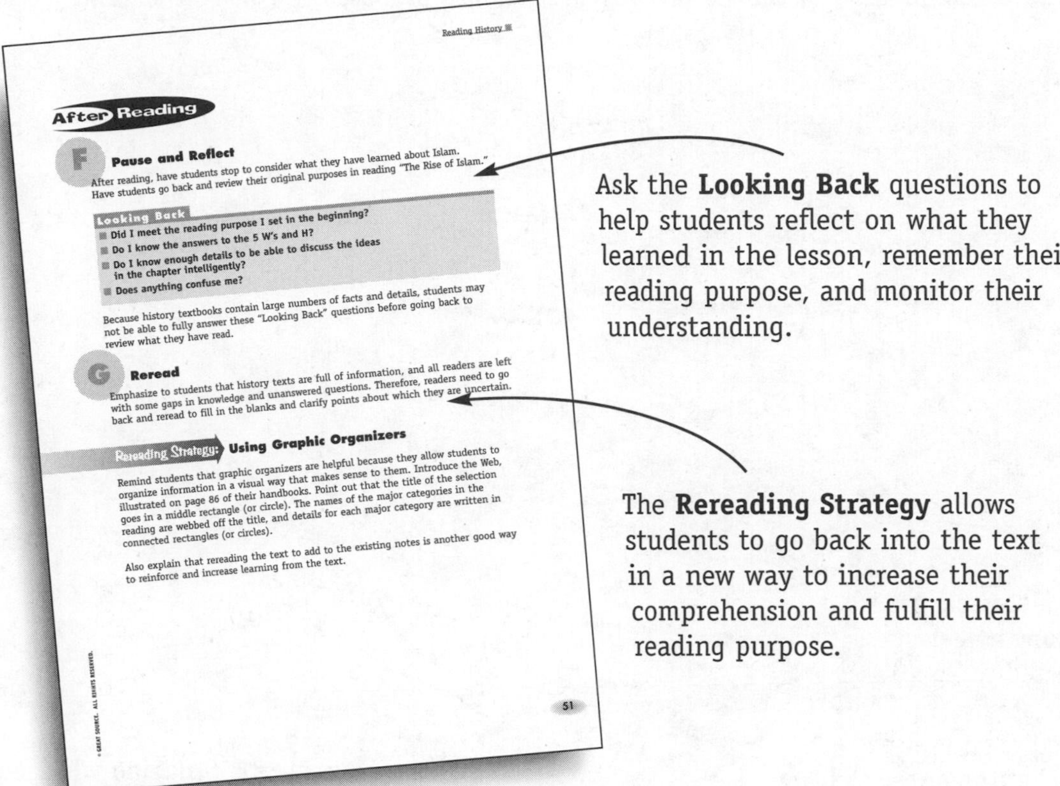

After Reading

F Pause and Reflect

After reading, have students stop to consider what they have learned about Islam. Have students go back and review their original purposes in reading "The Rise of Islam."

Looking Back

- **Did I meet the reading purpose I set in the beginning?**
- **Do I know the answers to the 5 W's and H?**
- **Do I know enough details to be able to discuss the ideas in the chapter intelligently?**
- **Does anything confuse me?**

Because history textbooks contain large numbers of facts and details, students may not be able to fully answer these "Looking Back" questions before going back to review what they have read.

G Reread

Emphasize to students that history texts are full of information, and all readers are left with some gaps in knowledge and unanswered questions. Therefore, readers need to go back and reread to fill in the blanks and clarify points about which they are uncertain.

Rereading Strategy: Using Graphic Organizers

Remind students that graphic organizers are helpful because they allow students to organize information in a visual way that makes sense to them. Introduce the Web, illustrated on page 86 of their handbooks. Point out that the title of the selection goes in a middle rectangle (or circle). The names of the major categories in the reading are webbed off the title, and details for each major category are written in connected rectangles (or circles).

Also explain that rereading the text to add to the existing notes is another good way to reinforce and increase learning from the text.

Ask the **Looking Back** questions to help students reflect on what they learned in the lesson, remember their reading purpose, and monitor their understanding.

The **Rereading Strategy** allows students to go back into the text in a new way to increase their comprehension and fulfill their reading purpose.

Use the suggested activity in the **Remember** section to help students "make the material their own" and recall what they've learned.

Use the **Summing Up** feature to review the key points of the lesson with students.

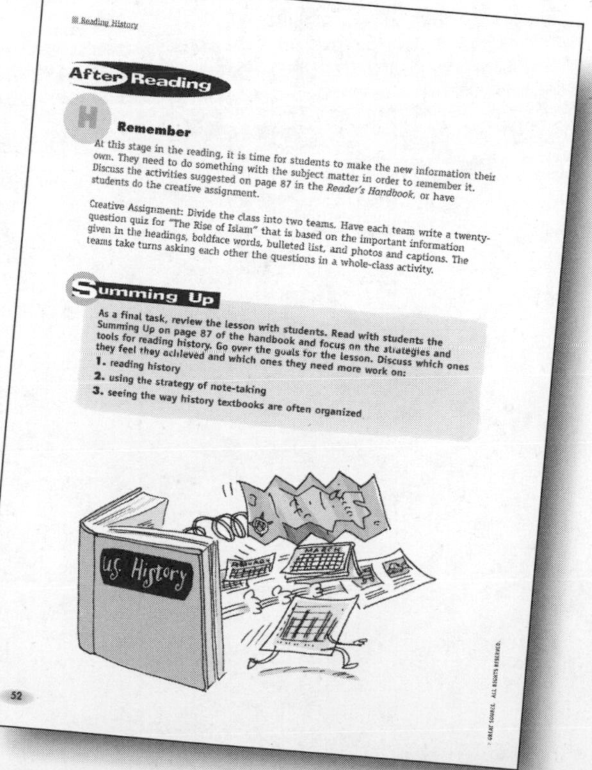

After Reading

H Remember

At this stage in the reading, it is time for students to make the new information their own. They need to do something with the subject matter in order to remember it. Discuss the activities suggested on page 87 in the *Reader's Handbook*, or have students do the creative assignment.

Creative Assignment: Divide the class into two teams. Have each team write a twenty-question quiz for "The Rise of Islam" that is based on the important information given in the headings, boldface words, bulleted list, and photos and captions. The teams take turns asking each other the questions in a whole-class activity.

Summing Up

As a final task, review the lesson with students. Read with students the Summing Up on page 87 of the handbook and focus on the strategies and tools for reading history. Go over the goals for the lesson. Discuss which ones they feel they achieved and which ones they need more work on:

1. **reading history**
2. **using the strategy of note-taking**
3. **seeing the way history textbooks are often organized**

After Reading

Assessment and Application includes a **Quick Assess** checklist that teachers can use to evaluate students' understanding of the lesson. This section also proposes two ways to extend the lesson.

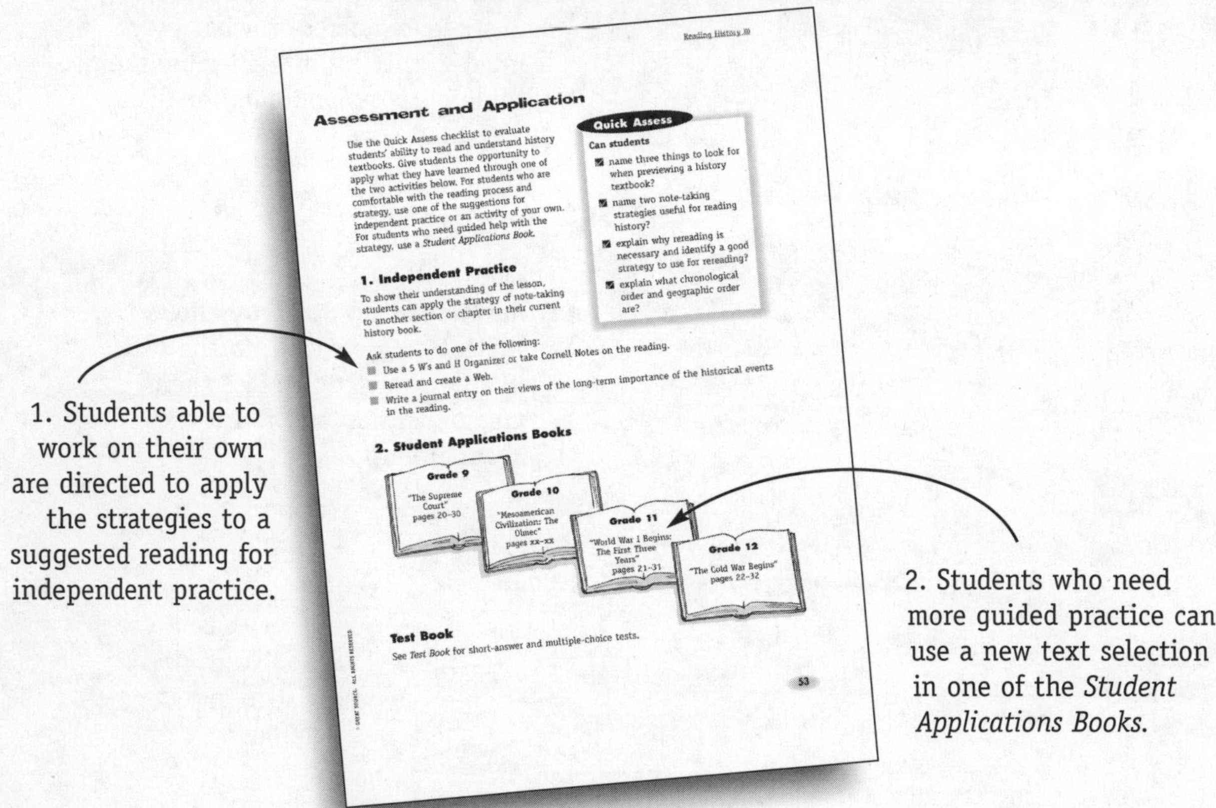

Reading History

Assessment and Application

Use the Quick Assess checklist to evaluate students' ability to read and understand history textbooks. Give students the opportunity to apply what they have learned through one of the two activities below. For students who are comfortable with the reading process and strategy, use one of the suggestions for independent practice or an activity of your own. For students who need guided help with the strategy, use a *Student Applications Book*.

Quick Assess

Can students

- name three things to look for when previewing a history textbook?
- name two note-taking strategies useful for reading history?
- explain why rereading is necessary and identify a good strategy to use for rereading?
- explain what chronological order and geographic order are?

1. Independent Practice

To show their understanding of the lesson, students can apply the strategy of note-taking to another section or chapter in their current history book.

Ask students to do one of the following:

- Use a 5 Ws and H Organizer or take Cornell Notes on the reading.
- Reread and create a Web.
- Write a journal entry on their views of the long-term importance of the historical events in the reading.

2. Student Applications Books

Test Book

See *Test Book* for short-answer and multiple-choice tests.

53

1. Students able to work on their own are directed to apply the strategies to a suggested reading for independent practice.

2. Students who need more guided practice can use a new text selection in one of the *Student Applications Books*.

Getting Started Activities

Reading Survey

The Reading Survey page explores students' thoughts and opinions about reading. Use it to determine which students will need additional support and encouragement over the course of the year. Supplement this activity with lessons from the appropriate *Student Applications Book,* Grades 9–12.

Brainstorm and Categorize

Here students work in pairs to activate prior knowledge of reading words, concepts, and ideas. The brainstorming part of the activity allows for a free flow of thoughts about reading. After brainstorming, students will categorize the words, thus creating a reading framework that they can modify and add to over the course of the year.

Reading as a Process

This activity introduces to students the idea that reading is a *process*—a series of steps that when repeated and perfected, can result in reader proficiency. Invite students to sketch their own reading process and then share their work with the class.

Preview the *Reader's Handbook*

In this activity, students complete a self-guided preview of the *Reader's Handbook* in order to familiarize themselves with its contents. In addition, the activity will serve as an important introduction to one of the initial steps of the reading process. Before they begin, direct students' attention to the Preview Checklist at the top of the page. Explain that these are the elements proficient readers look for when previewing a text.

NAME

Reading Survey

Everybody has reading likes and dislikes. Here's your chance to make yours known.
Directions: Complete these sentences.

1. To me, reading is

2. When I pick up a new book, I feel

3. The easiest type of reading is

4. The most challenging type is

5. The best book I ever read was

6. The worst book I ever read was

Directions: Answer these questions.

7. How much do you read at home?

8. Where is your favorite place to read?

9. Where is the first place you'd go to find a book to read?

10. What types of books do you enjoy most?

11. What types do you like the least?

12. What would you most like to improve about your reading abilities?

NAME

Brainstorm and Categorize

Brainstorm

Directions: Get together with a partner. Brainstorm a list of reading words. (For example, one word might be *fiction.*) Write as many words as you can think of in the Word Box.

Word Box

fiction

NAME

Brainstorm and Categorize (continued)

Categorize

Directions: With your partner, reread the words you wrote in the Word Box. Then make categories of words that go together. (For example, many reading words can be placed in a single category, called *Fiction Words.*)

Reading Categories

Write a head for each category here.

Category #1	Category #2	Category #3	Category #4	Category #5
Fiction Words				
plot				
setting				

Write words that belong in the category here.

NAME

Reading as a Process

Directions: Picture yourself sitting down to read. What do you do first? What do you do next? What about after that? Make a series of four sketches of you reading. Under each sketch, write a short explanation of the action.

Storyboard

NAME

Preview the *Reader's Handbook*

Directions: Thumb through the *Reader's Handbook*. Try to get a sense of what it's all about. Look at the items on the Preview Checklist and then answer the questions.

Preview Checklist

- ❑ the front and back covers
- ❑ the table of contents and chapter titles
- ❑ the first and last chapters
- ❑ any repeated words and phrases
- ❑ key words, headings, and words in boldface
- ❑ any illustrations

1. What grabbed your attention on the front and back covers?

2. What did you learn from the table of contents and chapter titles?

3. What is the first chapter about?

4. What is the last chapter about?

5. Which repeated words and phrases did you see?

6. What did you notice about the art?

7. What is the *Reader's Handbook* mostly about?

8. Why should you read it?

ANSWER KEY

Reading Survey

Some possible answers are:

1. To me, reading is a way of learning new things.
2. When I pick up a new book, I feel excited and nervous at the same time.
3. The easiest type of reading is the reading I do when I email.
4. The most challenging type is textbook reading.
5. The best book I ever read was Huckleberry Finn.
6. The worst book I ever read was Introduction to Algebra.
7. At home, I read only when I have time.
8. My favorite place to read is in my bed, late at night.
9. I'd probably check my mother's bookcase if I needed a book to read.
10. My favorite kinds of books are mysteries.
11. My least favorite kinds of books are textbooks.
12. I'd really like to learn to read faster and more efficiently.

Brainstorm and Categorize

Some possible reading words are:
fiction, nonfiction, textbooks, words, phrases, sentences, paragraphs, pages, chapters, acts, scenes, lines, stanzas, vocabulary, spelling, characters, setting, plot, climax, theme, main idea, and supporting details
Some possible categories are:
fiction, nonfiction, poetry, plays, essays, articles, school reading, free reading, challenging reading, and easy reading

Reading as a Process

Students may picture themselves reading the information on the book jacket, thumbing through a book to preview it, reading the book closely, stopping to think about what they have read, jotting down some notes, and so on.

Preview the *Reader's Handbook*

Some possible answers are:

1. I really like the illustrations on the front and back. The color of the book is an attention-grabber as well.
2. I see that the book is divided into major sections, like Reading Textbooks, Reading Fiction, and so on.
3. The first chapter is an introduction to reading.
4. The last chapter is about improving vocabulary.
5. Reading, reading process, books, literature, article, essay, fiction, nonfiction, Set a Purpose, Preview, Plan, Read with a Purpose, Connect, Pause and Reflect, Reread, Remember
6. Most of the art is cartoons, although I see a few photographs, charts, tables, and graphs.
7. The *Reader's Handbook* is mostly about learning to be a better reader.
8. I should read it because I really want to learn how to get more from every book I pick up.

Lessons

Introduction

- What Is Reading?
- Why You Read
- What You Read
- Reading as a Process
- The Reading and Writing Processes

Introduction

In this lesson, students will discuss what reading is, why people read, and what happens when people read.

What Is Reading?

Have students talk about what reading is. How would they define reading, in their own words? What is involved in reading? How would they describe reading? After they have shared their ideas, ask students to turn to page 26 of the *Reader's Handbook* and discuss with them the idea that reading is a complex process because all texts are different and pose different challenges for readers.

Reading Requires Tools

Ask a volunteer to read this section for the class. Then ask students to talk about some of the "tools" they use while reading. What do they do when they realize they are not understanding something they're reading? Do they just give up? Emphasize to students that even the best readers have difficulty understanding some kinds of texts. Comprehending a text is not magic or something they're born knowing how to do. It is simply a matter of having the right strategies and tools and knowing which ones to use when.

Reading Is a Set of Habits and Abilities

Now ask for another volunteer to read this section aloud. Then have students think about how reading is a set of habits and abilities. Ask them to tell how reading is a habit and how it is an ability. Emphasize that reading quickly and with good comprehension requires lots of practice. Like learning how to ride a bike or drive a car, reading efficiently results from some instruction and lots and lots of independent practice.

Reading Is Thinking

Have a student volunteer read the paragraph aloud. Allow students to sit and think about the meaning of this passage for a few seconds. Then ask students if they can paraphrase, or restate in their own words, what this paragraph has said. Point out that when people are thinking, they hear their own voices or someone else's voice speaking in their heads, and they see images of faces, places, and so on. Similarly, reading is also thinking, except that people hear the author's voice in their heads, and they picture what the author is describing.

Reading Is Power

Ask a student volunteer to read the paragraph. Then ask students what they think about the idea that reading is power. Give examples of people you know who have overcome problems and become successful through reading, not just in their vocational lives but also in their personal lives. Ask students if they can give examples of such people. Emphasize that knowledge is power, and that reading is the best avenue there is to gaining knowledge. Point out how much more information there is in books than on television. Invite students to jot down new things they have learned through reading, constructing a special, ongoing bulletin board if possible.

Why You Read

Ask students why they think all kids are taught to read. Why is reading so important? List reasons on the board. Then ask the students to imagine that they can't read at all. What things do they do now that they would not be able to do if they couldn't read?

Now read through the list of reasons to read on pages 27 and 28 of the handbook. Stop to discuss each one and get students' reactions.

1. Academic Reading

Obviously, academic reading is the type of reading students do in school. It includes narrative texts, expository texts, fiction, and nonfiction, as well as graphics such as charts and maps. The goal of academic reading is to prepare students for a good future with many options.

2. Personal Reading

Personal reading includes reading any type of material that is meaningful to a student—a story that gets a student thinking about his or her life, an article in the sports section of the newspaper, a magazine article on computers, or a book on relationships. Personal reading helps connect a student with subjects and interest areas that provide information and insights that are relevant to his or her own life. Ask students to give examples of fiction and nonfiction that they read because it's interesting to them. Give some of your own examples as well.

3. Workplace Reading

Workplace reading can include memos, emails, manuals, reports, professional journals, and so on. Ask students to give examples of the type of reading they need to do for their summer or after-school jobs. Give your own examples of the type of reading you have had to do, not only for your job as a teacher but for other kinds of jobs you've had in the past.

4. Functional Reading

Functional reading includes the type of reading that students must do to function every day in the world. Examples of functional reading are road signs, bus schedules, and lunch menus. Ask students to take note of what kind of reading they do in the course of a day simply to get around in the world.

What You Read

Now ask students to read silently "What You Read," on page 29 of the handbook. When they are finished, ask them to share their reading tastes, either with the student next to them or with the whole class. Then ask students to talk about how technology already has affected their reading.

Reading as a Process

Now ask students to turn to page 30 of their handbooks. Explain that reading is a process, and read aloud to the students the text explaining what this means. Emphasize that the reading process begins before even looking at the first word in a story, chapter, or article and continues long after they've read the last sentence.

Then direct students' attention to the lists of effective and ineffective reading practices, beginning at the bottom of page 30 and continuing to page 32. Invite students to rate themselves, privately on a page in their notes, to determine which of the two columns they fall into. Ask students to make a note of what they need to work on to improve their reading.

Emphasize to students that good readers are not "smarter" than not-so-good readers; they simply have better habits or practices. Also emphasize to the students that researchers in the past twenty years have identified good readers' practices or habits and have shown the benefits of teaching these practices to all students. Stress that it is within the power of *every student* to improve his or her reading ability.

The Reading and Writing Processes

Explain to students that the reading process is like the writing process. Read through the three introductory paragraphs on page 33 in the handbook. Explain that, like writing, reading can be broken down into parts or steps.

Have students compare the steps of the writing process and the reading process as shown on pages 33–35. Read through the steps outlined in the two columns, emphasizing the parallels between the processes.

Finally, explain that the *Reader's Handbook* presents one reading process to help students read more efficiently—that is, faster and with better comprehension. The ultimate goal is for each student to develop the best reading process to meet his or her own needs.

Quick Assess

Can students

- ☑ name three reasons to read?
- ☑ name at least three characteristics of effective reading?
- ☑ explain two or three ways in which the reading process parallels the writing process?

The Reading Process

Before Reading

During Reading

After Reading

The Reading Process

Getting Ready

Explain to students that everyone can improve in reading ability. Emphasize that improving comprehension, recall, and speed in reading is really not that difficult. All students need is to get in the habit of doing a few things before, during, and after reading.

Ask students:

- what they usually do before starting to read
  (Do you simply pick up the book and start reading?)
- what goes on in their minds during reading
  (Do you feel that what you're reading doesn't "sink in"?)
- what they do after reading
  (Do you ever stop and think about what you've read? Or do you tend to close the book and take off to do something else?)
- how they study for tests
  (Do you try to read the material over and over again and hope it "sticks"? Do you worry a lot?)

Tell students that the *Reader's Handbook* presents a reading process that they will practice again and again with different types of texts. This reading process has three main stages: Before Reading, During Reading, and After Reading. Explain that if students can get into the habit of doing a few simple things in each stage, they will be able to read faster with better comprehension and recall.

Before Reading

Tell students that three things need to be done before they begin to read. Emphasize that each of these steps takes no longer than a few minutes. Also explain that as students become more familiar with and practiced at these steps, the time they take decreases. These are the three steps:

A. Set a Purpose
B. Preview
C. Plan

A Set a Purpose

Explain that before starting to read, it's important to think about what the material is and what the purpose is. People have different purposes for reading different types of material. For example, reading a manual to repair a camera is different from reading a science chapter for homework.

Read through the Set a Purpose section on page 38 with students. Ask students to think about why they read different texts (for example, a favorite magazine, a newspaper, a history chapter, a novel for English class, a novel of their own choosing). Ask students to comment about different purposes and how they affect the way students read.

B Preview

After setting a purpose for reading, students should preview the material. Read through the Preview section on page 39 with the students. Emphasize that though previewing seems to add a few minutes to the reading process, readers who preview tend to read faster, with more confidence, and with better comprehension and recall. Tell students that previewing provides an overview, like a map, so they know when they'll need to slow down and concentrate.

Explain that previewing is simply a quick look at the material before actually beginning to read. Previewing a chapter in a textbook, for example, would include the things on this checklist.

Preview Checklist

- ✓ *reading the title, headings, and subheadings*
- ✓ *looking at the photos, illustrations, and graphics and their captions*
- ✓ *reading any terms or sentences that appear in the margin*
- ✓ *glancing through the material for boldface or repeated words*
- ✓ *skimming end-of-chapter questions*

Let students know that they will be practicing previewing as they work through the handbook and that, as with anything else, they will get faster and more efficient at it with practice.

C Plan

Explain to students that "planning" means thinking about and deciding on the best way to reach a goal. Before starting to read, students need to make a plan for getting the information they need from the selection. They also need the right tools. Read through the Plan section on page 39.

Explain that the handbook is full of strategies and tools to use for getting what students need from different types of reading. Remind them that the different kinds of reading require different strategies and tools.

Tell students that once they set a purpose for reading, preview, and make a plan, they are ready to start reading. There are two important things to remember to do while reading:

D. Read with a Purpose
E. Connect

D Read with a Purpose

Ask students if they've ever felt a bit lost in the middle of reading a chapter or book. All readers have felt this way at some point—even the best readers. It's easy to get overwhelmed by all the new information and ideas in a text. This is why it's important to read with a purpose.

Read through the Read with a Purpose section on page 40. Tell students that when they begin to read, they need to keep in mind the Setting a Purpose questions they decided on before reading. Reading with those questions in mind will help them focus on finding the most important information in the reading.

E Connect

Connecting means relating what students are reading to what they already have experienced or know. It also means being aware of their thoughts and feelings about what they are reading.

Read through the Connect section on page 41 with the students. Have them look at and think about the questions given to help students connect while reading. Also suggest the following questions as some ways of connecting with reading:

- Has something like this ever happened to you?
- Have you seen or read something like this before?
- What do you think about this?
- What is important or meaningful to you in this reading?

After Reading

Tell students that, after reading, there are three more steps to take to help them better understand and remember what they read:

F. Pause and Reflect
G. Reread
H. Remember

F Pause and Reflect

After reading, students need to pause and reflect on what they have just read. Explain to students that it only takes a moment to do this. They need to ask themselves if they understood what they just read. Were there parts that seemed confusing? Which parts were those?

Read through the Pause and Reflect section on page 41 with the students. In this step, students need to revisit their original Setting a Purpose questions. Did they get the information they need to answer those questions? Or are there still some gaps?

G Reread

Emphasize to students that all readers—even the best readers—need to look back at the text to clarify confusions and obtain additional information after reading. Go through the Reread section on page 42.

Tell students that, when reading for school, they will want to look back and reread carefully so that they understand and remember the information in the reading as well as they can. The *Reader's Handbook* contains many rereading strategies and tools to help students with their school reading. Emphasize that these strategies and tools are study aids that will help students do well on tests.

H Remember

Let students know that hardly anyone can remember everything read. However, everyone can increase how much they recall simply by "doing something" with the new information. Tell students that the goal is to make the new information "their own." Ways of doing this include summarizing, making a graphic organizer, or telling a friend about what they've read. Read through the Remember section on page 42 with students.

Summing Up

Now review this chapter with the students, using the Summing Up on page 43. Read this section aloud, or ask for volunteers to read aloud while the rest of the students follow along in their own books.

The entire reading process can be boiled down to a few easy-to-follow steps.

Before

- **Set a purpose.**
- **Preview the reading.**
- **Plan a reading strategy.**

During

- **Read with a purpose.**
- **Create some personal connection to the text.**

After

- **Pause, reflect, and look back to see if you found information that fits your purpose.**
- **Reread to find out things you might have missed the first time through.**
- **Remember what you learned.**

Emphasize the final point on page 43. Using the reading process in the handbook will help students with all the different kinds of reading they do, especially academic reading and workplace reading.

Quick Assess

Can students

- ☑ name the three main stages of the reading process?
- ☑ explain what it means to preview a reading?
- ☑ suggest some questions to connect to a reading?
- ☑ explain why it is a good idea to reread?

Reading Know-how

- Essential Reading Skills
- Reading Actively
- Reading Paragraphs
- Kinds of Paragraphs
- Ways of Organizing Paragraphs

Reading Know-how

Here students learn the basics of reading effectively. "Reading Know-how" will help students learn to:

- ✓ understand and use essential reading skills
- ✓ read actively
- ✓ recognize kinds of paragraphs and ways of organizing paragraphs

Essential Reading Skills

Emphasize to students that they already have many valuable reading skills. However, explain that they, like all readers, including adults, can improve their reading skills so that they better understand and recall what they read. Emphasize that better comprehension and recall will lead to better grades in school. Stress that, because *everyone* can improve reading skills, *everyone* can also improve academic performance.

Brainstorm with the students what effective readers do while reading. You may wish to make two lists on the board: "What Good Readers Do While Reading" and "What Not-So-Good Readers Do While Reading." If the students aren't sure what might go in these lists, start each list with items such as "Think about what they read" for what good readers do and "Daydream" or "Fall asleep" for what not-so-good readers do. Try to accept all student responses.

Now have students turn to pages 46–48 of their handbooks and talk about how they use the essential skills of making inferences, drawing conclusions, comparing and contrasting, and evaluating in their everyday lives.

Making Inferences

Explain that an inference is a reasonable guess about what the words in a text are saying. It is a logical conclusion based on the text. Another way to think of it is "reading between the lines." Have students take a moment to look at the graphic on page 46.

Drawing Conclusions

Point out that students easily draw conclusions from personal experiences. Good readers also draw conclusions while reading. It is simply a matter of putting "two and two" together. Read through the Drawing Conclusions section on page 47, pausing to look at and talk about the graphics.

Comparing and Contrasting

Remind students that *comparing* means "looking at likenesses" and *contrasting* means "looking at differences." Explain that understanding comparing and contrasting helps readers interpret information. Read through the Comparing and Contrasting section on page 48, pausing to discuss the Venn Diagram.

Evaluating

Tell students that *evaluating* means "judging" or "making a judgment." Students, like adults, do this all the time—they form opinions about music, movies, clothes, and so on. Good readers also apply the skill of evaluating to reading. They evaluate the quality of a writer's argument and information as well as the logic of characters' actions. Read through the Evaluating section on page 48 with students.

Reading Actively

Read page 49 with the students. Make sure students understand the importance of staying focused, or concentrating, while reading. Emphasize that active readers think about what the author is saying and take notes on important or interesting points.

Have students look at the example of how one reader annotated the text on page 50:

1. Mark
2. Question
3. Clarify
4. React
5. Visualize
6. Predict

You may wish to ask student volunteers to read the descriptions on page 51 aloud.

Finding a Place to Read

Let students know that because reading actively means concentrating fully, they need to find a good place to do their reading. This place should be quiet and comfortable, with good light. Students should have available supplies, such as their notebooks, sticky notes, and a pen, pencil, or highlighter. A glass of water at hand is helpful too.

Making Time for Reading

Remind students that time management is important to good reading and good studying. High school students need to allot 20 to 30 minutes a day for reading, apart from the time needed for studying.

Reading Paragraphs

Explain that good reading comprehension relies on students' ability to identify the most important points in a selection. Understanding paragraphs is key to this ability. Have students turn to pages 53–58 of the handbook to see how to find the subject and main idea of a paragraph.

Finding the Subject

Walk through what to look at to find the subject, or topic, of a paragraph:

- the title of a whole work
- a heading or subheading
- the first sentence of the paragraph
- any key words or repeated words or names
- the last sentence of the paragraph

Now have students read "The Battle of Gettysburg" on page 54 and go through the points, as detailed on page 54.

Finding the Main Idea

Explain that the main idea of a paragraph is not the same as the subject of a paragraph. The main idea is what the author says about the subject. Go over Finding the Main Idea, beginning on page 55, allowing students to read through and discuss each example. Emphasize that the main idea can be stated or implied.

Identifying an implied main idea is difficult for readers of all ages. Focus students' attention on the steps for finding an implied main idea, illustrated in the graphic on page 58. Read these steps aloud as the students follow along in their handbooks.

Kinds of Paragraphs

Recognizing the different ways that paragraphs can be organized will help students identify the subject and main idea in paragraphs as well as distinguish between important and unimportant information.

Explain to students that there are four kinds of paragraphs, which are explained in detail on page 59:

- *Narrative* paragraphs, which tell a story
- *Expository* paragraphs, which provide information and explanations
- *Descriptive* paragraphs, which provide specific details to create a picture
- *Persuasive* paragraphs, which express an opinion or try to convince the reader

Now ask students to turn to page 60 of their handbooks to look at how these types of paragraphs may be organized.

Ways of Organizing Paragraphs

Time Order

Explain that in this kind of organization details appear in the order in which they happen. Go through the example from *Roughing It* on page 61, and point out the Sequence Notes at the bottom of the page.

Geographic Order

Tell students that in this way of organizing, details are arranged in spatial order, such as left to right. Point out the example and map on page 62.

Order of Importance

Explain that details may be arranged from most to least important or from least to most important. Go over the examples and Main Idea Organizers on pages 63 and 64.

Comparison-Contrast Order

In this paragraph organization, the author tells how two things are alike and how they are different. Ask students to read the example on page 65. Show them how the information in this paragraph can be represented in a Venn Diagram.

Cause-Effect Order

Explain that in a cause-effect paragraph the writer portrays a logical relationship between a cause (or causes) and an effect (or effects). Have the students read the example on page 66 and discuss the Cause-Effect Organizer at the bottom of the page.

Classification Order

Tell students that classification order is used to explain a term or concept. Writers use this structure to put things into categories, often based on special characteristics. Have students read the example on page 67. When they are finished, direct their attention to the Classification Notes at the bottom of the page.

Listing Order

Explain that some paragraphs are simply lists of details in no particular order. Have students read the example on page 68. A good way to keep track of the information in a paragraph such as this is in a Web, illustrated at the bottom of page 68.

Mixed Order

Now explain that some paragraphs are difficult to classify because they have more than one kind of order in them. Have students look at the example of a mixed order paragraph on page 69 of the handbook.

Quick Assess

Can students

- ☑ name two or three essential skills?
- ☑ describe four ways to be an active reader?
- ☑ find the implied main idea in a paragraph?
- ☑ list four ways paragraphs are organized?

Reading Textbooks

Introduction to Reading Textbooks

Reading Different Subjects

Reading History
Reading Science
Reading Math

Focus on School Reading

Focus on Foreign Language
Focus on Science Concepts
Focus on Study Questions
Focus on Word Problems

Elements of Textbooks

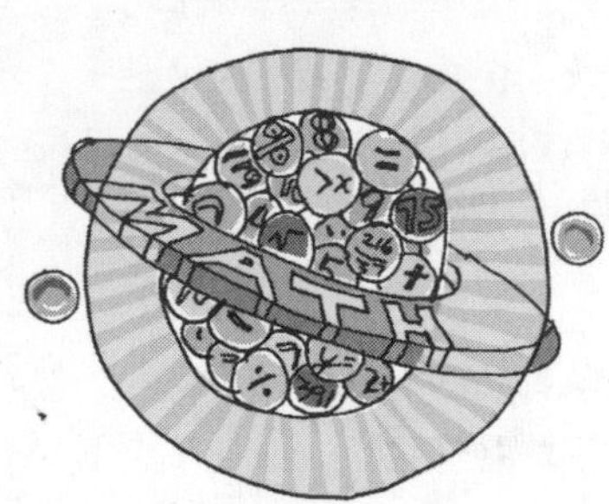

Introduction to Reading Textbooks

Ask students to describe some of the things that are alike in the textbooks they are using in different content areas. They may mention the division into units and chapters or sections as well as features such as footnotes, goals boxes, and review pages. Ask students to turn to page 72 and read the page. Then talk with them about what they can expect to learn from reading the chapter.

Reading History

Goals

Here students read a selection called "The Rise of Islam." This lesson will help them to learn to:

- ✔ read history
- ✔ use the strategy of note-taking
- ✔ see the way history textbooks are often organized

Background

Help students connect this lesson with their existing knowledge by asking them to:

- talk about how reading history is different from reading science books, math books, and literature
- name some special characteristics of history textbooks, including the different parts of these books
- discuss why reading a history textbook is sometimes difficult or uninteresting
- say what they like about reading history

Opening Activity

Using an example of a current history textbook, show students the different features of the book. Emphasize that a good history book not only tells *what* happened, *when* and *where* it happened, and *who* was involved, but *why* something happened. Also emphasize that looking for the 5 W's and the H (*who, what, when, where, why*, and *how*) while reading a history textbook can help students read faster and with better comprehension.

Overview

	Content	Teacher's Guide page	Reader's Handbook page
Selection	"The Rise of Islam"		75–79, 83, 84
Reading Strategy	Note-taking	48, 434	80, 81, 718
Rereading Strategy	Using Graphic Organizers	51, 439	85, 86, 734
Tool	5 W's and H Organizer Key Word or Topic Notes Web	48 48 51	80, 82, 745 81, 82, 746 86, 757

Ancillaries

	Grade	Content	Page
Overhead Transparency	9–12	Previewing History	Numbers 8 and 9
Lesson Plan Book	9 10 11 12	Reading History Reading History Reading History Reading History	64, 66–69 64, 66–69 55, 60–63 55, 60–63
Student Applications Book	9 10 11 12	"The Supreme Court" "Mesoamerican Civilization: The Olmec" "World War I Begins: The First Three Years" "The Cold War Begins"	20–30 20–30 21–31 22–33
Test Book	9–12	Short-answer Test Multiple-choice Test	
Website		www.greatsource.com/rehand/	
Content Area Guide		This lesson appears in the *Content Area Guide: Social Studies.*	

Before Reading

Set a Purpose

Have students set a purpose before they begin reading "The Rise of Islam." Suggest they put themselves in the role of an investigative reporter, asking *who, what, when, where, why*, and *how*. Direct students to the Setting a Purpose questions on page 74 in the *Reader's Handbook*.

Setting a Purpose

- **Who started Islam?**
- **What is Islam?**
- **When did Islam originate?**
- **Where is Islam important or practiced?**
- **Why is Islam important?**
- **How did Islam spread?**

B Preview

Ask students to look over "The Rise of Islam" before reading to familiarize themselves with the content and layout of the selection. Use the Preview Checklist on page 74 in the handbook. Have students find and point out each item in the Preview Checklist. Call attention to the color-coded annotations in the margin that students can use to find the appropriate bits of text.

Preview Checklist

- ✓ *the title, the list of terms and names, and the introductory information near the title*
- ✓ *the first and last paragraphs*
- ✓ *the headings*
- ✓ *any names, dates, words, or terms set in bold type or that are repeated*
- ✓ *any bulleted lists*
- ✓ *any photos, maps, or pictures and their captions*

Overhead Transparencies

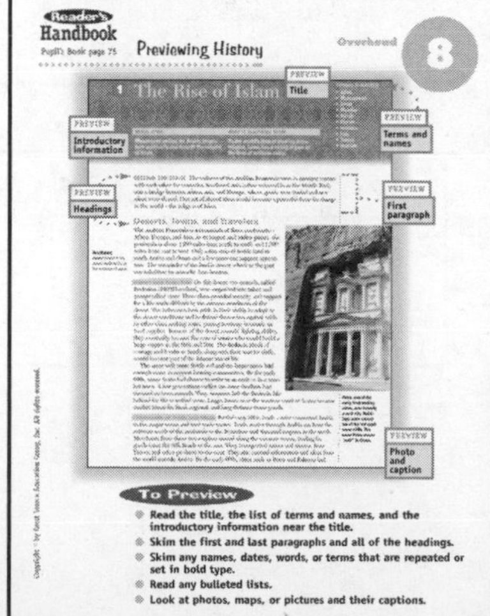

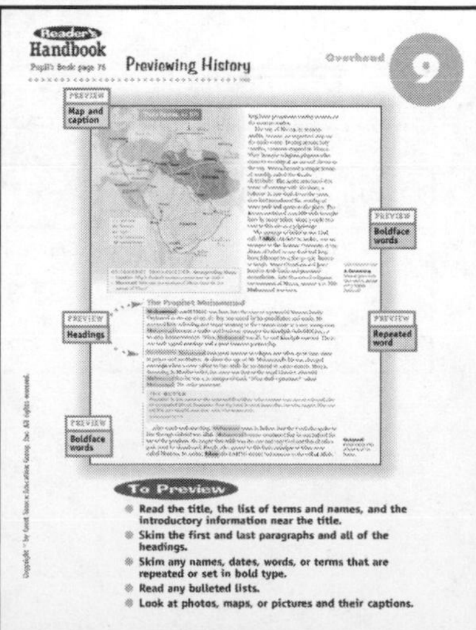

Before Reading

C Plan

Ask students to sum up what they learned about the selection by previewing it. Then have them make a plan for gathering the basic information from "The Rise of Islam." Explain that the strategy of note-taking is useful for collecting the most important information.

Reading Strategy: Note-taking

Introduce the strategy of **note-taking**. Emphasize that certain note-taking techniques help focus students' attention on the most important facts in the text, enabling them to read more efficiently. Emphasize that, while other reading strategies may also be helpful, here students learn and practice two note-taking techniques especially suitable for reading history textbooks.

The 5 W's and H Organizer focuses readers' attention on *who, what, when, where, why,* and *how.* Have students look at the example on page 80 of the *Reader's Handbook.*

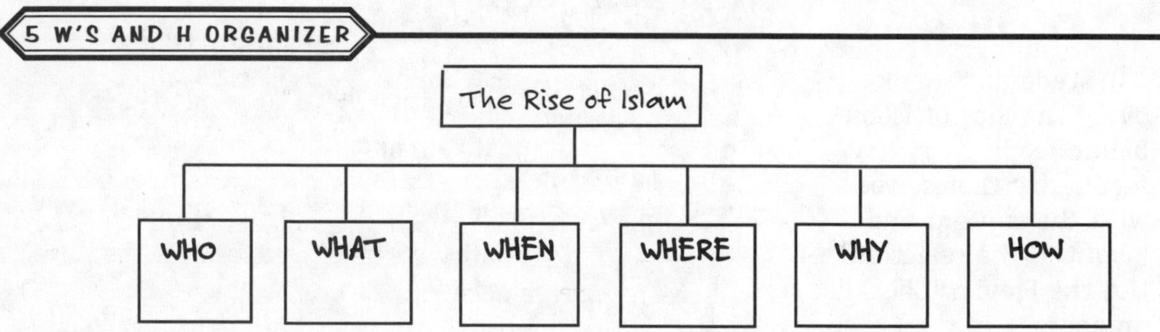

Now introduce the students to the Key Word or Topic Notes, sometimes called Cornell Notes. Direct them to the explanation on page 81 of the *Reader's Handbook.* Explain that they first divide notebook paper into two columns, roughly 2 inches on the left for key words and roughly 6 inches on the right for comments. Point out that this technique is also useful for taking notes during class lectures.

KEY WORD OR TOPIC NOTES

KEY WORDS OR TOPICS	COMPLETE NOTES

During Reading

D Read with a Purpose

Now students are ready to read. Ask them to read with the purpose of gathering the most important information from the selection. Have students choose whether to use the 5 W's and H Organizer or the Cornell Notes, whichever method they prefer.

Let students know that the 5 W's and H Organizer may be the best choice when they do not have a great deal of prior knowledge about the topic. Direct students to the example given on page 82 of the handbook.

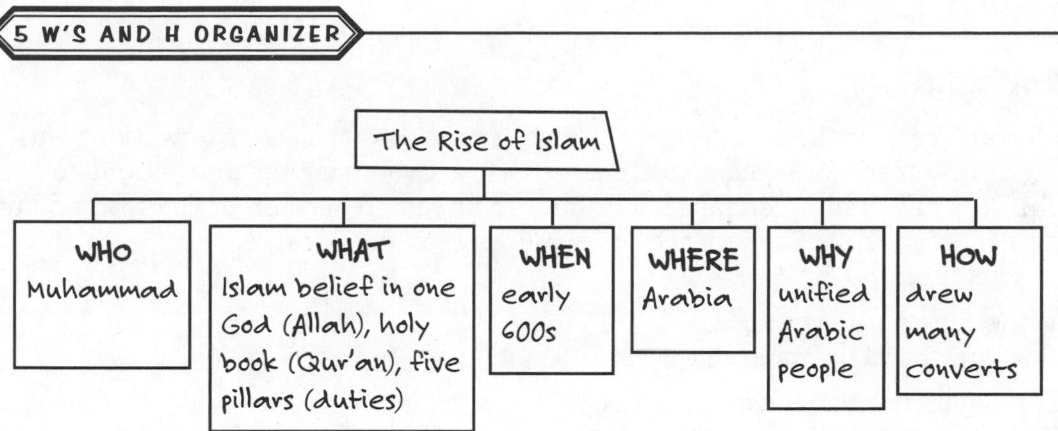

Key Word or Topic Notes may be the best choice when they already know something about Islam. Encourage these students to try this tool, directing them to the example given at the bottom of page 82.

Other Useful Tools

Point out to students that there are many useful tools for reading history. They do not need to use all of them, but it is good to know that they are available. As with any type of tool, students should be able to pull out the right one when needed. If students are not familiar with the tools below, they can find them in the Reader's Almanac. These reading tools are especially useful in reading history:

- **Cause-Effect Organizer**
- **Close Reading Organizer**
- **Study or Note Cards**

How History Textbooks Are Organized

Explain to students that knowing how history textbooks are organized will help them read faster and with better comprehension. Ask students to turn to page 83 in their handbooks to see the explanation of how history textbooks are organized.

Two common ways of presenting information in history texts are chronological (or time) order and geographical (or location) order. Looking at the example given on the bottom of page 83, point out to students which parts are chronologically organized and which are geographically organized.

E Connect

An important part of the reading process is to respond to or make connections with the text during reading. Explain to students that actively making connections to the information while reading enhances not only their comprehension of the reading but also their interest in it. Suggest the following ways students can connect with the current selection:

- ask themselves questions
  (What are the beliefs and practices of Islam?)
- think about the importance of Islam
  (How do Islamic beliefs affect me and our times?)
- think about causes and effects in the reading
  (The fears of the Meccans led to the persecution of Muhammad's early followers.)
- picture what is happening in the text
  (What did this region of the world look like?)
- compare historical figures with people they know or with other historical figures
  (How was Muhammad's life like other religious leaders' lives?)
- react personally to historical events and figures
  (How do I feel about Islam?)
- consider the effects that historical events have had on the world today
  (How is this religion perceived by members of other religions today? What conflicts still arise among members of different religions?)

F Pause and Reflect

After reading, have students stop to consider what they have learned about Islam. Have students go back and review their original purposes in reading "The Rise of Islam."

Looking Back

- **Did I meet the reading purpose I set in the beginning?**
- **Do I know the answers to the 5 W's and H?**
- **Do I know enough details to be able to discuss the ideas in the chapter intelligently?**
- **Does anything confuse me?**

Because history textbooks contain large numbers of facts and details, students may not be able to fully answer these "Looking Back" questions before going back to review what they have read.

G Reread

Emphasize to students that history texts are full of information, and all readers are left with some gaps in knowledge and unanswered questions. Therefore, readers need to go back and reread to fill in the blanks and clarify points about which they are uncertain.

Rereading Strategy: Using Graphic Organizers

Remind students that **graphic organizers** are helpful because they allow students to organize information in a visual way that makes sense to them. Introduce the Web, illustrated on page 86 of their handbooks. Point out that the title of the selection goes in a middle rectangle (or circle). The names of the major categories in the reading are webbed off the title, and details for each major category are written in connected rectangles (or circles).

Also explain that rereading the text to add to the existing notes is another good way to reinforce and increase learning from the text.

After Reading

H Remember

At this stage in the reading, it is time for students to make the new information their own. They need to do something with the subject matter in order to remember it. Discuss the activities suggested on page 87 in the *Reader's Handbook,* or have students do the creative assignment.

Creative Assignment: Divide the class into two teams. Have each team write a twenty-question quiz for "The Rise of Islam" that is based on the important information given in the headings, boldface words, bulleted list, and photos and captions. The teams take turns asking each other the questions in a whole-class activity.

Summing Up

As a final task, review the lesson with students. Read with students the Summing Up on page 87 of the handbook and focus on the strategies and tools for reading history. Go over the goals for the lesson. Discuss which ones they feel they achieved and which ones they need more work on:

1. **reading history**
2. **using the strategy of note-taking**
3. **seeing the way history textbooks are often organized**

Assessment and Application

Use the Quick Assess checklist to evaluate students' ability to read and understand history textbooks. Give students the opportunity to apply what they have learned through one of the two activities below. For students who are comfortable with the reading process and strategy, use one of the suggestions for independent practice or an activity of your own. For students who need guided help with the strategy, use a *Student Applications Book.*

Quick Assess

Can students

- name three things to look for when previewing a history textbook?
- name two note-taking strategies useful for reading history?
- explain why rereading is necessary and identify a good strategy to use for rereading?
- explain what chronological order and geographic order are?

1. Independent Practice

To show their understanding of the lesson, students can apply the strategy of **note-taking** to another section or chapter in their current history book.

Ask students to do one of the following:

- Use a 5 W's and H Organizer or take Key Word or Topic Notes on the reading.
- Reread and create a Web.
- Write a journal entry on their views of the long-term importance of the historical events in the reading.

2. Student Applications Books

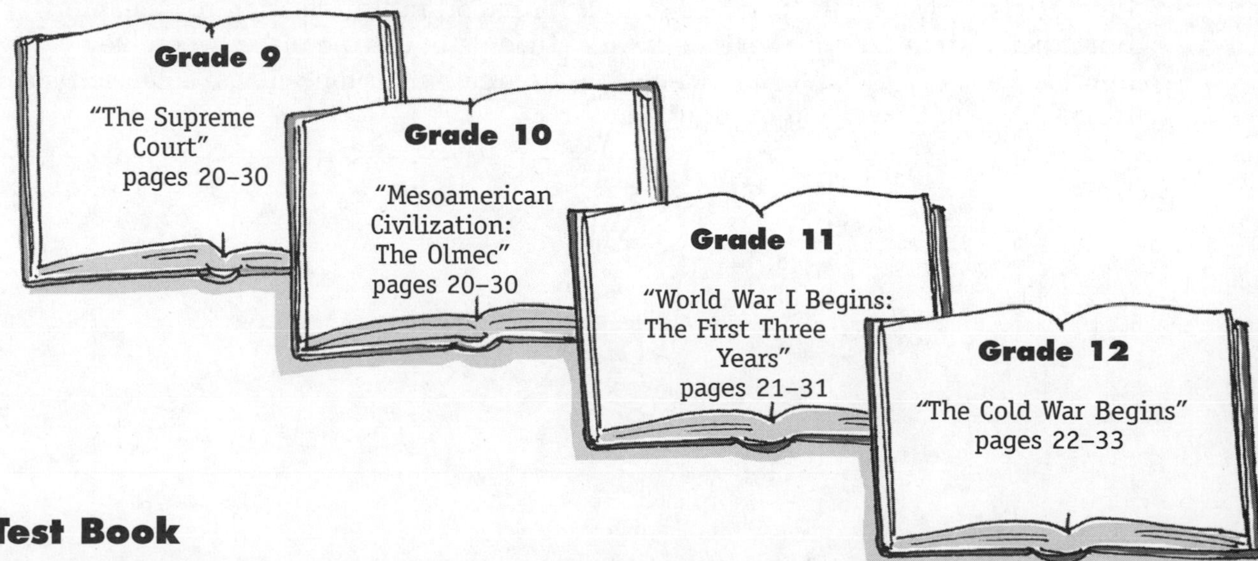

Test Book

See *Test Book* for short-answer and multiple-choice tests.

Reading Science

Goals

Here students read a section called "Biology in Your World" from a biology textbook. This lesson will help them learn to:

- determine what is important in a science textbook
- apply the strategy of outlining
- understand the organization of science textbooks and science writing

Background

Help students connect this lesson with existing knowledge by asking them to:

- talk about how reading science is different from reading other kinds of textbooks
- name some special characteristics of science textbooks, including different parts of these books
- discuss why reading a science textbook is sometimes difficult or uninteresting
- say what they like about reading science

Opening Activity

Have students work with partners to look for important information in a chapter from their current science textbooks. Ask students to list the places where key information can be found (for example, in headings and subheadings, boldface type, tables, figures, boxes, and other graphics).

Lesson Resources

Overview

	Content	Teacher's Guide page	Reader's Handbook page
Selection	"Biology in Your World"		90–93
Reading Strategy	Outlining	57, 435	94, 720
Rereading Strategy	Note-taking	60, 434	98, 718
Tool	Outline Cause-Effect Organizer Classification Notes Problem-Solution Organizer Study Cards	57 58 59 59 60	95, 749 96, 739 96, 741 96, 751 98, 754

Ancillaries

	Grade	Content	Page
Overhead Transparency	9–12	Previewing Science	Numbers 10 and 11
Lesson Plan Book	9 10 12	Reading Science Reading Science Reading Science	65, 70–73 65, 70–73 64, 66–69
Student Applications Book	9 10 11 12	"Igneous Rocks" "The Immune System" "Everyday Forces" "Chemical Reactions and Energy"	31–39 31–39 32–40 34–41
Test Book	9–12	Short-answer Test Multiple-choice Test	
Website		www.greatsource.com/rehand/	
Content Area Guide		This lesson appears in the *Content Area Guide: Science.*	

Before Reading

A Set a Purpose

Have students set a purpose before reading the selection. Point out the Setting a Purpose question on page 89 of the handbook.

Setting a Purpose

- **What are some real-world problems that biology can help solve?**

B Preview

Now have students preview the reading selection. Explain to the students that the main ideas in a science chapter are often clearly stated in the title, heads, and subheads. Remind students that previewing the chapter to get a general idea of what it's about will help them read faster and with better comprehension.

Read through the Preview Checklist on page 89 with the students. Then preview the selection beginning on page 90, focusing on the headings, the text in the margins, bold type, and the photographs, graphics, and boxed material.

Preview Checklist

- ✓ *the title*
- ✓ *the first and last paragraphs of the chapter*
- ✓ *the headings*
- ✓ *any words set in bold type or repeated*
- ✓ *any boxed material*
- ✓ *any photos, charts, or pictures and their captions*
- ✓ *the list of objectives and any review questions*

Overhead Transparencies

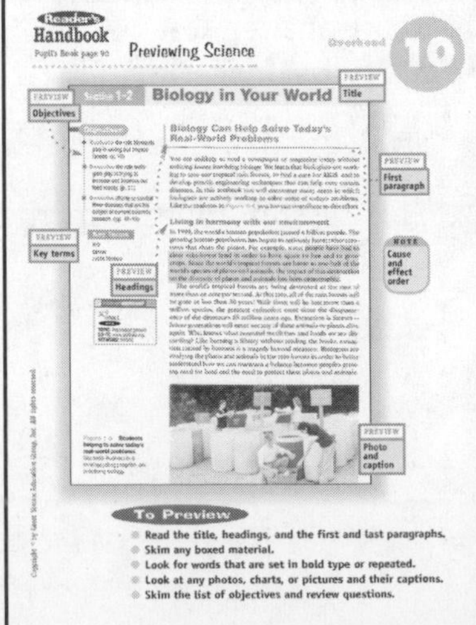

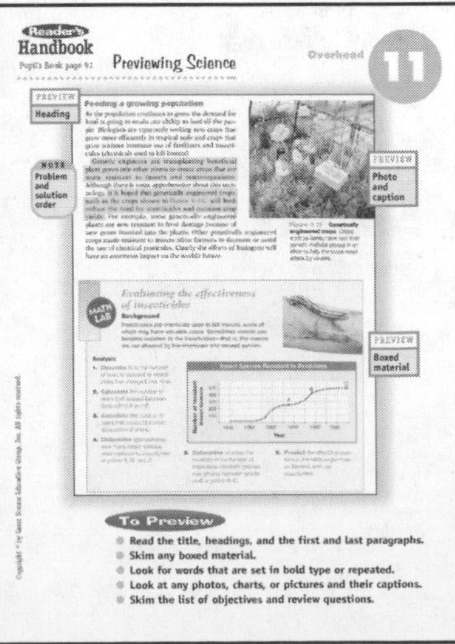

Before Reading

C Plan

Ask students to briefly tell some of the things they learned from their preview. Have them look at the bulleted list at the top of page 94 in their handbooks. Emphasize that after they have a general idea of what this chapter is about, they can make a plan to help them meet their purpose for reading.

Reading Strategy: Outlining

Explain that **outlining** is an excellent strategy for obtaining important information from science texts. This is a versatile strategy that can be used for reading several kinds of texts.

Let students know that Outlines can be formal or informal. An example of a formal Outline appears on the bottom of page 94. However, students may create an informal Outline, too, which would consist of simple indentations and bullets to show how ideas relate to one another.

OUTLINE

Title of Outline

I. ____________________

  A. ____________________

    1. ____________________

      a. ____________________

      b. ____________________

    2. ____________________

  B. ____________________

II. ____________________

During Reading

D Read with a Purpose

Remind students that, as they read, they need to keep in mind their purpose for reading. Their Outlines will help keep them focused on finding the important information in the text, which will enable them to answer their Setting a Purpose question.

Point out that the headings and subheadings in the selection can be used to create an effective Outline, as shown on page 95 of the handbook.

Other Useful Tools

Point out to students that there are other useful tools for reading science. As with any type of tool, students need to be able to pull out the right one when needed. If students are not familiar with the tools below, they can find them in the Reader's Almanac. These reading tools are especially useful in reading science:

- **Web**
- **Key Word or Topic Notes**

How Science Textbooks Are Organized

Explain to students that knowing how science writing is organized will help them locate important information faster and more efficiently. Three common organizations found in science writing are cause and effect, classification, and problem-solution.

Often, scientists try to explain how and why things happen. It makes sense, then, to look for causes and effects in the text. The Cause-Effect Organizer is useful for taking notes on this type of text. Show students the example of the Cause-Effect Organizer on page 96 of the handbook. Point out how this graphic organizer allows students to easily see and remember causes and effects.

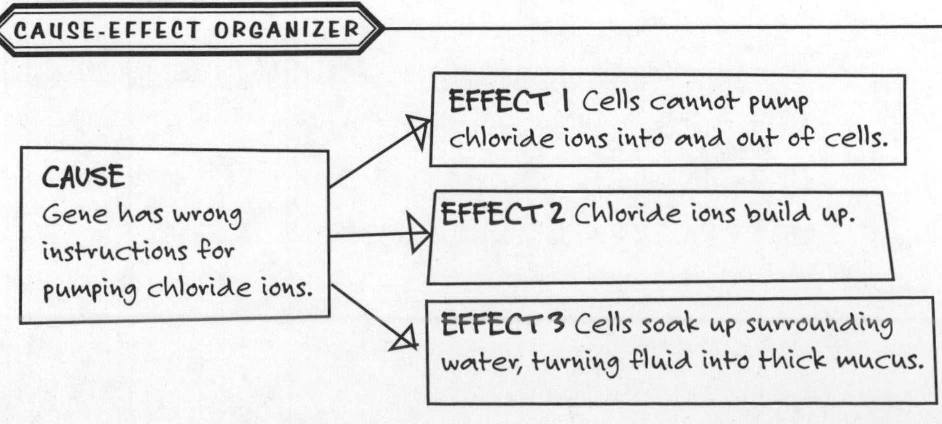

How Science Textbooks Are Organized

Another common way of organizing science writing is by classification. Science is often concerned with categories. Direct students' attention to the example of the Classification Notes graphic organizer on page 96. Point out that this graphic organizer helps students clarify and remember what they read in science textbooks.

CLASSIFICATION NOTES

BOTANISTS	ECOLOGISTS	MARINE BIOLOGISTS
study plants	study relationships between organisms and their environment	study organisms in the sea

Problem-Solution

Problem-solution is also a common way to organize science writing. Because scientists often concern themselves with the solutions to problems, the Problem-Solution Organizer is a good tool for readers. Show students the example of this organizer on the bottom of page 96.

PROBLEM-SOLUTION ORGANIZER

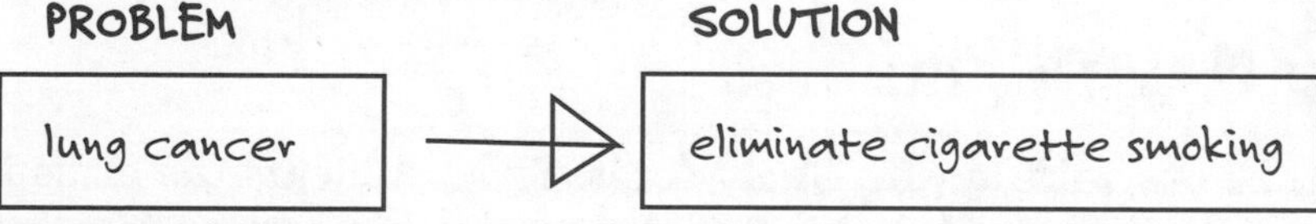

E Connect

Remind students that actively making connections to the text is an important part of effective reading. Suggest these ways of connecting to the science selection:

- ask themselves questions
  (What other real-world problems do biologists try to solve?)
- think about the meaning of what they learn
  (What would happen if the population keeps growing?)
- think about someone who would be interested in hearing about the information
  (Who can I tell about how biology helps fight diseases?)
- relate the new information to prior knowledge
  (What else do I know about protecting the environment?)
- compare what they learn to their own experience
  (Do I know anyone who has one of these diseases?)

Remind students that the study of science is important to our lives and the world. By connecting with science texts, students will learn important information.

After Reading

F Pause and Reflect

After reading, have students stop to consider what they have learned from the selection. Ask students to go back and review their original purpose for reading "Biology in Your World."

Looking Back

- **Did I accomplish the reading purpose I set in the beginning?**
- **Do I know what the main topics in the chapter are?**
- **Do I understand how the material is organized?**
- **Would I feel comfortable taking a test on this material now?**

Because science texts are packed with information, students will have to go back and reread to clarify their understandings and fill in any gaps in their knowledge. Emphasize to the students that rereading is something the best readers do.

G Reread

Encourage students to try a new strategy for gathering more information while rereading. Emphasize that using a different strategy will give them a fresh perspective on the selection.

Rereading Strategy: Note-taking

Introduce the strategy of **note-taking** with Study Cards. Show students the example on page 98. Study Cards are useful for helping students to recall important facts, work in groups, and study for quizzes and exams. Using index cards, students write a key word, term, or phrase on one side and a definition or explanation on the opposite side.

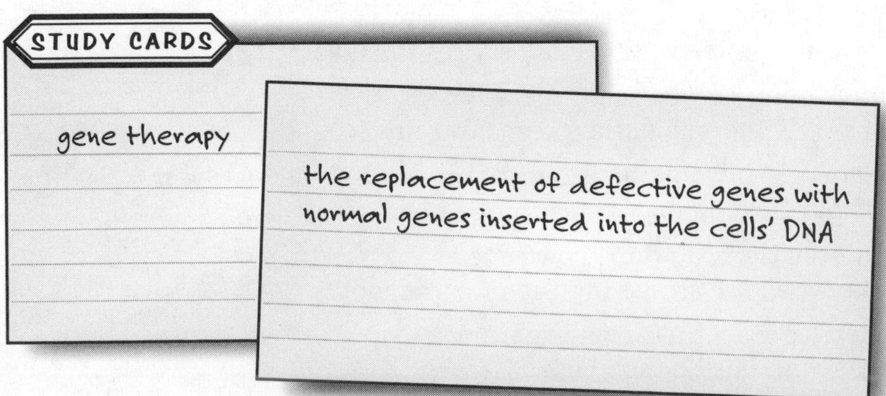

Remember

Now students need to make the reading their own. They need to do something with the subject matter in order to remember it. Read the activities suggested on pages 98 and 99 of the *Reader's Handbook,* or have students do the creative assignment below.

Creative Assignment: Working in pairs, have students choose a subtopic from "Biology in Your World" and do further research on the Internet. Students should look for two or three websites sponsored by recognized scientific organizations, institutions, or museums worldwide and gather more information on their topic. Students may talk about their research informally in groups of five or six.

Summing Up

Now review the lesson with the students, focusing on the points listed in the Summing Up on page 99 of the handbook. Discuss with them the strategies and tools for reading science. Go over the goals for the lesson. Ask the students which ones they feel they achieved and which ones they need more work on:

1. **determining what is important in a science textbook**
2. **applying the strategy of outlining**
3. **understanding the organization of science textbooks and science writing**

Assessment and Application

Use the Quick Assess checklist to evaluate students' ability to read and understand science textbooks. Give students the opportunity to apply what they have learned through one of the two activities below. For students who are comfortable with the reading process and strategy, use one of the suggestions for independent practice or an activity of your own. For students who need guided help with the strategy, use a *Student Applications Book*.

Quick Assess

Can students

- name three things to look for when previewing a science textbook?
- describe the strategy of outlining?
- explain why rereading is necessary and identify a good strategy to use for it?
- name three common ways of organizing science writing?

1. Independent Practice

Ask students to show that they understand the lesson by applying the strategy of **outlining** or the strategy of **note-taking** to a section or chapter in their current science book.

Ask students to do one of the following:

- Take notes on their next assigned science chapter using a formal or informal Outline.
- Create Study Cards for their next science chapter.
- Write a journal entry on the importance to their daily lives of the information in their next science reading.

2. Student Applications Books

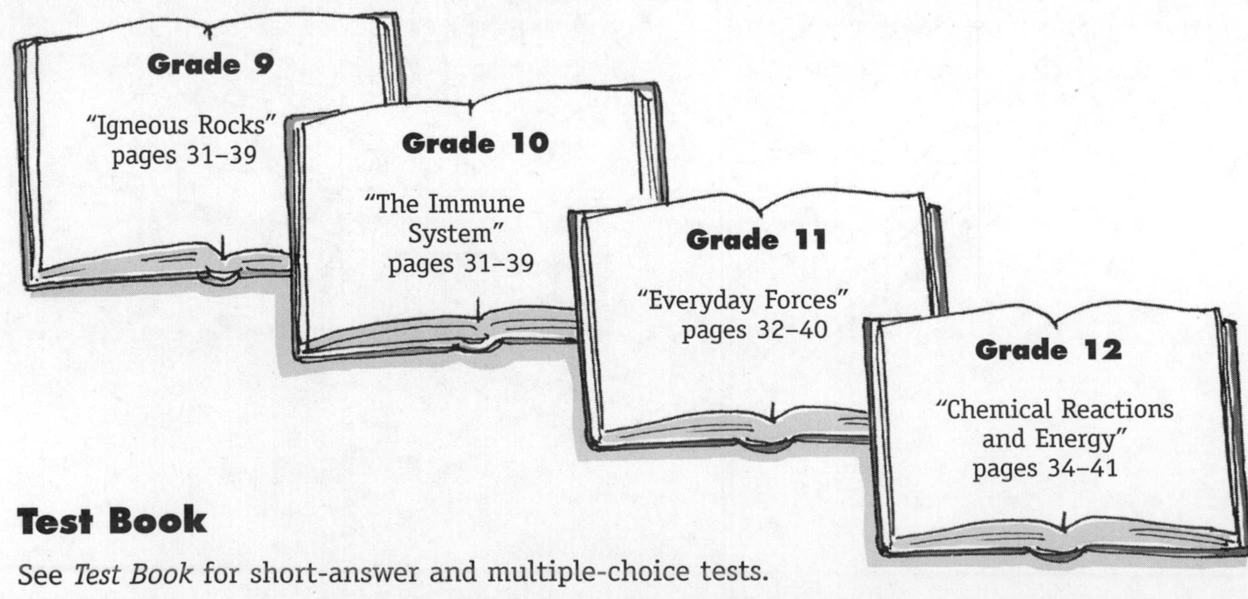

Test Book

See *Test Book* for short-answer and multiple-choice tests.

Reading Math

Goals

Here students read a section from a math textbook titled "Numbers and Number Operations." This lesson will help students learn to:

- read about math and understand concepts and operations
- use the strategy of visualizing and thinking aloud
- understand how math books are organized

Background

Help students connect this lesson with their existing knowledge by asking them to:

- talk about how reading a math textbook is different from reading other kinds of textbooks
- describe what they usually find in a math textbook
- discuss why reading math is sometimes difficult
- talk about ways that information is usually organized in a math textbook

Opening Activity

Using the students' current math textbook, flip through a chapter and point out the important features of the book, such as headings and subheadings, boldface terms, material in the margins, graphics, and example problems. Instruct students to be aware of these features while reading the current lesson's selection.

Overview

	Content	Teacher's Guide page	Reader's Handbook page
Selection	"Numbers and Number Operations"		102–104
Reading Strategy	Visualizing and Thinking Aloud	66	105–106, 736
Rereading Strategy	Note-taking	68, 434	110, 718
Tool	Key Word Notes	68	110, 746

Ancillaries

	Grade	Content	Page
Overhead Transparency	9–12	Previewing Math	Numbers 12 and 13
Lesson Plan Book	9 10 11 12	Reading Math Reading Math Reading Math Reading Math	74, 76–79 74, 76–79 65, 70–73 74, 76–79
Student Applications Book	9 10 11 12	"Solving Addition Equations" "Calculating the Surface Area of a Prism" "Graphing and Writing Equations of Circles" "Perpendicular Bisectors"	40–46 40–47 41–48 42–48
Test Book	9–12	Short-answer Test Multiple-choice Test	
Website		www.greatsource.com/rehand/	
Content Area Guide		This lesson appears in the *Content Area Guide: Math.*	

Before Reading

A Set a Purpose

Have students set a purpose before they read the selection. Direct them to the Setting a Purpose questions on page 101 of the handbook.

Setting a Purpose

- **What are number operations?**
- **What do I need to know about numbers and number operations?**

B Preview

Have students preview the reading selection. Remind them that previewing is just a quick look to get a general idea of what the chapter is about. Emphasize that previewing helps all readers read faster and with better comprehension.

Direct students' attention to the Preview Checklist on page 101. Then preview the selection beginning on page 102 of the handbook, focusing on the headings, the text in the margins, bold type, boxed material, and examples.

Preview Checklist

✓ *the title*
✓ *any listed goals*
✓ *the introductory paragraph*
✓ *the headings, boldface words, color, and highlighted items*
✓ *the models, diagrams, and examples*
✓ *the boxed items*
✓ *the review questions*

Overhead Transparencies

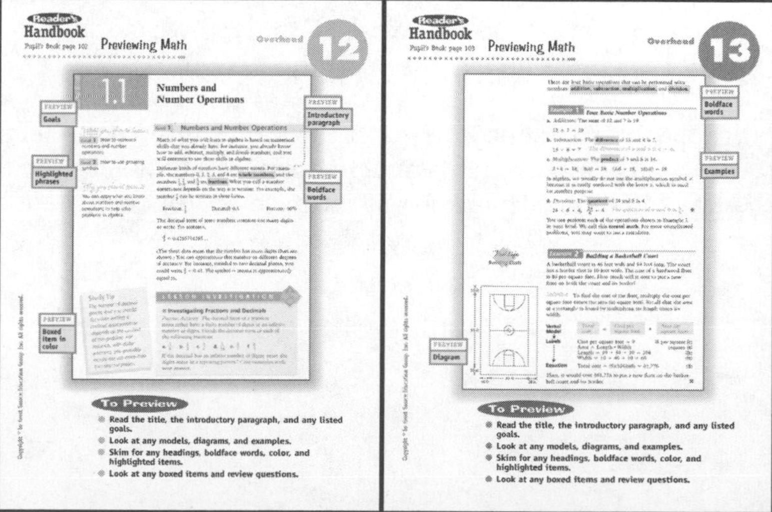

Before Reading

C Plan

Ask students to briefly tell some of the things they learned from their preview. Read the bulleted list at the top of page 105 in the handbook. Now that students have a general idea of what this chapter is about, they can make a plan to help them meet their purpose for reading.

Reading Strategy: Visualizing and Thinking Aloud

Introduce students to the strategy of **visualizing and thinking aloud** for reading math texts. Explain that this strategy is useful for understanding abstract concepts and reinforcing mental processes.

Visualizing helps students make an abstract idea (the math problem) concrete. Ask students to look at Example 2 in the reading selection, which includes a diagram. Point out that if this diagram were not included, it would be helpful for students to draw it themselves based on the information in the problem. Show them how one reader visualized and drew a diagram for the word problem at the top of page 106 of the handbook.

Thinking aloud is simply talking through what a diagram or equation means. Show students the example on page 106 of the handbook. Explain to students that thinking aloud enables them to concentrate on the math problem and to clarify for themselves what the problem is asking for.

During Reading

D Read with a Purpose

Remind students that they need to keep in mind their purpose questions as they read: "What are number operations?" and "What do I need to know about numbers and number operations?" Have students apply the strategy of visualizing and thinking aloud while reading the math selection.

Though visualizing the math problem can be done mentally, without making a drawing, have students practice this strategy by making drawings now. Walk through the diagram of the problem on page 107 of their handbooks.

How Math Textbooks Are Organized

Explain that understanding how math textbooks are organized will help students better understand their math lessons. They will be able to read their math textbooks with greater comprehension and speed when they know where to find the information they need.

Chapters in math textbooks usually begin with an opening explanation, followed by sample problems, which may include graphs and diagrams. These elements are followed by the exercises.

1. *opening explanation*
2. *sample problems*
3. *graphs and diagrams*
4. *exercises*

By identifying these parts of a math lesson, students will be able to find the information they need quickly and focus on it more clearly.

E Connect

A key part of the reading process is to respond to or make connections with the reading. Though students may not see initially how to connect to a math reading, students use math every day. To show students how math is relevant to their daily lives, turn an abstract problem into a real one, as shown in the chart at the top of page 109 in the handbook.

REAL-LIFE PROBLEM

ABSTRACT PROBLEM	REAL-LIFE PROBLEM
$(3 \bullet 4) + 8$	Suppose 3 different groups of 4 people each arrived at a party. Then 8 people came individually. How many people would be at the party?

Suggest these ways for students to connect with math texts:

- ask themselves questions (How would I use this in real life?)
- think about someone who would share an interest in this math selection (Who would be a good math study partner?)
- compare new information in a math reading to what they already know (How does this relate to what we learned last week?)

After Reading

F Pause and Reflect

After reading, have students return to their original Setting a Purpose questions to see if they can answer them. Also have students consider the Looking Back questions on page 109 of the handbook.

Looking Back

- **Do I understand the key vocabulary?**
- **Can I explain how to use grouping symbols?**
- **Are the sample problems clear to me?**
- **Would I do well on a test that covered this material?**

Because math concepts are complex and difficult for many students, rereading is necessary. Remind students that even the best readers go back to the text to clarify their understanding—this is part of what makes them good readers.

G Reread

Give students a fresh way to go back into the selection. Introduce the strategy of note-taking for rereading a math text.

Rereading Strategy: Note-taking

Explain to students that **note-taking** is a good way to record key terms and make sure that they understand the information. Using Key Word Notes enables students to focus on the most important information in the reading. Direct students to page 110 of the handbook, and show them the example of one reader's Key Word Notes.

KEY WORD NOTES

NUMBERS AND NUMBER OPERATIONS

Key Words	Examples
whole numbers	7, 8, 9
fractions	1/3, 5/8, 7/9
decimals	0.3, 0.8, 3.7
percent	25%, 42%, 100%
sum	10 + 3 = 13
difference	48 − 7 = 41
product	11 • 5 = 55
quotient	48 ÷ 6 = 8
grouping symbols	(6 • 7), (18 − 3)
numerical expression	(5 • 3) - (9 − 4) + [(2 + 7) ÷ 3]

After Reading

H Remember

Students must now make the reading their own. That is, they must do something with the new information to remember it. Discuss the activities highlighted on pages 110–111 in the *Reader's Handbook,* or suggest doing the creative assignment.

Creative Assignment: Have students teach one problem in the current lesson to a friend or family member unfamiliar with the operation, using the strategy of visualizing and thinking aloud. Have students report back to the class on how their "lesson" went.

Summing Up

Now review the lesson with students, reading the Summing Up on page 111 in the handbook. Go over the goals of the lesson. Discuss which ones the students feel they achieved and which ones they need more work on:

1. **reading about math and understanding concepts and operations**
2. **using the strategy of visualizing and thinking aloud**
3. **understanding how math books are organized**

Assessment and Application

Use the Quick Assess checklist to evaluate students' ability to read and understand math textbooks. Give students the opportunity to apply what they have learned through one of the two activities below. For students who are comfortable with the reading process and strategy, use one of the suggestions for independent practice or an activity of your own. For students who need guided help with the strategy, use a *Student Applications Book*.

Quick Assess

Can students

- name three things to look for when previewing a math chapter?
- explain the strategy of visualizing and thinking aloud?
- say why rereading is necessary and identify a good strategy to use for it?
- explain how a math text is usually organized?

1. Independent Practice

To show that they understand the lesson, ask students to apply the strategy of **visualizing and thinking aloud** to a section or chapter in their current math textbook.

Ask students to do one of the following:

- Work through the next section of their math books using the visualizing strategy.
- Write a Think Aloud in which they explain their thinking about how to solve a problem in the next section of their math books.
- Write a journal entry on how the math concepts presented in the next assigned chapter of their math book are relevant to their lives.

2. Student Applications Books

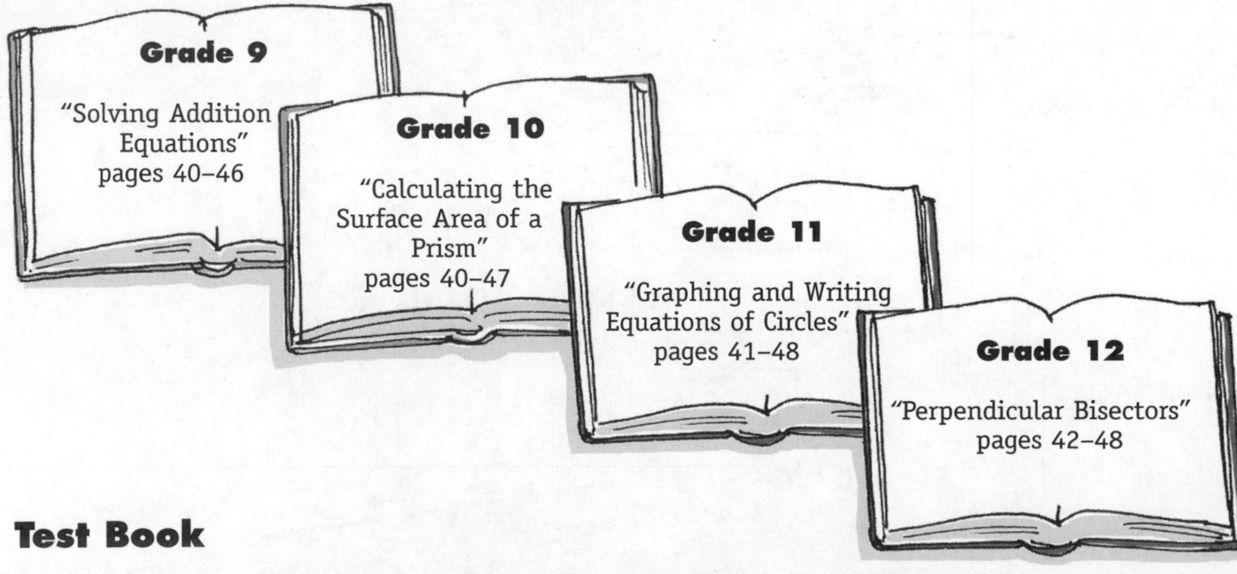

Test Book

See *Test Book* for short-answer and multiple-choice tests.

Focus on Foreign Language

Goals

Here students focus on reading a foreign language textbook. This lesson will help them learn to:

- read and understand foreign language textbooks
- remember new vocabulary and grammar rules

Background

Connect this lesson with students' existing knowledge by asking them to:

- talk about how a foreign language textbook is different from other textbooks
- discuss what features and sections they would expect to find
- discuss why studying a foreign language can be difficult
- say why learning a foreign language is important

Overview

	Content	Teacher's Guide page	Reader's Handbook page
Selection	"Vocabulario y gramática"		113–114
Reading Strategy	Note-taking	72, 434	116, 718
Tool	Web Study Cards	72 72	115, 117, 757 116, 754

Ancillaries

	Grade	Content	Page
Lesson Plan Book	11	Focus on Foreign Language	64, 66–69
Student Applications Book	9 10 11 12	"Comparativos y Superlativos" "Los Verbos *Ser* y *Estar*" "Preterite and Imperfect Tenses" "Indicative and Subjunctive Moods"	47–48 48–49 49–50 49–50
Test Book	9–12	Short-answer Test Multiple-choice Test	
Website		www.greatsource.com/rehand/	

Before Reading

Foreign language textbooks typically include new vocabulary, new grammar rules, and assignments in speaking and writing. Remind students of the importance of previewing to familiarize themselves with the content of a section or chapter. With the students, preview the excerpt from the Spanish book on pages 113 and 114 of the handbook.

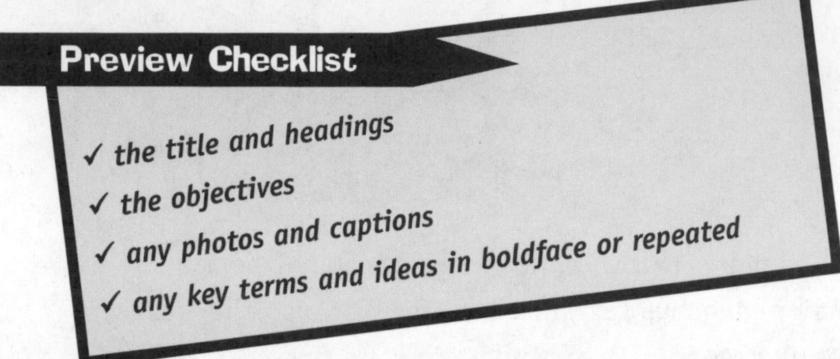

Ask students to say in their own words what they learned from the preview.

To plan how to get the needed information from this selection, students may use a Web, shown on page 115. Point out that this example shows boxes labeled with the main categories from the reading, which one reader picked up from the preview.

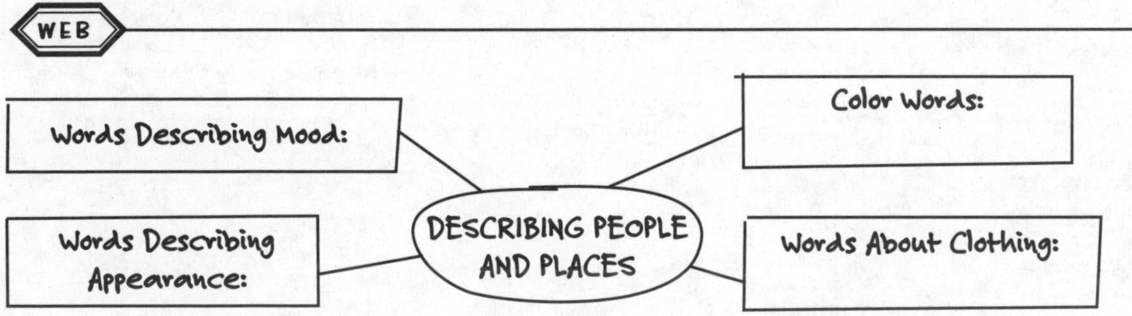

When a Web doesn't work for students' needs, they can choose a different reading tool.

Reading Strategy: Note-taking

Introduce the strategy of **note-taking** for reading foreign language textbooks. Point out that one of the biggest challenges in studying a foreign language is the number of new words and verb conjugations that must be learned. For this reason, Study Cards are a useful tool.

Study Cards are especially useful when studying for quizzes and tests. The English word may be written on one side and the Spanish equivalent on the opposite side. Have students look at the examples given on page 116 of the *Reader's Handbook*.

During Reading

As students read, ask them to take notes using a Web or the note-taking strategy. Emphasize to students that many strategies and tools can help them gain the important information from a reading. Students should select the technique that works best for them.

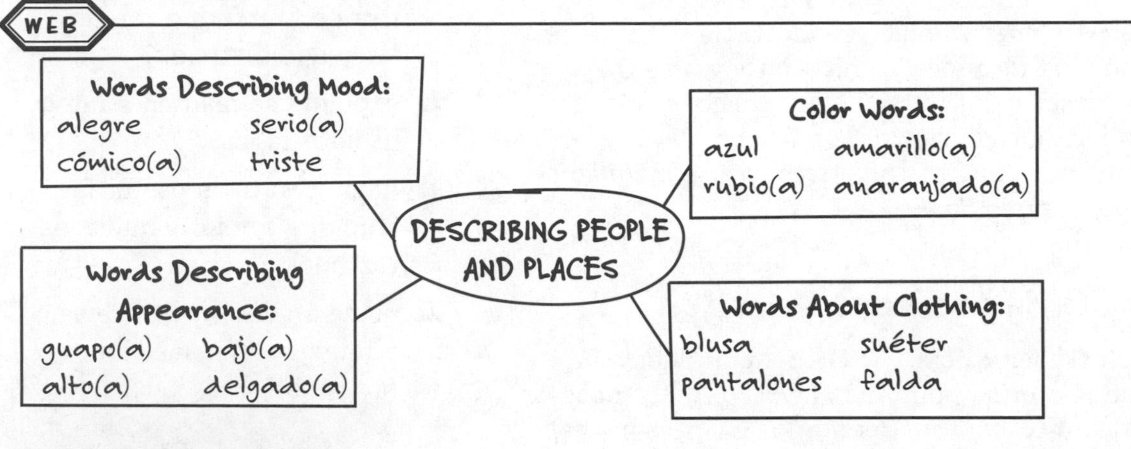

After Reading

After reading, have students stop to consider what they have learned from the selection. Because foreign language texts are packed with new words and new grammar rules, students will need to go back and reread.

Have students look at the review tips listed on page 117 of the handbook. Read the tips with the students, and then provide time for them to practice each one.

1. Look at your notes or organizers.
Do the students' notes make sense? Do there seem to be gaps in them? Is there information missing? Have students return to the selection to fill in the missing information.

2. Make up a practice test.
Have students make up a five- or ten-question practice test, find a partner, and exchange tests. The partners then take each other's tests. Emphasize to students that making up a practice test is an excellent study strategy because it requires them to anticipate possible test questions.

3. Play a game.
Students may use their Study Cards to invent and play word games. For example, students might take turns drawing a card and using the word on the card in a sentence.

Summing Up

Have students read over the points in the Summing Up on page 118. Ask students to say in their own words what they learned in this lesson.

Assessment and Application

Use the Quick Assess checklist to evaluate students' ability to read and understand foreign language texts. Give students the opportunity to apply what they have learned through one of the two activities below. For students who are comfortable with the reading process and strategy, use the suggestion for independent practice or an activity of your own. For students who need guided help with the strategy, use a *Student Applications Book.*

Quick Assess

Can students

- ☑ say what types of information can be found in a foreign language textbook?
- ☑ explain the reading strategy of note-taking?
- ☑ name two tools useful for studying foreign language textbooks?
- ☑ name a good way to review a foreign language chapter for a test?

1. Independent Practice

Ask students to show that they understand the lesson by applying the strategy of **note-taking** to another section or chapter in their current foreign language book.

2. Student Applications Books

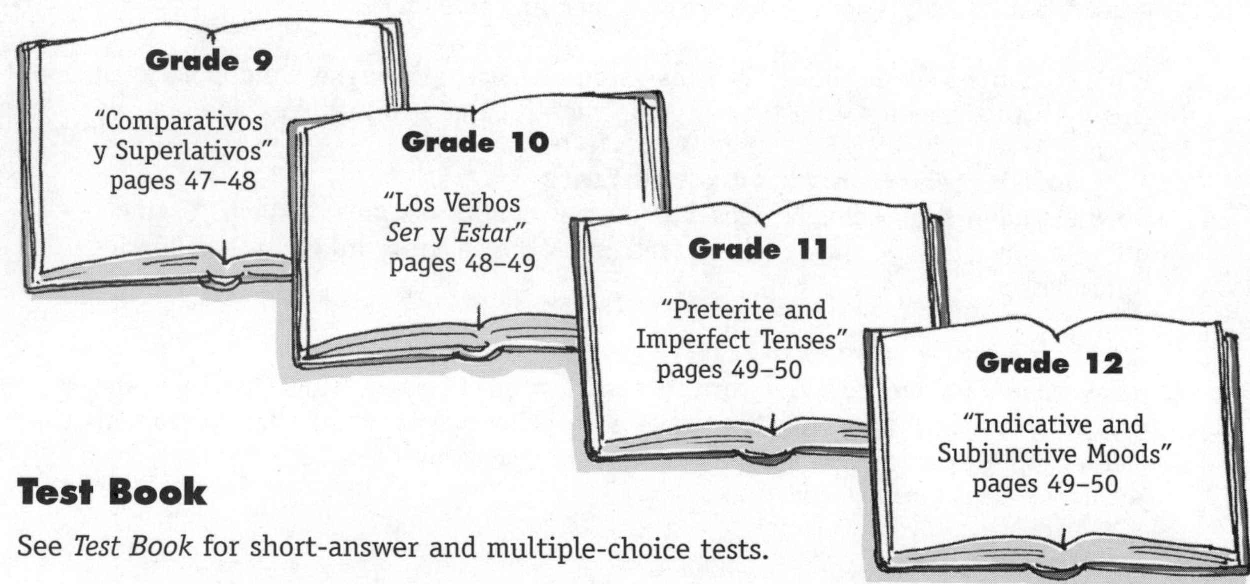

Test Book

See *Test Book* for short-answer and multiple-choice tests.

Focus on Science Concepts

Goals

Here students focus on understanding science concepts. This lesson will help students to:

- ✔ use tools that can help them read and understand science concepts
- ✔ use methods to help them memorize science terms

Background

Connect this lesson with students' existing knowledge by asking them to:

- define the term *concept* as it is used in science
- give an example or two of a science concept
- say why it's important to understand scientific concepts

Overview

	Content	Teacher's Guide page	Reader's Handbook page
Selection	"The Scientific Process"		120–122
Reading Strategy	Outlining	76, 435	122, 720
Tool	Outline Flow Chart	76, 77 77	122, 123, 749 123, 745

Ancillaries

	Grade	Content	Page
Lesson Plan Book	12	Focus on Science Concepts	65, 70–73
Student Applications Book	9 10 11 12	The Rock Cycle Understanding Inflammatory Response Displacement Photosynthesis	49–52 50–52 51–52 51–52
Test Book	9–12	Short-answer Test Multiple-choice Test	
Website		www.greatsource.com/rehand/	
Content Area Guide		This lesson appears in the *Content Area Guide: Science.*	

Before Reading

Explain to students that science textbooks usually include vocabulary and a process or series of steps to read and possibly follow. Remind students of the importance of previewing and direct them to the Preview Checklist.

Preview Checklist

- ✓ *the title and headings*
- ✓ *the first paragraph*
- ✓ *the objectives*
- ✓ *any photos and captions*
- ✓ *any key terms and ideas in boldface*
- ✓ *any bulleted lists*

Ask students to say in their own words what they learned from the preview. Then read the information from the preview at the top of page 122.

- The scientific process follows five steps or stages.
- Careful observation is important in the scientific process.
- Key terms include *observation, hypothesis,* and *prediction*.

Point out that the strategy of outlining can help students remember what they are reading.

Reading Strategy: Outlining

Emphasize that **outlining** will help students better remember the important information in a science chapter. Explain that the section or chapter headings and subheadings are used in the outline to direct students' attention to the important information.

OUTLINE

THE SCIENTIFIC PROCESS

I. Science Is Based on Careful Observation
   A.
   B.
II. Several Stages Are Common to Scientific Investigations
   A.
   B.

During Reading

As students read, they can achieve their reading purpose by using an Outline to jot down notes in their science notebooks.

Ask the students to turn to page 123 of the handbook. The example at the top of the page shows the beginning of one reader's Outline. Remind students that they should not attempt to write down everything in an Outline—only the main ideas are recorded.

OUTLINE

The Scientific Process

I. Science Is Based on Careful Observation
   A. David Bradford noticed that amphibians were disappearing.
   B. John Harte noticed that the number of tiger salamanders was declining.

II. Several Stages Are Common to Scientific Investigations
   A. Collecting observations is first stage.
   B. Asking questions is second stage.

Now show students the example of the Flow Chart at the bottom of page 123. A Flow Chart is an excellent tool for depicting a process. Suggest that students practice using this tool when a process is described in their science reading.

FLOW CHART

First	Next	Next	Next	Next
Make an observation.	Ask questions.	Form hypothesis.	Confirm predictions.	Draw conclusions.

Explain to students that science texts often describe processes, such as how a cell divides, how a volcano erupts, and so on. Knowing how to use a Flow Chart with science texts should help students better understand science processes.

After Reading

After reading, students need to think about what they have learned from the selection. Point out that, because science tests and concepts are complex, rereading probably will be necessary.

Have students look at the review tips given on page 124 of the handbook. Read over the tips with the students, and then work with them to do each one.

1. Review your Flow Chart and Outline.

Do the students' Outlines and Flow Charts make sense? Is some information missing? Have students return to the selection to fill in the missing information.

2. Have a conversation.

Tell students that simply talking about the material is a good way to better understand and remember it. Have students work in pairs, explaining concepts to one another. If one partner has some difficulty, the other partner can help to fill in the blanks or suggest where to reread to find the information.

Have students read the points in the Summing Up at the bottom of page 124. Ask students to say in their own words what they learned in this lesson.

Assessment and Application

Use the Quick Assess checklist to evaluate students' ability to read and understand science concepts. Give students the opportunity to apply what they have learned through one of the two activities below. For students who are comfortable with the reading process and strategy, use the suggestion for independent practice or an activity of your own. For students who need guided help with the strategy, use a *Student Applications Book*.

Quick Assess

Can students

- ☑ name three things to look for while previewing a science text?
- ☑ describe two tools that are useful for understanding science concepts?
- ☑ name two ways to review the important information in a science reading?

1. Independent Practice

Ask students to apply the strategy of **outlining** to another section or chapter in their current science textbook to show their understanding of the lesson.

2. Student Applications Books

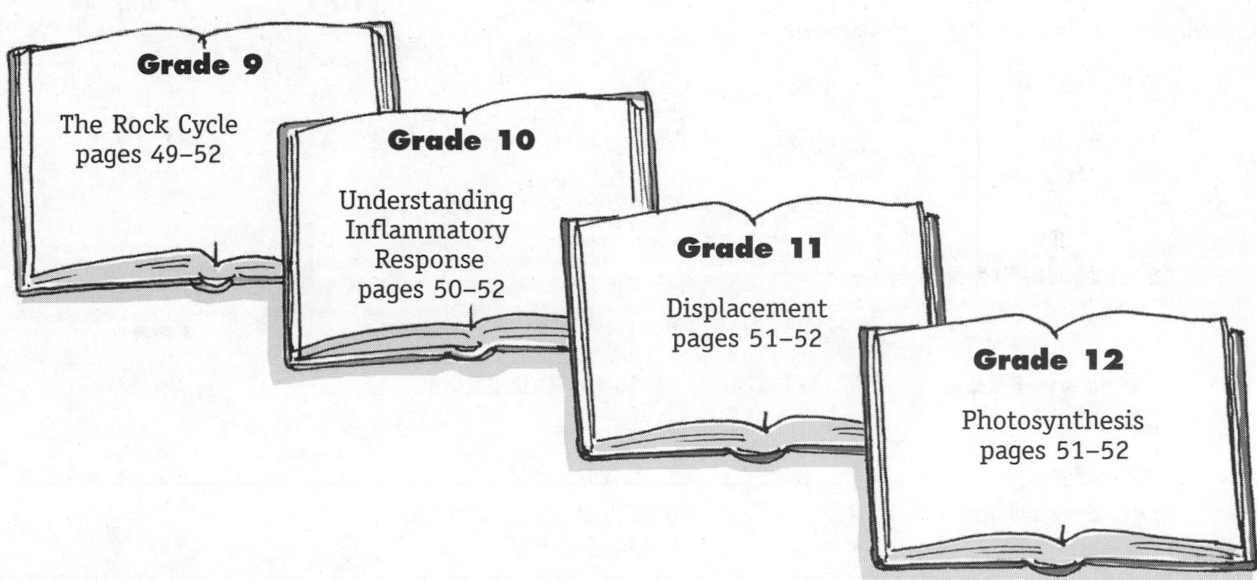

Test Book

See *Test Book* for short-answer and multiple-choice tests.

Focus on Study Questions

Goals

Here students will focus on understanding study questions. They will learn to:

- ✓ follow a four-step plan when answering study questions
- ✓ recognize and understand key words in questions

Background

Connect this lesson with students' existing knowledge by asking them to:

- talk about different types of questions they have had to answer in the past
- discuss why some questions are confusing
- say why it's important to understand how to read questions

Overview

	Content	Teacher's Guide page	Reader's Handbook page
Selection	Example Question		127
Reading Strategy	Visualizing and Thinking Aloud	81, 440	126, 736

Ancillaries

	Grade	Content	Page
Lesson Plan Book	12	Focus on Study Questions	75, 80–83
Student Applications Book	9	*Plessy* v. *Ferguson*	53–54
	10	The Protestant Reformation	53–54
	11	from "Self-Reliance" by Ralph Waldo Emerson	53–54
	12	The Bay of Pigs Incident	53–54
Test Book	9–12	Short-answer Test Multiple-choice Test	
Website		www.greatsource.com/rehand/	
Content Area Guide		This lesson also appears in the *Content Area Guide: Social Studies.*	

Before Reading

Explain that most, if not all, students sometimes misread questions, leading them to answer incorrectly. To avoid misreading questions, students need to have a plan.

Introduce the four-step plan explained on page 125 of the handbook. Read through each step with the students.

FOUR-STEP PLAN FOR STUDY QUESTIONS

Step 1: Read
Start by reading the question two or more times to make sure you know exactly what is being asked.

Step 2: Plan
Think of a way you can arrive at the answer.

Step 3: Write
Write your answer, following the strategy you chose.

Step 4: Reread and Edit
Reread the question and your answer, making sure it is clear and that it answers the question. Make any corrections that are necessary.

Reading Strategy: Visualizing and Thinking Aloud

Suggest the strategy of **visualizing and thinking aloud** during reading. This strategy helps ensure accurate understanding of the question.

During Reading

Explain to students that visualizing and thinking aloud allows them to focus on how to answer a question correctly. Have them turn to the example on page 126 of the handbook, and ask for a volunteer to read the Think Aloud.

Then direct students' attention to the list of key words in questions given at the bottom of page 126.

Understanding the meanings of certain key words commonly used in questions will greatly improve students' ability to answer questions correctly. Read over this list of verbs with the students and make sure they understand the definition of each. You may also wish to do other vocabulary activities with these words to help students learn them.

After Reading

Now ask students to turn to page 127 in their handbooks to look at the example question and one reader's answer. Point out how this reader marked up the sample question after finding the key words and phrases. Explain that key words in the question are circled, and words referring to the topic are underlined.

> Explain how Eliza is representative of the beginning of the women's movement at the start of the twentieth century.

Ask students to read silently the answer written below this question. Note how this reader went back over the answer to check its accuracy and correct mistakes.

Review tips for answering study questions are given on page 128 of the handbook. Read over the tips with the students.

1. Ask a partner for help.
Talking with a study partner about each question will help students clarify and elaborate their answers. Encourage students to do this, allowing class time for it when possible.

2. Review.
Suggest that students go back to the chapter and section introduction to review the big ideas. They can also look at the end of a chapter for a review or summary.

Summing Up

Have students read the points in the Summing Up on page 128. Ask students to say in their own words what they learned in this lesson.

Assessment and Application

Use the Quick Assess checklist to evaluate students' ability to read and answer questions. Give students the opportunity to apply what they have learned through one of the two activities below. For students who are comfortable with the reading process and strategy, use the suggestion for independent practice or an activity of your own. For students who need guided help with the strategy, use a *Student Applications Book*.

Quick Assess

Can students

- ☑ explain the four-step plan for answering a question?
- ☑ name and define two or three key words that commonly appear in questions?
- ☑ explain how to mark up a question to emphasize key words?

1. Independent Practice

Ask students to show that they understand the lesson by applying the **visualizing and thinking aloud** strategy or review tips to the study questions for an upcoming test.

2. Student Applications Books

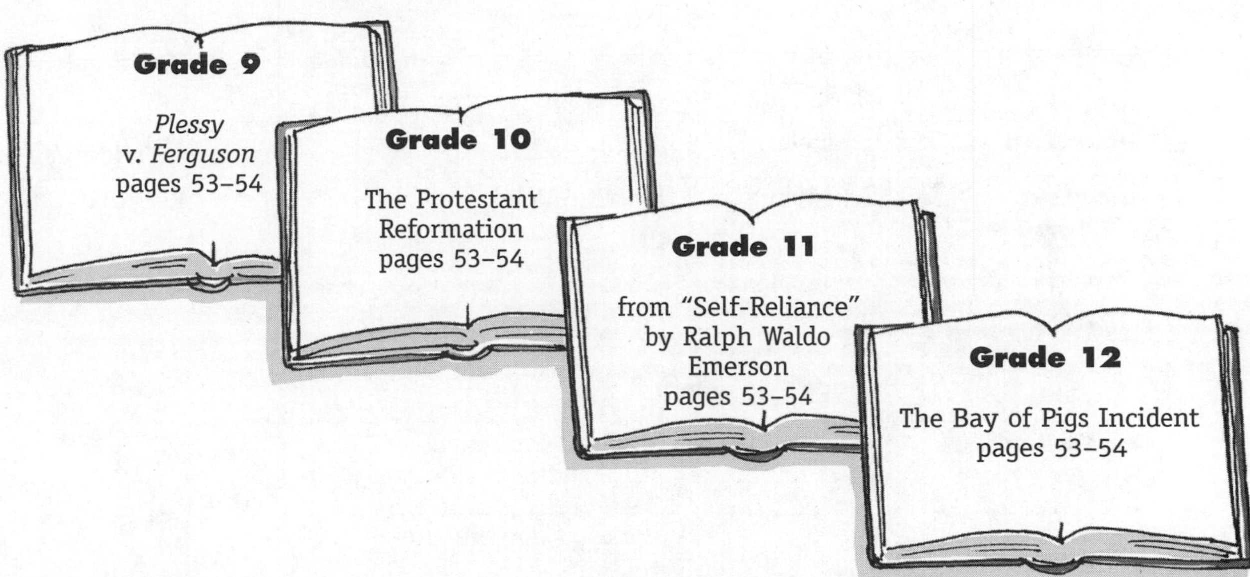

Test Book

See *Test Book* for short-answer and multiple-choice tests.

Focus on Word Problems

Goals

Here students focus on word problems in math. As students read and analyze sample word problems, they will learn to:

- ✓ use a four-step plan to solve word problems
- ✓ visualize what the problem asks for

Background

Connect this lesson with students' existing knowledge by asking them to:

- discuss why word problems can sometimes be difficult
- talk about the process they go through currently to solve word problems
- make up word problems as examples

Overview

	Content	Teacher's Guide page	Reader's Handbook page
Selection	Examples		130, 132, 133
Reading Strategy	Visualizing and Thinking Aloud	86, 44	130–131, 736

Ancillaries

	Grade	Content	Page
Lesson Plan Book	11	Focus on Word Problems	74, 76–79
Student Applications Book	9 10 11 12	Average Daily Temperature Computer Auto-save Bike Ride Problem Consumer Math	55–56 55–56 55–56 55–56
Test Book	9–12	Short-answer Test Multiple-choice Test	
Website		www.greatsource.com/rehand/	
Content Area Guide		This lesson appears in the *Content Area Guide: Math.*	

Explain that one trick to solving word problems is to read the question very carefully. Introduce the four-step plan explained on page 129 of the handbook. Read through each step with students.

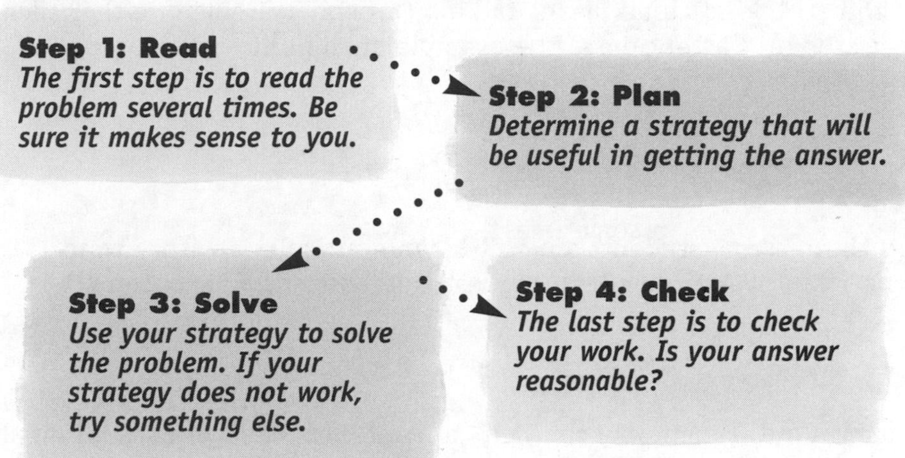

Understanding Word Problems

Because understanding the word problem exactly is so important to solving it, remind students that they need to read the problem more than one time. On the first reading, students should look for information on three questions:

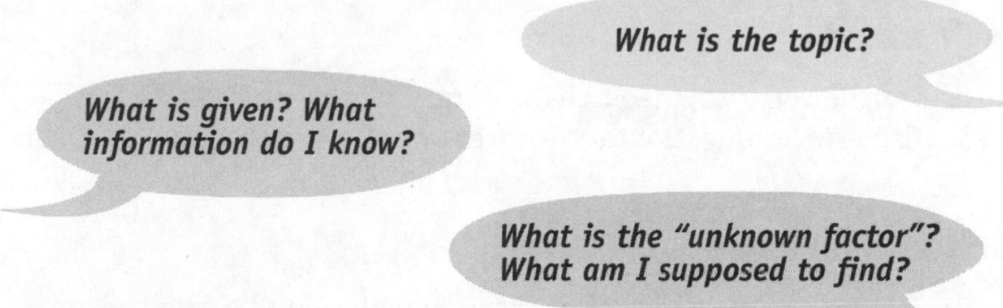

Making Notes

On the second reading, students may need to take notes. Show students the example of notes on page 130. Then suggest the strategy of **visualizing and thinking aloud** to solve the problem.

Reading Strategy: Visualizing and Thinking Aloud

Explain to students that visualizing means seeing a picture in the mind. Students may or may not actually make a drawing on paper like the one at the top of page 131.

During Reading

Remind students that thinking aloud means talking through a problem, either silently or out loud. Direct students' attention to the example of thinking aloud on page 131.

After Reading

If, after following these steps, students are still having difficulties with a word problem or are uncertain of their answers, suggest the following four options.

1. Solve in a Different Way

Solving the problem in a different way can help students see whether their original answers are correct. Have students look at the example on page 132.

2. Estimate, Using Simpler Numbers

Rounding off numbers and estimating the answer is also a good way of checking the original solution. If a student's initial answer is somewhat like the estimated answer, then the original answer is probably correct. Show students the example given on page 132.

3. Work Backward

Working backward is another way to check the accuracy of the initial answer, as shown on page 133. Discuss the question and process of working backward to solve it.

4. Work with a Partner

If the problems being solved are not part of a test, students may be allowed to work with partners. The partners can share their ideas, notes, and sketches with each other.

Summing Up

Have students read the points in the Summing Up at the bottom of page 133. Ask students to say in their own words what they learned in this lesson.

Assessment and Application

Use the Quick Assess checklist to evaluate students' ability to read and solve word problems. Give students the opportunity to apply what they have learned through one of the two activities below. For students who are comfortable with the reading process and strategy, use the suggestion for independent practice or an activity of your own. For students who need guided help with the strategy, use a *Student Applications Book*.

Quick Assess

Can students

- ☑ explain the four-step plan for solving a word problem?
- ☑ explain the strategy of visualizing and thinking aloud?
- ☑ name different ways to check their original answers?

1. Independent Practice

Ask students to apply the strategy of **visualizing and thinking aloud** to word problems in their current math text to show that they understand the lesson.

2. Student Applications Books

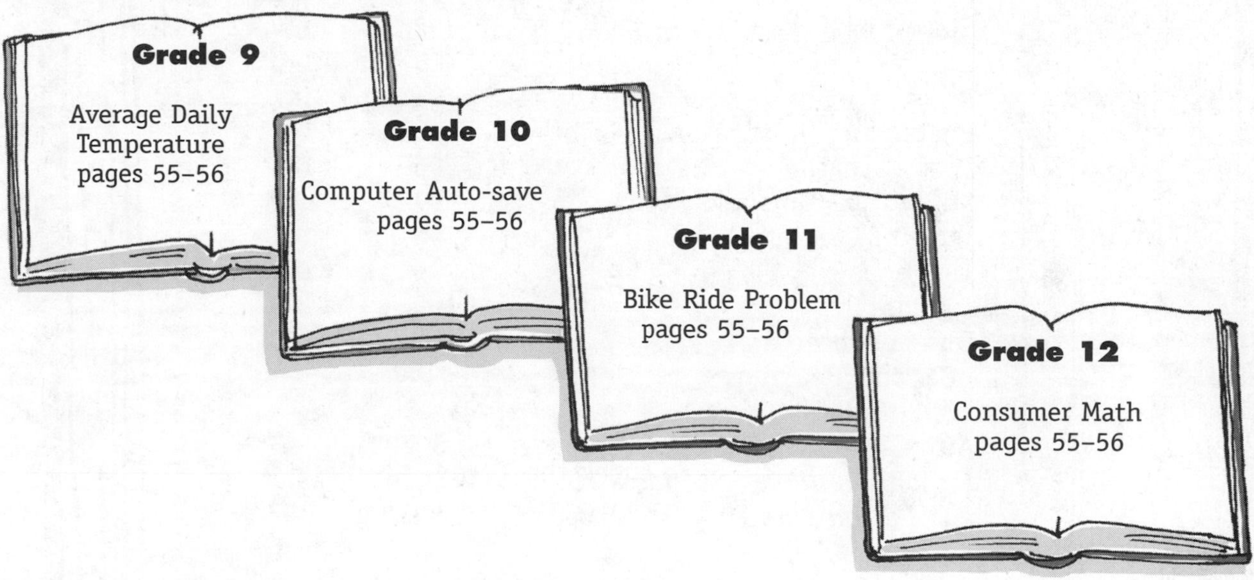

Test Book

See *Test Book* for short-answer and multiple-choice tests.

Elements of Textbooks

This section introduces and explains common elements in textbooks. The *Reader's Handbook* provides examples, descriptions, and definitions. Use this section to familiarize students with the terminology and the overall purposes of these elements of textbooks.

Element	***Teacher's Guide* page**	***Reader's Handbook* page**
Chapter Previews	89	135
Charts and Graphs	90	136
Footnotes	91	138
Glossaries	92	139
Indexes	93	140
Maps	94	141
Photos and Illustrations	95	142
Special Features	96	143
Study Questions and Reviews	97	145
Table of Contents	98	146
Timelines	99	148
Typography	100	149
Unit, Chapter, and Section Headings	101	150

Also see *Lesson Plan Book 9* (pages 75, 80–83), *Lesson Plan Book 10* (pages 75, 80–83), and *Lesson Plan Book 11* (pages 75, 80–83).

Chapter Previews

Set Goal

Students will learn that a chapter preview is an opening section that provides a quick summary of all the important points in the chapter.

Teach and Discuss

Have students look at the **Example** of a chapter preview on page 135 of the *Reader's Handbook*. Ask students to summarize what they learn just by reading and thinking about the chapter preview. Have them predict what they're likely to find in the material ahead. Also ask students if reading the preview made them think of questions that might be answered in the material that follows.

Read through the **Description** with the students. Emphasize that previews are designed to help improve students' reading comprehension and recall. By taking a moment to look over the chapter preview, students will be able to read not only faster but with better understanding.

Point out that the example chapter preview is for a history textbook. It lists themes in the chapter, provides two maps pertinent to the Industrial Revolution, and has a mini table of contents. Chapter previews in other textbooks may list objectives or goals and key terms or names. In addition, there may be study tips for the chapter and introductory or background information.

Check Understanding

Have students read the **Definition** at the bottom of page 135. Then have students look for chapter previews in their own classroom textbooks. Working in pairs, students can discuss what they found. Here are some good questions:

- What do you see in this chapter preview?
- What can you learn from the chapter preview?
- How might this chapter preview help you better understand the material that follows it?

Charts and Graphs

Set Goal

Students will learn that charts provide information, show processes, or make comparisons, usually in columns. Graphs show information using lines, symbols, and pictures.

Teach and Discuss

Have students look at the **Example** on page 136 of the handbook. One at a time, discuss the circle graph, the chart, the line graph, and the bar and line graphs. Ask students to describe or explain what they see in each one. Then ask them what interesting facts they have learned by studying the charts and graphs.

Read through the **Description** on page 137 with the students. Emphasize that charts and graphs are useful because they provide a visual display of information. This different type of presentation provides a great deal of information that can be absorbed faster—and often with better understanding. Ask students why it is important to summarize the main idea of a chart or graph. Explain the usefulness of creating a one-sentence summary, or conclusion, from a chart. Students do not need to remember every detail, but they should not just "look at" a chart or graph. They need to think about what it means. They should be sure to read the title and labels. They also need to take note of any colors, patterns, and symbols.

Check Understanding

Have students read the **Definition** at the bottom of page 137. Then have students look for charts and graphs in their current classroom textbooks. Working in pairs, students can discuss these points:

- Why is information represented in different ways in different types of charts and graphs?
- Why do textbook authors include charts rather than writing out the information in the body of the text?
- Which types of charts and graphs tend to be used in the different subject areas?

Footnotes

Set Goal

Students will learn that footnotes are numbered comments at the bottom, or sometimes at the side, of the page. Footnotes provide additional information, but they are not something that can just be skipped over.

Teach and Discuss

Have students look at the **Example** on page 138 of the handbook, and point out the small numbers in the text and the definitions of the words at the bottom of the page. Ask students to say what additional information these footnotes are providing. Have students think about and discuss the advantages of having footnotes in a textbook and taking the time to read the footnotes.

Read through the **Description** with the students. Emphasize that the numbers of the footnotes correspond to the small superscript numbers appearing in the text above. Also explain that, in addition to defining or explaining terms, footnotes are often used to cite sources or to further explain material in the text.

Point out that footnotes are very helpful in rereading or using the strategy of close reading. When readers return to a selection, they often reread the footnotes as a help in understanding or to clear up parts that have confused them.

Check Understanding

Have students read the **Definition** at the bottom of page 138. Then have students look through their current textbooks for examples of footnotes. Have students share the examples they find, as they find them, with the students sitting next to them. Ask students to note the following:

- What kind of information is the footnote providing?
- How can reading the footnote help increase comprehension of the material?

Glossaries

Set Goal

Students will learn that a glossary is an alphabetical listing of key words from the book, accompanied by the numbers of the pages on which the words appear.

Teach and Discuss

Have students turn to page 139 of the handbook and look at the **Example.** Point out the different parts of the glossary: the key terms, definitions, and page numbers. Explain how a glossary is like a dictionary.

Then read through the **Description** with the students. Emphasize that the glossary is useful for finding key words and improving reading comprehension. Discuss with students how glossaries differ from dictionaries.

Most of the time, a glossary contains the key words of the subject. For this reason, the glossary is often important for understanding the subject.

Check Understanding

Now have students read the **Definition** at the bottom of the page. To demonstrate understanding, have students look at their current science, history, or other textbook that contains a glossary. In a whole-group discussion, ask students:

- How can using the glossary help improve reading comprehension and recall?
- When would it be useful to look at the glossary?
- How could the glossary help in studying for a test?

Indexes

Set Goal

Students will learn that an index is an alphabetical list of words and terms followed by the numbers of the pages on which those words and terms can be found in the book.

Teach and Discuss

Have students look at the **Example** on page 140. Point out the page numbers listed after the entries. Ask students to talk about what other features they notice in this sample (for example, the explanation of the symbols used, the cross references to other entries, and the subentries under main entries).

Then read the **Description** with the class. Emphasize that an index is useful when they are looking for information on a particular term. Also stress that understanding how to use an index will save time when students study for tests and write reports.

Discuss with students how an index is like a search engine on the Internet. Point out that when students are searching for information on the Internet, they type a key word or two in a search engine. In a similar way, they can search an index for key terms. Further explain that indexes can often help in rereading. Suggest that students use the index the next time they think, "Where did I see that word before?"

Check Understanding

Now have students read the **Definition** at the bottom of page 140. To demonstrate their understanding, have students look at indexes in their current textbooks. Ask them questions such as these:

- How would you find information on ______?
- What are the subentries under ______?

Maps

Set Goal

Students will learn that a map is a reduced drawing of the world or part of the world showing the area as it would look from above. Maps are included in textbooks to show where an important place is or to show where an important event happened.

Teach and Discuss

Have students turn to page 141 in the handbook and look at the map in the **Example.** Ask what is shown in this map. What countries do the students see? Point out the map title, the labels for places, the legend, the arrow that points north, the scale, and the highlighted world map.

Read the **Description** with the students. Remind students that to interpret maps correctly they need to look at the special features, such as the symbols, legend, and scale.

Point out the importance of reading, not just looking at, a map. Suggest that students draw a conclusion about a map by writing a one-sentence summary of it.

Check Understanding

Have students quickly read the **Definition** at the bottom of page 141. Then have students find maps in their current history book. Working in pairs, students can find the legend or key, scale, labels, and other features that help them understand the map. Ask them questions:

- What is the purpose of this map?
- What parts of the map help you understand it better?
- Locate ________ on the map.

Photos and Illustrations

Set Goal

Students will learn that photographs and illustrations in a textbook are useful for previewing and understanding the material.

Teach and Discuss

Have students turn to page 142 of the handbook and look at the **Example**. Ask them to say all that can be learned about the material simply by looking at these pictures.

Then read through the **Description** with the students. Emphasize that photographs and illustrations are included in textbooks for visual interest and also to highlight important information. Remind students that taking the time to preview photographs and illustrations in textbooks before reading a chapter can help them read faster and with better comprehension. Ask them what purpose a caption serves.

Point out that students should look at the whole photograph or illustration first. Then they should look at the details. Suggest that students draw a conclusion by creating a one-sentence summary.

Check Understanding

Now have students read the **Definition** at the bottom of page 142. Have students work in pairs looking at the photos and illustrations in their current science, history, or other class textbook. Ask questions such as these:

- Based on the photographs or illustrations alone, what do you predict this chapter will be about?
- How much information can you learn simply by looking at the photographs and captions?
- How might you use photographs and illustrations to help you review for a test?

Special Features

Set Goal

Students will learn that special features in textbooks are used to clarify the material. These special features also provide additional information and visual interest.

Teach and Discuss

Have students turn to pages 143 and 144 of the handbook and look at the **Example** of special features. What do students notice? What kind of information do these special features provide and highlight?

Then read through the **Description** on page 144 with students. Emphasize that special features are often used to clarify and highlight important information in the text. Can students describe how a sidebar and a pullout box differ? Ask them to identify the purpose of symbols and icons and to explain how color can add to a text.

Point out that the additional related information in special features can help students see the content of the text in a new way.

Check Understanding

Have students read the **Definition** at the bottom of page 144. Then ask students to find examples of special features in a current textbook. In a whole-group discussion, ask students:

- How can the information given in special features help improve reading comprehension?
- How can special features be useful when studying for a test?

Study Questions and Reviews

Set Goal

Students will learn that most textbooks include study questions and reviews, which are designed to help students recall facts, apply the material, and think critically about what they have read.

Teach and Discuss

Have students turn to page 145 of the handbook and look at the **Example.** Point out the different types of questions asked in this selection. Emphasize that the timeline is included to help students review the sequence of important events.

Then read through the **Description** with the students. Point out that a list of key terms or names, study questions, and graphics can help students prepare for tests. Explain that study questions basically fall into one of two categories: questions that ask students to recall facts from what they have read and questions that ask students to use critical thinking skills to apply what they have learned.

Check Understanding

Have students read the **Definition** at the bottom of page 145. To demonstrate their understanding, have students compare the types of study questions and reviews in their classroom textbooks. Working in pairs, students can decide which questions ask for a literal recall of facts and which ask for higher-level thinking. They can consider these questions:

- Where do the study questions appear in these textbooks?
- What is an example of a recall question?
- What is an example of a critical thinking question?
- How will these questions help in studying for a test?

Table of Contents

Set Goal

Students will learn that a table of contents, located in the first few pages of a textbook, gives the major parts of the book, along with the page numbers. The table of contents gives the organization of the material.

Teach and Discuss

Ask students to turn to page 146 of the handbook and look at the **Example.** Ask them to explain what kinds of information can be found in a table of contents. Have them discuss the benefits of reading the table of contents before starting to read the book.

Read the **Description** on page 147 with the students. Then compare and contrast the table of contents to the examples of an index and glossary given earlier. Ask students to discuss the similarities, the differences, and how a table of contents might serve as a study aid.

Help students understand that a table of contents is not just a place listing page numbers. It also tells the topics and shows the organization. Explain how the table of contents embodies the organization of a book by putting the individual parts in the context of a larger whole.

Check Understanding

Have students read the **Definition** at the bottom of page 147. Then ask students to take a look at the table of contents in one of their current textbooks. Discuss the following questions in a whole-group session:

- What can you learn about a textbook just by looking at the table of contents?
- How can the table of contents help you read more efficiently—faster and with better comprehension?
- How might the table of contents help you take notes?

Timelines

Set Goal

Students will learn that a timeline is a type of chart that shows a sequence of events in a specified time frame.

Teach and Discuss

Ask students to turn to page 148 of the handbook and look at the **Example.** Briefly point out the different features of this timeline. Ask students to name a few interesting facts that they can learn from this timeline.

Read the **Description** with students. Emphasize that timelines provide an excellent review of important material that can be useful when studying for tests or writing papers. Guide students to see that they need to read timelines critically. They shouldn't just "look at" them.

Point out the need to look at end points. Remind students to read all the type. In addition to using timelines to preview or review, understand sequence, and learn dates, students can use them to find cause-and-effect relationships between events.

Check Understanding

Have students read the **Definition** at the bottom of page 148. Then ask students to find an example of a timeline in their current history textbook. Discuss the following questions in a whole-group session:

- Why do textbook authors include timelines?
- How can previewing timelines before you read a chapter help you read more efficiently?
- How might timelines be useful when studying for a test?

Typography

Set Goal

Students will learn that typography refers to the type styles, or fonts, used in books. The typography in a textbook can be plain, boldface, or italic.

Teach and Discuss

Have students turn to page 149 of the handbook. Ask them to point out the different type styles in the **Example.**

Read through the **Description** with the students. Emphasize that key words or terms in a textbook are usually printed in boldface type. Italics are usually used for picture captions, book titles, or other special features. Ask students to tell why textbook writers use boldface and italic type. Explain the idea that typography gives the reader signals by pointing out parts that are important or that need special emphasis.

Check Understanding

Have students read the **Definition** at the bottom of page 149. To demonstrate understanding, have students skim through a chapter of one of their current textbooks, noting boldface and italic type. Ask questions such as these:

- Why are certain words or terms set in boldface type?
- What are italics used for?
- What other variations in type style do you notice, and why do you think they are used?

Unit, Chapter, and Section Headings

Set Goal

Students will learn that the headings of units, chapters, and sections in textbooks announce the topics covered. These headings contain the main subject, idea, or concept that will be discussed.

Teach and Discuss

Have students turn to page 150 of the handbook. Ask them to read the different headings in the **Example.** Based on the headings, have students discuss in as much detail as they can what they would expect to find in the unit, chapter, and section that follow.

Read through the **Description** on page 151 with the students. Emphasize that the headings in a textbook follow a system of subordination, like an outline. The unit title will be broader than the chapter headings, which all relate to the unit title. Section headings are less important than the chapter heading and will all relate to the chapter heading. Emphasize that thinking about the unit, chapter, and section headings will help students sort out the order of importance of the ideas in the material.

Check Understanding

Have students read the **Definition** at the bottom of page 151. Then ask students to look through a unit of one of their current textbooks for the unit, chapter, and section headings. Students can work in pairs to create an Outline of a unit using the different levels of headings, taking note of which headings are subordinate to which. In a whole-group discussion, ask students:

- Why is it important to pay attention to unit, chapter, and section headings?
- How could you use these headings to outline or take notes on your textbook?
- How could you use the headings to clarify your understanding of the material during reading?

Reading
Nonfiction

Introduction to Reading Nonfiction

Begin by discussing with students what they already know about reading nonfiction. Then ask them to turn to page 154 in the handbook and read the page silently. Follow up by having volunteers read aloud the descriptions of expository nonfiction and narrative nonfiction. Ask students to tell about some nonfiction they have read recently and explain whether their examples are expository or narrative. Emphasize the importance of reading nonfiction critically.

Reading a Personal Essay

Goals

Here students will read a selection called "The Indian Dog." They will learn to:

- ✓ recognize the subject and main idea of an essay
- ✓ use the reading strategy of outlining
- ✓ identify the three main parts of an essay: introduction, body, and conclusion

Background

Explain that a personal essay is a short work of nonfiction that focuses on one topic or subject. Help students connect this lesson with their prior knowledge by asking them to:

- talk about essays they have read in the past
- discuss personal essays they have written for school or for their own reasons (What did they write about?)
- talk about reasons why people write and read personal essays

Opening Activity

Explain to students that in a personal essay the author is not just telling about a topic or subject but also telling what he or she thinks and feels about that subject. Readers then decide how they feel about the author's message. Remind students that posing questions before reading helps them to read more efficiently.

Take a moment and ask students to suggest questions that occur to them before reading a personal essay titled "The Indian Dog." Share the questions as a class so students are aware of the range of questions possible.

Overview

	Content	Teacher's Guide page	Reader's Handbook page
Selection	"The Indian Dog" by N. Scott Momaday		157–158, 161, 164
Reading Strategy	Outlining	106, 435	159, 720
Rereading Strategy	Questioning the Author	109, 436	165, 724
Tool	Outline Double-entry Journal Main Idea Organizer	106 109 110	159, 162, 749 166, 743 167, 747

Ancillaries

	Grade	Content	Page
Overhead Transparency	9–12	Previewing a Personal Essay	Numbers 14 and 15
Lesson Plan Book	9 10 11	Reading a Personal Essay Reading a Personal Essay Reading a Personal Essay	84, 86–89 84, 86–89 84, 86–89
Student Applications Book	9 10 11 12	"Going Out for a Walk" by Max Beerbohm from "Pleasure Boat Studio" by Ou-Yang Hsiu "About Barbers" by Mark Twain from "How Little We Know About Our Parents" by George Bernard Shaw	57–64 57–64 57–66 57–65
Test Book	9–12	Short-answer Test Multiple-choice Test	
Website		www.greatsource.com/rehand/	

Before Reading

A Set a Purpose

First students need to set a purpose for reading "The Indian Dog." Direct them to the Setting a Purpose questions on page 156 of the *Reader's Handbook*.

Setting a Purpose

- **What is the subject of the essay?**
- **What does the writer say about the subject?**
- **How do I feel about what the writer says?**

B Preview

Remind students of the importance of previewing before reading. Using the Preview Checklist on page 156 of the handbook, have students preview "The Indian Dog."

Point out that the annotations on pages 157 and 158 will help students find the items on the checklist.

Preview Checklist

✔ *the title and author*
✔ *the first and last paragraphs*
✔ *any key words or any words in boldface or italics*
✔ *any repeated words or phrases*

Overhead Transparencies

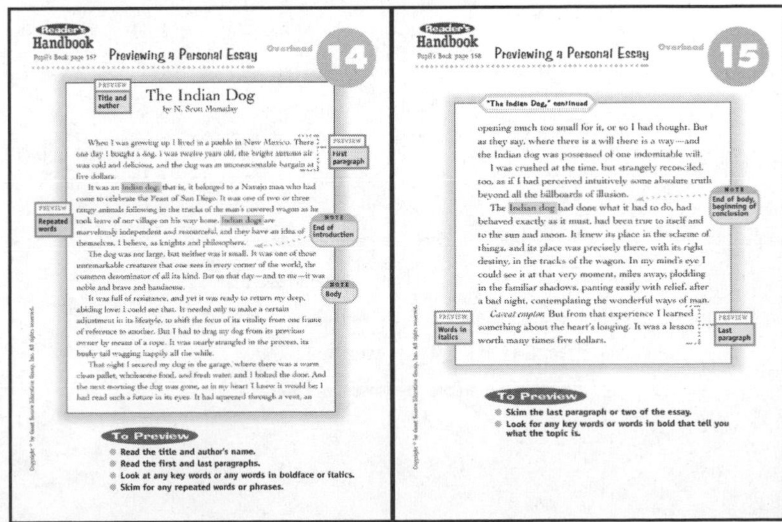

Reader's Handbook
Pupil's Book page 157
Previewing a Personal Essay
Overhead 14

The Indian Dog
by N. Scott Momaday

PREVIEW Title and author

When I was growing up I lived in a pueblo in New Mexico. There one day I bought a dog. I was twelve years old, the bright autumn air was cold and delicious, and the dog was an unconscionable bargain at five dollars.

PREVIEW First paragraph

It was an Indian dog; that is, it belonged to a Navajo man who had come to celebrate the Feast of San Diego. It was one of two or three rangy animals following in the tracks of the man's covered wagon as he took leave of our village on his way home. Indian dogs are marvelously independent and resourceful, and they have an idea of themselves, I believe, as knights and philosophers.

PREVIEW Repeated words

NOTE End of introduction

The dog was not large, but neither was it small. It was one of those unremarkable creatures that one sees in every corner of the world, the common denominator of all its kind. But on that day—and to me—it was noble and brave and handsome.

NOTE Body

It was full of resistance, and yet it was ready to return my deep, abiding love; I could see that. It needed only to make a certain adjustment in its lifestyle, to shift the focus of its vitality from one frame of reference to another. But I had to drag my dog from its previous owner by means of a rope. It was nearly strangled in the process, its bushy tail wagging happily all the while.

That night I secured my dog in the garage, where there was a warm clean pallet, wholesome food, and fresh water, and I bolted the door. And the next morning the dog was gone, as in my heart I knew it would be; I had read such a future in its eyes. It had squeezed through a vent, an

To Preview

- Read the title and author's name.
- Read the first and last paragraphs.
- Look at any key words or any words in boldface or italics.
- Skim for any repeated words or phrases.

Reader's Handbook
Pupil's Book page 158
Previewing a Personal Essay
Overhead 15

"The Indian Dog," continued

opening much too small for it, or so I had thought. But as they say, where there is a will there is a way—and the Indian dog was possessed of one indomitable will.

I was crushed at the time, but strangely reconciled, too, as if I had perceived intuitively some absolute truth beyond all the billboards of illusion.

NOTE End of body, beginning of conclusion

The Indian dog had done what it had to do, had behaved exactly as it must, had been true to itself and to the sun and moon. It knew its place in the scheme of things, and its place was precisely there, with its right destiny, in the tracks of the wagon. In my mind's eye I could see it at that very moment, miles away, plodding in the familiar shadows, panting easily with relief, after a bad night, contemplating the wonderful ways of man.

Caveat emptor. But from that experience I learned something about the heart's longing. It was a lesson worth many times five dollars.

PREVIEW Words in italics

PREVIEW Last paragraph

To Preview

- Skim the last paragraph or two of the essay.
- Look for any key words or words in bold that tell you what the topic is.

Before Reading

C Plan

Now have students sum up what they learned about the selection during their preview. Direct their attention to the bulleted list at the bottom of page 158. Then have students make a plan for finding the author's subject and main idea in "The Indian Dog."

Reading Strategy: Outlining

Introduce the strategy of **outlining.** Explain that outlining is helpful when reading a personal essay because it provides a framework for gathering important ideas and details. It organizes the material in the essay by grouping bits of information into main points and details.

Have students look at the example on page 159 of the *Reader's Handbook*. Point out that in this Outline the three major parts of the essay—the introduction, body, and conclusion—form the main Outline headings. This framework helps students know *where* to look for important information.

OUTLINE

I. Introduction (the writer's recollections)
  A. Introductory detail
  B. Introductory detail
  C. Introductory detail

II. Body (the writer's recollections)
  A. Detail
    1.
    2.
  B. Detail
    1.
    2.
  C. Detail
    1.
    2.

III. Conclusion (the writer's reflections)
  A. Main idea (if it appears here)
  B. Explanation of main idea
  C. Explanation of main idea

D Read with a Purpose

Now students are ready to read. Ask them to read with a purpose and to gather important ideas and details from the selection using the strategy of outlining.

Finding the Main Idea

Emphasize to students that to understand a personal essay they must go beyond knowing the subject of the piece. Clearly, the subject of "The Indian Dog" is the dog. However, the main idea is what the writer has to say about the dog, or the meaning the dog has in his life.

The main idea of a personal essay is usually implied. Ask students to turn to page 160 of their handbooks and read through the steps for finding an implied main idea in a personal essay:

1. Reread parts of the essay in which the writer reflects on the experience he or she has described. (This is usually toward the end of the essay.)
2. Watch for words and phrases that signal the author is going to say something important. For example: "This experience taught me . . . ," "Now I realize that . . . ," "My point is that . . ."
3. Ask yourself two important questions: How did the experience change the author's view of self or the world? What did the author learn from the experience described?

Go over the excerpt from "The Indian Dog" on page 161. Point out the highlighted words that help readers find the main idea.

Finding Supporting Details

Explain that supporting details may be examples, facts, statistics, quotations, or experiences. Have students look at the example of the completed Sentence Outline with supporting details on page 162. Let the students know that their own Outlines can be simpler. For instance, an Outline can be a list of words or phrases instead of a formal Sentence Outline using complete sentences.

Other Useful Tools

Encourage students to use other reading tools as they read "The Indian Dog." As with any type of tool, students need to be able to apply the right one when needed. If not familiar with the tools below, students can find them in the Reader's Almanac. These are especially useful tools for reading personal essays:

- **Evidence Organizer**
- **Argument Chart**

During Reading

How Personal Essays Are Organized

Explain to students that knowing how personal essays are organized will help them read faster and with better comprehension. Ask students to turn to page 163 in their handbooks to see how most personal essays are organized.

The funnel pattern is the most common organization found in personal essays. Typically, the essayist introduces the topic in the first few paragraphs, elaborates on the topic in the body using a great deal of rich detail, and concludes the essay in a paragraph or even in one sentence.

FUNNEL PATTERN

E Connect

Remind students that an important part of the reading process is to respond to or make connections with the text as they read. Actively making connections while reading enhances not only students' comprehension but also their interest in a text. Suggest the following ways students can connect with the current selection:

- find connections to their own lives
  (What do the animals that I encounter mean to me?)
- think about what the author is saying about the topic that relates to them
  (Is Momaday talking about something more than the dog? Is he talking about himself?)
- think about how the essay made them feel
  (Was I sad to read that the dog had disappeared?)
- evaluate the author's ideas against their own opinions
  (Do I agree with the author's point?)

After Reading

F Pause and Reflect

After reading, students need to stop and reflect on what they have read. Have students go back and review their original purpose in reading "The Indian Dog." Go over the Looking Back questions with them.

Looking Back

- **Can I name the subject of the essay?**
- **Do I know what the author says about the subject?**
- **Can I tell how I feel about the author's main idea?**

Students may still be uncertain of the author's reason for writing or what the author is saying about the Indian dog. Emphasize to students that finding an implied main idea is like solving a mystery. They need to go back to the reading and collect and study all the clues.

Reread

Emphasize to students that even the best readers need to go back and reread to clarify their understandings. In fact, this is one of the habits that *make* them the best readers. Explain that students should return to the text with a different strategy or tool so that they can get a fresh look at the material.

Rereading Strategy: Questioning the Author

Introduce students to the strategy of **questioning the author.** In this strategy, readers carry on a conversation with the author as though he or she is right there with them. Students are to ask the author some questions that will help to clarify the text. Direct students to the questions given on page 165 of the handbook, and read them aloud with the students.

AFTER-READING QUESTIONS

What does this detail mean?

What is the message of this essay?

How does this part of the essay relate to this other part?

What is the significance of this paragraph?

Answering your questions

Show students the example of the Double-entry Journal following the questions. Point out that this tool is excellent for asking and answering their own questions. Students can also write in their journals or discuss their questions with a friend.

After Reading

H Remember

At this stage in the reading, it is time for students to make the newly learned information their own. They need to do something with the subject matter in order to remember it. Discuss the activities highlighted on pages 166 and 167 of the *Reader's Handbook*. Go over the Main Idea Organizer with students. Have students do one of the activities, or suggest the creative assignment below.

MAIN IDEA ORGANIZER

"The Indian Dog" MAIN IDEA: The heart's longings can be extremely powerful.		
DETAIL #1 As a boy, Momaday buys a dog.	DETAIL #2 The dog longs for freedom.	DETAIL #3 The boy recognizes that the dog's longings and his own are not the same.

Creative Assignment: Have students work in pairs to brainstorm different possible endings for this essay. Suggest that they imagine Momaday successfully recovers the dog. What happens then? What revelation follows? Students may share their ideas in a whole-class discussion.

Summing Up

Review the lesson by reading the Summing Up on page 167 of the handbook. Focus on everything students have learned about strategies and tools for reading personal essays. Go over the initial goals for the lesson. Discuss which ones students feel they achieved and which ones they need more work on:

1. **recognizing the subject and main idea of an essay**
2. **using the reading strategy of outlining**
3. **identifying the three main parts of an essay: introduction, body, and conclusion**

Assessment and Application

Use the Quick Assess checklist to evaluate students' ability to read and understand personal essays. Give students the opportunity to apply what they have learned through one of the two activities below. For students who are comfortable with the reading process and strategy, use one of the suggestions for independent practice or an activity of your own. For students who need guided help with the strategy, use a *Student Applications Book*.

Quick Assess

Can students

- name two or three purpose-setting questions to guide their reading of a personal essay?
- name a useful strategy for reading a personal essay?
- explain why rereading is necessary and identify a good rereading strategy?

1. Independent Practice

Have students apply the strategy of **outlining** or the strategy of **questioning the author** to another essay of their choice to show that they understand the lesson.

Ask students to do one of the following:

- Create an Outline during reading, using the three parts of the essay as main outline heads.
- Apply the strategy of questioning the author, using the Double-entry Journal technique.
- Write a journal entry identifying the subject and main idea of an essay, including their own thoughts and feelings about the author's point.

2. Student Applications Books

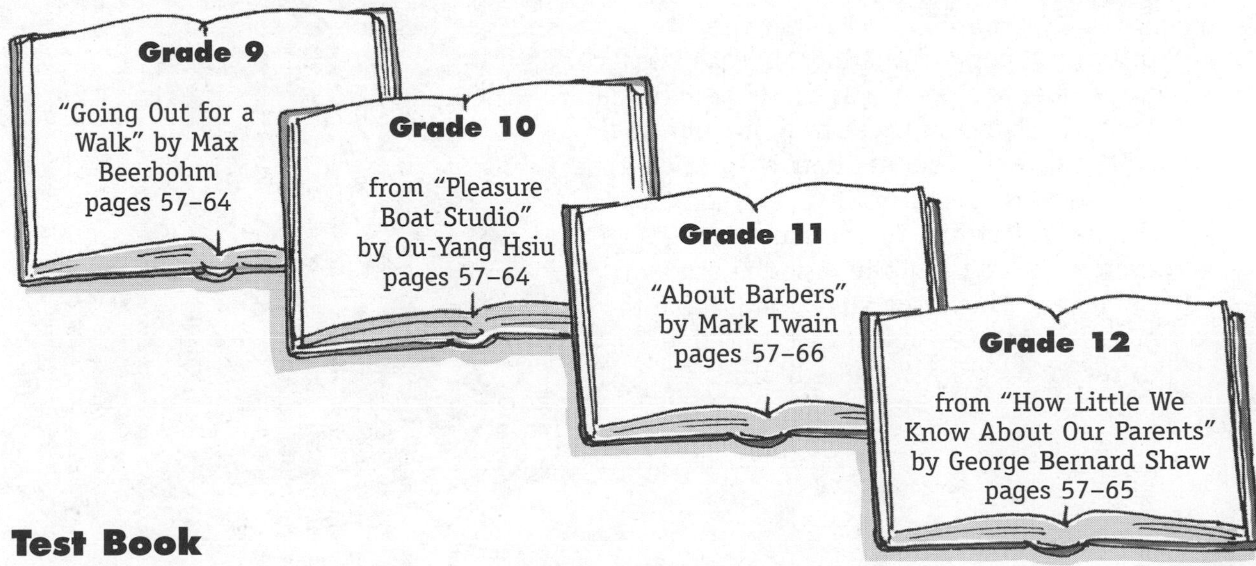

Test Book

See *Test Book* for short-answer and multiple-choice tests.

Reading an Editorial

Goals

Here students read an editorial titled "College Sports Myth Versus Math." This lesson will help them learn to:

- recognize the author's viewpoint or assertions
- use the strategy of questioning the author
- understand how an editorial is organized

Background

Help students connect this lesson with their existing knowledge by asking them to:

- explain what an editorial is and where they are likely to find one
- talk about editorials they have read in the past
- say what they like and dislike about reading editorials
- talk about editorials or letters to the editor that they have written, or have wanted to write but didn't
- discuss why editorials are important in a democratic society

Opening Activity

Bring in a copy of the day's local newspaper and ask students to help you find the editorial section. Then ask them to point out an editorial. Ask students how they know that the piece is an editorial. Then read aloud the day's editorial to the students. If there is more than one, ask the students to choose which one they'd most like to hear. Allow a few minutes for students to respond orally to the editorial.

Overview

	Content	Teacher's Guide page	Reader's Handbook page
Selection	"College Sports Myth Versus Math"		170–171, 173, 176
Reading Strategy	Questioning the Author	115, 436	172, 724
Rereading Strategy	Synthesizing	118, 439	179, 732
Tool	Double-entry Journal Critical Reading Chart Inference Chart Summary Notes	116 116 117 118	174, 743 174, 743 177, 746 179, 754

Ancillaries

	Grade	Content	Page
Overhead Transparency	9–12	Previewing an Editorial	Numbers 16 and 17
Lesson Plan Book	9 11	Reading an Editorial Reading an Editorial	94, 96–99 85, 90–93
Student Applications Book	9 10 11 12	"A Modest Rebuttal" "Let Us Reason Together" by W.E.B. DuBois "Freedom of Speech" by William Cullen Bryant from "The Value of Solitude"	65–74 65–73 67–76 66–73
Test Book	9–12	Short-answer Test Multiple-choice Test	
Website		www.greatsource.com/rehand/	

Before Reading

A Set a Purpose

Have students set a purpose before reading the selection. Point out the Setting a Purpose questions on page 169 of the handbook. Much of the time, the headline introduces the topic. In many instances, it tips off a reader to the viewpoint that will be argued in the editorial. Encourage students to use the headline to help them set their purpose.

Setting a Purpose

- **What is the college sports myth versus math?**
- **How do I feel about it?**
- **How persuasive is the editorial?**

B Preview

Now have students preview the editorial. Explain to the students that editorials are easy to preview because they are designed to be read by people who are in a hurry.

Have students follow the Preview Checklist on page 169 to preview the selection. Talk with them about where each checklist item is found in the editorial. Point out the annotations that help them locate the items on pages 170 and 171.

Preview Checklist

- ✓ *the headline and date*
- ✓ *any repeated words*
- ✓ *the writer's assertions*
- ✓ *the first and last paragraphs*

Overhead Transparencies

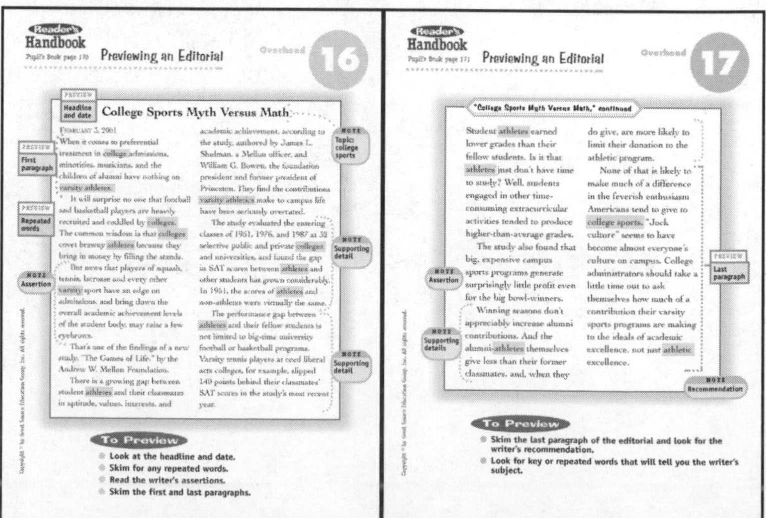

Reader's Handbook
Pupil's Book page 170
Previewing an Editorial
Overhead 16

College Sports Myth Versus Math

February 3, 2001

When it comes to preferential treatment in college admissions, minorities, musicians, and the children of alumni have nothing on varsity athletes.

It will surprise no one that football and basketball players are heavily recruited and coddled by colleges. The common wisdom is that colleges covet brawny athletes because they bring in money by filling the stands.

But news that players of squash, tennis, lacrosse and every other varsity sport have an edge on admissions, and bring down the overall academic achievement levels of the student body, may raise a few eyebrows.

That's one of the findings of a new study, "The Games of Life," by the Andrew W. Mellon Foundation.

There is a growing gap between student athletes and their classmates in aptitude, values, interests, and academic achievement, according to the study, authored by James L. Shulman, a Mellon officer, and William G. Bowen, the foundation president and former president of Princeton. They find the contributions varsity athletes make to campus life have been seriously overrated.

The study evaluated the entering classes of 1951, 1976, and 1987 at 32 selective public and private colleges and universities, and found the gap in SAT scores between athletes and other students has grown considerably. In 1951, the scores of athletes and non-athletes were virtually the same.

The performance gap between athletes and their fellow students is not limited to big-time university football or basketball programs. Varsity tennis players at coed liberal arts colleges, for example, slipped 140 points behind their classmates' SAT scores in the study's most recent year.

To Preview
- Look at the headline and date.
- Skim for any repeated words.
- Read the writer's assertions.
- Skim the first and last paragraphs.

Reader's Handbook
Pupil's Book page 171
Previewing an Editorial
Overhead 17

"College Sports Myth Versus Math," continued

Student athletes earned lower grades than their fellow students. Is it that athletes just don't have time to study? Well, students engaged in other time-consuming extracurricular activities tended to produce higher-than-average grades.

The study also found that big, expensive campus sports programs generate surprisingly little profit even for the big bowl-winners.

Winning seasons don't appreciably increase alumni contributions. And the alumni-athletes themselves give less than their former classmates, and, when they do give, are more likely to limit their donation to the athletic program.

None of that is likely to make much of a difference in the feverish enthusiasm Americans tend to give to college sports. "Jock culture" seems to have become almost everyone's culture on campus. College administrators should take a little time out to ask themselves how much of a contribution their varsity sports programs are making to the ideals of academic excellence, not just athletic excellence.

To Preview
- Skim the last paragraph of the editorial and look for the writer's recommendation.
- Look for key or repeated words that will tell you the writer's subject.

Before Reading

C Plan

Ask students to briefly tell some of the things they learned from their preview. Now that they have a general idea of what the reading is about, it's time to make a plan to help them meet their purpose for reading.

Reading Strategy: Questioning the Author

Explain that the strategy of **questioning the author** is good for reading editorials. In this strategy, the reader asks questions of the author as if the author were sitting right there. Some questions might be: "What do you mean by ______?" and "Are you saying that______?"

Ask students to read through the description of the strategy on page 172 of the handbook. Go over the questions to think about while reading an editorial.

1. Why does the author begin this way?

2. What point is the author making?

3. Why does the writer mention this detail?

4. What does the writer want me to believe?

5. What action can I take, or what am I supposed to do?

During Reading

D Read with a Purpose

Remind students that they need to keep in mind their purpose for reading as they read. The Setting a Purpose questions help guide students' reading. Call attention to the question and answer notes of one reader, shown on page 173.

Analyze

Now have students turn to page 174 of the handbook. Encourage students to identify key lines or sentences, copy them into their journals, and analyze them. Students' completed Double-entry Journals should be similar to this example when they have finished reading.

DOUBLE-ENTRY JOURNAL

QUESTIONS	MY THOUGHTS
1. Why does the author begin this way?	The first paragraph makes the reader want to read more about "preferential treatment."
2. What point is the author making?	College athletes of those sports besides football and basketball also get "preferential treatment" and bring down academic achievement levels.
3. Why does the writer mention the detail about alumni-athletes?	This detail supports the idea that an athlete's contributions to college life are overrated.
4. What does the writer want me to believe?	I'm to believe that athletes don't benefit colleges as much as was thought.
5. What action can I take, or what am I supposed to do?	The writer isn't clear about what readers can do.

Evaluate

Because reading critically is an essential skill for reading editorials, students may also prepare a Critical Reading Chart, with questions listed in the left-hand column and their thoughts in the right-hand column. Have students look at the example at the bottom of page 174.

Other Useful Tools

Encourage students to use other reading tools as they read "College Sports Myth Versus Math." As with any type of tool, students need to be able to apply the right one when needed. If not familiar with the tools below, students can find them in the Reader's Almanac. These are especially useful tools for reading editorials:

- **Evidence Organizer**
- **Argument Chart**
- **Close Reading Organizer**

How Editorials Are Organized

Emphasize that knowing how an editorial is organized will help students read more efficiently. Most editorials contain three parts: the author's *assertions*, the *support* for these assertions, and the author's *recommendation*. Though these three parts may appear in any order, they usually are arranged as shown on page 175.

Ask students to look at the graphic on page 175 of the handbook. Explain that "College Sports Myth Versus Math" follows this structure. Students should understand that an assertion is a strong belief, either written or spoken. Point out examples from the editorial.

EDITORIAL STRUCTURE

1. *assertion*
   supporting details
2. *assertion*
   supporting details
3. *recommendation*

E Connect

Remind students that actively making connections to the text is an important part of effective reading. Suggest these ways of connecting to the editorial:

- relate the information to their own life experiences
  (Do I know some kids who are going to college on athletic scholarships?)
- ask themselves why this topic is important
  (Will there be some negative long-term effects?)
- decide whether the author has made good points
  (Could the author have explained that study better?)
- decide whether they agree with the editorial or not
  (How do I feel about this?)

Decide

Show students the example of one reader's response to this editorial, given on page 176 of the handbook. Point out the journal entry and the Inference Chart on page 177. Then ask students to jot down their thoughts and feelings about the editorial quickly to refer to later. Emphasize that fast journaling does not have to be perfect writing, with complete sentences and perfect grammar. Jotting down phrases or items in list form is also fine.

JOURNAL

I think the argument this editorial writer makes is very clear. There is good support for the assertions.

F Pause and Reflect

After reading, have students stop to consider what they have learned from the editorial. Ask students to go back and review their original purpose for reading this selection.

Looking Back

- **Do I know what the college sports myth is?**
- **Can I explain how the writer refutes or challenges the myth?**
- **Do I know how I feel about the editorial?**

Students will need to go back to the selection to take a second look at how the author constructed the argument and what evidence he or she used to support the assertions. Let students know that good critical readers always glance back at the text.

G Reread

Encourage students to try a new strategy for rereading. Explain that using a different strategy will give them a fresh perspective on the selection.

Synthesizing

Introduce the strategy of **synthesizing.** This is the technique of pulling together all the facts, ideas, or assertions in a piece of writing.

Summary Notes, shown on page 179 of the handbook, is a useful tool for pulling together the information from a reading. Ask students to read this example carefully. Have them apply this tool when rereading the editorial.

SUMMARY NOTES

TOPIC: college sports
MAIN POINT: College athletes and expensive sports programs don't benefit schools as much as people thought.
1. College athletes have lower SAT scores than other students. 2. College athletes have lower grades than other students. 3. Alumni contributions don't increase even when teams win. 4. Former college athletes give less money to colleges than their former classmates do.

After Reading

H Remember

Now students need to do something with the subject matter to remember it and make it their own. Read and have students do one of the activities given on pages 179 and 180 of the *Reader's Handbook.* Alternatively, you may wish to have students do the creative assignment below.

Creative Assignment: Working in small groups, students brainstorm ideas for editorials on important issues in the school, community, or country. Combine the lists of the small groups into one large list, from which students may draw ideas. Then have students create an Outline of an editorial they would like to write, using the editorial structure described in this lesson. Point out that good editorials need facts and statistics to support assertions, not just opinions and impressions. If time permits, you may have students write their editorials to share with classmates or to submit to the school, or possibly the local, newspaper.

Summing Up

Now review the lesson with the students, focusing on the points listed in the Summing Up on page 180 of the handbook. Focus on everything students have learned about strategies and tools for reading editorials. Go over the goals for the lesson. Ask the students which ones they feel they achieved and which ones they need more work on:

1. **recognizing the author's viewpoint or assertions**
2. **using the strategy of questioning the author**
3. **understanding how an editorial is organized**

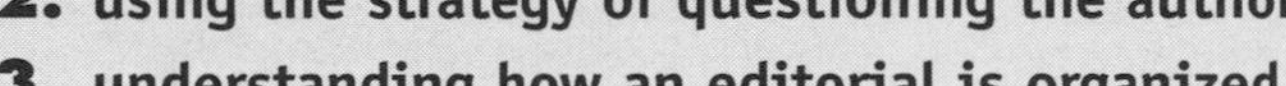

Assessment and Application

Use the Quick Assess checklist to evaluate students' ability to read and understand editorials. Give students the opportunity to apply what they have learned through one of the two activities below. For students who are comfortable with the reading process and strategy, use one of the suggestions for independent practice or an activity of your own. For students who need guided help with the strategy, use a *Student Applications Book*.

Quick Assess

Can students

- ☑ say how to identify the author's viewpoint?
- ☑ describe the strategy of questioning the author?
- ☑ explain why rereading is necessary and explain why synthesizing is a good strategy to use for it?
- ☑ describe how an editorial is usually organized?

1. Independent Practice

To show that they understand the lesson, have students apply the strategy of **questioning the author** to a recent editorial of their choice from the school or local newspaper.

Ask students to do one of the following:

- Apply the questioning the author strategy, using a Double-entry Journal.
- Complete a Critical Reading Chart.
- Write a journal entry agreeing or disagreeing with the editorial and explaining why.

2. Student Applications Books

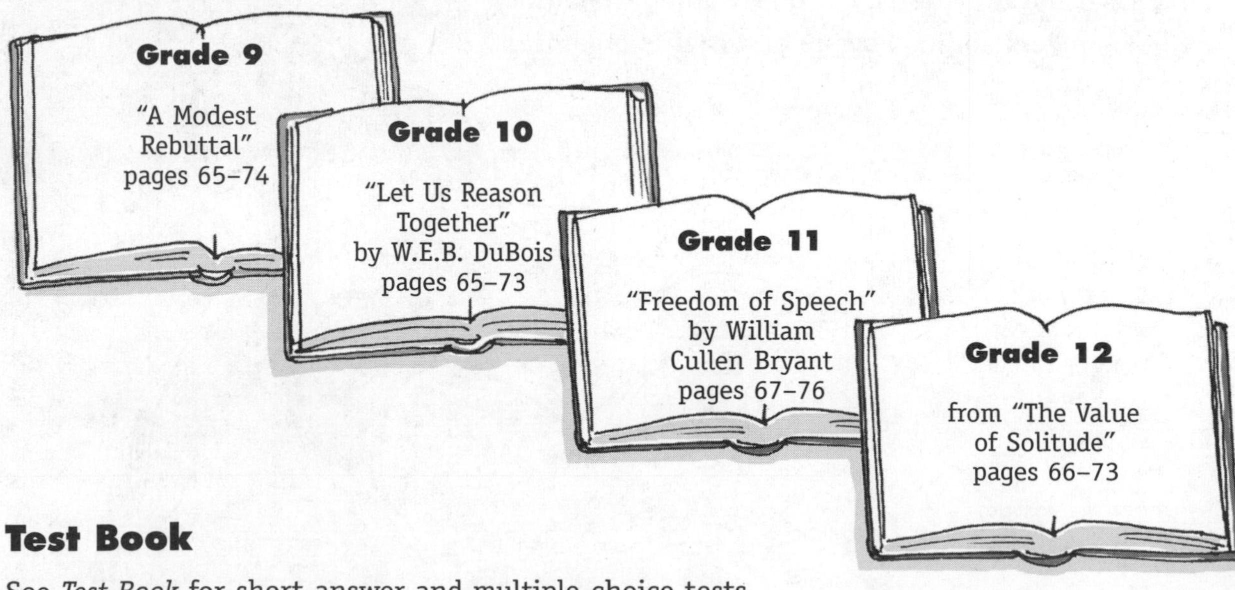

Test Book

See *Test Book* for short-answer and multiple-choice tests.

Reading a News Story

Goals

Here students read a news story titled "Violent Images May Alter Kids' Brain Activity." This lesson will help students learn to:

- recognize the major parts of a news story
- use the strategy of reading critically
- understand the organization of many news stories

Background

Help students connect this lesson to their prior knowledge by asking them to:

- define what a news story is
- talk about what types of information they expect to find in a news story
- discuss news stories they have recently seen or read
- talk about their experiences writing news stories for classroom or school newspapers

Opening Activity

Bring in a recent issue of the local newspaper and show students the front page. Ask them to say what the purpose of a news story is. Then read aloud to the students whichever story interests them the most. After you are finished, allow students a few minutes to respond to the article. Then ask if they noticed how the article was organized and what kinds of information were provided.

Do a quick survey to find out the kind of newspapers and news stories your students read. Ask how many read the school newspaper. Also ask how many read a daily newspaper and approximately how many minutes a day they spend reading. Some students may read only the comics or the sports pages. Increase students' awareness of this genre in order to build background before you begin the lesson. Explain also that reading a newspaper is one way to become an informed citizen who can participate thoughtfully in society.

Overview

	Content	Teacher's Guide page	Reader's Handbook page
Selection	"Violent Images May Alter Kids' Brain Activity"		183–184, 189
Reading Strategy	Reading Critically	124, 437	185, 726
Rereading Strategy	Summarizing	127, 438	190, 730
Tool	5 W's and H Organizer	124	185, 745
	Critical Reading Chart	124–125	186, 187, 743
	Summary Notes	127	191, 754
	Cause-Effect Organizer	128	191, 739

Ancillaries

	Grade	Content	Page
Overhead Transparency	9–12	Previewing a News Story	Number 18
Lesson Plan Book	10	Reading a News Story	94, 96–99
	12	Reading a News Story	84, 86–89
Student Applications Book	9	"Ghastly Deeds of Race Rioters Told"	75–84
	10	"Two Inmates Vanish from Alcatraz"	74–83
	11	"Heir to Austrian Throne Assassinated"	77–84
	12	"Defeat of Kaiser's Army Reported Near Nancy"	74–82
Test Book	9–12	Short-answer Test Multiple-choice Test	
Website		www.greatsource.com/rehand/	

Before Reading

A Set a Purpose

Have students set a purpose before they start reading the selection. Direct them to the Setting a Purpose questions on page 182 of the handbook.

Setting a Purpose

- **How do violent images alter kids' brain activity?** ***or***
- **Why do violent images alter kids' brain activity?**

B Preview

Have students preview the news story. Remind them that previewing is just a quick look to get a general idea of what the article is about. Emphasize that previewing helps all readers read faster and with better comprehension.

Have students turn to the Preview Checklist on page 182. Then preview the selection beginning on page 183 of the handbook, focusing on the headline, byline, lead, and key words.

Encourage students to use a finger or a file card to touch the key parts of the news story as they preview.

Preview Checklist

✓ *the headline*

✓ *the reporter's name (appears in what is called the byline)*

✓ *the lead*

✓ *any key words and phrases*

Overhead Transparency

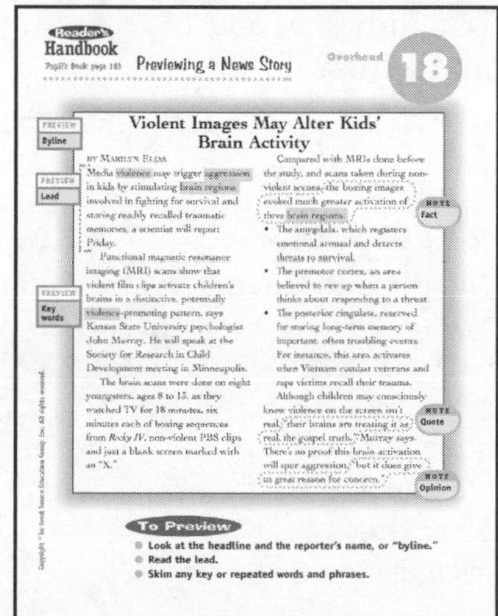

Reader's Handbook
Pupil's Book page 183 Previewing a News Story
Overhead 18

PREVIEW Byline

PREVIEW Lead

PREVIEW Key words

Violent Images May Alter Kids' Brain Activity

BY MARILYN ELIAS

Media violence may trigger aggression in kids by stimulating brain regions involved in fighting for survival and storing readily recalled traumatic memories, a scientist will report Friday.

Functional magnetic resonance imaging (MRI) scans show that violent film clips activate children's brains in a distinctive, potentially violence-promoting pattern, says Kansas State University psychologist John Murray. He will speak at the Society for Research in Child Development meeting in Minneapolis.

The brain scans were done on eight youngsters, ages 8 to 13, as they watched TV for 18 minutes, six minutes each of boxing sequences from *Rocky IV*, non-violent PBS clips and just a blank screen marked with an "X."

Compared with MRIs done before the study, and scans taken during non-violent scenes, the boxing images evoked much greater activation of three brain regions:

- The amygdala, which registers emotional arousal and detects threats to survival.
- The premotor cortex, an area believed to rev up when a person thinks about responding to a threat.
- The posterior cingulate, reserved for storing long-term memory of important, often troubling events. For instance, this area activates when Vietnam combat veterans and rape victims recall their trauma.

Although children may consciously know violence on the screen isn't real, "their brains are treating it as real, the gospel truth," Murray says. There's no proof this brain activation will spur aggression, "but it does give us great reason for concern."

NOTE Fact

NOTE Quote

NOTE Opinion

To Preview

- **Look at the headline and the reporter's name, or "byline."**
- **Read the lead.**
- **Skim any key or repeated words and phrases.**

Before Reading

C Plan

Ask students to tell briefly some of the things they learned from their preview. Now have them look at the 5 W's and H Organizer on the top of page 185 of the handbook. They are probably able to fill in much of this graphic organizer after their preview.

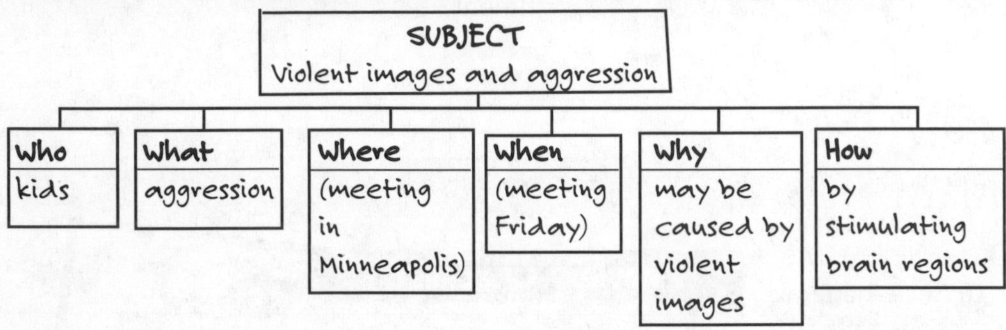

Remind students that, after they preview, they make a plan for reading. Ask students why reading critically would be important when reading a news story.

Reading Strategy: Reading Critically

Explain that **reading critically** means looking at the facts presented by a writer and deciding how believable they are. Reading critically also means being able to spot bias by looking at the writer's words and thinking about the information the writer chose to put in and to leave out of the article. Questioning is essential to reading critically.

Have students look at the Critical Reading Chart on the top of page 186. This chart provides a list of questions that students should ask while reading a news story. Read this chart with the students, making sure they are clear on such terms as *viewpoint, evidence, authoritative*, and *reliable*. Then have students take a quick look at the example of a completed Critical Reading Chart on page 187.

During Reading

D Read with a Purpose

Remind students that they need to keep in mind their purpose as they read. Their purpose for reading this selection is to find out how or why violent images alter kids' brain activity.

Let students know that if they're reading a news story simply because they're interested, they aren't expected to take notes or write things down. However, if they're reading a news story for a class assignment, taking notes is a good idea.

CRITICAL READING CHART

1. Is the main idea or viewpoint clear?	Yes. Violence can alter brain activity in kids.
2. What evidence is presented?	MRI scans, flashback information, Yale University study
3. Are the sources authoritative and reliable?	Yes. She quotes doctors from good universities.
4. Is the evidence convincing?	It's pretty convincing. Television images can be powerful.
5. Is there another side of the story?	Singer says study is too small. Another study says real violence causes more trouble than TV violence.

Other Useful Tools

Encourage students to use other reading tools as they read "Violent Images May Alter Kids' Brain Activity." As with any type of tool, students need to be able to apply the right one when needed. If not familiar with the tools below, students can find them in the Reader's Almanac. These are especially useful tools for reading news stories:

- **Evidence Organizer**
- **Main Idea Organizer**
- **Double-entry Journal**

How News Stories Are Organized

The organization of a news story has long been described as an inverted pyramid. Instruct students to turn to page 188 to see the illustration. The pyramid is inverted because the biggest, or most important, information goes at the top, or beginning, of the article, followed by progressively less important details. The lead paragraph usually contains information on *what, who, where, when, why,* and *how.* The current trend in news writing is to start a story with an *indirect* or *soft* lead intended to get the reader's attention. It does not necessarily include the essential information.

INVERTED PYRAMID

Lead

Most important details

Less important details

Least important details

E Connect

A key part of the reading process is to respond to or make connections with the reading. Connecting with current events is often not difficult, as news stories are clearly about real life and what is of local interest. Since many students lack prior knowledge of particular subject areas, such as foreign affairs or the workings of local politics, they may initially feel uninterested in these topics. Connecting with the text is a good way to help students acquire some knowledge of unfamiliar topics. Suggest these ways for students to connect with news stories:

- ask themselves questions
  (How might this affect me?)
- think about someone who would share an interest in this news story
  (I should mention this to ________ the next time I see her!)
- compare new information to what they already know
  (This reminds me of the debate we had last year on the effects of watching a lot of TV.)

Have students look at how one reader responded to this article, illustrated on page 189 of the handbook.

After Reading

F Pause and Reflect

After reading, have students consider the Looking Back questions on page 190 of the handbook.

Looking Back

- **Have I met my reading purpose?**
- **Can I restate the reporter's main idea?**
- **Do I understand the facts in the story?**
- **Can I give my own opinion of what was written?**

Remind students that some rereading may be needed to meet their reading purposes, especially when they want to evaluate a news story or sum it up.

G Reread

Give students a fresh way to go back into the selection. Introduce the strategy of summarizing for rereading the article.

Rereading Strategy: Summarizing

Explain that **summarizing** is a good rereading strategy for many types of texts, including news stories. Summarizing a piece of writing greatly improves students' ability to understand and recall what they read.

Have students look at the Summary Notes on page 191 of the handbook. Emphasize that there is only one sentence for each paragraph and that it contains the main idea of the paragraph.

SUMMARY NOTES

1. Violence in the media may cause aggression in kids.
2. MRI scans show that violent film clips activate a violence-promoting mechanism in children's brains.
3. For the study, scientists had eight children watch violent and non-violent TV for 18 minutes.
4. The violent show caused a reaction in three brain regions: the amygdala, premotor cortex, and posterior cingulate.
5. A child's brain thinks the violence on TV is real.
6. The result may be post-traumatic stress in kids.
7. One study showed kids reacting aggressively after an aggressive TV show.
8. Some researchers question whether media violence really does trigger aggression in kids.
9. They say that exposure to real violence has a far worse effect on children.
10. Most studies show that too much TV is bad for kids.

After Reading

H Remember

Students must now somehow make the reading their own, or do something with the new information to remember it. Discuss the activities highlighted on pages 191 and 192 in the *Reader's Handbook*. Assign students to make a Cause-Effect Organizer or use the Internet to learn more about a news story. Students might also do the creative assignment below.

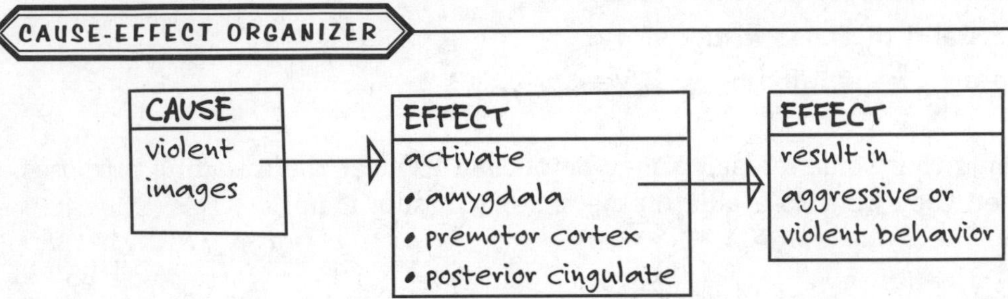

Creative Assignment: Working in pairs, students research, outline, and write a short news story on a local event for the school or a classroom newspaper. A "classroom newspaper" may simply be pages copied and stapled together.

Summing Up

Now review the lesson with students, reading the Summing Up on page 192 in the handbook. Focus on everything students have learned about strategies and tools for reading news stories. Go over the goals of the lesson. Discuss which ones the students feel they achieved and which ones they need more work on:

1. **recognizing the major parts of a news story**
2. **using the strategy of reading critically**
3. **understanding the organization of many news stories**

Assessment and Application

Use the Quick Assess checklist to evaluate students' ability to read and understand news stories. Give students the opportunity to apply what they have learned through one of the two activities below. For students who are comfortable with the reading process and strategy, use one of the suggestions for independent practice or an activity of your own. For students who need guided help with the strategy, use a *Student Applications Book.*

Quick Assess

Can students

- ☑ say where they are likely to find information on the 5 W's and H in a news story?
- ☑ explain how to read critically?
- ☑ say why rereading may be necessary and identify a good strategy to use for it?
- ☑ describe how a typical news story is organized?

1. Independent Practice

Ask students to show that they understand the lesson by applying **critical reading** or **summarizing** to a news story from a fairly recent issue of the local newspaper. Bring several newspapers to class, and allow students to choose which news story they want to read.

Ask students to do one of the following:

- Apply the strategy of critical reading using a Critical Reading Chart.
- Summarize using the Summary Notes technique.
- Write a journal entry responding to a news story, giving clear reasons why they think the article represents good reporting.

2. Student Applications Books

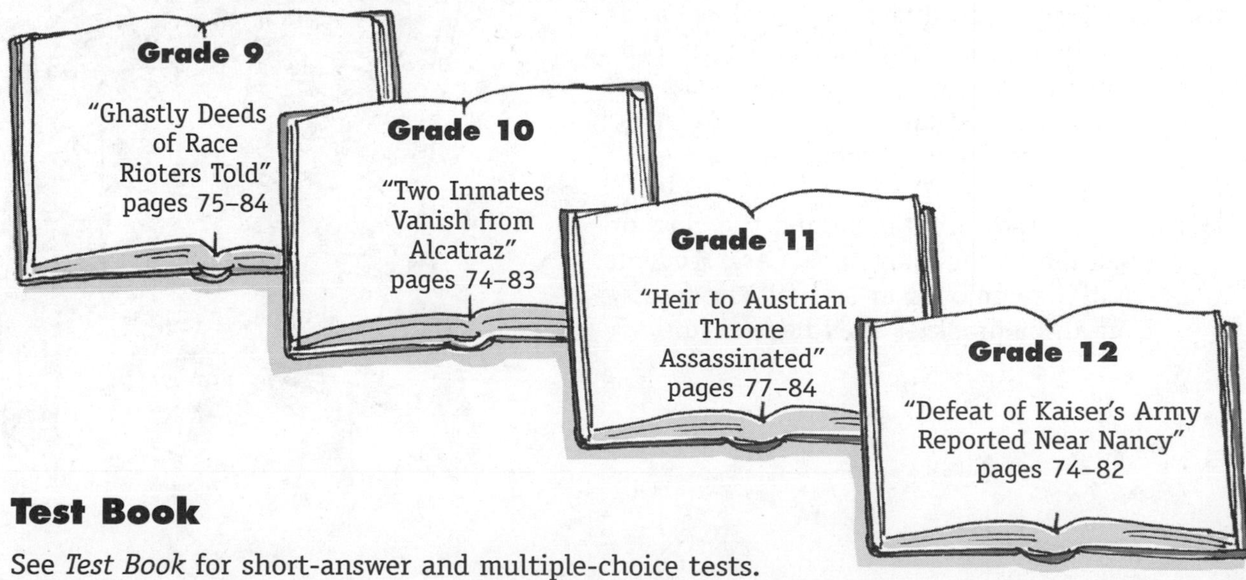

Test Book

See *Test Book* for short-answer and multiple-choice tests.

Reading a Biography

Goals

Here students read an excerpt from *Rickey & Robinson* by John C. Chalberg. Students will learn to:

- ✓ appreciate the two major goals of a biography
- ✓ use the strategy of looking for cause and effect
- ✓ understand the organization biographers use in telling the story

Background

Explain that a biography is a work of nonfiction written by one person about another person's life. Help students connect this lesson with their prior knowledge by asking them to:

- discuss some biographies they have read
- talk about why people write and read biographies
- list a few people whose biographies students would be interested in reading

Opening Activity

Talk about what students can expect to find in a biography, such as when and where the subject of the biography lived and key events and accomplishments in the subject's life. Emphasize that a good biographer has at least two goals: to tell an interesting story and to create a portrait or impression of the subject so that readers can understand what he or she was truly like.

Spend a few minutes polling the class on biographies they have read. Ask students what they enjoyed or learned the most from in biographies they have read.

Overview

	Content	Teacher's Guide page	Reader's Handbook page
Selection	From *Rickey & Robinson* by John C. Chalberg		196–198, 200–201, 206
Reading Strategy	Looking for Cause and Effect	133, 433	199, 716
Rereading Strategy	Outlining	137, 435	208, 720
Tool	Cause-Effect Organizer	133	199, 202, 739
	Inference Chart	134	202, 746
	Sequence Notes	134	203, 751
	Character Map	135	204, 740
	Topic Outline	137	208, 749
	Timeline	138	209, 755

Ancillaries

	Grade	Content	Page
Overhead Transparency	9–12	Previewing a Biography	Numbers 19–21
Lesson Plan Book	12	Reading a Biography	85, 90–93
Student Applications Book	9	from *The Life of Phineas Taylor Barnum* by Joel Benton	85–93
	10	from *Spotted Tail* by Charles A. Eastman	84–93
	11	from *Indian Heroes and Great Chieftans* by Charles A. Eastman	85–93
	12	excerpt from "Florence Nightingale" from *Eminent Victorians*	83–92
Test Book	9–12	Short-answer Test Multiple-choice Test	
Website		www.greatsource.com/rehand/	

Before Reading

Set a Purpose

Have students set a purpose for reading the selection. Direct students to the Setting a Purpose questions on page 194 of the *Reader's Handbook*.

Setting a Purpose

- **What kind of life has this person had?**
- **What was he or she really like?**

B Preview

Have students preview before reading, starting with the book cover, jacket copy, and table of contents as shown on pages 196–198. Refer to the Preview Checklist on page 195.

Point out to students that previewing a biography can give them an excellent idea of what the book will be about. You might even demonstrate this point by bringing several biographies to class. Have students preview them and report the results to the class.

Preview Checklist

✓ *the title and author*
✓ *the front, back, and inside covers*
✓ *the table of contents and chapter titles*
✓ *any photographs or illustrations*
✓ *any dedication, preface, introduction, or note to the reader*
✓ *the first paragraph or two of the text*
✓ *any repeated words*

Overhead Transparencies

Before Reading

C Plan

Now have students sum up what they learned about the biography by previewing it. Direct their attention to the list at the top of page 199. Then have students make a plan for reading the excerpt.

Reading Strategy: Looking for Cause and Effect

Point out that biographers try to show how certain life experiences affected the subject of the biography. For this reason, **looking for cause and effect** is a good strategy to use for reading biographies.

Have students look at the Cause-Effect Organizer at the bottom of page 199 of the *Reader's Handbook*. As students read, they should note a major event in a cause box. After reading, students can think about what the effects were of these major events and write them in the effects boxes.

During Reading

D Read with a Purpose

Now students are ready to read. Go over with them the questions at the top of page 200. Tell students they are to read the excerpt on pages 200 and 201 to gather important information using the Cause-Effect Organizer.

CAUSE-EFFECT ORGANIZER

CAUSE	EFFECTS
became the only black player in baseball	stayed alone in black hotels
	had to eat alone
	hit by a ball six times

During Reading

D Read with a Purpose continued

Students may also wish to practice taking notes using other graphic organizers. Allow them to choose the tools they want to use.

Sometimes students have to read between the lines, or make inferences, to determine how certain events produced certain effects. The Inference Chart, as shown at the bottom of page 202, is useful for this purpose. Ask students to read through the completed example of the Inference Chart.

INFERENCE CHART

TEXT	WHAT I CONCLUDE
1. He had to stay alone in black hotels and eat alone.	He was probably lonely and angry because of segregation.
2. He was hit by pitches.	He must have been bruised and realized how dangerous this was.
3 He was insulted on the field.	It must have been hard for him to keep his temper.
4. Reese puts his hand on Robinson's shoulder.	Robinson was probably surprised and grateful.

Details about Key Events

Making Sequence Notes, as illustrated on page 203, can help students keep track of the major events in a biography. This organizer is simple for students to use, and it helps in understanding cause and effect.

SEQUENCE NOTES

1947: Robinson begins playing for the Dodgers.

▼

He travels to major cities with the team.

▼

Robinson thrown at constantly and hit a total of six times.

▼

He sharpens skills as base runner.

▼

He is heckled and abused in Cincinnati and Boston.

▼

Pee Wee Reese stands beside Robinson to silence crowd.

▼

Event is a turning point in Robinson's career.

During Reading

Read with a Purpose continued

Details about the Subject

Another useful tool for reading biographies is a Character Map. This graphic organizer can help students clarify their understanding of what the subject of the biography is like. Show the students the completed example on page 204, and have them read the information recorded in it.

CHARACTER MAP

WHAT HE SAYS AND DOES
1. He's "explosive" and fast.
2. He "dances" and "charges."

WHAT OTHERS THINK ABOUT HIM
1. Fans and opposing teams heckle him because he's black.
2. Management is confident enough in him to hire him.
3. Only Pee Wee Reese tries to defend him.

JACKIE ROBINSON

HOW HE LOOKS AND FEELS
1. Picture shows him as a young man.
2. humiliated by racism
3. disappointed in his teammates
4. tries not to let insults bother him

HOW I FEEL ABOUT HIM
1. I think he was brave.
2. In a lot of ways, he was a hero.

Other Useful Tools

Encourage students to use other reading tools as they read the passages from *Rickey & Robinson*. As with any type of tool, students need to be able to apply the right one when needed. If not familiar with the tools below, students can find them in the Reader's Almanac. These are especially useful tools for reading biographies:

- **Double-entry Journal**
- **Summary Notes**
- **Character Web**

How Biographies Are Organized

Most biographies are written in chronological order. Details about time and place are important to note, as they often signal important changes in the subject's life.

READING A BIOGRAPHY

Read through pages 204 and 205 with the students, and point out the key details noted about time and place in the excerpt. Emphasize that highlighting text or making notes about it can help students understand the subject of a biography.

E Connect

Remind students that it is important to respond to or make connections with the text as they read. Suggest the following ways students can connect with the current selection:

- find connections to their own lives (Do I know anyone with experiences like these?)
- think about the importance of Robinson's life (Why has this author chosen to write a biography of Robinson?)
- think about how the excerpt made them feel (Would I like to read more of this book?)
- ask themselves how they would respond in this situation (What would I do if I'd experienced this?)

After Reading

Pause and Reflect

After reading, students stop and reflect on what they have read. Have students go back and review their original purposes in reading this excerpt. Go over the Looking Back questions with them.

Looking Back

- **Can I name several important events in the subject's life?**
- **Do I understand how these events affected the subject?**
- **Do I have a sense of what the person was really like?**
- **Can I say how I feel about the subject?**
- **Can I support how I feel with evidence from the text?**

Students may still be uncertain of the answers to these questions. At this point, students need to return to the text to obtain more information.

Reread

Explain that when rereading students need to use a different strategy or tool to get a fresh look at the material. Suggest the strategy of outlining.

Rereading Strategy: Outlining

Remind students that **outlining** requires them to pull the most important information from the text and organize it in some way. Have them look at the example on page 208. This is a Topic Outline that uses the biography's chronological structure to organize the most important events in the subject's life.

TOPIC OUTLINE

Title or Subject
- *I. Early Years*
  - *A. important event*
  - *B. important event*
- *II. School-age Years*
  - *A. important event*
  - *B. important event*
- *III. Young Adulthood*
  - *A. important event*
  - *B. important event*
- *IV. Adulthood*
  - *A. important event*
  - *B. important event*
  - *C. important event*

IV. Adulthood: Robinson's 1947 season with the Dodgers
- A. encounters racism on the field and off
  - 1. insults
  - 2. forced to obey unfair segregation laws
- B. ignores taunts and jeers of the crowd
  - 1. stays quiet but refuses to back down
  - 2. must prove himself
- C. Reese incident
  - 1. crowd silent
  - 2. turning point

After Reading

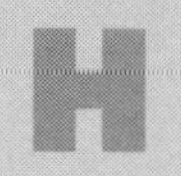

Remember

Now students must make the newly learned information their own. Discuss the activities on page 209 of the *Reader's Handbook*. Suggest that students make a Timeline or draw a map. As an alternative, students may do the creative assignment below.

Creative Assignment: Have students work in pairs to become each other's "biographers." Have the students create Timelines of the important events in each other's lives. Timelines can be displayed on a classroom bulletin board. If time permits, students may write short biographies of their partners.

Summing Up

Review the lesson by reading the Summing Up on page 209. Discuss everything students have learned about strategies and tools for reading a biography. Go over the initial goals for the lesson, discussing which ones students feel they achieved and which ones they need more work on:

1. **appreciating the two major goals of a biography**
2. **using the strategy of looking for cause and effect**
3. **understanding the organization biographers use in telling the story**

Assessment and Application

Use the Quick Assess checklist to evaluate students' ability to read and understand biographies. Give students the opportunity to apply what they have learned through one of the two activities below. For students who are comfortable with the reading process and strategy, use one of the suggestions for independent practice or an activity of your own. For students who need guided help with the strategy, use a *Student Applications Book*.

Quick Assess

Can students

- ☑ name two major goals of a biographer?
- ☑ identify a useful strategy for reading a biography?
- ☑ explain why rereading is necessary and name a good rereading strategy?

1. Independent Practice

Have students apply the strategy of **looking for cause and effect** to another biography of their choice to show their understanding of the lesson.

Ask students to do one of the following:

- Complete a Cause-Effect Organizer or a Topic Outline.
- Write Sequence Notes.
- Write a journal entry about the subject of the biography, explaining how certain major events affected the subject.

2. Student Applications Books

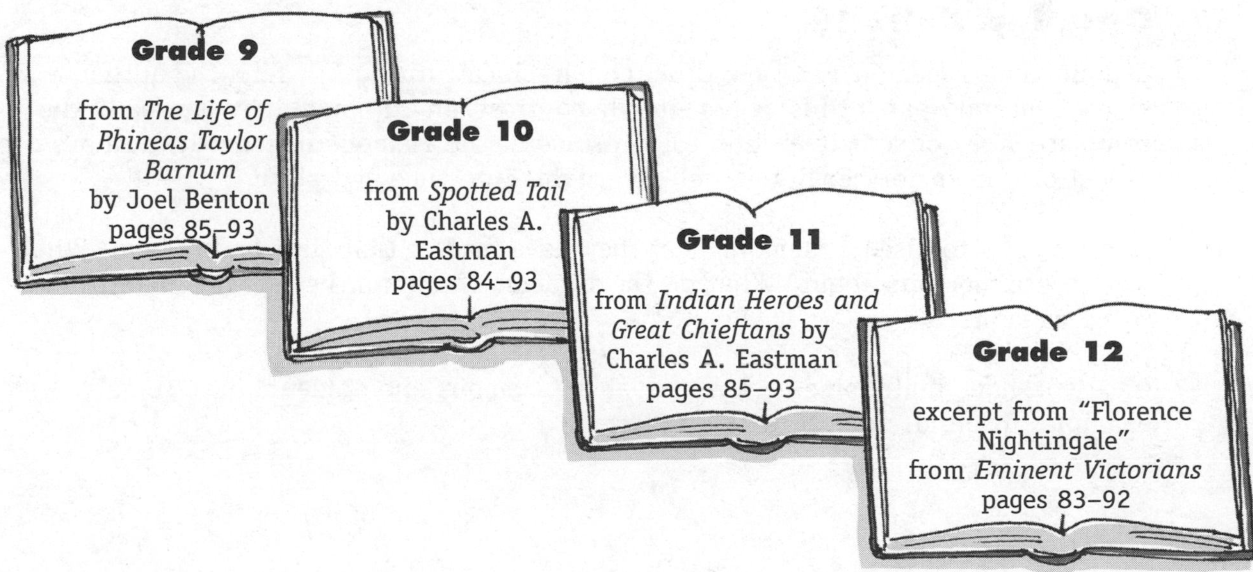

Test Book

See *Test Book* for short-answer and multiple-choice tests.

Reading a Memoir

Goals

Here students read an excerpt from Isak Dinesen's memoir, *Out of Africa*. Students will learn to:

- ✓ recognize the major topics of a memoir
- ✓ use the strategy of synthesizing (pulling together key topics)
- ✓ understand the organization of most memoirs

Background

Help students connect this lesson with their prior knowledge by asking them to:

- explain what a memoir is and how it differs from an autobiography
- discuss memoirs they have read in the past
- talk about what events in their own lives they have put down in writing
- discuss why people would write and read memoirs

Opening Activity

Explain that a memoir is a type of autobiographical writing in which the author focuses on only part of his or her life. By contrast, an autobiography is usually the complete story of someone's life, told in some detail. Memoirs include the author's reflections on his or her life as well as insights into time and place.

Ask students to discuss memoirs that they have read or that they know about. What were these memoirs about? What do the students think are the reasons for writing these memoirs?

Once you have built some background about memoirs and students have some examples in mind, proceed with the lesson.

Overview

	Content	Teacher's Guide page	Reader's Handbook page
Selection	from *Out of Africa* by Isak Dinesen		212–213, 216–218
Reading Strategy	Synthesizing	143, 439	214, 732
Rereading Strategy	Visualizing and Thinking Aloud	147, 440	223, 736
Tool	Key Word or Topic Notes	143–144	215, 219, 746
	Web	144	220, 757
	Inference Chart	145	221, 746
	Timeline	146	222, 755

Ancillaries

	Grade	Content	Page
Overhead Transparency	9–12	Previewing a Memoir	Numbers 22 and 23
Lesson Plan Book	9	Reading a Memoir	85, 90–93
	10	Reading a Memoir	85, 90–93
	12	Reading a Memoir	94, 96–99
Student Applications Book	9	from *Incidents in the Life of a Slave Girl* by Harriet Jacobs	94–103
	10	from *When the Sea-Asp Stings* by Irving S. Cobb	94–104
	11	from *Travels Through North and South Carolina, Georgia, East and West Florida* by William Bartram	94–102
	12	from *Memoirs of My Life and Writings* by Edward Gibbon	93–101
Test Book	9–12	Short-answer Test Multiple-choice Test	
Website		www.greatsource.com/rehand/	

Before Reading

Set a Purpose

First students need to set a purpose for reading the selection. Have them read the Setting a Purpose questions on page 211 of the *Reader's Handbook*.

Setting a Purpose

- **What kind of life did this person have at this time?**
- **How do I feel about him or her and the places, times, and events described?**

B Preview

Have students preview before reading, starting with the book cover and jacket copy shown on pages 212 and 213. Call attention to the annotations that highlight things to look for in previewing. Guide students through the Preview Checklist on page 211. Talk with them about where they might find each item that is listed.

Preview Checklist

- ✓ *the title and author*
- ✓ *front and back cover*
- ✓ *any summaries, quotations, or reviews*
- ✓ *any dedication, preface, introduction, or note to the reader*
- ✓ *the title of each chapter*
- ✓ *any photographs or illustrations*
- ✓ *the opening paragraph or two of the first chapter*

Overhead Transparencies

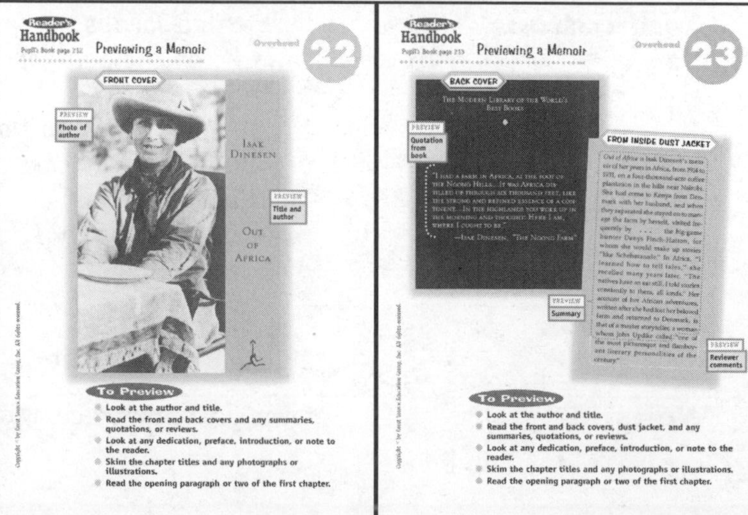

Before Reading

C Plan

Ask students to tell what they learned about this memoir simply by previewing it. Direct their attention to the list at the top of page 214. Then have students make a plan for reading.

Reading Strategy: Synthesizing

Explain to students that **synthesizing** is an important skill for many types of reading. Synthesizing means pulling together the important information in a text. It's like gathering up puzzle pieces and putting them all together to reveal the "big picture."

Knowing the key topics that tend to be present in most memoirs can help students identify the important information they need to collect for their synthesis. Ask students to look at the bottom of page 214 and read the six key topics listed there.

KEY TOPICS IN A MEMOIR

1. *reasons for the focus on this particular period in the writer's life*
2. *physical surroundings*
3. *actions and personalities of people the writer knew*
4. *work and major achievements*
5. *major problems and how they were overcome*
6. *opinions and actions that reveal the writer's character and personality*

Finding Key Topics

Students can better organize the information they find by using a note-taking technique called Key Word or Topic Notes.

Ask students to look at the example of Key Word or Topic Notes on page 215 of the *Reader's Handbook.* They can make their own charts to use during reading. As students read the memoir excerpt, they note information on the right-hand side of their charts for each of the key topic categories on the left.

During Reading

D Read with a Purpose

As students read, they gather important information from the excerpt on pages 216–218. Using Key Word or Topic Notes helps them keep track of important details.

KEY WORD OR TOPIC NOTES

KEY TOPICS	NOTES
reasons for the focus on this period in the writer's life	• experiences may be of historical interest
physical surroundings	• plantation was near the equator • over six thousand feet high
work and major achievements	• successfully ran a coffee plantation
major problems	• drought, weeds, and diseases • transportation difficult
personality and character traits	• feels pride in her achievements • loves the beauty of Africa • is strong and determined

Students may also wish to practice taking notes in other ways. Allow students to choose which tools to use.

Show students the example of the Web on page 220. Point out that this tool will help them form an opinion about the author of the memoir. Dinesen's name is written in the center circle of the Web, with circles describing character traits connected to it. Attached to the character trait circles are proof circles, which contain examples from the text showing that Dinesen has these traits.

WEB

ISAK DINESEN

Trait: hard-working
- **Proof:** manages coffee plantation on her own after her husband leaves
- **Proof:** battles difficulties, such as drought, disease, weeds

Trait: intelligent
- **Proof:** has a broad vocabulary; uses elaborate sentence structures
- **Proof:** understands her own reasons for farming

Trait: highly observant
- **Proof:** describes her surroundings in a very detailed way

Trait: sympathetic to others' circumstances
- **Proof:** has respect for government officials who had to work in hot rooms

D Read with a Purpose continued

An Inference Chart is designed to help students draw conclusions about important aspects of the author's life. Have students look at the example given on page 221.

INFERENCE CHART

TEXT	WHAT I CONCLUDE
Writer She took over management of the coffee plantation after her husband left.	She was determined and brave. It probably wasn't easy to run that plantation on her own.
Places She describes her farm in detail. Nairobi, where the government offices were, was the nearest town.	Her descriptions of the farm and the surrounding countryside make them sound beautiful. Nairobi must have been where she bought supplies.
Times When she first arrived (1914), there were no cars there.	It must have been hard to run a farm without a car, and it must have taken a long time to travel the twelve miles to town.

Other Useful Tools

Encourage students to try out other reading tools as they read the passages from *Out of Africa*. As with any type of tool, students need to be able to apply the right one when needed. If not familiar with the tools below, students can find them in the Reader's Almanac. These are other especially useful tools for reading memoirs:

- **Double-entry Journal**
- **Character Map**

How Memoirs Are Organized

Though every memoir is organized a little differently, all memoirs have certain features in common. For instance, nearly all are written in first person and focus on a major period or periods in the author's life.

MEMOIR FACTS

***Almost all memoirs are written in the first person. Watch for pronouns such as* I, we, *and* our.**

A memoir often focuses on one or more major periods in the writer's life. Look for them.

Because memoirs are not necessarily told in chronological order, creating a Timeline may be useful, as shown on page 222 of the handbook.

TIMELINE

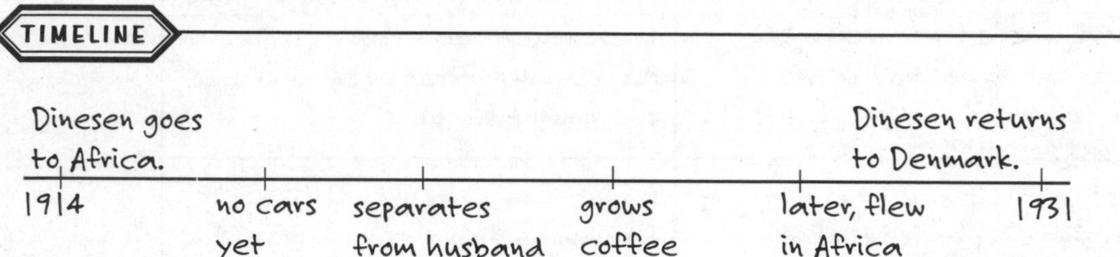

E Connect

Remind students that making connections to the text as they read is an important part of reading actively. Suggest the following ways students can connect with the current selection:

- find connections to their own lives
  (Do I know anyone with experiences like these?)
- think about the importance of Dinesen's life in relation to their own lives
  (How do her experiences help me understand what's going on today?)
- think about how the excerpt made them feel
  (Would I like to read more of this book?)
- ask themselves how they would respond in this situation
  (What would I do if I'd been living in Africa in 1920?)

On the bottom of page 222, an example of one reader's journal response to this excerpt is shown. Ask students to read and think about this response.

F Pause and Reflect

After reading, students need to stop and reflect on what they have read. Have students go back and review their original purposes in reading this excerpt. Go over the Looking Back questions with them.

Looking Back

- **Do I have a good portrait of the writer?**
- **Do I have a clear impression of the people, places, times, and events?**
- **Do I know how I feel about the writer?**
- **Do I understand the purpose of the memoir?**

Students may still be uncertain of the answers to these questions. At this point, they may need to return to the text to obtain more information.

G Reread

When rereading, students need to use a different strategy or tool to get a fresh look at the material. Suggest the strategy of visualizing and thinking aloud.

Rereading Strategy: Visualizing and Thinking Aloud

Remind students that **visualizing** is picturing in their minds what they are reading, and **thinking aloud** is talking to themselves about what they are reading. Suggest that, as they read, they make sketches of the places Dinesen describes. Invite them to think out loud while they sketch.

Take time here to explain to students the strategy and why it's helpful to readers. Point out that, by thinking aloud, they put ideas into their own words and in doing so make the ideas clear for themselves. Visualizing works by making something abstract more concrete, helping the brain "see" what's there so that they can build upon what is visualized.

After Reading

Remember

Now students need to do something with the reading to make it their own. Assign one of the activities on page 224 of the *Reader's Handbook,* or suggest the creative assignment below.

Creative Assignment: Ask students to think about some important times and events in their own lives. What places, times, or happenings have had an influence on who they are today? Have students read their Key Word or Topic Notes for inspiration. Then ask them to write informal journal entries about the events and times in their own lives, which they may use in the future as a basis for a memoir.

Summing Up

Review the lesson by reading over the Summing Up on page 224. Focus on everything students have learned about strategies and tools for reading memoirs. Go over the initial goals for the lesson, discussing which ones students feel they achieved and which ones they need more work on:

1. **recognizing the major topics of a memoir**
2. **using the strategy of synthesizing (pulling together key topics)**
3. **understanding the organization of most memoirs**

Assessment and Application

Use the Quick Assess checklist to evaluate students' ability to read and understand memoirs. Give students the opportunity to apply what they have learned through one of the two activities below. For students who are comfortable with the reading process and strategy, use one of the suggestions for independent practice or an activity of your own. For students who need guided help with the strategy, use a *Student Applications Book*.

Quick Assess

Can students

- ☑ explain what a memoir is?
- ☑ identify a few key topics found in most memoirs?
- ☑ define synthesizing and explain why it's a useful strategy for reading memoirs and other narratives?
- ☑ describe one or two good tools for reading or rereading a memoir?

1. Independent Practice

To show that they understand the lesson, students can apply the strategy of **synthesizing** to another memoir of their choice.

Ask students to do one of the following:

- Complete a set of Key Topic Notes.
- Complete a Web, an Inference Chart, or a set of sketches.
- Write a journal entry explaining how certain major events affected the author of a memoir and describing what the author was really like as a person.

2. Student Applications Books

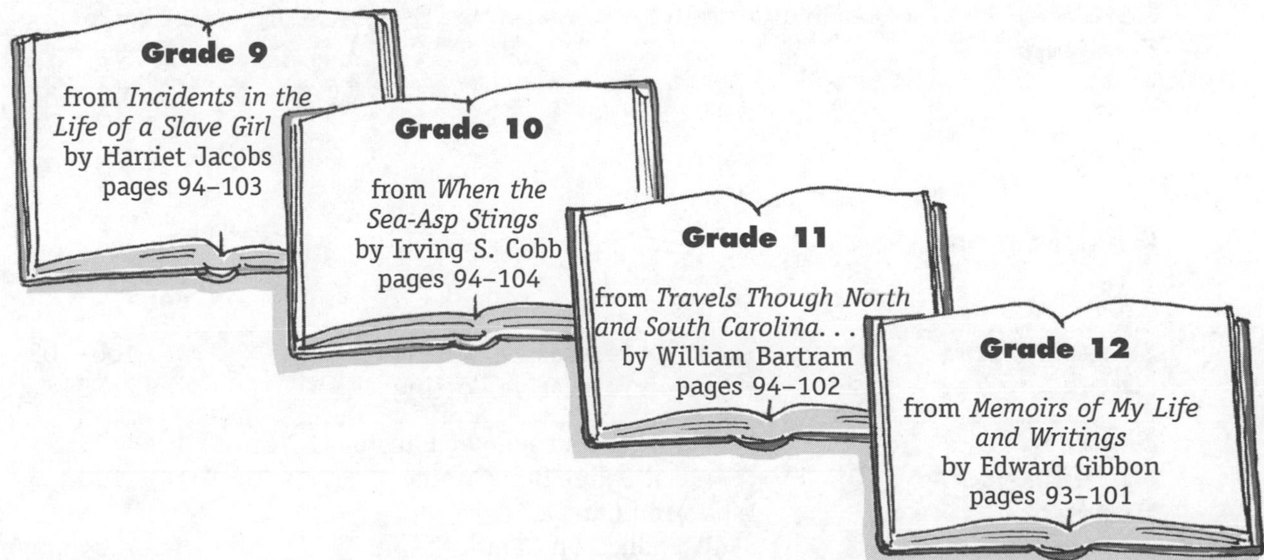

Test Book

See *Test Book* for short-answer and multiple-choice tests.

Focus on Persuasive Writing

Goals

Here students focus on how to read persuasive writing. This lesson will help them learn to:

- recognize the topic and the author's assertion and viewpoint
- identify the three parts of an argument
- use the strategy of reading critically to evaluate the argument

Background

Like most adults, students rarely think of advertisements, speeches, or emails from friends as persuasive writing. Help students connect this lesson with their prior knowledge by asking them to:

- give examples of persuasive writing
- recall a piece of persuasive writing that changed their thinking
- discuss how persuasive forms of writing affect the attitudes and beliefs of their friends and family members

Overview

	Content	Teacher's Guide page	Reader's Handbook page
Selection	"Appearances Are Destructive" by Mark Mathabane		227–228, 231
Reading Strategy	Reading Critically	151, 437	229, 726
Tool	Argument Chart	151, 152	230, 739

Ancillaries

	Grade	Content	Page
Lesson Plan Book	10	Focus on Persuasive Writing	95, 100–103
	11	Focus on Persuasive Writing	94, 96–99
Student Applications Book	9	"Cell Phone and Beeper Ban for the Birds"	104–105
	10	"Eastern Ballet Bankruptcy: What You Can Do"	105–106
	11	"Cell Phones on Campus"	103–104
	12	"New Library Needed"	102–103
Test Book	9–12	Short-answer Test Multiple-choice Test	
Website		www.greatsource.com/rehand/	

Before Reading

Introduce students to the three-step plan for reading persuasive writing, explained on page 226 of the *Reader's Handbook*.

THREE-STEP PLAN

Step 1. *Find the topic.* ▶ **Step 2.** *Find what the writer says about the topic (his or her assertion or viewpoint).* ▶ **Step 3.** *Decide what you think about the writer's argument.*

Then ask the students to preview "Appearances Are Destructive" on pages 227 and 228 of the handbook.

Preview Checklist

- ✓ *the title or headline*
- ✓ *the first and final paragraphs*
- ✓ *any repeated words and phrases*

Ask students to say in their own words what they learned from the preview. Point out the Preview Checklist on page 226 and the Preview Chart on page 229.

Point out the need to read persuasive writing critically. Emphasize that if readers don't have the skills they need to make up their own minds about certain issues, they can be easily swayed by any piece of persuasive writing.

Reading Strategy: Reading Critically

Remind students that the strategy of **reading critically** requires understanding and evaluating what the writer is saying. Students must be able to judge the strength of the argument being presented.

During Reading

Ask students to study the Argument Chart at the top of page 230. A good argument consists of three parts: the assertion, the support, and a consideration of the opposing viewpoint. These parts may appear in any order and can even be mixed together. Reading critically means checking that all three parts of the argument are present. The argument is flawed if one part is missing or weak.

Have students complete their own Argument Charts while reading the current selection.

After reading, have students stop and think about the points the author makes in "Appearances Are Destructive." Students should ask themselves:

What's my opinion of Mathabane's assertion?

Is his support strong and convincing?

Has his argument changed my view of the topic?

1. Connect to the Topic

Ask students to think about how this topic relates to their own lives. Have they had any similar experiences? Have students informally jot down their responses to the selection, as illustrated on page 231.

2. Evaluate the Argument

Have students also make notes on how persuasive they thought the author's argument was. What might he have included in his piece to strengthen his argument? Show students the example on page 232.

Understanding Propaganda Techniques

Students must be familiar with common propaganda techniques if they are to read and think critically.

Ask students to read about eight of the most common propaganda techniques on page 233 of the handbook. Carefully go over with students the examples. Ask students if they can think of any other examples of propaganda they've heard or read.

3. Decide How You Feel

Students need to ask themselves how they feel about the author's assertion. An opinion chart can help them organize their thoughts. Review the example of an opinion chart on page 234.

Summing Up

Have students read the points in the Summing Up at the bottom of page 234. Ask students to say in their own words what they learned in this lesson.

Assessment and Application

Use the Quick Assess checklist to evaluate students' ability to read and understand persuasive writing. Give students the opportunity to apply what they have learned through one of the two activities below. For students who are comfortable with the reading process and strategy, use the suggestion for independent practice or an activity of your own. For students who need guided help with the strategy, use a *Student Applications Book*.

Quick Assess

Can students

- ☑ give several examples of persuasive writing?
- ☑ explain why reading critically is an important strategy for reading persuasive writing?
- ☑ give three or more examples of common propaganda techniques?

1. Independent Practice

To show that they understand the lesson, students can apply the strategy of **reading critically** to an advertisement from a popular teen magazine.

2. Student Applications Books

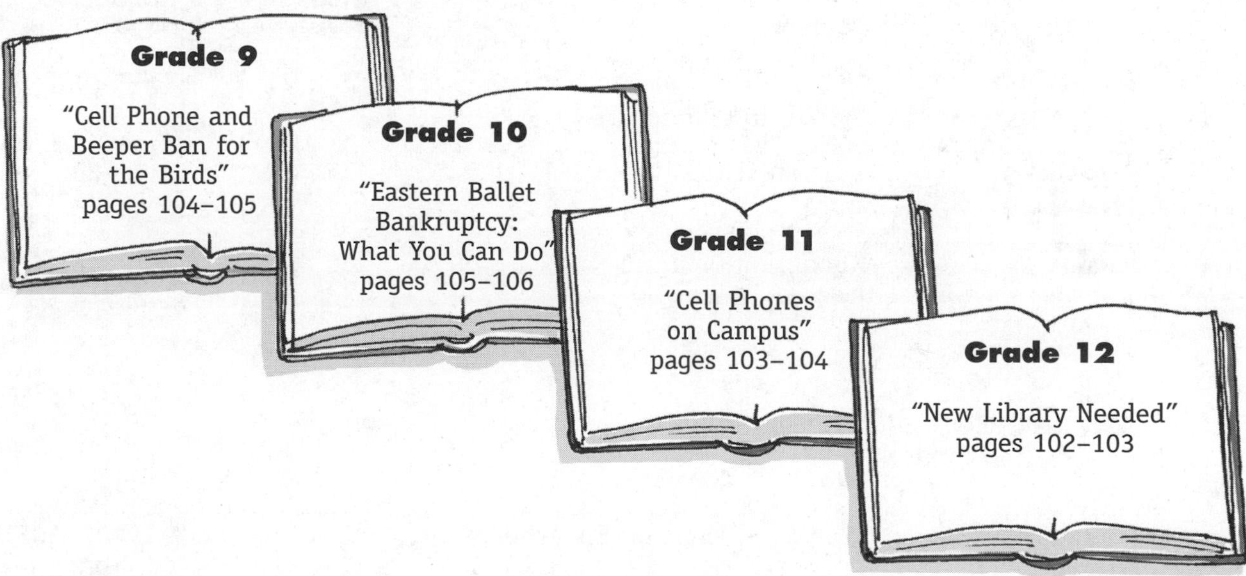

Test Book

See *Test Book* for short-answer and multiple-choice tests.

Focus on Speeches

Goals

Here students focus on analyzing speeches. This lesson will help students to:

- find the speaker's purpose
- use the strategy of reading critically
- understand how speeches are organized
- recognize common stylistic devices

Background

Help students connect this lesson with their prior knowledge by asking them to:

- tell what a speech is
- talk about a speech or part of a speech they have heard or read
- discuss a time when they had to write and give a speech in class

Overview

	Content	Teacher's Guide page	Reader's Handbook page
Selection	"Blood, Toil, Tears, and Sweat" by Winston Churchill		238–239, 243
Reading Strategy	Reading Critically	155, 437	239, 726
Tool	Nonfiction Organizer Evidence Organizer	156 156	241, 748 242, 744

Ancillaries

	Grade	Content	Page
Lesson Plan Book	9 11	Focus on Speeches Focus on Speeches	95, 100–103 95, 100–103
Student Applications Book	9	"Let Me Be a Free Man" by Chief Metea	106–108
	10	"Child Labor and Women's Suffrage" by Florence Kelley	107–109
	11	Carrie Chapman Catt's Speech in Favor of Women's Suffrage	105–106
	12	The Empress Theodora's Speech During the Invasion of Constantinople	104–106
Test Book	9–12	Short-answer Test Multiple-choice Test	
Website		www.greatsource.com/rehand/	

Before Reading

Explain to students that a speech is like any other work of nonfiction. The reader must determine the topic and purpose of the speech. Point out that most speeches have one of two purposes: to inform or to persuade.

Have students turn to page 236 of the handbook and read the characteristics of these two types of speeches. Point out that some of the characteristics overlap.

Reading a Speech

To read a speech, students should follow the four-step plan outlined on page 237.

FOUR-STEP PLAN

Step 1. *Figure out the occasion or purpose of the speech.* ▶ **Step 2.** *Understand the organization.* ▶ **Step 3.** *Find out the speaker's main idea or viewpoint and support for that idea or viewpoint.* ▶ **Step 4.** *Evaluate the speech.*

Previewing

Remind students of the need to preview a selection before reading. Point out that the background information with a published speech will often give clues to its subject and purpose. Quickly review the checklist on page 237.

Preview Checklist

- ✓ *the title*
- ✓ *the topic*
- ✓ *the context (time, place, and audience)*
- ✓ *the introduction and conclusion*
- ✓ *any repeated words and phrases*

Call attention to the annotations that will help students preview the speech. After previewing, ask students to say in their own words what they learned from the preview.

Step 1. Look at the Occasion or Purpose of the Speech

Have students silently read Step 1 on page 239 and talk about Churchill's purpose in making the speech. Emphasize the need to read a speech critically.

Reading Strategy: Reading Critically

Remind students that **reading critically** begins with understanding the text and ends with an evaluation of it. Understanding how a speech is organized helps students to read critically.

Step 2. Understand the Organization

Ask the students to turn to page 240 of their handbooks. Point out that a speech has three parts: an introduction, a body, and a conclusion. Important information in each part of the speech can be recorded in a Nonfiction Organizer, illustrated on page 241.

NONFICTION ORGANIZER

Title: "Blood, Toil, Tears, and Sweat"
Subject: War against Hitler
Introduction: • says the battle is just beginning • apologizes for his informality • stresses the importance of the situation
Body: • says long struggle ahead • emphasizes that victory is the aim
Conclusion: • urges audience to join him in seeking victory against Hitler

Step 3. Find Out the Viewpoint and Support

Identifying the speaker's viewpoint is essential to reading critically. Often that viewpoint is implied. Show students the formula for discovering an implied viewpoint, shown on page 241.

Evaluating the quality of the support or evidence the speaker provides is also crucial to critical reading. Have students turn to page 242 and read about common types of support. Keeping track of the evidence or support is easier when students have an Evidence Organizer. Point out to students how the organizer clearly presents the important information, revealing a lack of facts and statistics in Churchill's speech.

EVIDENCE ORGANIZER

VIEWPOINT: Great Britain can win a war against Hitler.			
SUPPORTING DETAIL #1 We will wage war everywhere.	SUPPORTING DETAIL #2 God will give us strength.	SUPPORTING DETAIL #3 We will win because we must. There will be no British Empire without victory.	SUPPORTING DETAIL #4 Churchill himself feels confident of victory.

After Reading

After reading, students need to think about and evaluate the speech. To evaluate the speech, students analyze the speaker's stylistic devices and judge the effects of those devices.

Step 4. Evaluate the Speech

Ask students to turn to page 244 in the handbook. Have them take turns reading the table about common stylistic devices aloud. After each device is explained, pause and ask students if they can think of any examples of these devices used in a speech they heard recently.

Then ask students to use the evaluation form on page 245 to "grade" Churchill's speech. Students may prefer to do this as a whole-class activity.

Evaluation Form

Speaker's Name ______________________________

Speaker's Topic ______________________________

	Poor	*Fair*	*Good*	*Very Good*	*Excellent*
1. Clear organization	❑	❑	❑	❑	❑
2. Clear viewpoint	❑	❑	❑	❑	❑
3. Use of support	❑	❑	❑	❑	❑
4. Language appropriate to audience	❑	❑	❑	❑	❑
5. Topic appropriate to audience	❑	❑	❑	❑	❑

Summing Up

Have students read the points in the Summing Up at the bottom of page 245. Then ask students to say in their own words what they learned in this lesson.

Assessment and Application

Use the Quick Assess checklist to evaluate students' ability to analyze speeches. Give students the opportunity to apply what they have learned through one of the two activities below. For students who are comfortable with the reading process and strategy, use the suggestion for independent practice or an activity of your own. For students who need guided help with the strategy, use a *Student Applications Book.*

Quick Assess

Can students

- ☑ name the two most common types of speeches?
- ☑ name the three parts in the standard organization of a speech?
- ☑ list at least three common types of support for a viewpoint?
- ☑ list at least three common stylistic devices found in speeches?

1. Independent Practice

To show that they understand the lesson, students can apply the strategy of **reading critically** to a recent speech by a local politician or by the U.S. President.

2. Student Applications Books

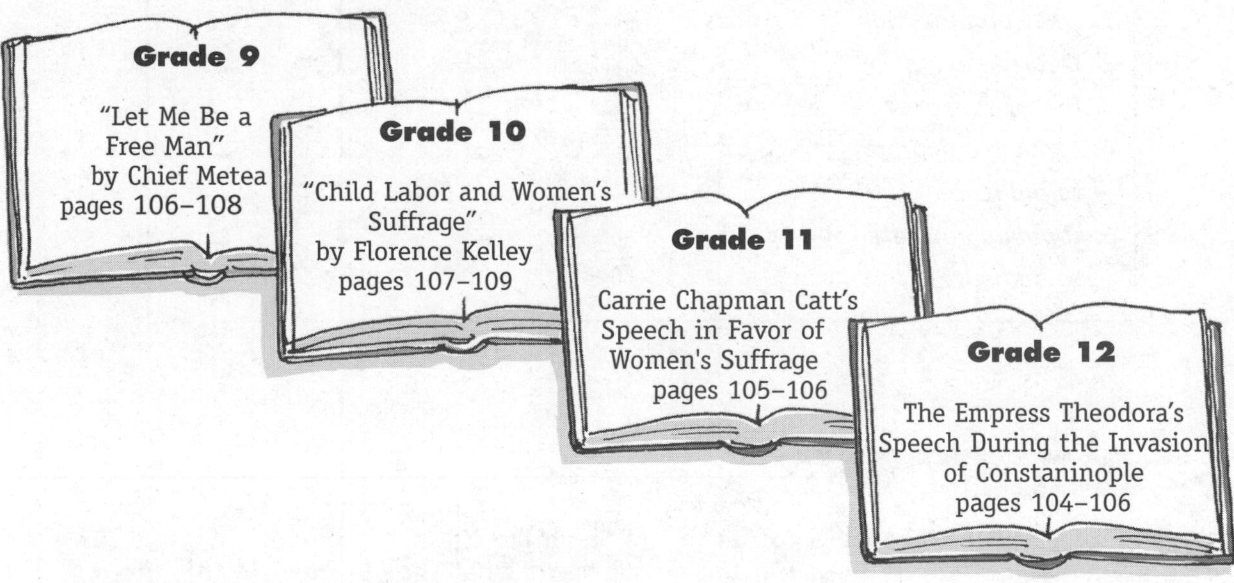

Test Book

See *Test Book* for short-answer and multiple-choice tests.

Elements of Nonfiction

This section introduces and explains common elements in nonfiction. The *Reader's Handbook* provides examples, descriptions, and definitions. Use this section to familiarize students with the terminology and the overall purposes of these elements.

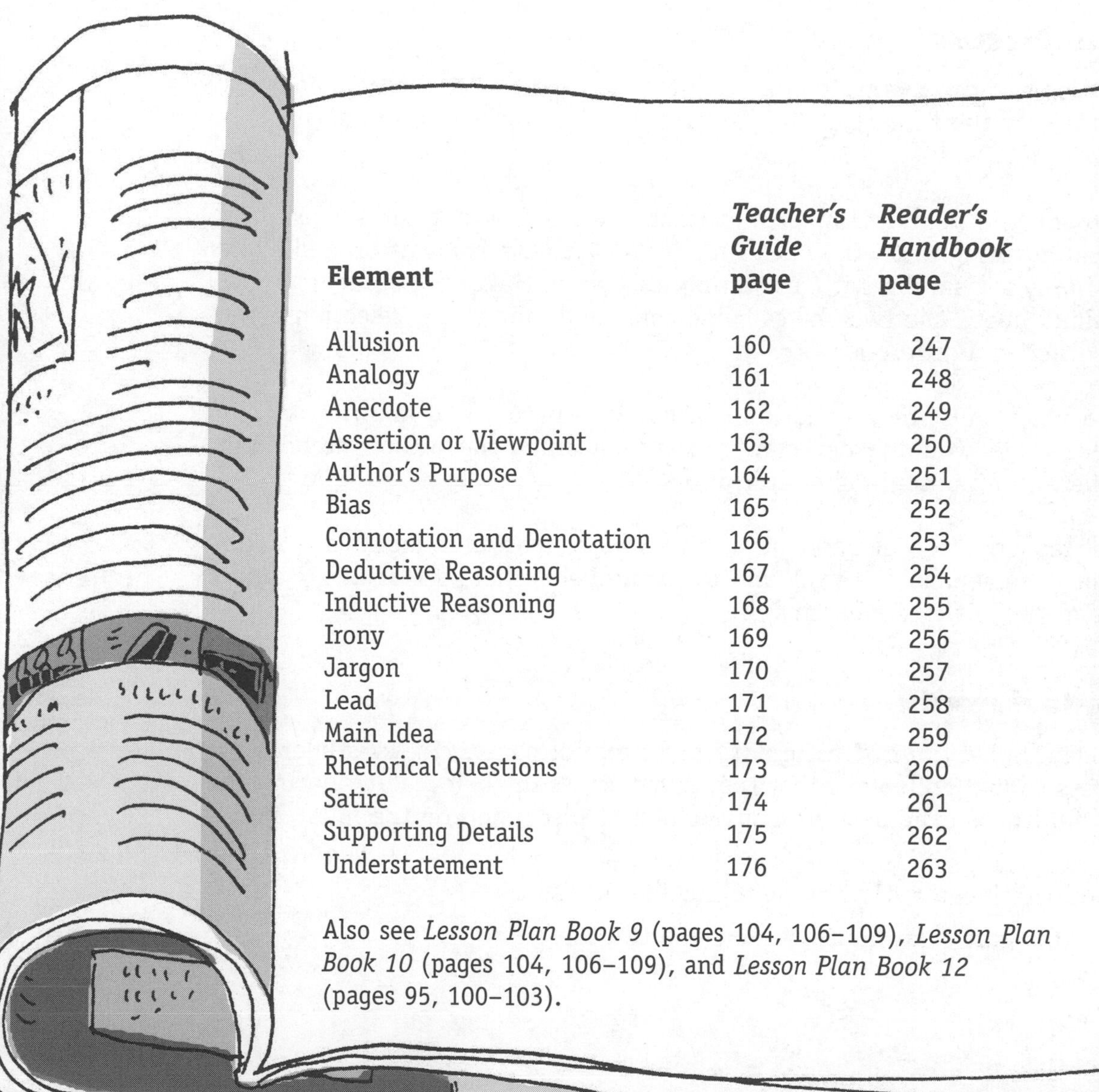

Element	***Teacher's Guide* page**	***Reader's Handbook* page**
Allusion	160	247
Analogy	161	248
Anecdote	162	249
Assertion or Viewpoint	163	250
Author's Purpose	164	251
Bias	165	252
Connotation and Denotation	166	253
Deductive Reasoning	167	254
Inductive Reasoning	168	255
Irony	169	256
Jargon	170	257
Lead	171	258
Main Idea	172	259
Rhetorical Questions	173	260
Satire	174	261
Supporting Details	175	262
Understatement	176	263

Also see *Lesson Plan Book 9* (pages 104, 106–109), *Lesson Plan Book 10* (pages 104, 106–109), and *Lesson Plan Book 12* (pages 95, 100–103).

Allusion

Set Goal

Students will learn that an allusion is a reference to a literary, artistic, or musical work.

Teach and Discuss

Have students look at the **Example** of an allusion on page 247 of the handbook. Ask them to identify the subject of the paragraph and the reference to another literary work.

Then read through the **Description** with students. Emphasize that authors use allusions to add meaning to their works. An allusion makes a comparison and allows the writer to imply a meaning without stating it directly. Make sure students know they should think about the two things being compared, one in the selection being read and the other in a different work.

Talk with students about why an allusion is usually made to a well-known work. Bring out that readers wouldn't necessarily get the meaning the author intended if the allusion were to an obscure character or event.

Point out that readers often like to look up the work suggested in an allusion. They may only vaguely remember the work and rereading helps them better understand the allusion and the author's meaning.

Check Understanding

Now have students read the **Definition** at the bottom of page 247. Ask students to use sticky notes to mark allusions that they come across in their reading during the next week. Using these examples, have a whole-class discussion on the following questions:

- Why do you think the author chose to include this allusion?
- What does this particular allusion make you think of?

Analogy

Set Goal

Students will learn that an analogy is a comparison of something unfamiliar with something familiar in an attempt to explain the former to readers.

Teach and Discuss

Ask for a volunteer to read aloud the **Example** on page 248 of the handbook. Then ask students to say what two things are being compared in this excerpt. Do the students find the analogy helpful in comprehending the excerpt?

Now read through the **Description** with the students. Emphasize that focusing on key words, such as *knockout* and *referees* in the example, can help students better understand what the author is trying to convey through the analogy. Ask students which is more familiar to them, the war in Vietnam or a boxing match. Most students will be more familiar with boxing. Help students understand that Walter Cronkite is using a comparison to make clear his point about the Tet offensive.

Bring out that the comparison in an analogy is often an extended one. In "We Are Mired in a Stalemate," the writer provides numerous examples of the standoff between the Vietcong and America.

Check Understanding

Have students read the **Definition.** Then have students work in pairs to create analogies of their own. The partners talk about their interests until they find one that is unfamiliar to the other student. Each partner then attempts to explain some aspect of that interest using an analogy to something familiar to the other. Students then report back to the whole group, saying:

- what each partner was attempting to explain to the other partner
- what analogy was used
- whether or not it was successful, and why

Anecdote

Set Goal

Students will learn that an anecdote is a brief story told to make a point or to entertain.

Teach and Discuss

Have students look at the **Example** of an anecdote on page 249 of the handbook. Ask students to say why they think the author told this story.

Read through the **Description** with students. Emphasize that anecdotes can be used to illustrate a point or to entertain the reader. Ask students if this anecdote was more likely written to entertain or to make a point.

Discuss with students how an anecdote can help a writer make a point. Bring out that a story illustrates the point by putting it in a context. An anecdote often provides a real-life situation to which readers can relate.

Have students tell about anecdotes that they themselves have used in conversation in order to entertain others or to make a point.

Check Understanding

Have students read the **Definition** at the bottom of page 249. Ask students to spend the next week looking and listening for anecdotes in magazines and newspapers, on television and the radio, or in conversations with friends or family members. Have students bring at least one example back to class and discuss:

- What was the anecdote that you found?
- Who was using it?
- Why was it being used? (To make a point? To persuade you of something? To make you laugh?)

Assertion or Viewpoint

Set Goal

Students will learn that an assertion is a claim, statement, or declaration that a writer makes and supports with evidence or details.

Teach and Discuss

Have a student volunteer read aloud the **Example** on page 250 of the handbook. Emphasize that an assertion can be a statement of opinion, a claim, a hypothesis, or a conclusion. If necessary, explain the subtle differences among these terms. An opinion is an idea or judgment about something. A claim is a statement that something is true. A hypothesis is an idea that explains something that hasn't yet been proven true. A conclusion is a decision or belief reached after considering the available information. None of these statements is fact. However, assertions should be backed up with some sort of evidence or supporting details.

Ask students what they think of Carson's assertion and whether she effectively backs it up. Then read through the **Description** with the students. What is said to be the purpose of the assertion in the first line of Carson's book?

Discuss with students why assertions are particularly relevant for reading nonfiction. Help them see that editorials, essays, and news stories are often based on assertions.

Check Understanding

Now have students read the **Definition** at the bottom of the page. To demonstrate understanding, have students look through magazines and newspapers for examples of assertions. (Students may do this in class or at home.) After everyone has at least one example, have students work in groups of three or four, sharing what they found and discussing the following questions:

- What is the assertion being made?
- What evidence or details does the author provide to support the assertion?
- Do you think the assertion is adequately supported?

Author's Purpose

Set Goal

Students will learn that the author's purpose is his or her reason for writing.

Teach and Discuss

Have students read the **Example** on page 251 from "Letter from Birmingham Jail" by Martin Luther King, Jr. Ask students, "What do you think was King's purpose in writing this letter?" Have students explain their responses. Point out that authors seldom state their purpose as directly as Dr. Martin Luther King, Jr., does in this paragraph.

Now read the **Description** with the class. Explain that there are several purposes for writing: to explain or inform, to entertain, to persuade, and to enlighten or reveal an interesting truth. Though it may seem like an author has several purposes in mind, he or she usually has one primary purpose.

Discuss with students why it is difficult to know for sure an author's purpose. Bring out that if the writer does not state a purpose, then it may be nearly impossible to be certain about what the author really intended. Nevertheless, the four reasons for writing are a useful guide for interpreting nonfiction.

Check Understanding

Now have students read the **Definition** at the bottom of page 251. Have students find a magazine article, a newspaper article, an essay, or another work of nonfiction that interests them and decide what the author's purpose is. To demonstrate understanding, students may express their opinions in a journal entry, or they may discuss them in a small-group or a whole-class situation. Ask students to consider these questions:

- How did you decide what the author's purpose was? (For example, what evidence from the text backs up your opinion?)
- In your opinion, what did the author hope the reader would think, feel, or do after reading his or her piece?
- In what way was the author's purpose related to your interest in the piece?

Bias

Set Goal

Students will learn that a bias is an inclination or prejudice toward one point of view.

Teach and Discuss

Have students turn to page 252 of the handbook and read the **Example** from *Coming into the Country* by John McPhee. Then ask students if they think the author has a particular bias. What is it? What clues in the text (words, phrases, and information) tell the reader about this author's bias?

Now read the **Description** with the students. Emphasize that some authors easily reveal their biases, whereas other authors attempt to conceal them. Review how McPhee reveals his bias in the current selection.

Help students see how being aware of an author's bias can make them more effective readers. Bring out that once they have determined a writer is biased in a certain direction, then they are better prepared to evaluate the author's viewpoint. Students can compare the author's bias or inclination to their own.

Check Understanding

Have students read the **Definition** at the bottom of page 252. Then ask students to find a magazine article, a newspaper article, an essay, or another work of nonfiction that they feel shows the author's bias. Working in pairs, students can share the writing samples they found and discuss whether or not the author is biased and what that bias is. Ask questions such as these:

- What is the author's bias?
- What in the text makes you think the author has this bias?
- Is this author up front about his or her bias, or does the author try to conceal it? And what in the text is the basis of your opinion?
- Why would some authors try to conceal their biases?

Connotation and Denotation

Set Goal

Students will learn that while a denotation is the dictionary definition of a word, a connotation includes thoughts and feelings that readers associate with a word. Students will also learn why nonfiction writers use words with connotations.

Teach and Discuss

Have students turn to page 253 of the handbook. Ask a student volunteer to read the **Example.** Have students identify words with particular connotations. What feelings do these words evoke? How does Scott Simon's use of strong words affect his writing about the use of weapons by the U.S. military in the Gulf War?

Now read the **Description** with the students. Point out how the tone of the piece would be different had Simon chosen different words (for example, *kill* instead of *slaughter, cruel* instead of *diabolical*). The author makes his feelings clear through his choice of words with certain connotations.

Discuss with students how an understanding of the connotations of words can help them evaluate the viewpoint in a piece of nonfiction. Once they have identified words with strong emotional feelings attached to them, then they are prepared to decide for themselves whether or not they agree with the writer.

You may want to use a thesaurus to demonstrate how words with a similar meaning can have very different connotations.

Check Understanding

Have students read the **Definition** at the bottom of page 253. To demonstrate understanding, students can look for words with positive or negative connotations in magazine articles. Here are some questions to consider:

- What are the connotations of the word chosen?
- What is the denotation of this word?
- Why do you think the author chose this particular word?

Deductive Reasoning

Set Goal

Students will learn that deductive reasoning is a way of thinking that proceeds from the known to the unknown, from the general to the specific, or from a premise to a logical conclusion.

Teach and Discuss

Have students turn to page 254 of the handbook and read the **Example** from Charles Darwin's *On the Origin of Species.* Point out that the passage begins with a general statement about how quickly living things reproduce and moves to specific examples about how fast people multiply and how fast plants multiply.

Then read through the **Description** with the students. Ask them if they've heard about "deductive reasoning" or "deduction" in the past and in what context. Remind students that this is the type of thinking portrayed in Sherlock Holmes stories and other murder and crime mysteries in which the investigator reasons out the solution to the mystery based on what is known.

In using deductive reasoning, a writer begins with a belief or assertion that something is true. This hypothesis is then followed up by proof.

Check Understanding

Have students read the **Definition** at the bottom of page 254. Then ask students to spend the upcoming week looking for examples of deductive reasoning in books or magazines, on television shows, or in other people's attempts to make sense of a puzzling event in their lives. At the end of the week, discuss students' examples as a whole class. Use questions such as these:

- What example did you find?
- How did you know it was an example of deductive reasoning?
- How was deductive reasoning being used?
- Did you notice yourself engaging in deductive reasoning? (When and why?)

Inductive Reasoning

Set Goal

Students will learn that inductive reasoning, in contrast to deductive reasoning, is a way of thinking that proceeds from small, specific details or reasons to a broader, more general conclusion.

Teach and Discuss

Have students turn to page 255 of the handbook and read the **Example** from Chief Joseph's "I Will Fight No More." Point out how the passage moves from specific details about the fighting in which Chief Joseph's people have been engaged to a general conclusion Chief Joseph has made. Have students note the author's use of details.

Then read through the **Description** with the students. Ask them if they've ever heard of inductive reasoning. If so, what was the context? Point out that because inductive reasoning is the opposite process of deductive reasoning, it is not difficult to remember.

Bring out through discussion that students use inductive reasoning in science when they perform a number of experiments and then draw a general conclusion from those experiments. A writer using inductive reasoning begins with the details and ends with the general statement, or conclusion.

Check Understanding

Have students read the **Definition** at the bottom of page 255. Then ask students to spend the upcoming week looking for examples of inductive reasoning in books or magazines, on television shows, or in conversations with other people. At the end of the week, discuss students' examples as a whole class. Ask students:

- What example did you find?
- How did you know your example shows inductive reasoning?
- How was inductive reasoning being used?
- Have you ever noticed yourself engaging in inductive reasoning? (If so, under what circumstances?)

Irony

Set Goal

Students will learn that irony is a sarcastic or humorous way of saying the opposite of what they mean.

Teach and Discuss

Have students read the **Example** on page 256 from *The Happiness of Getting It Down Right* edited by Michael Steinman. Point out Frank O'Connor's use of irony in his letter to Gus Lobrano.

Then read through the **Description** with the students. Emphasize that students use this device all the time, possibly without knowing what it's called. When students jokingly say one thing but mean the opposite, knowing that their friends know what they really mean, they are using irony. Help students see that statements such as "What a great day" when it is stormy outside or "I just love my neighbor's dog" when the dog is barking loudly are examples of irony. It would be an ironic situation if a student worked all summer to buy a used car and then failed the driver's test. Invite students to offer other ironic statements or situations. The obvious difference between what is said and what is meant in an ironic statement is the source of the humor.

Point out that readers must be on the lookout for irony in order to understand the meaning in back of the writer's words. Finding irony takes practice and thought.

Check Understanding

Have students read the **Definition** at the bottom of page 256. Then say you know how happy they'll be to get an additional homework assignment (this is irony). Ask students to spend one evening on the lookout for irony in people's conversation, on television or the radio, or in any reading material. The next day, ask students to share their examples in a whole-class discussion. Here are some good discussion questions:

- What is one example that you found?
- What was said, and what was really meant?
- Why do you think the speaker or author used irony at that time?

Jargon

Set Goal

Students will learn that jargon is the technical or specialized vocabulary of a particular group, especially a profession.

Teach and Discuss

Ask students to turn to page 257 of the handbook, and ask a volunteer to read aloud the **Example** from "Freshman Shows the Way" by Bob Sakamoto. Point out the jargon, which is highlighted, as the student reads.

Now read the **Description** with the students. Emphasize that writers need a good sense of audience to know how to use jargon effectively. In the current example, readers who are knowledgeable about baseball and its terminology will have no difficulty constructing the author's meaning. However, people who are not baseball fans will not understand the passage very well. Emphasize that a writer for a general audience needs to be careful about using jargon. Make sure students know that any group may have its own particular jargon.

Suggest that students practice using the two methods for making sense of jargon, guess/go and context clues. They might try them with a manual for electronic equipment or a magazine for computer users.

Check Understanding

Have students read the **Definition** at the bottom of page 257. Then ask students to look for magazine articles that contain a lot of jargon. Because most magazines are targeted to very specific audiences, such as computer, car, or music enthusiasts, they are a good source of jargon-laden writing. Working in pairs or small groups, students can discuss the following questions:

- Who is the intended audience for this article?
- What are some examples of jargon in this article?
- Do you know someone who would have a difficult time making sense of this article?
- How can someone who does not know a lot of this jargon try to make sense of the article?

Lead

Set Goal

Students will learn that a lead is the opening paragraph or paragraphs of a news story. It usually contains essential information on *who, what, when, where, why,* and *how.*

Teach and Discuss

Ask a student volunteer to read the **Example** on page 258. Point out that the highlighted information answers the essential 5 W's and H questions in a news story.

Now read the **Description** with the students. Explain that, many years ago, the lead of a news article was always the first paragraph, which contained the essential information, so that readers could get the basic information without necessarily reading on. This is a traditional lead. Now, however, the trend is to begin a news story with an indirect or "soft" lead. Then, lead paragraphs are often found further down in news articles. This is called a buried lead, and it encourages readers to keep reading. The first few sentences or paragraphs in contemporary news stories tend to set a scene or attempt to draw the reader in without immediately revealing what the article is about. Point out that in the example given readers initially think the article will be about terrorism.

Check Understanding

Have students read the **Definition** at the bottom of page 258. Then have students work in pairs or small groups, looking through an issue of the local newspaper. Students are to choose an article that looks interesting to them and discuss the following with their peers:

- Where is the lead in this article?
- How is all the important information given?
- If the lead is not the first paragraph, how does the news story begin, and why?

Main Idea

Set Goal

Students will learn that the main idea in nonfiction is the author's main point, or what the author wants you to remember most.

Teach and Discuss

Have students turn to page 259 of the handbook. Read the **Example** from Lorraine Hansberry's "To Be Young, Gifted and Black" aloud to the students. Ask students to say the author's main point in their own words.

Then read through the **Description** with the students. Emphasize that identifying the main idea in a piece is essential to fully comprehending it. Also stress that some writers state the main idea directly, but others only imply it. When the main idea must be inferred, the reader must pull together many details and draw his or her own conclusion based on those details.

Suggest that students reread the pages about main idea in the Reading Know-how chapter. Information on finding a stated main idea is found on page 55. Information on finding an implied main idea is found on pages 56–58. Call students' attention to the Main Idea Organizers on pages 56 and 57.

Check Understanding

Have students read the **Definition** at the bottom of page 259. To demonstrate understanding, have students choose a personal essay, memoir, or biography that looks interesting to them and read the first few pages. Then have them write a journal entry about the author's main idea. Here are some questions to address:

- What is the author's main idea?
- What evidence or clues, such as words or phrases, make me think that this is the main idea?
- What are some other ways to convey this idea?

Rhetorical Questions

Set Goal

Students will learn that a rhetorical question is one asked to make a point, not to be answered.

Teach and Discuss

Have students turn to page 260 of the handbook and read the **Example** from D. H. Lawrence's *"Benjamin Franklin"* in *Studies in Classic American Literature.* Ask students to stop and take note of the rhetorical questions.

Point out that students use rhetorical questions in everyday life. If, for example, they have been given the chore of doing the dishes, they may wash and dry the dishes and then say, "I suppose I have to put them away, too?" Or, after hearing an unbelievable story, they might ask, "Who would be foolish enough to think that really happened?"

Read through the **Description** with the students. Then return to the example and read aloud some of the rhetorical questions. Ask students to say what point Lawrence is trying to make with each one—in other words, ask students to rephrase the rhetorical questions as statements. Ask students why a writer would use rhetorical questions to make a point rather than simple statements.

Check Understanding

Have students read the **Definition** at the bottom of page 260. Then have students look for examples of rhetorical questions in works of nonfiction as well as in people's speech. Instruct students to pay special attention to the speech of their teachers, school administrators, parents, and other adult authority figures for examples of rhetorical questions. In a whole-class discussion, ask students:

- What examples of rhetorical questions did you find?
- What statement was that person actually making?
- Why do you think the writer or speaker used a rhetorical question instead of making a more direct statement?

Satire

Set Goal

Students will learn that satire is a literary device used to make fun of human vices or weaknesses, usually in an attempt to correct or change the subject of the ridicule.

Teach and Discuss

Have students turn to page 261 of the handbook and ask them to follow along as you read the **Example** aloud. As you read, emphasize the more satiric parts.

Now read the **Description** with the students. Explain that writers use satire to poke fun at large institutions in society or society in general. Though satire is intended to be funny, it is also a serious attempt to draw attention to and correct problems in society.

Check Understanding

Have students read the **Definition** at the bottom of page 261. Then have students work in pairs to create a satirical paragraph or two of their own. Have them think about problems they see in the world around them, choose one, and poke fun at it.

You may first need to model this briefly. For example, use the issue of excessive standardized testing. Talk through a possible editorial you'll write for the local newspaper. You might argue that because standardized tests are such valuable indicators of a person's progress and ability, and so much more reliable than teachers' assessments, such tests should not be limited to schoolchildren. In fact, standardized tests should be given to adults too—all adults in all kinds of jobs—so that promotions and raises may be more objectively given to the high scorers.

Ask students to discuss:

- What societal problem or issue did you satirize?
- How was your actual position on the issue different from your argument?
- Did you accomplish your purpose?

Supporting Details

Set Goal

Students will learn that details are used to provide evidence, describe a process, or create an impression in a work of nonfiction.

Teach and Discuss

Have students turn to page 262 of the handbook. Ask a volunteer to read aloud the **Example** from "The Lantern-Bearers" by Robert Louis Stevenson. Instruct the rest of the students to read along silently, taking note of the details as they go.

Then read through the **Description** with the students. Emphasize that supporting details, such as facts, statistics, and expert opinions, back up or support an author's points. Discuss with students the different kinds of supporting details used in nonfiction. Point out that facts and statistics are used to prove or show something stated is true. Examples and opinions may be offered as evidence. Details can be used to provide a complete description of a process. Details that appeal to the senses, as in the current example, create clear impressions of a person, place, time, object, or action.

Check Understanding

Have students read the **Definition** at the bottom of page 262. To demonstrate understanding, students may choose a work of nonfiction that interests them and read it for details. With a partner, students can discuss:

- What type of details are these? (Are they facts, statistics, or details that appeal to the senses?)
- What point or idea does the author support with the details?

Understatement

Set Goal

Students will learn that an understatement is a statement that is intentionally less than complete.

Teach and Discuss

Have students turn to page 263 of the handbook and read the **Example** from *The Universe* by Isaac Asimov. Then ask students to explain how it illustrates understatement.

Read through the **Description** with the students. Emphasize that an understatement is the opposite of an exaggeration. Point out that students probably use understatements in their everyday conversations. Rather than saying, "I'm so hungry I could eat a horse," a very hungry person may make an understatement, "I could eat a bite or two," to be humorous or surprising, or to emphasize the point. Have students look back at the example from *The Universe* and explain how Asimov uses understatement to make a point about humans' understanding of the universe.

Check Understanding

Have students read the **Definition** at the bottom of page 263. Then have students work in pairs to create a list of understatements about upcoming events in their lives. For example, to describe their feelings about driving lessons, students might write, "I'm not unhappy," or "I might be a little nervous." Have students share their understatements with each other. You may wish to display them on a class bulletin board. In a discussion, ask students:

- How do you really feel?
- What are some other ways of expressing your feelings?
- What effect does an understatement have on your peers when you use it?

Reading Fiction

Introduction to Reading Fiction

Have students name a few of the novels and stories they have read recently, either for a class assignment or for pleasure. Ask students to tell why they like—or do not like—fiction. Direct students to read the first paragraph on page 266 to see if they agree with what Willa Cather wrote about human stories. After students have read the paragraph, discuss with them Cather's comment as well as the points made by Muriel Rukeyser and William Faulkner. Then, have students read the rest of the page and ask volunteers to explain each of the five points made about fiction.

Reading a Short Story

Goals

Here students will read a short story titled "Powder" by Tobias Wolff. They will learn to:

- ✔ appreciate the short story genre
- ✔ use the reading strategy of synthesizing
- ✔ understand the structure of a short story

Background

Help students connect this lesson with their prior knowledge by asking them to:

- name different short stories they have read
- say how a short story is different from other genres, such as a novel or a personal essay
- discuss a short story they particularly liked and one they particularly disliked, explaining why
- talk about why people read and write short stories

Opening Activity

Explain to students that a short story is usually about a moment in someone's life. Some short stories are as long as 30 pages, and others as short as one page. Ask students to think about how writers can bring a character or a whole world to life in so few pages. Have them continue to think about this while reading the short story in this lesson.

Overview

	Content	Teacher's Guide page	Reader's Handbook page
Selection	"Powder" by Tobias Wolff		270–275
Reading Strategy	Synthesizing	181, 439	277, 732
Rereading Strategy	Close Reading	186, 433	284, 714
Tool	Web	180	268, 757
	Fiction Organizer	181, 182	278, 279, 744
	Cause-Effect Organizer	183	279, 739
	Character Development Chart	183	280, 740
	Plot Diagram	184	280, 281, 750
	Making Connections Chart	185	282, 748
	Close Reading Organizer	186	284, 742
	Setting Chart	186	285, 752
	Venn Diagram	186	286, 756

Ancillaries

	Grade	Content	Page
Overhead Transparency	9–12	Previewing a Short Story	Numbers 24 and 25
Lesson Plan Book	9	Reading a Short Story	105, 110–113
	10	Reading a Short Story	114, 116–119
	11	Reading a Short Story	104, 106–109
	12	Reading a Short Story	104, 106–109
Student Applications Book	9	"The Last Leaf" by O. Henry	109–122
	10	"The Voyage" by Katherine Mansfield	110–123
	11	"A Wagner Matinée" by Willa Cather	107–119
	12	"Marriage à la Mode" by Katherine Mansfield	107–122
Test Book	9–12	Short-answer Test Multiple-answer Test	
Website		www.greatsource.com/rehand/	

Before Reading

A Set a Purpose

First, students need to set a purpose for reading "Powder." Direct them to the Setting a Purpose questions on page 268 of the *Reader's Handbook*. Then, have them look over the Web that one reader created based on the title of the story. Point out that brainstorming is a good way to activate prior knowledge and spark interest in what a story is about.

Setting a Purpose

- **What kind of powder is this story about?**
- **Who are the main characters, and what are they like?**
- **What is the setting?**
- **What are the main events?**

B Preview

Remind students of the importance of previewing before reading. Using the Preview Checklist on page 269 of the handbook, have students preview "Powder."

Preview Checklist

✓ *the title and author*
✓ *any background or biographical material about the author*
✓ *the point of view from which the story is told*
✓ *any names of characters or places*
✓ *the first few paragraphs*
✓ *any repeated words*
✓ *any questions printed at the end*

Overhead Transparencies

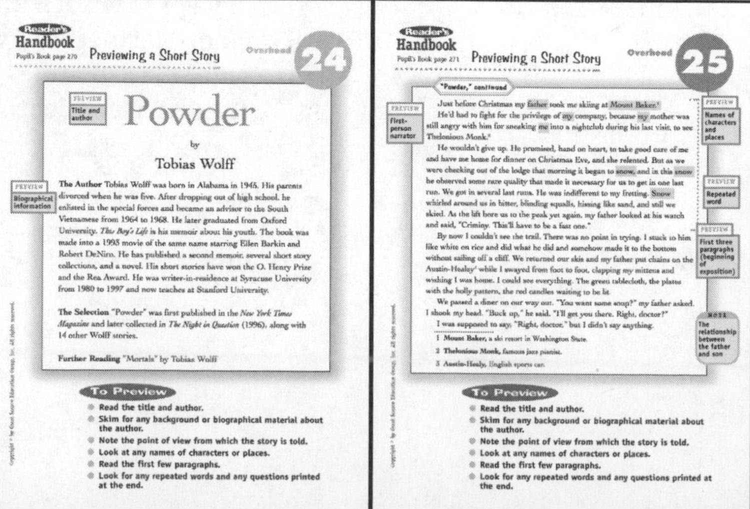

Reader's Handbook
Pupil's Book page 270
Previewing a Short Story
Overhead 24

PREVIEW: Title and author

Powder

by

Tobias Wolff

PREVIEW: Biographical information

The Author Tobias Wolff was born in Alabama in 1945. His parents divorced when he was five. After dropping out of high school, he enlisted in the special forces and became an advisor to the South Vietnamese from 1964 to 1968. He later graduated from Oxford University. *This Boy's Life* is his memoir about his youth. The book was made into a 1993 movie of the same name starring Ellen Barkin and Robert DeNiro. He has published a second memoir, several short story collections, and a novel. His short stories have won the O. Henry Prize and the Rea Award. He was writer-in-residence at Syracuse University from 1980 to 1997 and now teaches at Stanford University.

The Selection "Powder" was first published in the *New York Times Magazine* and later collected in *The Night in Question* (1996), along with 14 other Wolff stories.

Further Reading "Mortals" by Tobias Wolff

To Preview

- Read the title and author.
- Skim for any background or biographical material about the author.
- Note the point of view from which the story is told.
- Look at any names of characters or places.
- Read the first few paragraphs.
- Look for any repeated words and any questions printed at the end.

Reader's Handbook
Pupil's Book page 271
Previewing a Short Story
Overhead 25

"Powder," continued

PREVIEW: First-person narrator

Just before Christmas my father took me skiing at Mount Baker.[1]

He'd had to fight for the privilege of my company, because my mother was still angry with him for sneaking me into a nightclub during his last visit, to see Thelonious Monk.[2]

PREVIEW: Names of characters and places

He wouldn't give up. He promised, hand on heart, to take good care of me and have me home for dinner on Christmas Eve, and she relented. But as we were checking out of the lodge that morning it began to snow, and in this snow he observed some rare quality that made it necessary for us to get in one last run. We got in several last runs. He was indifferent to my fretting. Snow whirled around us in bitter, blinding squalls, hissing like sand, and still we skied. As the lift bore us to the peak yet again, my father looked at his watch and said, "Criminy. This'll have to be a fast one."

PREVIEW: Repeated word

By now I couldn't see the trail. There was no point in trying. I stuck to him like white on rice and did what he did and somehow made it to the bottom without sailing off a cliff. We returned our skis and my father put chains on the Austin-Healey[3] while I swayed from foot to foot, clapping my mittens and wishing I was home. I could see everything. The green tablecloth, the plates with the holly pattern, the red candles waiting to be lit.

PREVIEW: First three paragraphs (beginning of exposition)

We passed a diner on our way out. "You want some soup?" my father asked. I shook my head. "Buck up," he said. "I'll get you there. Right, doctor?"

I was supposed to say, "Right, doctor," but I didn't say anything.

NOTE: The relationship between the father and son

1 **Mount Baker,** a ski resort in Washington State.

2 **Thelonious Monk,** famous jazz pianist.

3 **Austin-Healy,** English sports car.

To Preview

- Read the title and author.
- Skim for any background or biographical material about the author.
- Note the point of view from which the story is told.
- Look at any names of characters or places.
- Read the first few paragraphs.
- Look for any repeated words and any questions printed at the end.

C Plan

Ask students to sum up what they learned about the selection during their preview. Direct their attention to the bulleted list at the top of page 276. Emphasize that previewing a story helps students make a plan for reading efficiently—with speed and good comprehension. Ask students to:

1. Use Prior Knowledge
Consider what they know about snow, father-son relationships, and separated parents to make some predictions about the conflicts in the story.

2. Focus on One Part
Identify one part, such as the author's language, that they would like to focus on. Alternatively, students can focus on one character.

3. Watch What Changes
Look for changes that occur in the story, either in a character, between characters, in the setting, or in the mood.

4. Appreciate the Story
Consider the important elements that make up a story: plot, setting, characters, theme, style, and mood. The reading strategy of synthesizing will help students keep track of all these elements.

Reading Strategy: Synthesizing

Introduce the strategy of **synthesizing.** Explain that synthesizing means pulling together many parts or elements to see the whole picture. Compare the process to putting together the pieces of a jigsaw puzzle.

Have students read the description of synthesizing on page 277 of the handbook. Then have them look at the Fiction Organizer on page 278. Read through each short story element listed in the chart.

During Reading

D Read with a Purpose

Now students are ready to read. Tell students to read with a purpose. To synthesize, students look at different aspects of a story and evaluate their importance.

Have students look at the completed chart on page 279. Their own Fiction Organizers should look similar to that one.

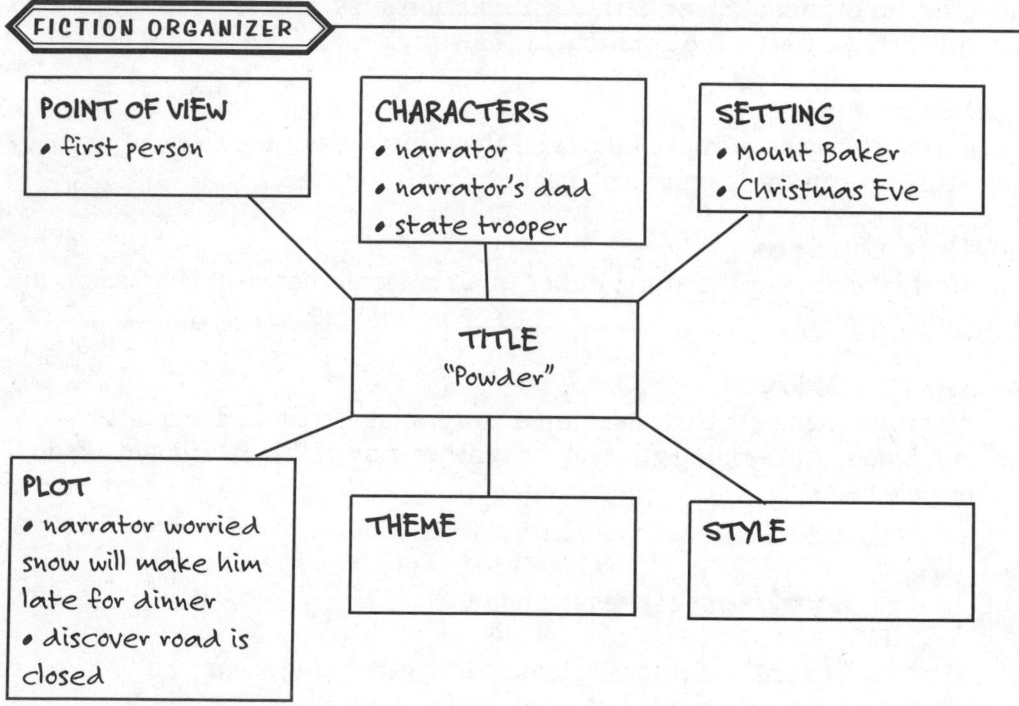

Explain that, as students read, additional graphic organizers may be useful for identifying important information in the story. Have students look at and read through the Cause-Effect Organizer on page 279.

CAUSE-EFFECT ORGANIZER

CAUSE
Road is closed.

EFFECT
Son is more worried he'll be late for dinner.

EFFECT
Father decides to drive down road anyway.

D Read with a Purpose continued

The Character Development Chart is another helpful tool for identifying and recording important information from the story. Ask students to look at and read through this chart at the top of page 280.

CHARACTER DEVELOPMENT CHART

BEGINNING	MIDDLE	END
Narrator wants to be home and is annoyed with father.	Narrator worried they won't be home in time and is afraid.	Narrator learns to trust and like his father during the drive.
POSSIBLE THEME Learning to trust can sometimes result in a better understanding of oneself and others.		

Other Useful Tools

Point out to students the wide variety of graphic organizers in the lesson on "Powder." Be sure students understand that they do not have to use all of them. As with any type of tool, students need to be able to pull out the right one when they need it. Other useful tools for short stories include the following:

- **Paraphrase or Retelling Chart**
- **Inference Chart**
- **Story Organizer**

How Stories Are Organized

Explain to students that knowing how short stories are organized will help them read faster and with better comprehension. Have students look at page 280 in the handbook to see how short stories are typically organized.

Though short stories may follow one of several organizational patterns, the Plot Diagram on page 280 displays the classic structure. This includes exposition (the background information), rising action (characters face or try to resolve a problem), climax (the tension reaches a peak), falling action (the consequences of the climax), and resolution (the story's central problem is resolved).

Now, point out how the Plot Diagram, illustrated on page 281, can serve as a graphic organizer for identifying and organizing the important events in "Powder." Have the students read through the illustration to see how story information can be plotted.

PLOT DIAGRAM FOR "POWDER"

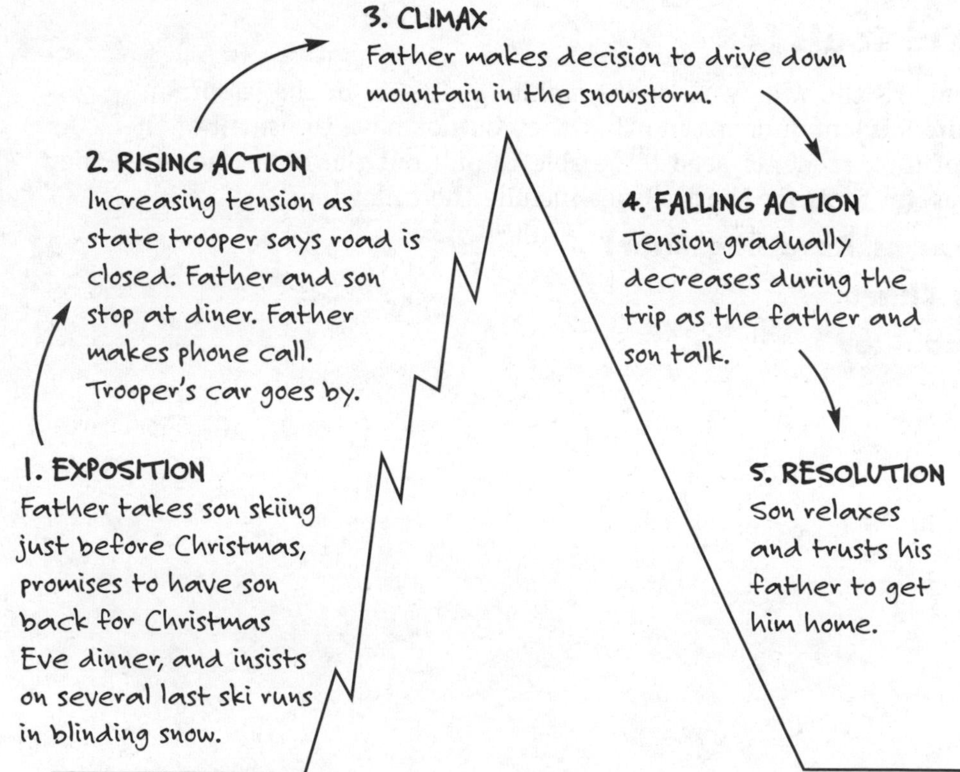

During Reading

E Connect

Remind students that an important part of the reading process is to respond to or make connections with the text as they read. Actively making connections while reading enhances not only students' comprehension of but also their interest in a story. Suggest the following ways to connect with the current selection:

- find connections to their own lives
  (Have I been in a similar situation?)
- compare and contrast characters to people they know
  (Do I know anyone like the father? How is my father similar or different?)
- think about how the story made them feel
  (Am I angry at this father?)
- evaluate the story
  (Do I like or dislike this story? What about it is good, and what's not?)

Students may also use the Making Connections Chart to make connections to this story. Show them the example at the top of page 282. Another way to clarify their thoughts and feelings is by journaling about the story. Have students read over one reader's journal entry, appearing on the bottom of page 282.

MAKING CONNECTIONS CHART

Prompts	Example from "Powder"
I wonder why . . .	I wonder why the father wanted to take his son skiing ?
I think . . .	I think the father is very nervous. Maybe he is afraid this is his last chance to patch up his marriage.
I can relate to this because . . .	I can relate to this because I know people like the father, and they are so frustrating because you like them and hate them at the same time.
What caused . . .	What caused the son to relax and enjoy himself and trust his father? For one thing, he admired his father's driving.
This is similar to . . .	This is similar to The Catcher in the Rye, except this kid's father is still with him. Both are about a time when a son's life changed.
This reminds me of . . .	This reminds me of a trip I took with my mom when I was twelve.

After Reading

F Pause and Reflect

After reading, students need to stop and reflect on what they have read. Have students go back and review their original purposes in reading "Powder." Go over the following Looking Back questions with them.

Looking Back

- **Can I describe the main characters?**
- **What do the main characters want most?**
- **How does the title fit the story?**
- **How is the setting significant?**
- **Does the ending make sense? Why or why not?**
- **What is the theme of the story?**

Students may still be uncertain of the answers to some of these questions. Emphasize that even the best readers go back to the text after reading to clarify their understandings.

G Reread

Explain that students should return to the text with a different strategy or tool so that they can get a fresh look at the material. Introduce the strategy of close reading.

Rereading Strategy: Close Reading

Instruct students to give this strategy a try when rereading. Have them read through the description of **close reading** on page 284 of the handbook.

Close reading provides a way for students to think more carefully and more deeply about what they have read. With this strategy, students choose part of the story to reread. The Close Reading Organizer, shown on page 284, helps scaffold students' close reading.

As they reread, students may want to look more closely at settings and characters. The Setting Chart, shown on page 285, and the Venn Diagram, shown on page 286, will help direct students' attention to these two important elements.

After Reading

H Remember

At this stage in the reading, it is time for students to make the story "their own." They need to do something with it in order to remember it. Assign one of the activities (talking about it or writing a sequel to the story) described on pages 286 and 287 of the *Reader's Handbook,* or ask students to do the creative assignment below.

Creative Assignment: Have students work in pairs or groups of three to create movie posters for "Powder." Display and discuss the students' creations. Why would the posters be likely to attract an audience? What elements of the story do the posters highlight?

Summing Up

Quickly review the many tools covered in this lesson. Review the lesson by reading the Summing Up on page 287 of the handbook. Go over the initial goals for the lesson. Discuss which ones students feel that they achieved and which ones that they need more work on:

1. **appreciating the short story genre**
2. **using the reading strategy of synthesizing**
3. **understanding the structure of a short story**

Assessment and Application

Use the Quick Assess checklist to evaluate students' ability to read and understand a short story. Give students the opportunity to apply what they have learned through one of the two activities below. For students who are comfortable with the reading process and strategy, use one of the suggestions below for independent practice. For students who need guided help with the strategy, use a *Student Applications Book*.

Quick Assess

Can students

- ☑ name a reading and a rereading strategy useful for reading short stories?
- ☑ name two or three useful tools for reading short stories?
- ☑ explain ways that they can make connections to a short story?

1. Independent Practice

To show that they understand the lesson, students can apply the strategies and tools to a short story of their choice.

Ask students to do one of the following:

- Create a Fiction Organizer while reading the story.
- Apply the strategy of **close reading**, using a Close Reading Organizer.
- Complete a Making Connections Chart and write a short journal entry showing the connections they were able to make to the story.

2. Student Applications Books

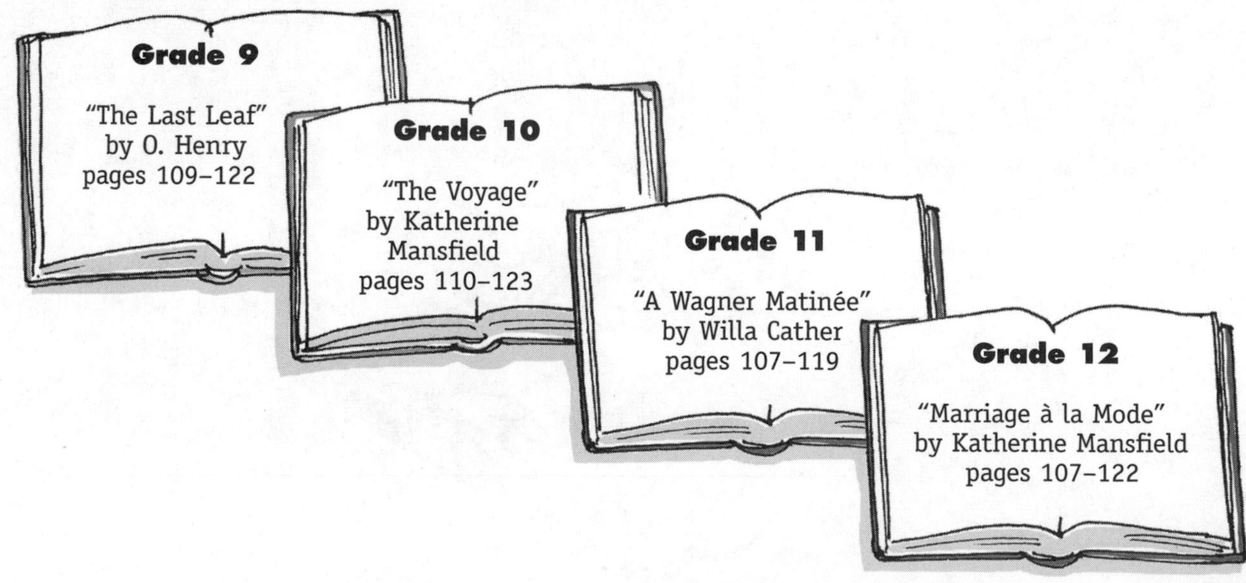

Test Book

See *Test Book* for short-answer and multiple-choice tests.

Reading a Novel

Getting Ready

Goals

Here students will read passages from *All Quiet on the Western Front,* the World War I novel by Erich Maria Remarque. This lesson will help them to learn to:

- examine the basic elements of a novel
- use the reading strategy of using graphic organizers
- recognize the plot structure of a novel

Background

Help students connect this lesson with their prior knowledge by asking them to:

- define *novel* in their own words
- name novels they have read and liked in the past
- discuss what they like and dislike about reading novels
- name some elements of novels, such as character, theme, and plot

Opening Activity

Bring one of your favorite novels to class to show the students. Show them the front cover, read any jacket or summary copy, and read a short passage from it. Talk about why you like it. Remind students of the basic elements of a novel: characters, setting, conflict or plot, theme, and point of view. Talk about each of these elements in the novel you are showing them.

Overview

	Content	Teacher's Guide page	Reader's Handbook page
Selection	from *All Quiet on the Western Front* by Erich Maria Remarque		291–293, 295, 296, 299, 300, 301
Reading Strategy	Using Graphic Organizers	192, 439	293, 734
Rereading Strategy	Synthesizing	198, 439	310, 732
Tool	Web	191	290, 757
	Fiction Organizer	192, 198	293, 310, 744
	Classification Notes	193	297, 741
	Character Map	194, 198	298, 311, 740
	Setting Chart	194	301, 752
	Summary Notes	194–195	302, 754
	Sequence Notes	194–195	303, 751
	Plot Diagram	196	304, 305, 750
	Topic and Theme Organizer	196	306, 755
	Double-entry Journal	196	307, 743

Ancillaries

	Grade	Content	Page
Overhead Transparency	9–12	Previewing a Novel	Numbers 26 and 27
Lesson Plan Book	9	Reading a Novel	125, 130–133
	10	Reading a Novel	134–143
	11	Reading a Novel	124–133
	12	Reading a Novel	124, 126–129
Student Applications Book	9	from *Great Expectations* by Charles Dickens	123–134
	10	from *Tarzan of the Apes* by Edgar Rice Burroughs	124–136
	11	from *The Red Badge of Courage* by Stephen Crane	120–133
	12	from *Jane Eyre* by Charlotte Brontë	123–135
Test Book	9–12	Short-answer Test Multiple-answer Test	
Website		www.greatsource.com/rehand/	

Before Reading

A Set a Purpose

Remind students that they need to set a purpose before reading. Point out the Setting a Purpose questions on page 289 of the *Reader's Handbook*.

Setting a Purpose

- **Who is telling the story?** ***(point of view)***
- **Who are the main characters, and what are they like?** ***(characters)***
- **Where and when does the story take place? What is this place, culture, or historical period like?** ***(setting)***
- **What happens?** ***(plot)***
- **What is the author's central idea or message?** ***(theme)***
- **How does the author express his or her ideas?** ***(style)***

B Preview

Now, have students preview the selection following the Preview Checklist on page 289.

As part of the preview, students may use a Web to explore the associations evoked by the title of the novel. Point out one reader's use of this organizer on page 290.

Then have students preview the book cover and jacket copy on pages 291 and 292. Read the author's statement of purpose on page 293.

Preview Checklist

✓ *the title and author*

✓ *the front and back covers or the book jacket*

✓ *any summaries or excerpts from book reviews*

✓ *any information about the author*

✓ *any introductory material, such as a dedication, introduction, epigraph, or foreword*

✓ *the chapter names and any illustrations*

Overhead Transparencies

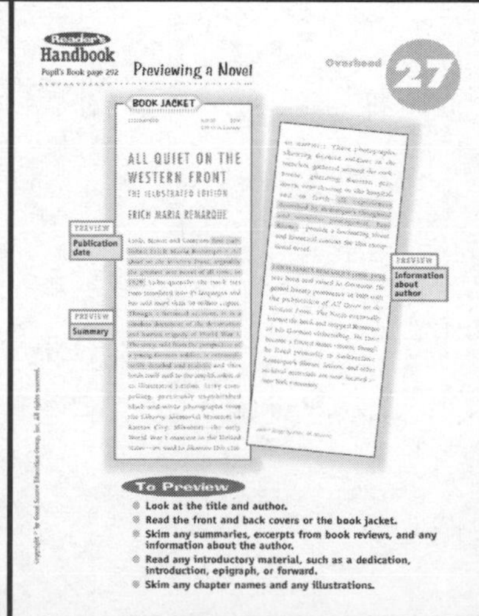

Before Reading

C Plan

Ask students to briefly tell what they learned from their preview. Remind them that, now that they have a general idea of what the novel is about, it's time to make a plan to help them meet their purpose for reading.

Reading Strategy: Using Graphic Organizers

Explain that **using graphic organizers** is an excellent way to keep track of important information in a novel. Show students the Fiction Organizer on the bottom of page 293. Point out that this organizer includes all the main elements of a novel and that completing it will result in a good summary of the book.

FICTION ORGANIZER

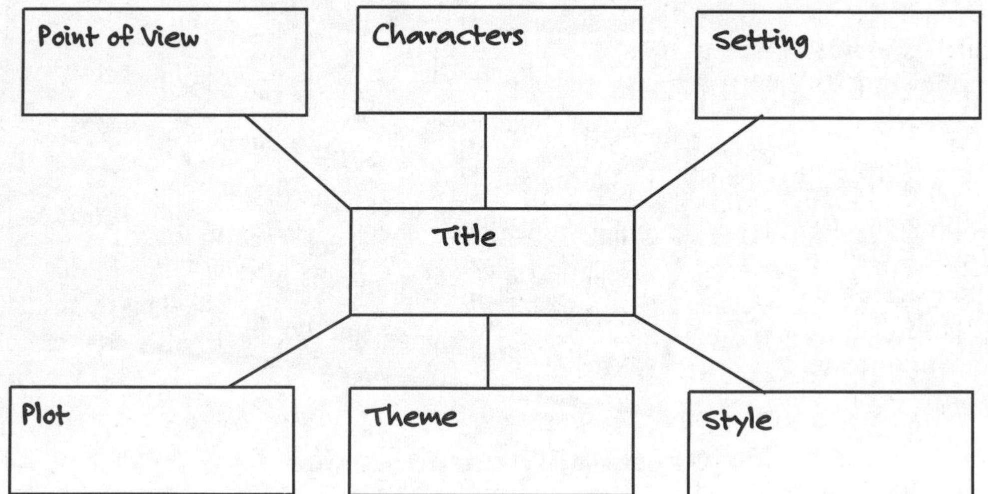

During Reading

D Read with a Purpose

Now students are ready to read. Ask them to read with the purpose of gathering the most important information from the selection. Students will learn about a number of tools that can be used for taking notes while reading a novel.

1. Point of View

Remind students that **point of view** refers to the person who is telling the story. Have students read the passage, looking at the two notes beside it.

2. Characters

Remind students that keeping track of the **characters** is important in order to read a novel efficiently. Have students read the passage on page 296, noting the information given about characters.

Now, have students look at the two graphic organizers given, the Classification Notes on page 297 and the Character Map on page 298, to help them keep track of all this information about characters. Read through the examples to show students how these organizers are to be completed.

CLASSIFICATION NOTES

Main Character: Paul Bäumer		
School Friends	**Teacher**	**Army Friends**
Albert Kropp Müller Leer Franz Kemmerich	Kantorek	Tjaden Haie Westhus Detering Stanislaus Katczinsky (aka Kat)
Officer	**Family**	**"Enemies"**
Himmelstoss	Mother Father Sister	Russians French Girls Gérard Duval

Read with a Purpose continued

CHARACTER MAP

WHAT KAT SAYS AND DOES	WHAT OTHERS THINK ABOUT HIM
• argues with the cook • helps his young friends • says the war would not be so bad if they could just get a bit more sleep	• leader of the group • others rely on him for insight
HOW HE LOOKS AND FEELS	**HOW I FEEL ABOUT HIM**
• shrewd • 40 years old • blue eyes • bent shoulders • thinks all officers are fools	• amusing • the one who shakes things up

STANISLAUS "KAT" KATCZINSKY

3. Setting

Remind students that **setting** refers to where and when the story takes place. Have students read the excerpts on pages 299, 300, and 301 for information about setting. Point out the simple Setting Chart on page 301.

SETTING CHART

ALL QUIET ON THE WESTERN FRONT	
TIME: • toward end of World War I • many soldiers in their twenties	PLACE: • Western Front in World War I • Opens with them at camp behind the front (to rest) • not under attack but can hear and see the war

4. Plot

Explain that novels usually have one main **plot** and one or more subplots. Reinforce that plot is what happens as a result of conflicts and the characters' responses to conflicts.

Then, point out the example of Summary Notes on page 302, explaining that such notes are useful for keeping track of what happens in novels. Another good tool for this purpose is Sequence Notes, shown on page 303.

During Reading

Read with a Purpose continued

SUMMARY NOTES

CHAPTER ONE

Paul Bäumer and his friends have come from the front, where they have been fighting for two weeks. They lost 80 men. Paul introduces us to his friends. They go to visit Kemmerich, whose leg has been amputated.

CHAPTER TWO

Paul remembers life before the war. He visits Kemmerich, who dies. Paul tells about joining the army and training under Corporal Himmelstoss. The men hate Himmelstoss, who hates them.

SEQUENCE NOTES

Paul and friends join the army at age 19. → Himmelstoss attacked for humiliating Tjaden. → They go to training camp for ten weeks. →

Assigned to Second Company (150 men). → Assigned to No. 9 platoon under Himmelstoss for six weeks of training. → Second Company loses 80 men in battle with British. →

Kemmerich dies from wounds. → New recruits arrive to replace the dead. → Second Company returns to front. →

Major bombardment: five killed, eight wounded. → Himmelstoss arrives to serve as commanding officer. → Tjaden and Kropp are punished for disrespecting Himmelstoss.

Other Useful Tools

Point out to students how many organizers appear in this lesson. Here are a few more possibilities for organizers that work well with novels:

- **Character Development Chart**
- **Double-entry Journal**
- **Story String**

How Novels Are Organized

Emphasize that knowing how a novel is organized will help students read more efficiently. Have students look at page 304 in their handbooks to see how novels are typically organized.

As in short stories, the classic structure of a novel includes exposition (the background information), rising action (characters face or try to resolve a problem), a climax (the tension reaches a peak), falling action (the consequences of the climax), and a resolution (the story's central problem is resolved). However, novels may follow other structures also.

Point out how the Plot Diagram, illustrated on page 305, can serve as a graphic organizer for identifying and organizing the important events in *All Quiet on the Western Front.* Have the students read the notes to see how the information can be plotted.

5. Theme

Explain that **theme** is the main idea or ideas developed in a novel or other literary work. Have students ask themselves the questions at the bottom of page 305. Then show students the completed Topic and Theme Organizer on page 306.

6. Style

An author's **style** is based on how he or she expresses ideas. The use of certain words and literary devices helps create an author's unique style. Read through the categories given on page 307 to help students see the ways in which styles can vary. Then, read through the Double-entry Journal at the bottom of that page.

AUTHOR'S STYLE

Sentence Structure: *Does the author use mostly short sentences or long, complex sentences?*

Word Choice: *Does the author use simple words or long, formal ones?*

Tone: *What sort of feeling do you have about the writing? Is it loose and casual, formal and proper, or something different?*

Dialogue: *Do the characters speak in slang or dialect? Does their language seem realistic and believable?*

Sensory Details: *Does the author use words that appeal to your five senses?*

Figurative Language: *Does the author use words to paint pictures? Are similes and metaphors an important part of the author's style?*

During Reading

E Connect

Remind students that good readers connect what they read to themselves and the world in which they live. Read through the questions given on page 308. Let students know that asking themselves questions such as these as they read can help them make connections to the text.

What do I think of these characters?

What was the most interesting moment or event in the story?

Which characters interest me the most?

What experiences or people in my life can I compare to this story?

Which characters do I dislike or even hate?

Show students the example at the bottom of page 308. Point out the two notes that show the way one reader connected to the passage from *All Quiet on the Western Front.*

F Pause and Reflect

After reading, have students stop to consider what they have read. Ask students to go back and review their original purpose for reading this selection.

Looking Back

- **Do I know the point of view?**
- **Can I describe the characters?**
- **Can I visualize the setting?**
- **Do I understand the plot?**
- **Do I know the central idea or message?**
- **Can I describe the author's style?**

Remind students that their notes and graphic organizers will help them answer most of these questions. However, they will probably need to go back and reread to clarify their understanding and obtain more information.

G Reread

Encourage students to try another strategy for rereading. Explain that using a different strategy will give them a fresh perspective on the selection.

Rereading Strategy: Synthesizing

Introduce the strategy of **synthesizing.** This is the technique of pulling together the important elements of a novel to see "the big picture."

The Fiction Organizer, shown on page 310 of the handbook, is a useful tool for synthesizing information from a reading. Ask students to read this example carefully.

Next, have students turn to the Character Map on page 311. Emphasize that when a reader goes back to reread, he or she does so to clarify or organize the most important parts of the text. In this graphic organizer, the character of Katczinsky and his relationship with the main character are further defined.

Remember

Now students need to do something with the subject matter to remember it and make it their own. Read and have students do one of the three activities given on page 312 of the *Reader's Handbook*. Alternatively, you may wish to have students do the creative assignment below.

Creative Assignment: Imagine that you and your friends are sent back through time to fight on the Western Front in World War I. Write a letter home describing the conditions in which you are living. Also describe your thoughts and feelings about what is happening.

Summing Up

Review the lesson with the students. Read the list of tools in the Summing Up section on page 312. Ask the students which ones they feel comfortable with and would like to use again. Then, go over the three goals for the lesson. Ask students which ones they feel they achieved and which ones need more work:

1. **examining the basic elements of a novel**
2. **using the reading strategy of using graphic organizers**
3. **recognizing the plot structure of a novel**

Assessment and Application

Use the Quick Assess checklist to evaluate students' ability to read and understand novels. Give students the opportunity to apply what they have learned through one of the two activities below. For students who are comfortable with the reading process and strategy, use one of the suggestions below for independent practice. For students who need guided help with the strategy, use a *Student Applications Book*.

Quick Assess

Can students

- ☑ name some of the elements of a novel?
- ☑ describe the strategy of using graphic organizers?
- ☑ name two or three tools useful for reading a novel?
- ☑ identify a good rereading strategy for novels?

1. Independent Practice

To show that students understand the lesson, they can apply the strategy of **using graphic organizers** to a novel of their choice.

Ask students to do one of the following:

- Complete a Fiction Organizer on a novel of their choice.
- Choose and complete two graphic organizers on the main characters of the novel.
- Create a Plot Diagram or complete a set of Sequence Notes or Summary Notes on the plot of the novel.

2. Student Applications Books

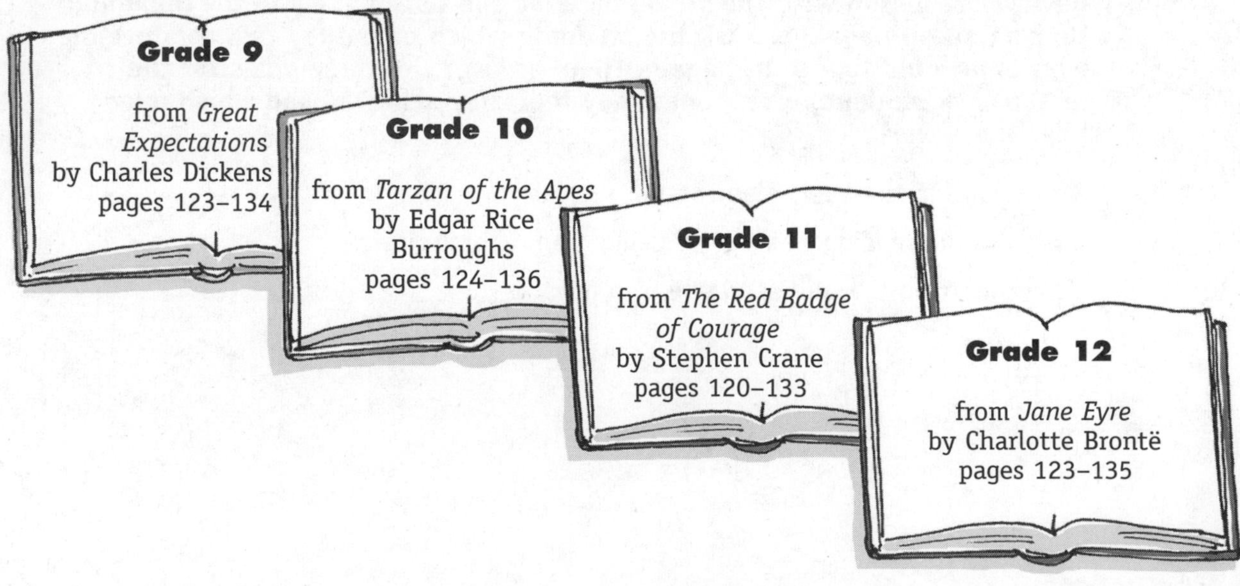

Test Book

See *Test Book* for short-answer and multiple-choice tests.

Focus on Plot

Goals

Here students focus on understanding plot. This lesson will help them learn to:

- ✓ follow the events of a plot
- ✓ identify the story's subplots and how these relate to the main plot
- ✓ consider how plot contributes to a story's theme

Background

Remind students that plot refers to what happens in a story, usually as a result of conflicts and the resolution of conflicts. Help students connect this lesson with their prior knowledge by asking them to:

- retell the plot of a favorite story, novel, or movie
- define *subplot* and discuss subplots they recall

Overview

	Content	Teacher's Guide page	Reader's Handbook page
Selection	from "Blues Ain't No Mockinbird" by Toni Cade Bambara		315–316, 318
Reading Strategy	Using Graphic Organizers	203, 439	316, 734
Tool	Plot Diagram Story String	202, 204 203	314, 322, 750 317, 753

Ancillaries

	Grade	Content	Page
Lesson Plan Book	9 12	Focus on Plot Focus on Plot and Setting	114, 116–119 105, 110–113
Student Applications Book	9 10 11 12	from "Pandora" by Edith Hamilton from "Pegasus and Chimaera" by Thomas Bulfinch from *Riders of the Purple Sage* by Zane Grey from "Beware of the Dog" by Roald Dahl	135–136 137–138 134–135 136–137
Test Book	9–12	Short-answer Test Multiple-answer Test	
Website		www.greatsource.com/rehand/	

Before Reading

Explain that understanding the parts of a plot is helpful for following the action in a story. Read through the five parts of a plot on page 314 of the *Reader's Handbook*. Note that not all works of fiction contain all five parts, but many will. Also review the Plot Diagram at the bottom of page 314.

PLOT DIAGRAM

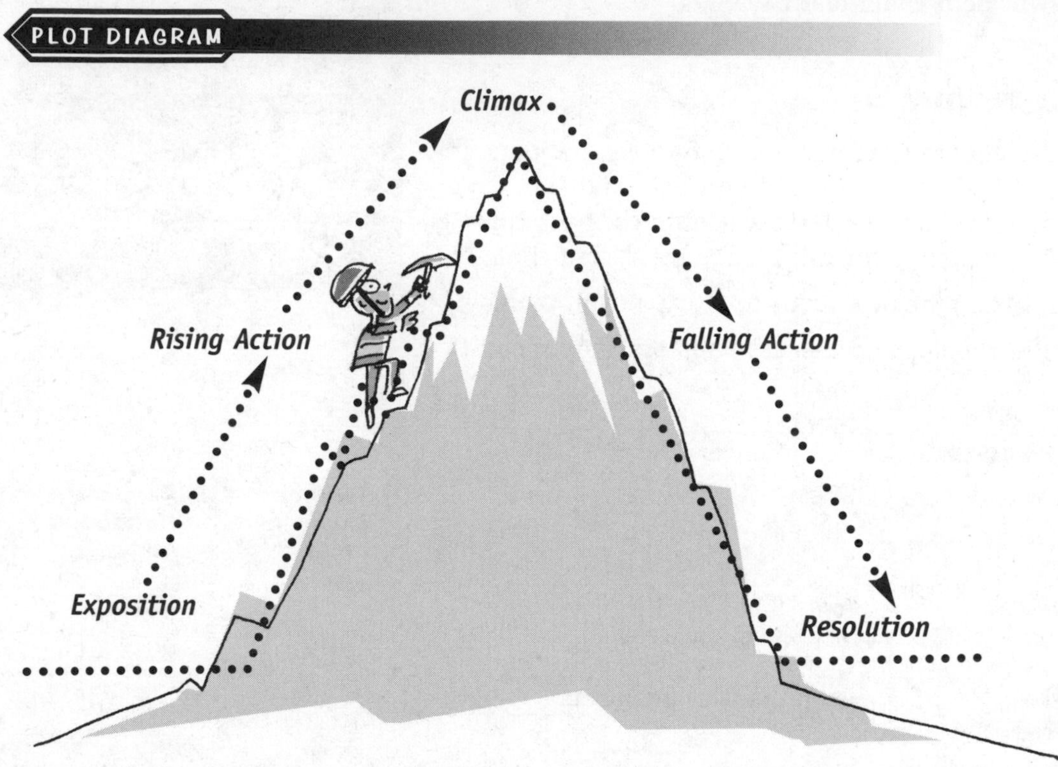

Getting Background Information

Explain that in the beginning of a story or novel the author often gives important information on setting, character, and the source of the conflict or problem. Tell students to watch for this information as they skim the opening paragraphs. Remind students to mark this information in the margins of their books or on sticky notes. Now ask them to read the excerpt on pages 315 and 316.

Instruct students to note, as they read, how the events relate to one another as well as to characters and theme. A strategy that will help them do this is using graphic organizers.

Reading Strategy: Using Graphic Organizers

Explain that **using graphic organizers** can help students identify and record the most important information in a story or novel. Remind students that transitional words, such as *then* and *later*, signal movement in time through a story. Introduce the Story String as a good tool for keeping track of the important events in the story.

Ask students to look at the Story String on page 317 of the handbook. Read the notes in the boxes to illustrate how to use this graphic organizer.

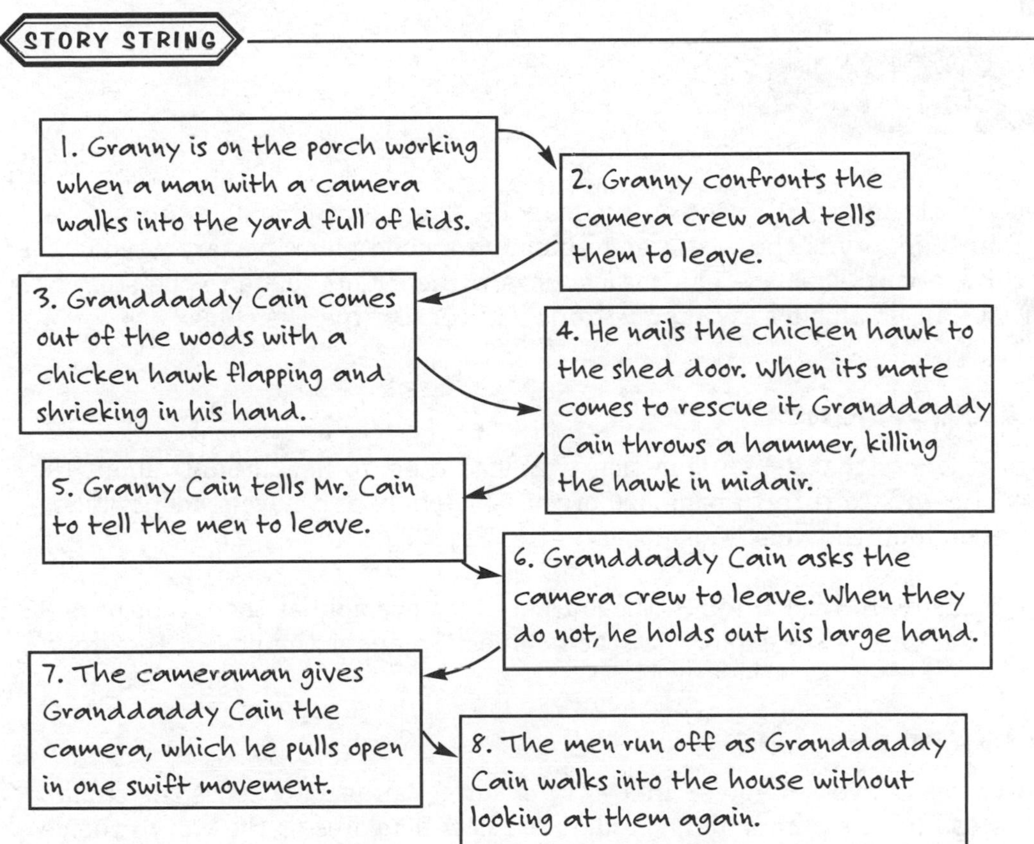

During Reading

Understanding Flashbacks

Virtually all students will understand the concept of a flashback, if only from movies and television shows. Note that "Blues Ain't No Mockinbird" also contains a flashback. Have students read the excerpt on page 318. Let students know that flashbacks are included to explain or underscore an important point in the story. When continuing their reading after a flashback, students need to think about what in the story has changed or what they have learned because of it.

Understanding Subplots

Most students will also be familiar with the concept of subplots from movies and television. Explain that a subplot is simply a smaller story in a story. Students may think of subplots as smaller plots that orbit the main plot. Although "Blues Ain't No Mockinbird" is primarily about the conflict between the Cains and the camera crew, it is also about the relationship between Granny and Granddaddy Cain.

After Reading

After reading, students will focus on summarizing the plot. Being able to say what happened in the story is the first step to building a good plot summary. Students also need to think about what the plot means, or how the events relate to the story's theme. They can do this by asking questions and considering the climax.

1. Ask Questions

Explain to students that asking questions will lead them to new insights about the story. Ask students to turn to page 320 of the handbook, and have students take turns reading aloud the questions listed on the page.

Next, ask students to read through the journal entry example at the top of page 321. Emphasize that this entry explores a specific question about the plot of the story.

2. Consider the Climax

Readers who are actively involved in a story or novel can usually sense the climax coming. Rereading the climax helps readers see how it relates to the story's theme.

Ask students to turn to page 322 and look at the completed Plot Diagram. Read through each part, from exposition to resolution. Point out how the incident with the chicken hawks works symbolically in the context of the overall theme.

Have students read the points in the Summing Up at the bottom of page 322. Ask students to say in their own words what they learned in this lesson.

Assessment and Application

Use the Quick Assess checklist to evaluate students' ability to understand plot. Give students the opportunity to apply what they have learned through one of the two activities below. For students who are comfortable with the reading process and strategy, use the suggestion for independent practice or an activity of your own. For students who need guided help with the strategy, use a *Student Applications Book*.

Quick Assess

Can students

- ☑ name the five parts of the classic plot structure?
- ☑ define *flashback* and explain why it is used?
- ☑ define *subplot*?
- ☑ explain how the plot of a story or novel relates to theme?

1. Independent Practice

Students can show they understand the lesson by applying the strategy of **using graphic organizers** to the plot of a short story of their choice.

2. Student Applications Books

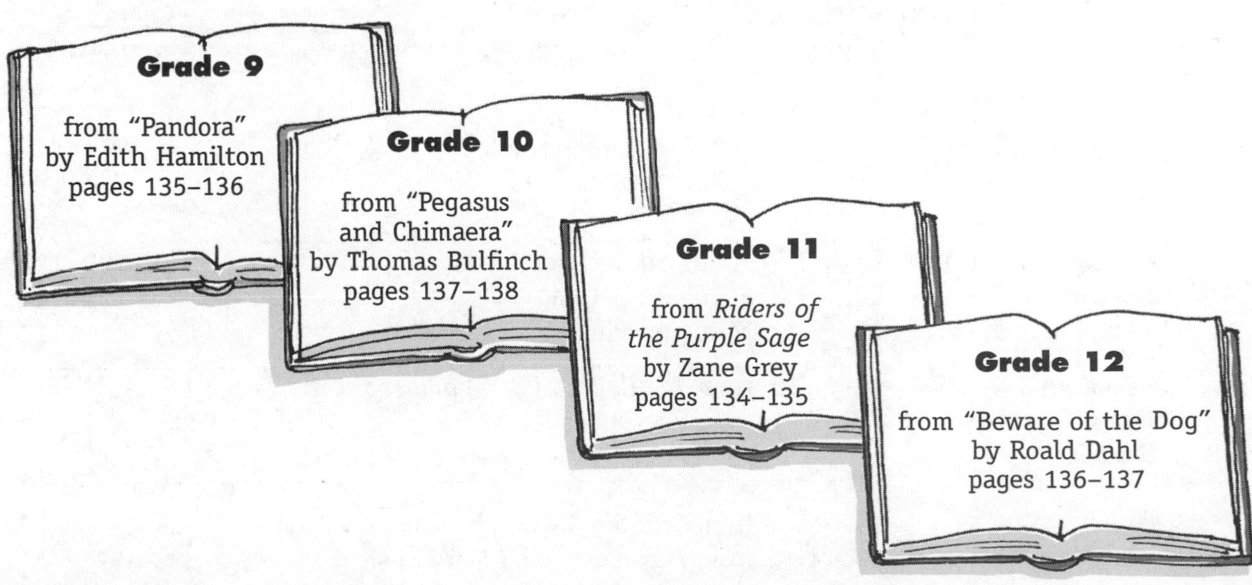

Test Book

See *Test Book* for short-answer and multiple-choice tests.

Focus on Setting

Goals

Now students will focus on understanding setting. This lesson will help them to:

- identify and evaluate details of setting that matter most
- understand how setting relates to the mood, characters, and plot
- use the strategy of close reading to analyze the setting

Background

Help students connect this lesson with their prior knowledge by asking them to:

- discuss stories they have read in which the setting is important

Overview

	Content	Teacher's Guide page	Reader's Handbook page
Selection	from *Cry, the Beloved Country* by Alan Paton		324, 326, 327, 329
Reading Strategy	Close Reading	207, 433	325, 714
Tool	Inference Chart	207, 208	325, 328, 746
	Web	208	327, 757
	Setting Chart	209	330, 752
	Storyboard	209	331, 753

Ancillaries

	Grade	Content	Page
Lesson Plan Book	9	Focus on Setting	115, 120–123
	10	Focus on Setting	115, 120–123
	12	Focus on Plot and Setting	105, 110–113
Student Applications Book	9	from *The House of Sand and Fog* by Andre Dubus III	137–139
	10	from "Death of a Traveling Salesman" by Eudora Welty	139–140
	11	from *Lord Jim* by Joseph Conrad	136–137
	12	from *Frankenstein* by Mary Shelley	138–139
Test Book	9–12	Short-answer Test Multiple-answer Test	
Website		www.greatsource.com/rehand/	

Before Reading

Emphasize that the setting of a story or novel is usually very important to understanding character, plot, and theme. During their preview, students should note where and when the story takes place. Have students preview the excerpt on page 324, looking for descriptions or physical details about the place or landscape and descriptions of the climate or weather.

After they preview, ask students to say in their own words what they learned about the setting.

Reading Strategy: Close Reading

Explain that the strategy of **close reading** enables readers to examine the author's choice of words, phrases, and sentence structure. Understanding this will help students see how important the setting is to the story.

Using sticky notes or a graphic organizer will help students read closely. One excellent tool for close reading is the Inference Chart, shown on page 325.

INFERENCE CHART

Title: Cry, the Beloved Country

DETAILS ABOUT SETTING	POSSIBLE MEANINGS OR IMPORTANCE
• rich, thick grass	• beautiful land • people there probably well-off
• hills change and grow red and bare	• Soil near the valley is washing away and crops don't grow well.
• too many cattle and fires • soil not "kept"	• People there probably poor
• Only old men and women there	• Young people have gone because the land cannot support them.

Setting and Mood

Remind students that **mood** is the feeling a story produces in a reader. Draw a parallel to listening to music, pointing out that different types of music create different moods in the listeners. Allow students to talk briefly about what kinds of music they listen to and how music makes them feel.

Now ask students to read the excerpt from *Cry, the Beloved Country* on the bottom of page 326. Ask them to take note of how the reading makes them feel. Then have them look at the Web at the top of page 327. This is how one reader felt about the passage.

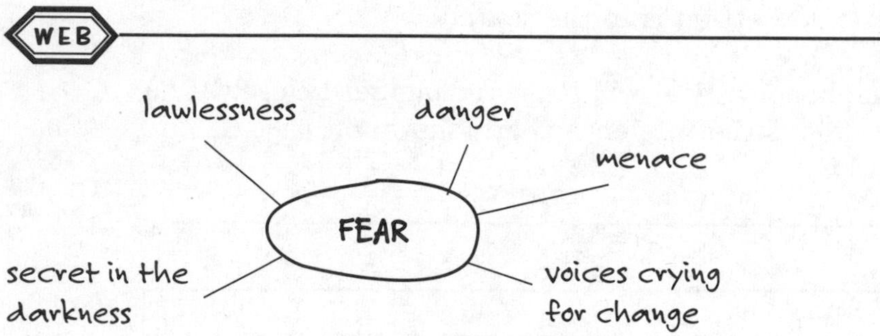

Point out that authors use sensory details to create mood and setting. Have students read the excerpt on page 327, noting the sensory details.

Setting and Characters

Setting also affects characters or readers' perceptions of characters. Have students look at the Inference Chart on page 328 to see how setting and characters are connected in *Cry, the Beloved Country.* Call students' attention to the inferences that can be made from what a character says and does.

Setting and Plot

Point out that changes in setting usually affect the plot in some way. Students need to think about why such changes occur. Have students read the excerpt on page 329 to see how change in setting can bring about other changes as well.

After Reading

After reading, ask students to stop and think for a moment about what they learned about setting and its effect on the novel. To better help them draw conclusions about setting in *Cry, the Beloved Country,* have them list key settings or make sketches.

1. List Key Settings

Ask students to turn to page 330 and look at the completed Setting Chart. Emphasize that using a tool such as this one can help students appreciate the importance of setting in a novel or story.

SETTING CHART

TITLE: Cry, the Beloved Country	
GENERAL TIME: • period when segregation policies were enforced by the government • wide differences in income and housing between blacks and whites	GENERAL PLACES: • Johannesburg, South Africa • South African countryside
IMMEDIATE TIME: • not given	IMMEDIATE PLACES: • place where Kumalo's sister lives • Ezenzeleni

2. Sketch the Setting

A good alternative to the graphic organizer is making sketches. Many students may prefer to draw rather than to fill out a graphic organizer. Have students look at the Storyboard on page 331 and suggest this as an alternative.

Summing Up

Have students read the points in the Summing Up at the bottom of page 331. Then, ask students to say in their own words what they learned in this lesson.

Assessment and Application

Use the Quick Assess checklist to evaluate students' ability to understand setting. Give students the opportunity to apply what they have learned through one of the two activities below. For students who are comfortable with the reading process and strategy, use one of the suggestions below or one of your own. For students who need guided help with the strategy, use a *Student Applications Book.*

Quick Assess

Can students

- ☑ define *setting*?
- ☑ say why setting is important to mood, character, and plot?
- ☑ explain close reading and say why it is a good strategy for understanding the significance of setting?

1. Independent Practice

To show that they understand the lesson, students can use a Web, Inference Chart, Setting Chart, or Storyboard to apply the strategy of **close reading** to the setting of a novel or short story of their choice.

2. Student Applications Books

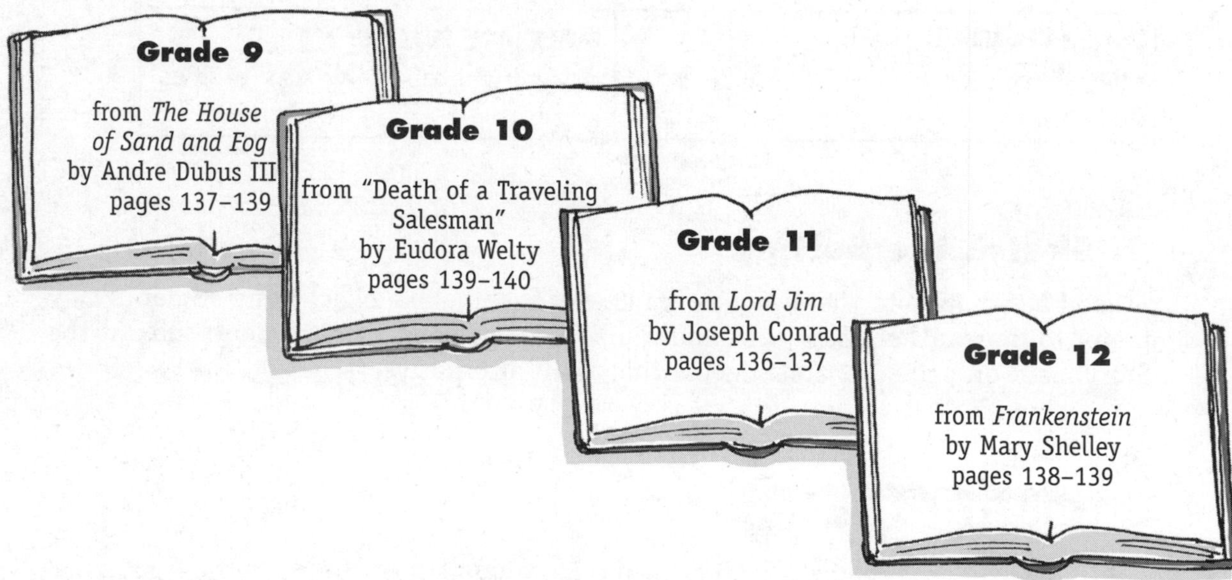

Test Book

See *Test Book* for short-answer and multiple-choice tests.

Focus on Characters

Goals

Here students focus on understanding characters. This lesson will help them learn to:

- identify and understand different character types
- recognize how characters affect plot, other characters, and theme
- use graphic organizers to analyze characters and track changes in them

Background

Help students connect this lesson with their prior knowledge by asking them to:

- discuss memorable characters in stories, movies, or television shows
- name a favorite character and say why he or she is a favorite

Overview

	Content	Teacher's Guide page	Reader's Handbook page
Selection	from "The Necklace" by Guy de Maupassant		335, 336, 337, 339–340, 341, 342
Reading Strategy	Using Graphic Organizers	213, 439	334, 734
Tool	Character Map Character Web Inference Chart Character Development Chart	213 213 214 216	334, 336, 740 338, 741 340, 746 344, 740

Ancillaries

	Grade	Content	Page
Lesson Plan Book	9 10 12	Focus on Characters Focus on Characters Focus on Characters	124, 126–129 124, 126–129 125, 130–133
Student Applications Book	9 10 11 12	from *Stuck in Neutral* by Terry Trueman from *Song of Solomon* by Toni Morrison from *The Accidental Tourist* by Anne Tyler from *Women in Love* by D. H. Lawrence	140–141 141–142 138–139 140–141
Test Book	9–12	Short-answer Test Multiple-answer Test	
Website		www.greatsource.com/rehand/	

Before Reading

Explain that characters serve a variety of purposes in a story, novel, or movie. The main character, often the hero, is called the *protagonist*. A character who works against the protagonist is called the *antagonist*. Also, some characters play a bigger role than others. Major characters are usually fully developed and complete, or *round* characters. Minor characters who are not fully developed are called *flat* characters.

Sometimes characters who are intended to play a major role are not very well developed because of the author's or screenwriter's lack of skill. Applying the term *flat* to major characters is a criticism. Invite students to discuss examples of flat major characters in teen movies.

Major and Minor Characters

Tell students that identifying the main characters in a story or novel is usually easy. When previewing a work of fiction, students should take note of the character name or names most often repeated.

Clues about Characters

Explain that authors create characters using a variety of techniques. This is called *characterization*. Read through the "Character Clues" listed on the bottom of page 333.

CHARACTER CLUES

1. physical appearance and personality

2. speech, thoughts, feelings, actions, and desires

3. interactions with other characters

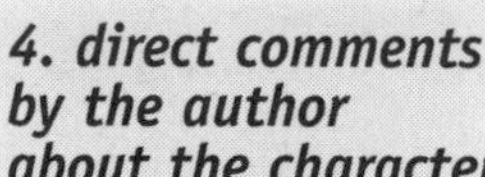

4. direct comments by the author about the character

5. personal history or other background information

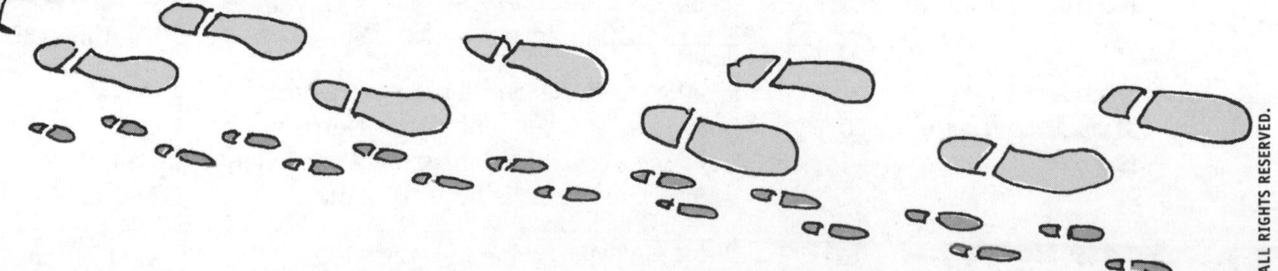

Before Reading

When reading passages from "The Necklace," students should take note of clues about the characters. Explain to students that using a graphic organizer, such as a Character Map, will help them record the important character clues more efficiently.

Reading Strategy: Using Graphic Organizers

Remind students that **using graphic organizers** can help them to better understand and remember what they have read.

Ask students to look at the Character Map on page 334 of the handbook. Read through the boxes to remind students of what specific information they should look for to understand characters.

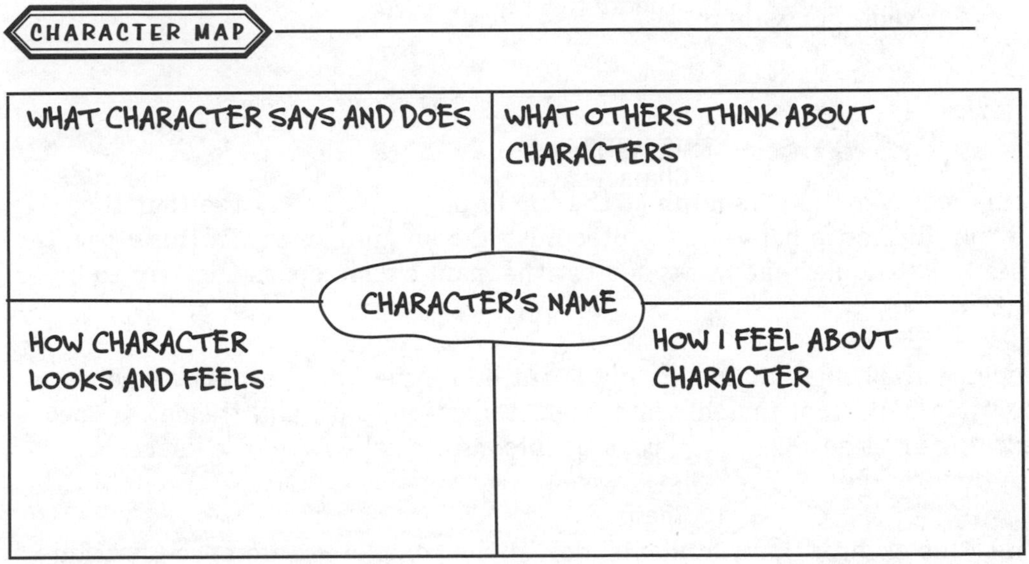

CHARACTER MAP

WHAT CHARACTER SAYS AND DOES	WHAT OTHERS THINK ABOUT CHARACTERS
CHARACTER'S NAME	
HOW CHARACTER LOOKS AND FEELS	HOW I FEEL ABOUT CHARACTER

During Reading

Now have students read the excerpt on page 335. When they have finished, have them look at the Character Map shown on page 336. Students then continue reading the story, this time focusing on a passage about Matilda's husband. Character Webs for Matilda and Matilda's husband appear on page 338.

Point out to students that they can look for details about Matilda as they read short excerpts from "The Necklace." They should notice how she looks, acts, feels, talks, interacts with others, and also how others feel about her.

Character and Plot

Explain that characters make the plot happen. Characters have conflicts with one another, or problems arise that characters must solve. As students continue to read excerpts from "The Necklace," encourage them to ask themselves the questions on page 338.

What is this character's role in the plot?

How do the events in the plot affect this character?

How would the plot change if this character were taken out of the story?

Character and Other Characters

With students, go over the paragraph at the top of page 339. Make sure that they understand the difference between a protagonist and an antagonist. In this story, the antagonist is the struggle that works against the main characters as they try to pay back a debt.

Remind students that what characters say about each other and how they react to one another give important insights into characterization, plot, and theme. As they read the excerpt on pages 339–340, ask students also to take note of characters' reactions to one another.

After reading this excerpt, have students look at the completed Inference Chart on page 340. Point out that this reader's conclusions provide insight into the characters.

INFERENCE CHART

WHAT CHARACTERS SAID OR DID	WHAT I CAN CONCLUDE ABOUT THEM
• Matilda discovers her necklace is missing. • She says she had it when she left the party.	• Matilda is in a panic. • She tries to reassure her husband.
• Her husband questions her. • He says it must be in the cab. • He leaves to look for the necklace.	• Her husband is also in a panic. • He doesn't blame her, however. • He takes action.

Character and Theme

Explain that characters act out a story's themes. The story's themes are usually the themes that run through the main character's life. Tell students that there are two major sources of clues to these themes: (1) characters' actions, feelings, or thoughts about life, and (2) a change in a character.

1. Characters' Actions, Feelings, or Thoughts about Life

Emphasize that students should take note of the places in the story (or novel) where a character talks about life in general or reveals his or her feelings and beliefs. In addition, a character's thoughts and feelings about life can be inferred from his or her actions. These are clues to the themes in the character's life and in the story. Have students read the short excerpt on the top of page 341 for practice.

2. A Change in a Character

Explain that a *dynamic* character is one who changes and grows throughout the story. A *static* character is one who stays the same. Both types can reveal the themes of a story, but students should pay particular attention to changes that occur in a character. Read through the questions given at the bottom of page 341.

Does the character feel different about herself or himself at the end of the story?

Do other characters notice differences in him or her?

Does the character's appearance, condition, or status change?

Does the character learn anything by the story's end?

Then, ask students to read the excerpts on page 342 for examples of how characters change.

After Reading

After reading, students should ask themselves what they have learned about the characters in this selection. Review the questions on page 343 with the students.

Can I identify the major and minor characters?

Do I know what the main characters want most of all and why?

Do I know why they act the way they do?

Do I know which characters change by the end of the story?

Can I tell how the main characters affect the plot, other characters, and themes?

Then, introduce students to the Character Development Chart on the top of page 344. Read through the notes made by one reader.

Summing Up

Have students read the points in the Summing Up at the bottom of page 344. Ask students to say in their own words what they learned in this lesson.

Assessment and Application

Use the Quick Assess checklist to evaluate students' ability to understand characters. Give students the opportunity to apply what they have learned through one of the two activities below. For students who are comfortable using graphic organizers to understand characters, use the suggestion below for independent practice. For students who need guided help with the strategy, use a *Student Applications Book*.

Quick Assess

Can students

- ☑ name different types of characters?
- ☑ name some techniques authors use to create a character?
- ☑ name one or two graphic organizers that can help readers understand characters?

1. Independent Practice

To show that they understand the lesson, ask students to apply the strategy of **using graphic organizers** to the main character(s) in a short story of their choice. They may want to use a Character Map, Character Web, Inference Chart, or Character Development Chart.

2. Student Applications Books

Grade 9

from *Stuck in Neutral*
by Terry Trueman
pages 140–141

Grade 10

from *Song of Solomon*
by Toni Morrison
pages 141–142

Grade 11

from *The Accidental Tourist*
by Anne Tyler
pages 138–139

Grade 12

from *Women in Love*
by D. H. Lawrence
pages 140–141

Test Book

See *Test Book* for short-answer and multiple-choice tests.

Focus on Theme

Goals

Here students will focus on understanding theme. This lesson will help students to:

- identify and understand themes in fiction
- find details that develop these themes in a literary work
- see the difference between a subject or topic and a theme

Background

Help students connect this lesson with their existing knowledge by asking them to:

- give examples of themes from novels or short stories they have read
- discuss why understanding the themes of a literary work is important

Overview

	Content	*Teacher's Guide* page	*Reader's Handbook* page
Selection	from *Jasmine* by Bharati Mukherjee		
Reading Strategy	Using Graphic Organizers	220, 439	347, 734
Tool	Summary Notes Double-entry Journal Topic and Theme Organizer	220 220 221	348, 754 348, 743 349, 755

Ancillaries

	Grade	Content	Page
Lesson Plan Book	9 10 11 12	Focus on Theme Focus on Theme Focus on Theme Focus on Theme	134, 136–139 144, 146–149 105, 110–113 114, 116–119
Student Applications Book	9 10 11 12	from "Pandora" by Edith Hamilton from *Lord of the Flies* by William G. Golding from "The Gift of the Magi" by O. Henry from *Around the World in Eighty Days* by Jules Verne	142–144 143–145 140–141 142–143
Test Book	9–12	Short-answer Test Multiple-answer Test	
Website		www.greatsource.com/rehand/	

Before Reading

Finding the theme or themes of a literary work can sometimes be difficult. Explain to students that there is a three-step plan that can help them greatly.

Step 1: Identify the "big ideas" or central topics

Read through the description and the list of common topics for themes in literary works on page 346. Emphasize that identifying the topic is not difficult.

COMMON TOPICS FOR THEMES

ambition	*friendship*	*loyalty*
change	*future*	*money*
childhood	*growing up*	*power*
choices	*hope*	*prejudice*
courage	*human needs*	*relationships*
culture	*identity*	*secrets*
differences	*independence*	*success*
faith	*justice*	*trust*
family	*loss*	*truth*
freedom	*love*	*war*

During Reading

As students read, they can take notes about the topics that recur. This gives them an additional purpose for reading and helps focus their reading.

Step 2: Find out what the characters do or say that relates to the central topics

Explain that the author and/or the characters will say things about the topic that provide clues to understanding theme.

- repeated words, ideas, or symbols
- images and metaphors
- important plot events or dialogue
- changes in characters' actions, beliefs, or values

During Reading

Reading Strategy: Using Graphic Organizers

Emphasize to students that the strategy of **using graphic organizers** helps direct readers' attention to important details in the text and provides a way to record details relating to a topic. Summary Notes and a Double-entry Journal are two useful tools.

Ask students to look at the example of the completed Summary Notes at the top of page 348. Read through the notes.

SUMMARY NOTES

Book: JASMINE
Topic: IDENTITY
Chapter 1 In India a fortune-teller says Jasmine will be a widow and live in exile. The chapter ends with her living in Iowa years later.
Chapter 4 She compares herself as a girl in India with herself as a woman in America.
Chapter 12 Prakash, her Indian husband, changes her name from Jyoti to Jasmine.

Next, have students look at the Double-entry Journal at the bottom of page 348. Read through the quotes and one reader's thoughts.

DOUBLE-ENTRY JOURNAL

BOOK: JASMINE
TOPIC: IDENTITY

QUOTES	WHAT I THINK ABOUT IT
"Masterji, you are here to tell me that there is a lotus blooming in the middle of all this filth, no?" (p. 50)	Jasmine's teacher comes to tell her father that she is not a common village girl and should not be married off. They have a discussion about Jasmine's future and what she really is. This is important because identity is based not only on what you are or where you are from, but what you know and can do.
"Yogi's in a hurry to become all-American, isn't he?" (p. 28)	"Yogi" is the nickname school friends give to Jasmine and Bud's adopted Vietnamese son. His real name is Du. This quote brings up the question of what it means to be American now. Kids like Du change identities to meet the needs of the situation. Jasmine is always saying Du does whatever he must to survive. Changing names, identities—these are not big problems or sacrifices for him.

Step 3: State what the author says about life that relates to the central topics

In the final step, students synthesize the information gathered in the first two steps to determine the theme, or what the author feels is important to know about life. Point out that a good statement of the theme does not include any character names.

After reading, students can use their notes and organizers to figure out and write about the theme or themes in the literary work. Have students look at the Topic and Theme Organizer on page 349. Show them that the first two steps lead to the third step.

Ask students to turn to page 350 and look at the tips for making a theme statement.

TIPS FOR MAKING THEME STATEMENTS

Tip 1. State your idea. *Try not to summarize the story. Your theme statement should be a complete sentence that expresses the story's theme. Try completing the following sentence: "The point the author makes is that ____________."*

Tip 2. Use precise words. *Vague words—such as* good *or* important *or* bad*—make it hard to get your point across.*

Tip 3. Avoid using characters' names. *Good theme statements are about the book and its ideas, not one particular character.*

Have students take turns reading the tips and explanations out loud.

Summing Up

Now read the points in the Summing Up at the bottom of page 350. Then, ask students to say in their own words what they learned in this lesson.

Assessment and Application

Use the Quick Assess checklist to evaluate students' ability to understand theme. Give students the opportunity to apply what they have learned through one of the two activities below. For students who are comfortable with the reading process and strategy, use the suggestion below for independent practice. For students who need guided help with the strategy, use a *Student Applications Book*.

Quick Assess

Can students

- ☑ define *theme*?
- ☑ explain the three-step plan for finding the theme in a literary work?
- ☑ name one or two tools that help readers figure out the theme?
- ☑ say why theme is important?

1. Independent Practice

Ask students to show that they understand the lesson by applying the strategy of **using graphic organizers** to the theme of a novel or short story of their choice. They may use Summary Notes, a Double-entry Journal, or a Topic and Theme Organizer.

2. Student Applications Books

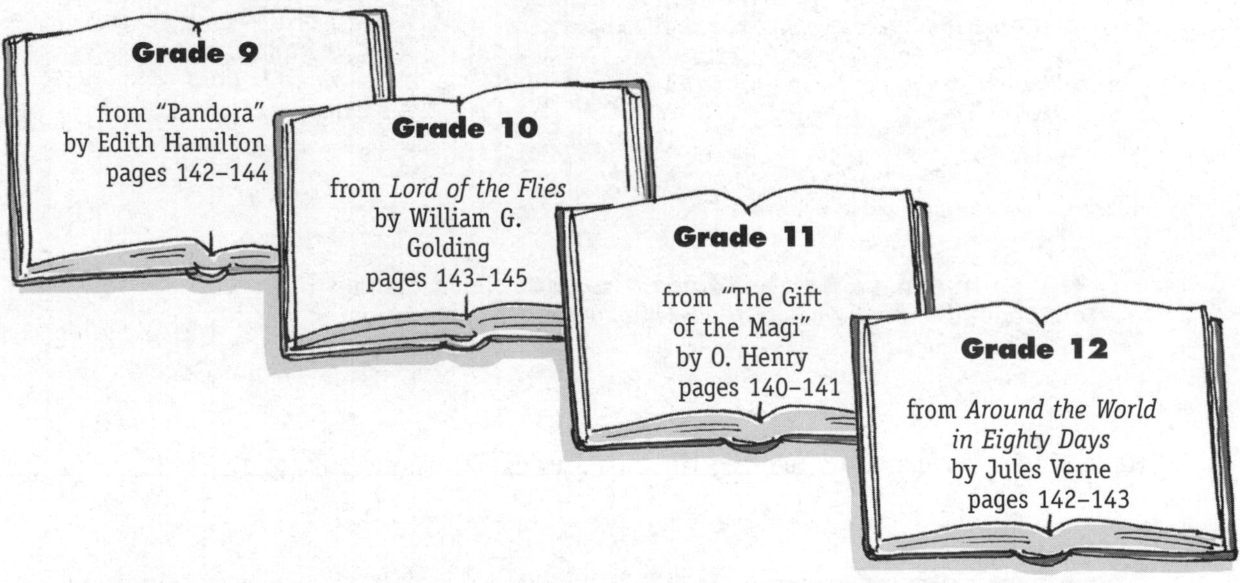

Test Book

See *Test Book* for short-answer and multiple-choice tests.

Focus on Dialogue

Goals

Here students focus on understanding dialogue. This lesson will help them learn to:

- understand the forms of dialogue
- see how dialogue affects the characters, mood, and plot of a literary work
- understand the different ways dialogue is shown

Background

Help students connect this lesson with their prior knowledge by asking them to:

- discuss why dialogue is important
- talk about what readers can learn from how characters speak
- discuss how dialogue can explain and advance the plot

Overview

	Content	*Teacher's Guide* page	*Reader's Handbook* page
Selection	from "Blues Ain't No Mockinbird"		352, 353, 356, 357
	from *Cry, the Beloved Country*		354
	from *All Quiet on the Western Front*		354
Reading Strategy	Close Reading	225, 433	355, 714
Tool	Double-entry Journal	226	358, 743

Ancillaries

	Grade	Content	Page
Lesson Plan Book	10	Focus on Dialogue	125, 130–133
	12	Focus on Dialogue	115, 120–123
Student Applications Book	9	"What Means Switch" by Gish Jen	145–147
	10	from "The Golden Honeymoon" by Ring Lardner	146–147
	11	from *The Shipping News* by E. Annie Proulx	142–143
	12	from *Some Tame Gazelle* by Barbara Pym	144–145
Test Book	9–12	Short-answer Test Multiple-answer Test	
Website		www.greatsource.com/rehand/	

Before Reading

Explain that dialogue includes what characters say out loud and what they think. Both are important to understanding characters and themes in works of fiction. Remind students that writers may use different conventions to indicate a character's speech or thoughts.

Quotation Marks and Speech Tags

Tell students that usually dialogue is set off by quotation marks. However, authors may also use italics, dashes, or even no special punctuation.

Have students read the excerpt on the bottom of page 352 to see an example of how speech is usually indicated. Ask students to note the speech tags, which tell the reader who is speaking. Also point out that the beginning of the dialogue is indented when the speaker changes.

1. Extended Quotations: Ask students to turn to page 353. Explain that in "extended quotations" in which one character's speech goes on for more than one paragraph, there are no closing quotation marks at the end of each paragraph. Closing quotation marks will not appear until the speaker is finished speaking.

2. Embedded Quotations: Now explain how authors punctuate embedded quotations. When a character is speaking and quotes another character, the embedded quote is set off in single quotation marks. Have students look at the example in the excerpt.

3. Representative Dialogue: Explain that some dialogue is not spoken by a particular character; rather, it is meant to represent what people in general are saying. Have students look at the excerpt from *Cry, the Beloved Country* at the top of page 354 to see an example of this.

4. Internal Dialogue: Explain that "internal dialogue" takes place only inside a character's head. Authors often use internal dialogue to show readers the discrepancy between what a character is thinking and what he or she is saying.

5. No Speech Tags: Have students look at the example at the bottom of page 354. Tell students that most authors would italicize thoughts or simply follow a line of thought with "he thought" or "she thought."

Before Reading

Reading Strategy: Close Reading

Emphasize that **close reading** is a good strategy for focusing on dialogue in a story or novel. Close reading can help students hear in their own minds how the characters sound.

Read through the questions on page 355 that students should ask themselves while reading dialogue. Remind students to ask themselves these questions when they come to dialogue in a story or novel.

What does this remark reveal about the character?

Do the other characters understand why the character makes this statement?

Why does this character say this?

How does the dialogue influence the mood of the story?

How do the characters' comments affect the outcome of the story?

During Reading

Clues about Character

Remind students that readers learn a lot about characters by how they speak and what they say. Emphasize that good writers are very careful when choosing the words that a character says and thinks.

Ask students to read the excerpts from "Blues Ain't No Mockinbird" on page 356. Have students say what they infer about Granddaddy's character from his speech. Then, ask the students to read through the journal entry at the bottom of the page.

Clues about Plot

Explain that dialogue can also give important information about background, conflicts, and plot. Have students read the excerpts on page 357 to see examples.

After Reading

After reading, students should look back and reflect on the dialogue in a story or novel they have read. To better understand what dialogue says about the characters and the story, students can complete a Double-entry Journal. With the students, read the sample on page 358.

DOUBLE-ENTRY JOURNAL

QUOTE	MY THOUGHTS
"Now aunty," Camera said, pointin the thing straight at her. "Your mama and I are not related."	Granny insists on respect in the way people speak to and treat her. The man's informal tone and familiar use of "aunty" and his pointing his camera right at her show little respect for her.

Summing Up

Have students read the points in the Summing Up at the bottom of page 358. Ask students to say in their own words what they learned in this lesson.

Assessment and Application

Use the Quick Assess checklist to evaluate students' ability to understand dialogue. Give students the opportunity to apply what they have learned through one of the two activities below. For students who are comfortable with reading dialogue, use the suggestion below for independent practice. For students who need guided help with the strategy, use a *Student Applications Book*.

Quick Assess

Can students

- ☑ explain how dialogue is typically punctuated?
- ☑ give an example of how dialogue helps readers better understand a character?
- ☑ give an example of how dialogue can help readers understand the background of a story and its conflicts?

1. Independent Practice

To show that they understand the lesson, students can apply the strategy of **close reading** to the dialogue in a short story of their choice. Alternatively, have students work in pairs to write a dialogue between two imaginary characters.

2. Student Applications Books

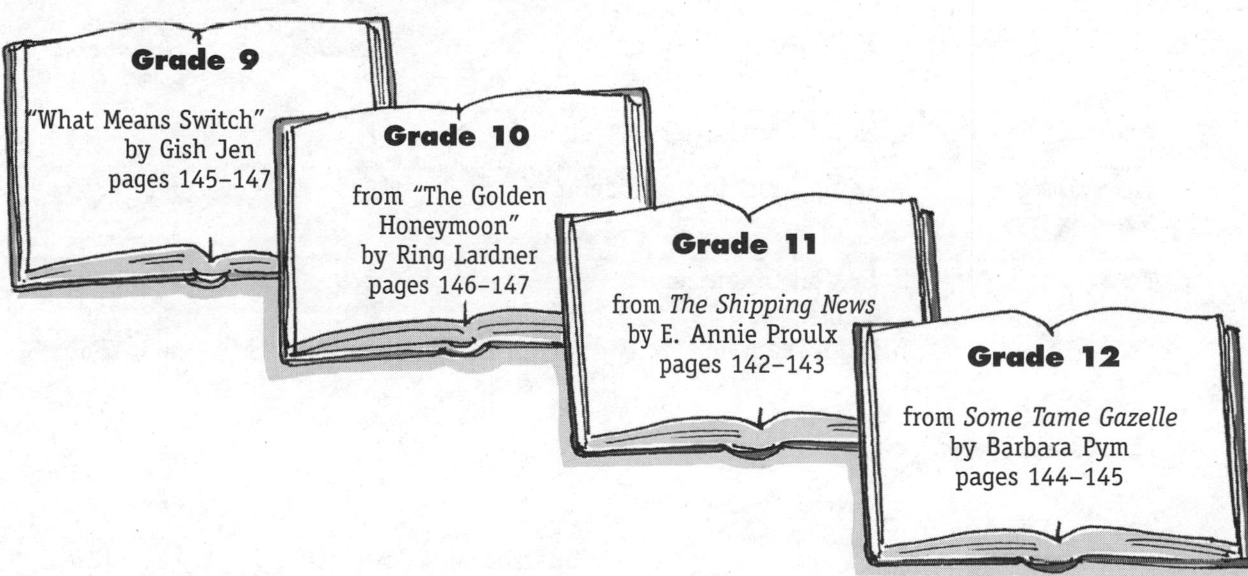

Test Book

See *Test Book* for short-answer and multiple-choice tests.

Focus on Comparing and Contrasting

Goals

Here students will compare and contrast two pieces of literature. This lesson will help students to:

- use the reading process to make strong comparisons and contrasts
- use different reading tools to analyze works or elements
- find and organize details from the literary works to support their points

Background

Help students connect this lesson with their existing knowledge by asking them to:

- name two stories or novels that seem similar and talk about the similarities
- name two stories or novels that seem very different and discuss the differences

Overview

	Content	Teacher's Guide page	Reader's Handbook page
Selection	Novels by Charles Dickens		
Reading Strategy	Using Graphic Organizers	229, 439	361, 734
Tool	Fiction Organizer Two-novel Map Venn Diagram	229 230 230	361, 744 362, 756 363, 756

Ancillaries

	Grade	Content	Page
Lesson Plan Book	11	Focus on Comparing and Contrasting	114, 116–119
Student Applications Book	9	from *A Tree Grows in Brooklyn* by Smith and *The Catcher in the Rye* by Salinger	148–149
	10	from *A Tale of Two Cities* by Dickens and *The Garden of Eden* by Hemingway	148–149
	11	from "The Fall of the House of Usher" by Poe and *The Aspern Papers* by James	144–145
	12	from *Gulliver's Travels* by Swift	146–147
Test Book	9–12	Short-answer Test Multiple-answer Test	
Website		www.greatsource.com/rehand/	

Before Reading

Emphasize that comparing and contrasting require students to find a number of ways in which two novels are alike and different. Students should keep this goal in mind when previewing the works.

Read the Preview Checklist on page 360 with the students. Each item on the list would be a good point to compare and/or contrast.

Preview Checklist

- ✔ *the characters and what they are like*
- ✔ *when and where the story takes place*
- ✔ *the plot*
- ✔ *the themes*
- ✔ *who tells the story*
- ✔ *any words, phrases, or ideas that are repeated throughout the novel*

During Reading

Reading Strategy: Using Graphic Organizers

Emphasize that **using graphic organizers** is an excellent strategy for gathering the information students will need to compare and contrast two literary works.

Have students turn to page 361 to see an example of a Fiction Organizer on Dickens's novel *David Copperfield.* The Fiction Organizer enables students to identify and record the most important elements in works of fiction.

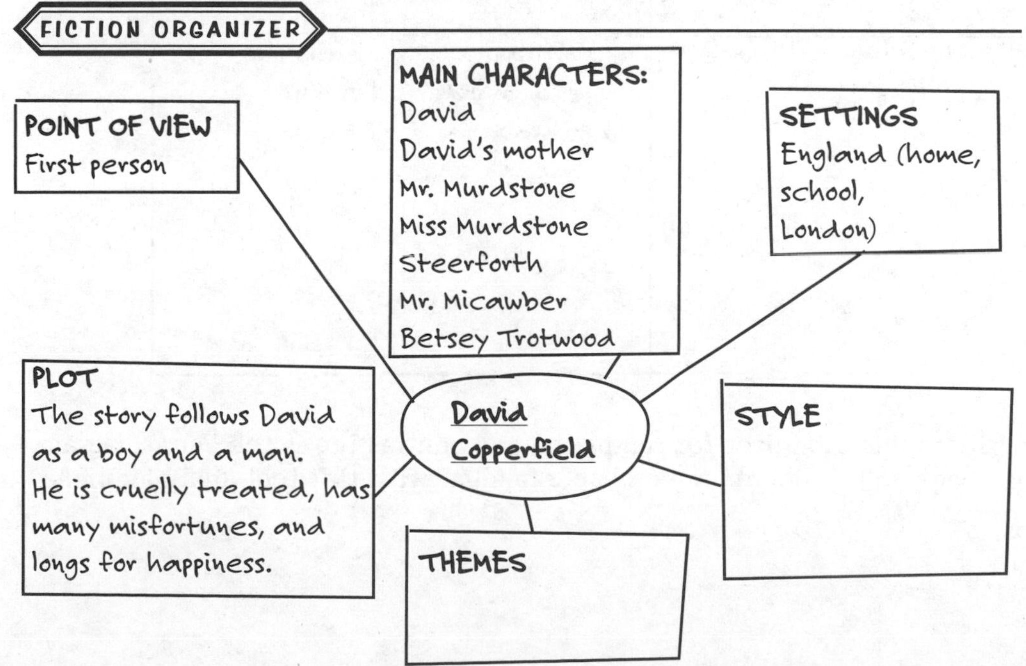

During Reading

Explain that a variety of graphic organizers will be useful for comparing and contrasting works.

Then have students turn to page 362 to see a Two-novel Map, which simply aligns the elements from two works. Read through this example, which compares and contrasts Dickens's *David Copperfield* and *Great Expectations*.

TWO-NOVEL MAP

DAVID COPPERFIELD	GREAT EXPECTATIONS
Background	
written 1849–1850 somewhat autobiographical	written 1860–1861
Main Characters	
David David's Mother The Murdstones Steerforth Mr. Micawber Uriah Heep Betsey Trotwood	Pip Joe Gargery Miss Havisham Magwitch Estella
Main Setting	
London, England	London, England
Main Plot	
• David orphaned at an early age • lives with stepfather	• Pip orphaned at an early age • Lives with older sister and her husband
Main Events	
Main Themes	
Ending	

Another useful graphic organizer for comparing and contrasting is the Venn Diagram, illustrated on page 363. Students are probably familiar with this tool and may prefer to use it for that reason.

After Reading

After reading and taking notes, students will need to look back at the two literary works to clarify anything they don't understand and gather more information. Have students turn to page 364 and read through the questions given.

Which literary elements did I find most interesting?

Did I find the minor characters, if any, more appealing than the major ones? Why?

Which antagonists were more fully characterized or described?

Which protagonists did I find most realistic?

What were the motives of the characters?

What were some important themes?

Which work gave a clearer picture of immediate settings, and what were these settings?

Was the dialogue realistic?

What were some key aspects of the styles? (sentence structure and figurative language, for example)

How believable were the plots?

Before turning their notes into a composition or discussion, students need to look at the model of comparison and contrast on page 365. Stress to students that knowing the format of a composition in advance enables them to write more efficiently—faster and better.

Summing Up

Read the points in the Summing Up at the bottom of page 365. Then, ask students to say in their own words what they learned in this lesson.

Assessment and Application

Use the Quick Assess checklist to evaluate students' understanding of comparison and contrast. Give students the opportunity to apply what they have learned through one of the two activities below. For students who are comfortable with comparing and contrasting, use the suggestion for independent practice or another of your own. For students who need guided help with the strategy, use a *Student Applications Book.*

Quick Assess

Can students

- define *compare* and *contrast*?
- name two or three graphic organizers that will help them compare and/or contrast literary works?

1. Independent Practice

To show that they understand the lesson, students can apply the strategy of **using graphic organizers** to compare and/or contrast two short stories of their choice.

2. Student Applications Books

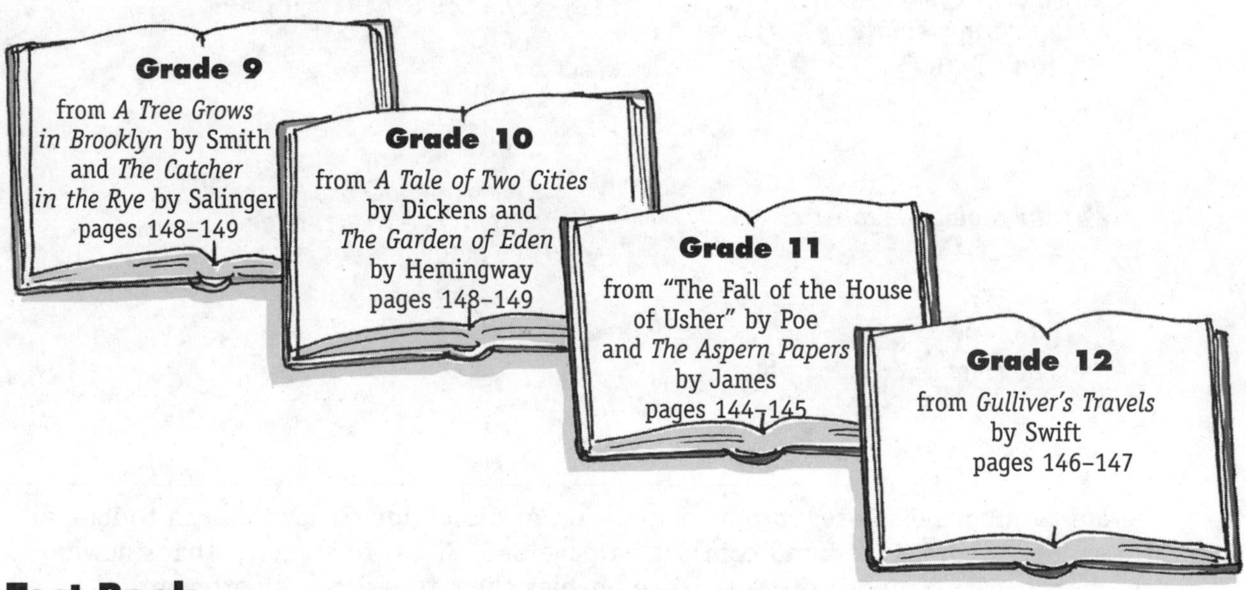

Test Book

See *Test Book* for short-answer and multiple-choice tests.

Elements of Fiction

This section introduces and explains common elements in fiction. The *Reader's Handbook* provides examples, descriptions, and definitions. Use this section to familiarize students with the terms and the overall purposes of these elements.

Also see *Lesson Plan Book 9* (pages 135, 140–143), *Lesson Plan Book 10* (pages 105, 110–113), and *Lesson Plan Book 11* (pages 115, 120–123).

Antagonist and Protagonist

Set Goal

Students will learn that the protagonist is the main character, or hero, of a literary work, and that the antagonist is that which opposes him or her.

Teach and Discuss

Emphasize that all literature involves some kind of conflict, often a conflict between two characters. Ask a student to read aloud the **Example** from Edgar Allan Poe's "The Cask of Amontillado" on page 367 of the handbook. Then discuss who is the protagonist (the narrator) and who is the antagonist (Fortunato) in this example.

Read through the **Description** with the students. Emphasize that an antagonist is not necessarily another character—it could be a group of people, a force of nature, or even something within the protagonist's personality. Have them apply the information about protagonist and antagonist to the excerpt from "The Cask of Amontillado." Ask them:

- What problem is the narrator facing?
- Is the antagonist a person or something else?
- What does the protagonist feel compelled to do?

Check Understanding

Then have students read the **Definition** at the bottom of page 367. After that, in a whole-class discussion, have students discuss the protagonists and antagonists in short stories, books, and movies that they have recently read and seen. Focus on the following questions:

- Who was the protagonist, and how do you know he or she was the protagonist?
- Who (or what) was the antagonist, and how do you know?
- What was the conflict between the two?
- How was the conflict resolved?

Character

Set Goal

Students will learn that a character (a person, animal, or imaginary creature in a literary work) can be understood by what he or she says, does, thinks, and feels as well as by what other characters and the author say about him or her.

Teach and Discuss

Ask for a volunteer to read aloud the **Example** on page 368 of the handbook. Then, ask students what clues the reader can use to understand the characters in this passage.

Next, read the **Description** with the students. Have them apply the information to the excerpt from "The Adventure of the Speckled Band." Ask them:

- How does the woman speak?
- What does she say about how she feels?
- What does Sherlock Holmes notice about her?

Emphasize the four aspects of a character that an author may choose to describe. These are listed at the top of page 369. Then, read through the different character types, pausing to give examples of major and minor characters from recently read literature. Discuss what makes these characters dynamic or static.

Check Understanding

Have students read the **Definition** on page 369. Then, have students work in pairs to brainstorm characters from favorite stories, books, movies, and television shows. Have them list at least ten characters from different sources (for example, not all from one television show). Have the partners choose three characters from their lists, identify their types (major or minor, dynamic or static), and write a short description of what their characters are like and *how they know.* Ask students to give an example or two, as evidence from the text or television show, to support their interpretation of these characters. Then, have the partners informally present one of their characters to the whole class. Questions for discussion include these:

- What type of character is this?
- What is the character like?
- What are some examples to support your interpretation?
- What characterization techniques did the writer use to make this character vivid?

Conflict and Complication

Set Goal

Students will learn that conflict is the struggle between two opposing forces and that complication is the part of the plot that becomes tense or entangled as a result of the conflict.

Teach and Discuss

Ask for a volunteer to read aloud the **Example** from *A Lesson Before Dying* on page 370. Ask students to note the conflict as their classmate is reading. Make sure they understand that Wiggins is the teacher.

Then read the **Description** on page 371 with the students. Ask them to distinguish between a complication (a problem or situation that is difficult to deal with) and a conflict (the major struggle in a plot). Emphasize that there are different types of conflicts—not all involve two people or two groups of people. Read through the five types of conflict on page 371, pausing when possible to give examples of recently read literature containing a particular conflict type.

Check Understanding

Have students read the **Definition** at the bottom of page 371. As a whole class, ask students to jot down movies, television shows, books, and short stories that they particularly liked or recently read or saw. Have them list as many as possible in a given time (two or three minutes). Then, ask them to look at their lists to find examples of each conflict type. Make five lists on the board. Here are some interesting questions:

- What type of conflict is most common in the movies you see?
- What type of conflict is most common in the literature you read for school?
- What complications arise from the conflicts?
- If you were to write a story about your life now, what type of conflict would it have?

Dialogue and Dialect

Set Goal

Students will learn that dialogue is the conversation of characters in a literary work and that dialect is a form of language spoken in a particular culture.

Teach and Discuss

Read aloud the **Example** from "B. Wordsworth" on page 372 as students follow along, modeling for students how the dialogue and dialect in this passage should sound. Ask students what they noticed about the speech patterns and what they learned about the two characters. Then, ask students what they think the rest of this story might be about.

Read the **Description,** emphasizing the difference between *dialogue* and *dialect.* Have students apply the information to the passage by V. S. Naipaul. Make sure they understand that the dialogue is the conversational exchange between the narrator and B. Wordsworth. The words spoken by the narrator depart grammatically from standard language and are an example of dialect. Give examples and ask students for examples of literary works that include unusual dialects.

Check Understanding

Ask students to read the **Definition** at the bottom of the page. Then, have them read excerpts from books or stories in your classroom library and write informally in their journals about what they learned from the dialogue. Students can then share what they learned with a partner, focusing on the following questions:

- What does the dialogue tell you about the characters?
- Is there dialect in the excerpt? If so, can you identify it?
- What does the dialogue tell you about the possible plot or conflict in the story?

If time permits, ask a few pairs to rehearse and perform a piece of dialogue, as though they were actors in a play. Emphasize the need to "get the sound right."

Flashback

Set Goal

Students will learn that a flashback is an interruption in the narrative to show something that happened before that time.

Teach and Discuss

Read aloud the **Example** on page 373. Ask students to identify the flashback in this paragraph from *All Quiet on the Western Front.*

Next, read the **Description** with the class. Point out that a flashback is an interruption in the order of events in a story. Sometimes a story opens with events that happen later in time than the event in the flashback. Emphasize that the purpose of a flashback is to help the reader understand the current situation or characters. For that reason, flashbacks are important. Attending to them will help students better understand the literary work.

Check Understanding

Then have students read the **Definition** at the bottom of page 373. To demonstrate understanding, have students write their own flashbacks. Have them begin their narratives as themselves—as students sitting in class. Let them know they will be sharing their flashbacks with classmates. Point out that their flashbacks ought to be about something fairly meaningful or important. Ask them to write about a page and not to worry about mechanics. After they are finished, they may share their flashbacks with a partner or in a small group. Ask the groups to discuss:

- What was the author trying to convey in his or her flashback? Why is it important to the author?
- What are the similarities and differences in the flashbacks shared?
- What words did each author use to signal that the flashback was beginning? How did the author signal a return to the present time?

Foreshadowing

Set Goal

Students will learn that foreshadowing is text that provides hints about what is to come.

Teach and Discuss

Have a student volunteer read aloud the **Example** on page 374 of the handbook. Ask the rest of the students to watch for clues or hints about what lies ahead in the story. Make sure students understand what worries the grandmother in "A Good Man Is Hard to Find" and what she tries to do about it.

Then read the **Description** with the students. Have them apply the information to the passage by Flannery O'Connor. Ask them:

- What is the grandmother trying to do?
- What do her actions and words tell about the conflict that will develop in the plot?

Emphasize that foreshadowing creates suspense in a story, contributes to mood, and makes the end seem plausible or believable.

Check Understanding

Have students read the **Definition** at the bottom of page 374. Then, give them an assignment to complete over the next week: watch for foreshadowing in television shows, movies, books, and stories. Students must jot down the examples, including the title of the show or story containing the examples. You may make it a contest, awarding a small prize to the person or team who brings in the most examples of foreshadowing. The examples may be posted on the bulletin board for discussion. Here are some good questions:

- What did the foreshadowing make you think would happen?
- How did the foreshadowing make you feel? How did it contribute to the mood?
- What happened in the end?
- Did the foreshadowing make the ending more plausible?
- What would the story or show have been like without the foreshadowing?

Genre

Set Goal

Students will learn that genre is a type or form of writing.

Teach and Discuss

Have students turn to page 375 of the handbook and talk with them about the word *genre*. Ask them to give examples of literary genres. Help them see that *subgenres* are more specific kinds of writing than the major literary genres.

Then, have students take turns reading aloud each row in the table. Ask students to think of other examples of the genres given as you go. Contribute examples of your own. Discuss the characters, plot, setting, and theme in the example.

Check Understanding

Then have students read the **Definition** at the bottom of page 375. To demonstrate their understanding, have students work in pairs or small groups to brainstorm examples of different genres. When they have written down as many examples as they can, have them jot down their favorite books, stories, movies, and television shows and identify the genres of these favorites. Ask them questions such as these:

- How do you know __(title)__ is an example of __(genre)__?
- Do you have a favorite genre? Do your favorite stories and shows belong to the same one or two genres?
- What do you like about your favorite genre(s)?
- What do you dislike about other genre(s)?

Irony

Set Goal

Students will learn that irony is the contrast between what something seems to be and what it really is.

Teach and Discuss

Ask students to read the **Example** from "Indian Education" on page 376 and then have a student volunteer read it aloud. Discuss what is opposite of the expected in the situation described by the narrator.

Read the **Description** with the students, emphasizing the three types of irony: verbal irony, irony of situation, and dramatic irony. Ask students to describe each of the types of irony. Have them provide additional examples for each type, either from literature or from everyday life.

Check Understanding

Have students read the **Definition** at the bottom of page 376. Then, ask students to spend the upcoming week looking for examples of the three types of irony in literature, in movies or television shows, or in real life. Students need to jot down their examples. At the end of the week, discuss students' examples as a whole class. Here are some questions to ask:

- What example did you find?
- What type of irony does it exemplify?
- Why do you think the author, screenwriter, or speaker used irony in that situation?

Persona

Set Goal

Students will learn that persona is the voice through which an author tells a story.

Teach and Discuss

Have students turn to page 377 of the handbook and read the **Example** silently. Then, ask the students to comment on the "voice" they heard while reading the selection from *Great Expectations*.

Read through the **Description** with the students. Have them apply the information to the passage by Charles Dickens.

- What voice does Dickens take on to tell the story?
- How will telling the story through Pip's eyes affect the story itself and the reader's feeling about Pip?

Emphasize that authors take on a persona, or become a character, while writing. Even a first-person narrator in a work of fiction is *not* the author himself or herself. Explain that in Latin *persona* means "person." Students can think of persona as the person an author assumes in order to tell a particular story.

Check Understanding

Have students read the **Definition** at the bottom of page 377. Then, working in pairs, have students choose a short story or novel from your class or school library and take turns reading the first few pages aloud to one another. The pairs then describe the persona they think the author has adopted, focusing on the following questions:

- What persona has the author adopted?
- Why do you think the author chose this particular persona?
- Imagine the author taking on a different persona. How would it change the story?

Plot and Subplot

Set Goal

Students will learn that plot is what happens in a story and that subplot is a smaller, less important plot within the main plot.

Teach and Discuss

After students silently read the **Example,** a summary of *Bless Me, Ultima*, on page 378, ask a volunteer to read it aloud. Have students restate what this summary tells about the plot of Anaya's novel.

Then, read the **Description** with the students. Make sure they understand the difference between the plot, or what happens in the story, and the subplots, in which less important events are told. Emphasize that the events of the story usually result from the main conflict. Review the five parts of plot carefully. You may want to refer to the Plot Diagram on page 750 in the Reader's Almanac.

Check Understanding

Have students quickly read the **Definition** at the bottom of the page. Then, ask students to give examples of interesting plots and/or subplots in books, stories, movies, or television shows that they have read or seen recently. Some good discussion questions are as follows:

- What happened in the story, movie, or show to cause that event or series of events?
- What did the subplot add?
- If the main character or a major character had reacted differently to a conflict or occurrence, how might the plot have been changed?

Point of View

Set Goal

Students will learn that point of view is the vantage point or perspective from which a story is told.

Teach and Discuss

Ask two students to volunteer to read the two **Examples** on page 379 of the handbook. Have the rest of the class note the difference in point of view between the two passages. Call attention to the pronouns that are clues to point of view.

Then, read with the students the **Description** of first-person and third-person points of view on page 380. Explain that point of view is a term used by literary critics. Understanding the point of view is important in identifying the angle from which the author chooses to tell a story. Emphasize the differences between first- and third-person points of view. Discuss the distinction between an omniscient narrator, in which the author is all knowing, and a limited point of view, in which the story is told from one character's perspective. Ask students to cite examples of books and stories told from the first- and third-person points of view.

Check Understanding

After reading the **Definition,** have students choose a book or short story of interest from your classroom or school library. Working in pairs, students can discuss the following questions:

- Is the point of view first or third person?
- If it is first-person narration, does the narrator appear to be reliable? Why do you think he or she is or is not reliable?
- If the point of view is third person, is it limited or omniscient? Tell how you know which it is by citing evidence from the text.
- Imagine the story or novel is written from a different point of view. How would it change?

Setting

Set Goal

Students will learn that setting is the time and place in which a literary work takes place.

Teach and Discuss

Ask students to read the **Example** from *1984* on page 381, and then have a student volunteer read it aloud. Point out that the highlighted information gives important information about the time of year, the place, and what the place is like.

Now read the **Description** with the students. Go over the details in the passage by George Orwell that establish the time and place. (It is a day in April at a place called Victory Mansions.) Point out that setting can be established through description, as in the example, or it may be suggested through action or dialogue. Emphasize that setting is an important literary element that helps readers better understand characters, mood, and the major themes in a literary work. You may want to point out that setting can include the general social situation of the characters and time.

Check Understanding

Have students read the **Definition** at the bottom of page 381. Then, working in pairs, have students choose a story or novel and, reading together, gather information about the setting. Ask students to jot down phrases in list form. Then, have students discuss with their partners:

- How might this setting be important to character development and theme?
- What mood does the setting create?
- How would the story change if the setting were changed?

Style

Set Goal

Students will learn that style refers to the way an author writes—the language and literary devices that he or she chooses to tell a story.

Teach and Discuss

Have students turn to page 382 of the handbook and read aloud the **Example** from *The House on Mango Street* as the students follow along. Then, ask them to say what they notice about the author's style, especially her choice of words and her sentence structures. They can note that the dialogue doesn't have quotation marks and that italic type is used for emphasis.

Then, read through the **Description** with the students. It is important for them to know that style is the way the author writes. Style is a result of the idea the author wants to express as well as a reflection of the author's unique way of putting words together. Emphasize that the main elements of style to look for are word choice, sentence structure and length, and literary devices such as figurative language, symbols, dialogue, and imagery.

Check Understanding

Have students read the **Definition** at the bottom of page 382. Then, working in pairs, have students analyze the author's style in a short story or novel of their choice. Ask the pairs to consider each of the three categories of style—word choice, sentence structure and length, and literary devices. Some questions for discussion are as follows:

- How would you describe the author's style?
- How does the style make you feel? What mood does it create?
- Do you like this style? Do you find it easy or difficult to read, and why?
- Why do you think the author chose this style?

Symbol

Set Goal

Students will learn that a symbol is a person, place, thing, or event used to stand for something abstract, such as an idea or emotion, in a literary work.

Teach and Discuss

Have students turn to page 383 of the handbook and read the **Example** silently. Ask them to look for the symbols in the highlighted sentences.

Read the **Description** with the students. Help them see that the car is a symbol in the excerpt from *The Bean Trees*. It is a concrete object, but it represents for the narrator of the novel an opportunity to venture out from her home in Kentucky. Discuss with students what they can infer about the mother's feelings and attitude. Emphasize that a symbol is something concrete—an object, a place, or even a person—that stands for or represents something abstract, such as an idea or emotion.

Check Understanding

Have students read the **Definition** at the bottom of page 383. Then, ask them to think about objects, places, or people in their own lives that may serve as a symbol for an idea or a feeling. Share with them something you have that symbolizes something more abstract. Have students jot down possessions they have, places they have been, or people they have known that are special to them. In a whole-class discussion, ask for volunteers to share an item, place, or person from their list and think aloud about what it may represent. Here are some good questions:

- Why is this thing (place, person) special to you?
- What feelings do you associate with this thing (place, person)?
- What idea might it symbolize?
- What can we learn about ourselves from this exercise?

Theme

Set Goal

Students will learn that a theme is the author's statement about life in a literary work.

Teach and Discuss

Have a student volunteer read the **Example** from "Like the Sun" on page 384 of the handbook while the others follow along. Ask students to watch for clues about the theme, and discuss what theme is suggested by the clues.

Then read the **Description** with the students. Distinguish between a topic (or subject) and a theme (a statement about the topic). A theme is the underlying meaning in a literary work. Point out that most themes are implied and not directly stated. Students may want to review the pages on making inferences and drawing conclusions on pages 46–47 in their handbooks. Also refer them to pages 56–58 on finding an implied main idea. Emphasize that novels may have more than one theme. Also emphasize that, although not all fiction has a theme, paying attention to the characters' words, the key scenes, or the symbols will help them identify the theme in a piece of literature.

Check Understanding

Have students read the **Definition** at the bottom of page 384. In a whole-group discussion, generate a list of themes that students have encountered in books and short stories they have read previously. You may spark students' memories by mentioning a literary work that the students read recently and discussing its theme. Here are some good questions for remembering or generating common themes:

- What did the main character come to learn or appreciate by the end of the story or novel?
- How was the conflict resolved and what, if anything, can you infer from it?
- What attitude did the author convey about the characters and their conflicts?

Tone and Mood

Set Goal

Students will learn that tone is an author's attitude toward the subject, while mood is the feeling that a work conveys.

Teach and Discuss

Have students turn to page 385 of the handbook and read the **Example** from "The Sniper" silently. Then, ask students how the scene made them feel. Discuss how the author's choice of words and sentence structures creates a certain feeling.

Then, read the **Description** with the students. Go over the terms commonly used to describe tone and the terms commonly used to describe mood. Invite students to suggest additional terms to describe tone (*playful, folksy, straightforward, bitter, ridiculing*, and so on) and to describe mood (*calm, mellow, dark, hopeless,* and so on). Emphasize that *tone* and *mood* do not mean the same thing. Explain that the tone of the passage from "The Sniper" might be considered serious, but the mood is tense.

Knowing the distinction between these two terms allows students to analyze literature in a more sophisticated and subtle way. Encourage students to apply what they know about tone and mood to stories or movies they know. Discuss their examples as a class until you are comfortable that students understand the meaning of both terms.

Check Understanding

Have students read the **Definition** at the bottom of page 385. To demonstrate understanding, students may choose a short story or novel that looks interesting to them and read the first few pages silently. Then, with a partner, students can discuss these points:

- the mood of the story they chose
- how the author succeeded in creating the mood
- the author's tone
- how they can identify the author's tone

Introduction to Reading Poetry

Ask students to tell what a poem is. During discussion, clarify that poems can be long or short, written in free verse or with rhyme, describe a single object or tell a story, and so on. Direct students to page 388 and have them read the first paragraph in the introduction. Then, ask a volunteer to read the paragraph aloud. Talk about the two things that all poems have in common: short lines and saying a lot in a few words. Ask students to read the rest of the page. Emphasize that song lyrics and rap music are forms of poetry. If any students have attended a poetry slam, ask them to describe it for the class. Conclude by having students tell what they expect to gain from studying the chapter.

Reading a Poem

Goals

Here students will read a sonnet by Elizabeth Barrett Browning. This lesson will help them learn to:

- ✓ enjoy and understand poems
- ✓ use the strategy of close reading
- ✓ understand how poems are organized

Background

Help students connect this lesson with their prior knowledge by asking them to:

- say what a poem is
- name some poems they have read
- name different types of poems they have learned about or read
- discuss what they like and what they dislike about reading poetry
- say why reading poetry is sometimes difficult for them

Opening Activity

Explain to students that most readers don't understand a poem on their first reading of it. This is partly because poems pack a lot of meaning into a short space—like too many clothes stuffed into a small duffel bag. Explain that readers of a poem must "unpack" it to see and appreciate what's there.

Explain that, in this lesson, students will read a sonnet. Originating in Italy, a sonnet is only one of many types of poems. Because sonnets are always 14 lines and follow specific rules about rhyme and rhythm, writing them is challenging.

Overview

	Content	Teacher's Guide page	Reader's Handbook page
Selection	Sonnet 43 by Elizabeth Barrett Browning		391, 395, 397
Reading Strategy	Close Reading	254, 433	392, 714
Rereading Strategy	Paraphrasing	258, 435	398, 722
Tool	Double-entry Journal Paraphrase Chart	254, 255, 256 258	392, 393, 394 396, 743 399, 749

Ancillaries

	Grade	Content	Page
Overhead Transparency	9–12	Previewing a Poem	Number 28
Lesson Plan Book	9 10 11 12	Reading a Poem Reading a Poem Reading a Poem Reading a Poem	145, 150–153 154, 156–159 134, 136–139 134, 136–139
Student Applications Book	9 10 11 12	"Sympathy" by Paul Laurence Dunbar "The Charge of the Light Brigade" by Alfred, Lord Tennyson "Richard Cory" by Edwin Arlington Robinson "Sonnet 29" by William Shakespeare	150–156 150–156 146–153 148–155
Test Book	9–12	Short-answer Test Multiple-answer Test	
Website		www.greatsource.com/rehand/	

A Set a Purpose

First, students need to set a purpose for reading the sonnet. Direct students to the Setting a Purpose questions on page 390 of the *Reader's Handbook.*

Setting a Purpose

- **What is the poem about?**
- **What's the mood or feeling of the poem?**
- **What meaning can I take from the poem?**

B Preview

Remind students of the importance of previewing before reading. Using the Preview Checklist on page 390 of the handbook, have students preview Elizabeth Barrett Browning's sonnet on page 391. Point out the annotations that will help in previewing.

Preview Checklist

✓ *the title of the poem and name of the poet*

✓ *the structure and shape of the poem on the page*

✓ *any rhymes*

✓ *any words and names that are repeated or that stand out*

✓ *the first and last lines*

Overhead Transparency

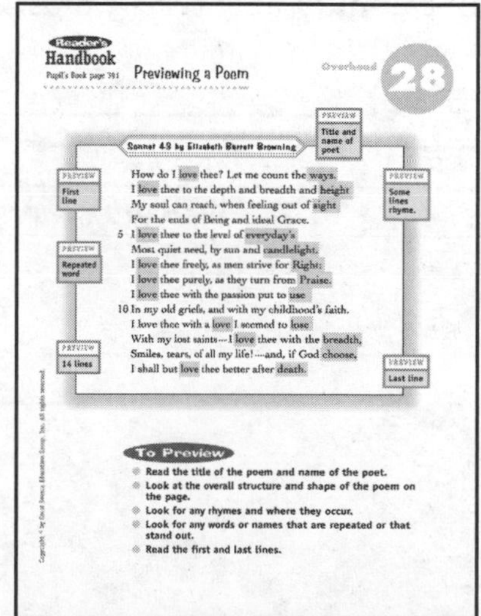

Reader's Handbook

Pupil's Book page 391

Previewing a Poem

Overhead 28

PREVIEW Title and name of poet

Sonnet 43 by Elizabeth Barrett Browning

How do I love thee? Let me count the ways.
I love thee to the depth and breadth and height
My soul can reach, when feeling out of sight
For the ends of Being and ideal Grace.
I love thee to the level of everyday's
Most quiet need, by sun and candlelight.
I love thee freely, as men strive for Right;
I love thee purely, as they turn from Praise.
I love thee with the passion put to use
In my old griefs, and with my childhood's faith.
I love thee with a love I seemed to lose
With my lost saints—I love thee with the breadth,
Smiles, tears, of all my life!—and, if God choose,
I shall but love thee better after death.

PREVIEW First line

PREVIEW Repeated word

PREVIEW 14 lines

PREVIEW Some lines rhyme.

PREVIEW Last line

To Preview

- Read the title of the poem and name of the poet.
- Look at the overall structure and shape of the poem on the page.
- Look for any rhymes and where they occur.
- Look for any words or names that are repeated or that stand out.
- Read the first and last lines.

Before Reading

C Plan

Ask students to sum up what they learned about the poem during their preview. Invite students to answer the questions in boldface type on page 391. Emphasize that what readers learn from previewing a poem helps them make a plan for reading. Often the plans start when readers ask themselves questions about what they will be reading.

Why are certain words capitalized?

To whom is the poem addressed?

Let students know that all readers, even the world's best readers, have to read a poem several times to fully understand and appreciate it. Therefore, they need to plan to read the sonnet more than once.

Have students turn to page 392. Read through the plan for reading a poem with them. Stress that looking at a different aspect each time helps readers better understand and appreciate a poem.

Reading Strategy: Close Reading

Now introduce the strategy of **close reading.** Explain that this strategy is perfectly suited to reading poetry because each and every word in a poem is very important.

Have students read the description of close reading on page 392 of the handbook. Then, explain how the Double-entry Journal, illustrated at the bottom of the page, will help students think carefully about the words and phrases in the sonnet.

DOUBLE-ENTRY JOURNAL

QUOTE	MY THOUGHTS ABOUT IT

During Reading

D Read with a Purpose

Now students are ready to read. Remind them that they will be reading slowly and then rereading the sonnet several times.

First Reading—Enjoyment

First, students should read the poem straight through, simply for enjoyment, without worrying too much about what it means. After this reading, students are ready to think more about what the poem means. They can record their initial reactions in a Double-entry Journal.

DOUBLE-ENTRY JOURNAL

QUOTE	MY THOUGHTS ABOUT IT
"How do I love thee? Let me count the ways."	I know that the word "thee" is an old-fashioned way of saying "you," and it is used only for people one is close to. I like the second sentence. It hints that there are many ways to love, perhaps too many to count.

Second Reading—Meaning

Remind students that paraphrasing the lines of a poem is a good aid to comprehension. Paraphrasing requires the reader to actively process what he or she has read. Have students look at the sample Double-entry Journal at the top of page 394 to see how one reader paraphrased a line of Elizabeth Barrett Browning's sonnet.

DOUBLE-ENTRY JOURNAL

QUOTE	MY THOUGHTS ABOUT IT
"I love thee to the depth and breadth and height/ My soul can reach, when feeling out of sight/ For the ends of Being and ideal Grace."	I think the speaker means that when she stretches her soul in all directions, the effort she puts forth is the same effort she puts forth in her love.

Third Reading—Structure and Language

Explain to students that the structure and language of a poem contribute to its overall meaning. Students should think about why a poet chose a certain structure or a certain word. Have students read the journal entry at the bottom of page 394 to see what one reader thought about these issues.

How Poems Are Organized

Explain to students that sonnets follow certain rules. Depending in part on how a sonnet is rhymed, it is called Italian or English. Elizabeth Barrett Browning's Sonnet 43 is Italian. Have students look at page 395 to see the rhyme scheme in this sonnet. Point out that the *abba* rhyme scheme is followed in lines 5–8.

Also explain that sonnets follow a certain rhythm, called *iambic pentameter.* Read through the explanation of iambic pentameter on page 395 with the students. Also read aloud the line from the sonnet, exaggerating the stressed syllables, so that students can hear which ones are to be accented.

Understanding a Poet's Choices

With students, read this paragraph about the lines in Sonnet 43 that are not in iambic pentameter. Make sure students understand that poets often depart from a pattern for a reason.

Fourth and Fifth Readings—Mood, Tone, and Enjoyment

In the fourth and fifth readings, students should look for words or phrases that evoke emotion in the reader. How does the sonnet make them feel? Ask students to read through the Double-entry Journal completed by one reader. Emphasize that all readers respond differently to poems and that it's fine if their thoughts and feelings about Sonnet 43 are different.

DOUBLE-ENTRY JOURNAL

QUOTE	MY THOUGHTS ABOUT IT
"I love thee with the passion put to use / In my old griefs. . . ."	Recalling sad times of the past gives a serious feeling to the poem. It makes her love sound true and sincere.

During Reading

Connect

Remind students that responding to or making connections with the poem as they read is very important. Good readers actively try to relate and respond to what they read. Have students look at the reactions of one reader, illustrated by the sticky notes on page 397. Journaling is another good way to respond to poetry.

Help students by telling them to:

- ask themselves questions (What do I like about Sonnet 43?)
- connect again with the meaning of the poem (What do I think Elizabeth Barrett Browning is saying about love?)
- restate why the poet chose the structure and language she did (What do I feel is special about the structure and language of Sonnet 43?)

After Reading

Pause and Reflect

After reading, students need to stop and reflect on what they have read. Have students go back and review their original purposes in reading Sonnet 43. Go over the following Looking Back questions with them.

Looking Back

- **Do I have a clear understanding of the poem?**
- **Can I remember any specific words, images, or phrases?**
- **How would I express the "big idea" of the poem?**
- **What mood or feeling did the poet create?**

Students may still be uncertain of the answers to some of these questions. If so, they need to return to the poem and reread in order to achieve understanding.

After Reading

G Reread

Explain that students should return to the text with a different strategy or tool so that they can get a fresh look at the sonnet.

Rereading Strategy: Paraphrasing

Encourage students to give the strategy of **paraphrasing** a try when rereading. Read the description of paraphrasing on page 398, and have students look at the Paraphrase Chart on page 399.

PARAPHRASE CHART

LINES	MY PARAPHRASE
"I love thee with the passion put to use / In my old griefs, . . .	I used to have strong feelings about some sad things, but now my strong feelings are directed toward you. These strong feelings have changed to love.

H Remember

After rereading, it is time for students to make the sonnet "their own." Discuss the activities of giving a dramatic reading or writing a poem on page 399 of the *Reader's Handbook,* or ask students to do the creative assignment below.

Creative Assignment: Have students work in pairs to find other sonnets by Elizabeth Barrett Browning. Ask them to choose one and talk with each other about its meaning, structure, and language. Then ask the pairs to share their sonnets by reading them aloud to the whole class or reading them to a small group of peers.

Summing Up

Review the lesson by reading the Summing Up on page 399 of the handbook. Go over the initial goals for the lesson. Discuss which ones students feel they achieved and which ones need more work:

1. **enjoying and understanding poems**
2. **using the strategy of close reading**
3. **understanding how poems are organized**

Assessment and Application

Use the Quick Assess checklist to evaluate students' ability to read and understand a poem. Give students the opportunity to apply what they have learned through one of the two activities below. For students who are comfortable with the reading process and strategy, use the suggestion below for independent practice or an activity of your own. For students who need guided help with the strategy, use a *Student Applications Book.*

Quick Assess

Can students

- ☑ explain why reading a poem more than once is necessary?
- ☑ explain why close reading and paraphrasing are good reading and rereading strategies for poetry?
- ☑ name two useful tools for reading poetry?

1. Independent Practice

Ask students to show they understand the lesson by applying the strategy of **close reading** or the strategy of **paraphrasing** to a poem of their choice.

Ask students to:

- Complete a Double-entry Journal while reading the poem.
- Apply the strategy of paraphrasing using a Paraphrase Chart.
- Complete journal entries for each reading of the poem, focusing on the different aspects of the poem in each reading.

2. Student Applications Books

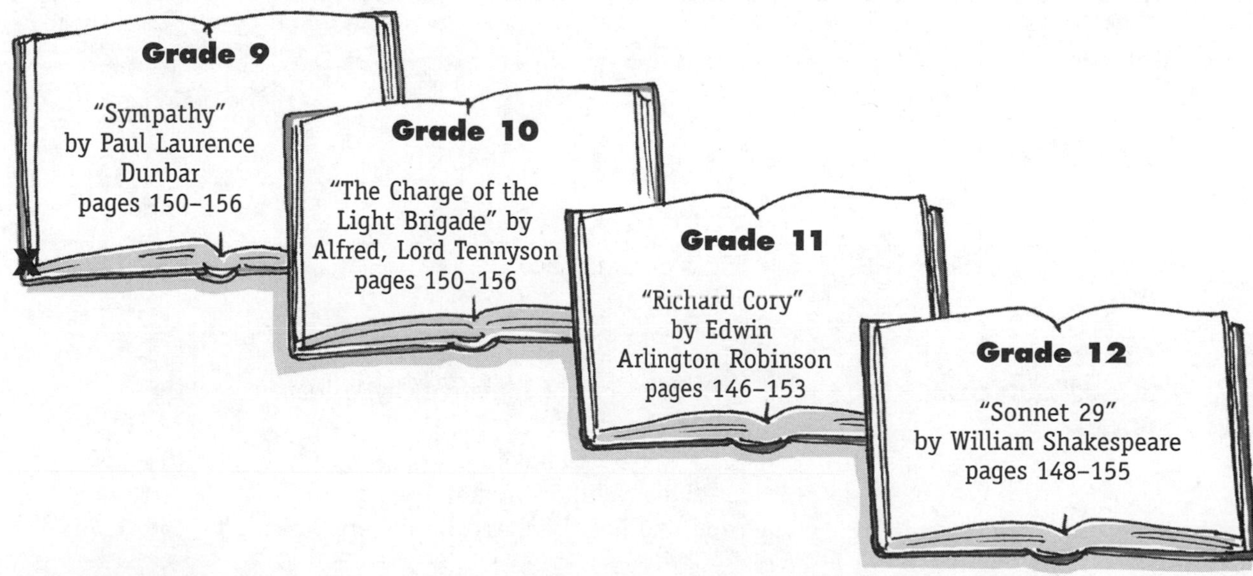

Test Book

See *Test Book* for short-answer and multiple-choice tests.

Focus on Language

Goals

Here students focus on understanding poetic language. This lesson will help them learn to:

- ✓ recognize symbols and other figurative language
- ✓ appreciate imagery
- ✓ understand how language affects tone and mood

Background

Help students connect this lesson with their prior knowledge by asking them to:

- discuss how the language in poetry generally differs from language in novels, short stories, and essays
- comment on whether the language used in poetry can sometimes make it difficult to read
- define *symbol, figurative language*, and *imagery*

Overview

	Content	*Teacher's Guide page*	*Reader's Handbook page*
Selection	"Identity" by Julio Noboa Polanco		401, 403, 404, 405
Reading Strategy	Close Reading	261, 433	402, 714

Ancillaries

	Grade	Content	Page
Lesson Plan Book	12	Focus on Language	135, 140–143
Student Applications Book	9	"The Tyger" by William Blake	157–159
	10	"The Lake Isle of Innisfree" by William Butler Yeats	157–159
	11	"The Death of Lincoln" by William Cullen Bryant	154–155
	12	from "My Last Duchess" by Robert Browning	156–157
Test Book	9–12	Short-answer Test Multiple-answer Test	
Website		www.greatsource.com/rehand/	

Before Reading

Explain that, when focusing on the language of a poem, students need to look for:

- word meanings
- figurative language, such as symbols, metaphors, and similes
- repetition
- imagery that jolts, surprises, and makes them say "wow"
- words that convey attitude, tone, or mood

Have students take a look at the notes that one reader made while reading "Identity," shown on page 401.

Reading Strategy: Close Reading

Explain that the strategy of **close reading** is good for focusing on the language in a poem. This strategy enables the reader to look at the poem word by word and line by line.

Encourage students to use the strategy of close reading when reading "Identity." While reading closely, students need a variety of ways to understand and think about words.

During Reading

1. Use a Dictionary

Let students know that they will probably have to look up a few words while reading a poem. Comprehension relies on understanding precisely what the words mean. Read through the description of using a dictionary with the students, pointing out the journal entry on page 402.

JOURNAL ENTRY

guarded—protected from danger; cautious
harnessed—fastened or held in place

2. Think about Connotations

Remind students that connotations are the thoughts and feelings that a word suggests, while a denotation is the literal meaning of the word. Read through the description on page 403 with the students and talk about the denotation and connotations of the word *eagle*.

DENOTATION AND CONNOTATION

DENOTATION

- *"a large bird of prey"*

CONNOTATION

- *a wild creature*
- *a symbol of the United States*

3. Examine Figurative Language

Explain that figurative language adds dimension to the literal meanings of words. Examples are given on page 404. Read through the examples, reminding students of the definitions of metaphor and simile.

4. Look for Imagery

Poets use imagery not only to stimulate a reader's senses but also to emphasize the poem's meaning. Have students look at the excerpt from "Identity" on page 405. Read the inference made by one reader and recorded on the sticky note.

5. Look for Repetition

A repeated word or line in a poem signals that it contains an important thought or idea. Have students look for repeated words, phrases, or lines in "Identity."

6. Look for Tone and Mood

Remind students that mood is the feeling that the poem creates in the reader, whereas tone is the author's attitude toward the subject matter he or she is writing about. Read through the sample journal entry at the bottom of page 405.

After Reading

After reading, students should identify key words, look up the meaning of unfamiliar words, and think about connotations, figurative language, and imagery. Students should ask themselves:

- Do I understand how the language affects the way I read the poem?
- Are there words or lines in the poem that are still not clear to me?

1. Write about the Poem

Read through the tips for writing about poetry given on the bottom of page 406. Direct students' attention to how one reader began a paper on "Identity," at the top of page 407.

2. Write a Poem of Your Own

You may also ask students to respond to the poem by writing poems of their own, following the same format. Have students read the poem based on "Identity."

POEM BASED ON "IDENTITY"

Let them be like sheep,
always guided, fed, protected, cared for,
but kept in a pen.
I'd rather be a deer, running free.

Summing Up

Now ask students to read over the points in the Summing Up at the bottom of page 407. Have students say in their own words what they learned in this lesson.

Assessment and Application

Use the Quick Assess checklist to evaluate students' ability to understand poetic language. Give students the opportunity to apply what they have learned through one of the two activities below. For students who are comfortable with poetic language, use the suggestion for independent practice or an activity of your own. For students who need guided help with the strategy, use a *Student Applications Book*.

Quick Assess

Can students

- ☑ give some examples of poetic language?
- ☑ explain why the strategy of close reading is well-suited for understanding poetic language?

1. Independent Practice

To determine whether students understand the lesson, ask them to apply the strategy of **close reading** to the language in a poem of their choice.

2. Student Applications Books

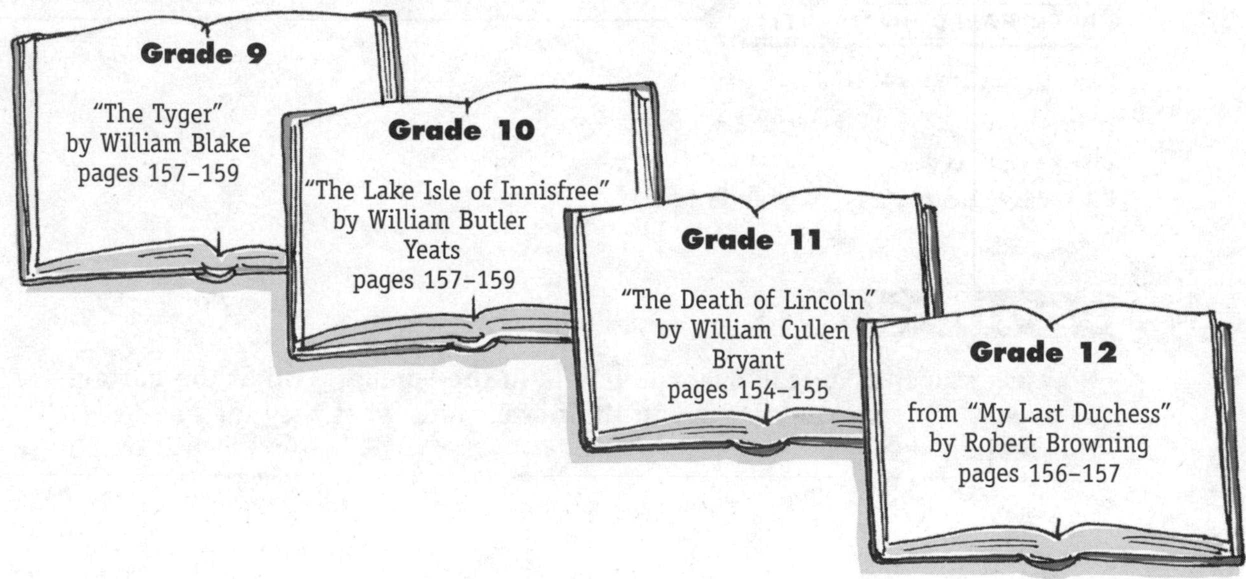

Test Book

See *Test Book* for short-answer and multiple-choice tests.

Focus on Meaning

Goals

Now students will focus on understanding the meaning of a poem. This lesson will help students to:

- ✔ use the strategy of close reading to unlock the meaning of a poem
- ✔ recognize clues to a poem's meaning
- ✔ see the difference between the subject of a poem and its meaning

Background

Help students connect this lesson by asking them:

- why the meanings of poems are often hard to figure out
- how they have figured out the meanings of poems in the past

Overview

	Content	*Teacher's Guide* page	*Reader's Handbook* page
Selection	"Ex-Basketball Player" by John Updike		409, 414
Reading Strategy	Close Reading	266, 433	410, 714
Rereading Strategy	Paraphrasing	267, 435	413, 722
Tool	Double-entry Journal	266	412, 743
	Inference Chart	266	412, 746
	Paraphrase Chart	267	413, 749

Ancillaries

	Grade	Content	Page
Lesson Plan Book	9	Focus on Meaning, Sound, and Structure	154, 156–159
	10	Focus on Meaning	155, 160–163
	11	Focus on Meaning	144–153
	12	Focus on Meaning	145, 150–153
Student Applications Book	9	"'For oh,' say the children, 'we are weary'" by Browning	160–162
	10	"After Death" by Rossetti	160–161
	11	"Success Is Counted Sweetest" by Dickinson	156–158
	12	"Loveliest of Trees" by Housman	158–160
Test Book	9–12	Short-answer Test/Multiple-answer Test	
Website		www.greatsource.com/rehand/	

Encourage students to read the poem initially just for fun. On the second reading, students can begin to think about what it means. Have students pay attention to the title, any unfamiliar words, words that express emotion or feeling, and the first and last several lines.

Now ask students to read "Ex-Basketball Player" on page 409.

Form a First Impression

Discuss with students their impressions after a first reading of the poem. They should immediately identify the subject as an ex-basketball player whose life seems empty now.

Emphasize to students that an appropriate reading strategy will help them unlock the meaning of a poem. Point out that close reading would be good for this purpose.

Reading Strategy: Close Reading

Close reading, which involves reading the poem slowly and carefully, word by word and line by line, is one of the best ways to focus on the meaning of a poem. Read through the description of this reading strategy with the students.

Go over with students the four ways to focus on the meaning of a poem.

1. Look at Denotations and Connotations

Remind students that words have connotations as well as denotations. Readers need to understand both in order to unlock the poet's intended meaning. Read the description of denotations and connotations on page 411 with the students, pointing out the journal entry for word definitions. Then, have students look at the sample Double-entry Journal, at the top of page 412, made by one reader to keep track of word connotations.

2. Think about the Style

Now have students think about the style of "Ex-Basketball Player." Ask how they would describe or characterize the style. Explain that a writer achieves a particular style by the way he or she uses language—figurative language, imagery, rhythm, and so on. Have students look at the Inference Chart at the bottom of page 412 to see how one reader recorded thoughts about John Updike's style.

After reading the poem a number of times and responding in journals, students should ask themselves whether they know what this poem means. Understanding the poet's attitude will help students better understand this poem's meaning.

3. Look for the Poet's Attitude

Point out that the subject of "Ex-Basketball Player" is a particular character, Flick, but that the subject of a poem is not the same as the meaning of the poem. Emphasize that the meaning comes through the emotion or feeling in the words used to talk about the subject. Ask students to think about how the speaker of the poem feels about Flick. What does he want the reader to think about Flick?

Rereading Strategy: Paraphrasing

Explain that, if students are still unclear about the meaning of the poem, they need to reread the poem again. Suggest a different strategy to help them get a fresh look at the poem. **Paraphrasing** is a good strategy for figuring out the meaning of a poem because it requires readers to understand the lines in the poem. Have students look at the Paraphrase Chart at the bottom of page 413.

PARAPHRASE CHART

QUOTE	MY PARAPHRASE
"Flick seldom speaks to Mae, just sits and nods/Beyond her face towards bright applauding tiers/Of Necco Wafers, Nibs, and Juju Beads."	Flick and Mae don't talk. He just sits there and looks past her at the rows of candy boxes. The phrase "applauding tiers" makes me think maybe he's imagining that they are an audience, clapping for him. Maybe the speaker feels a little sorry for Flick.

4. Listen to Your Own Feelings

Emphasize to students the importance of listening to and trusting their own feelings about a poem to figure out its meaning. Show them the reader's comments about the last stanza of the poem on page 414. Also emphasize that readers will have different reactions to and come up with different meanings for a poem. This is to be expected, and it is all right. Differences in viewpoints lead to rich, meaningful discussions about important issues in life.

Summing Up

Now read the points in the Summing Up at the bottom of page 414. Then, ask students to say in their own words what they learned in this lesson.

Assessment and Application

Use the Quick Assess checklist to evaluate students' ability to understand the meaning of a poem. Give students the opportunity to apply what they have learned through one of the two activities below. For students who are comfortable with the reading process and strategy, use the suggestion for independent practice or an activity of your own. For students who need guided help with the strategy, use a *Student Applications Book*.

Quick Assess

Can students

- ☑ distinguish between the subject of a poem and its meaning?
- ☑ say why close reading and paraphrasing are good strategies for understanding the meaning of a poem?
- ☑ name one or two tools that can help readers figure out the meaning of a poem?

1. Independent Practice

Students can apply the strategy of **close reading** to another poem of their choice. They should demonstrate how close reading helps them understand the meaning of the poem.

2. Student Applications Books

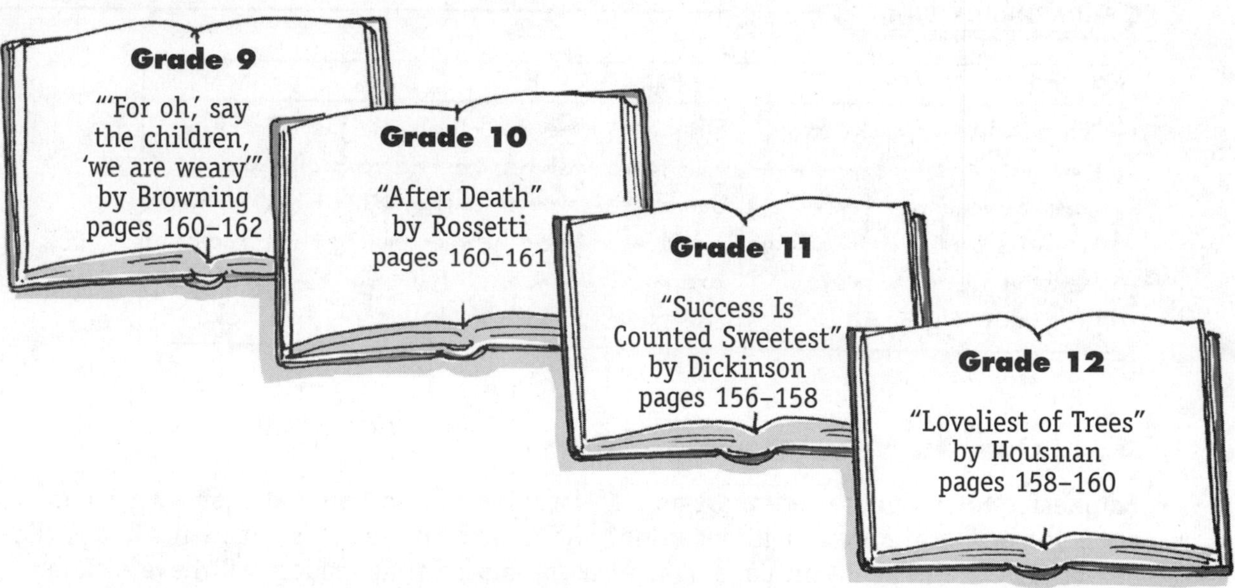

Test Book

See *Test Book* for short-answer and multiple-choice tests.

Focus on Sound and Structure

Goals

Here students focus on the sound and structure of a poem. This lesson will help them learn to:

- ☑ notice rhyme patterns and the use of sound devices
- ☑ understand the rhythm or meter of a poem
- ☑ recognize the structure of a poem

Background

Help students connect this lesson with their prior knowledge by asking them to:

- discuss what they know about sound and structure in poetry
- say why they think some poets use rhyme while others don't
- talk about the sound and structure of poems that they have liked or disliked

Overview

	Content	*Teacher's Guide* page	*Reader's Handbook* page
Selection	"Suicide in the Trenches" by Siegfried Sassoon	271	416, 418, 419, 420, 421
Reading Strategy	Close Reading	270, 433	416, 714

Ancillaries

	Grade	Content	Page
Lesson Plan Book	9	Focus on Meaning, Sound, and Structure	154, 156–159
	10	Focus on Sound and Structure	164, 166–169
	11	Focus on Sound and Structure	135, 140–143
	12	Focus on Sound and Structure	144, 146–149
Student Applications Book	9	"Throwing a Tree" by Thomas Hardy	163–165
	10	from "The Bells" by Edgar Allan Poe	162–164
	11	from "Snow-bound" by John Greenleaf Whittier	159–160
	12	from "The Rime of the Ancient Mariner" by Samuel Taylor Coleridge	161–162
Test Book	9–12	Short-answer Test Multiple-answer Test	
Website		www.greatsource.com/rehand/	

Before Reading

Tell students that, as they preview the poem, they should watch for the way lines are grouped, repeated sounds and rhyming words, and the rhythm or meter. Remind students that the first time they read a poem, they should read simply for enjoyment, without worrying too much about what it means. Ask students to preview "Suicide in the Trenches" by noticing the elements on the Preview Checklist.

Preview Checklist

- ✓ *the way the lines are grouped*
- ✓ *any repeated sounds and rhyming words*
- ✓ *the rhythm or meter*

Emphasize that close reading is a good strategy for focusing on sound and structure in poetry.

Reading Strategy: Close Reading

Close reading, which involves looking carefully at each word, phrase, and line in the poem, can help students understand sound and structure.

During Reading

As they read poems, students need to pay attention to four things:

1. organization of lines
2. repeated sounds
3. rhymes
4. rhythm or meter

1. Organization of Lines

Point out that "Suicide in the Trenches" has three stanzas, each with four lines. Explain to students that, like a paragraph, a stanza generally contains its own main idea, image, or thought. A shift in stanzas signals a change in idea or thought, just as the start of a new paragraph does. Have students read through the sample notes on the bottom of page 417.

2. Repeated Sounds

Explain that the sounds in a poem are intended to create certain effects in the reader. Repetition of sounds in poetry is important. Have students read through the section on page 418. Remind them of the meanings of **alliteration** and **assonance.**

Alliteration

Point out that alliteration is the repetition of sounds at the beginnings of words.

Assonance

Have students look at and say aloud the examples that show the repetition of vowel sounds in accented syllables that are close together.

Purpose of Sound Devices

Discuss lines in the poem that show how alliteration and assonance create a unified, melodic effect. These lines give the poem a musical quality.

3. Rhymes

Now read through the section on **rhyme** on page 419 of the handbook. Make sure that students take note of the rhyme scheme used in "Suicide in the Trenches."

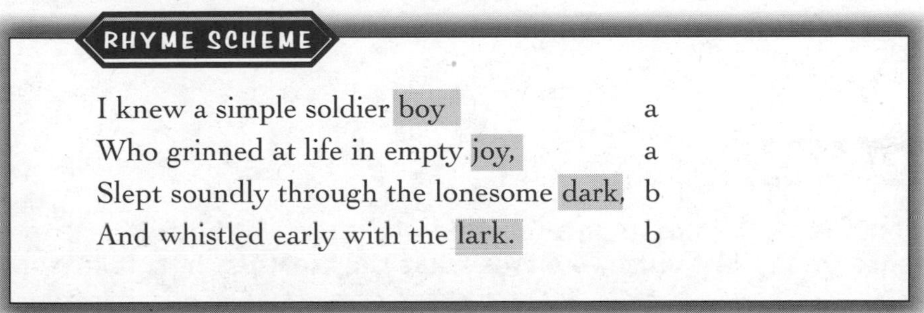
RHYME SCHEME

I knew a simple soldier boy a
Who grinned at life in empty joy, a
Slept soundly through the lonesome dark, b
And whistled early with the lark. b

4. Rhythm or Meter

Ask students to turn to page 420 to read the section on **rhythm,** or meter. Read the stanza from "Suicide in the Trenches" aloud, exaggerating the beat so that all students can hear it.

After Reading

After reading the poem, encourage students to think more deeply about it. They can do this by connecting to and/or responding to the poem in some way.

Connect to the Poem

Remind students that they will get more out of a poem if they make personal connections to it. Ask students to read one reader's response to "Suicide in the Trenches" at the bottom of page 421.

Write a Poem

Encourage students to respond to the sound and structure of Sassoon's poem by writing their own poems using the same rhyme scheme and organization. Students may write about whatever they like, as did the reader whose poem appears on page 422.

JOURNAL ENTRY

She was a girl from Boston town.
Her eyes were blue, her hair was brown.
She liked the feel of Venice Beach,
The cool salt air, the seagull's screech.

She stayed a year, wrote letters home.
Said, "Mom, I'm here and I won't roam.
I like my friends. The surf's not bad.
Good-bye to Boston. Don't be sad."

Summing Up

Now have students read the points in the Summing Up at the bottom of page 422. Ask students to say in their own words what they learned in this lesson.

Assessment and Application

Use the Quick Assess checklist to evaluate students' ability to understand sound and structure in poetry. Give students the opportunity to apply what they have learned through one of the two activities below. For students who are comfortable with reading poetry and the reading strategy, use the suggestion for independent practice or an activity of your own. For students who need guided help with the strategy, use a *Student Applications Book.*

Quick Assess

Can students

- say what is meant by sound and structure in poetry?
- define *alliteration* and *assonance*?
- explain how understanding structure can help readers understand the meaning of a poem?

1. Independent Practice

Ask students to show that they understand the lesson by applying the strategy of **close reading** to the sound and structure of a poem of their choice.

2. Student Applications Books

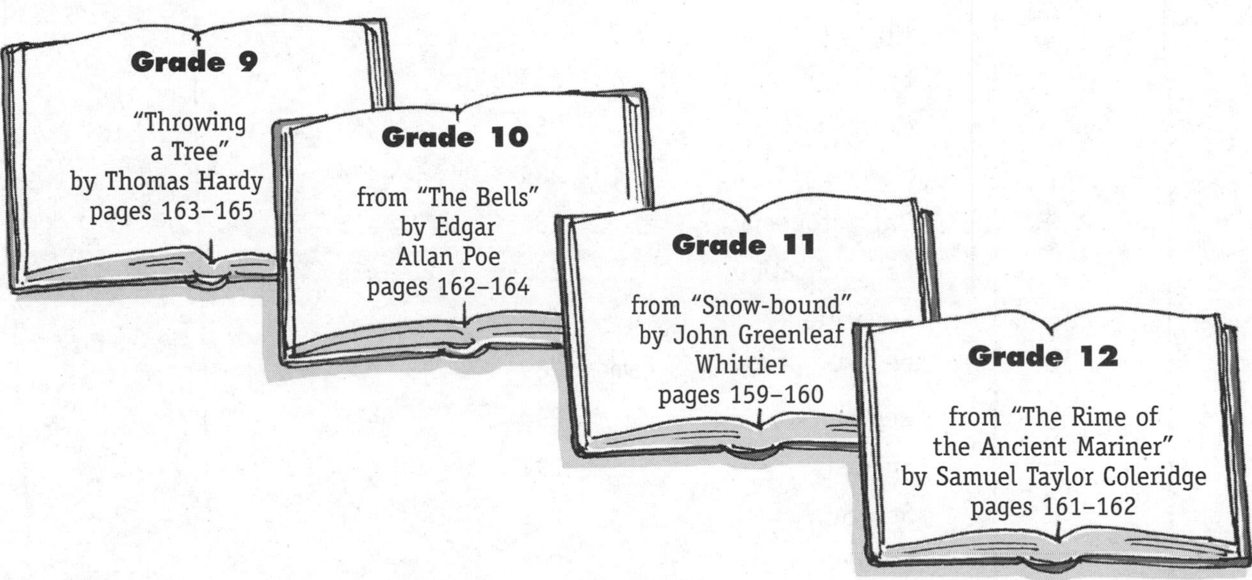

Test Book

See *Test Book* for short-answer and multiple-choice tests.

Elements of Poetry

This section introduces and explains common elements in poetry. The handbook provides examples, descriptions, and definitions. Use this section to familiarize students with the terms and the overall purposes of these elements.

Also see *Lesson Plan Book 9* (pages 144, 146–149), *Lesson Plan Book 10* (pages 145, 150–153), *Lesson Plan Book 11* (pages 154–163), and *Lesson Plan Book 12* (pages 154–163).

Alliteration

Set Goal

Students will learn that alliteration is the repetition of consonant sounds at the beginnings of words.

Teach and Discuss

Ask a student to read aloud the **Example** from "The Rime of the Ancient Mariner" on page 424 while the others follow along. Ask students to take note of any repetition of sounds they hear.

Then, read the **Description** with the students. Ask them to say aloud the words *fair, foam, flew, furrow, followed*, and *free* so that they can hear the repetition of the initial *f* sound. Do the same for *silent* and *sea*. Point out that alliteration can be used to reinforce meaning or for musical effect. Emphasize that alliteration is common in the English language. In addition to being used in poetry, it is also commonly used in advertising and popular songs.

Check Understanding

Have students read the **Definition** at the bottom of page 424. Then, have the students work in pairs to write their own original lines of alliteration. Suggest that they start with their first names and write one sentence about themselves, using as much alliteration as possible. Ask students to share their creations with the whole class by reading them aloud. Discuss the following:

- What sounds do you hear repeated?
- What feeling does the repetition of that sound evoke?
- What else does the line make you think of?

Allusion

Set Goal

Students will learn that an allusion is a reference to a person, place, or event from history or literature that the writer expects to be familiar to the reader.

Teach and Discuss

Read aloud the **Example** from "On First Looking into Chapman's Homer" on page 425 of the handbook while the students follow along. Ask students to note the allusions to other works. In addition to the references in the annotations, there is an allusion to Darien, the former name of Panama, the isthmus linking South America with Central and North America.

Then read the **Description** with the students. Point out that an allusion is a brief, casual reference. Allusions add layers of meaning to a poem. Emphasize that recognizing allusions helps readers better understand the meaning of a poem. Also stress that the more a student reads, the more allusions he or she will be able to understand or recognize.

Check Understanding

Have students read the **Definition** on page 425. Then, have students work in pairs to brainstorm a list of possible allusions to people, places, or things in their own, contemporary culture. (As an example, you might suggest allusions to the World Trade Center and the events of September 11, 2001.) Have students share their lists with the class. Ask questions such as these for discussion:

- What does this allusion suggest to you? What associations do you make with it?
- How could this allusion be used in a poem?
- Would most readers understand this allusion? What type of reader might not get it?

Consonance

Set Goal

Students will learn that consonance is the repetition of consonant sounds preceded by different vowel sounds.

Teach and Discuss

Read aloud the **Example** on page 426. Ask students to take note of the ending consonant sounds in the highlighted words. Point out that the vowels coming before the consonant sounds differ.

Next, read the **Description** with the students. Emphasize that consonance is almost a rhyme, but not quite. Discuss with students the reason why poets sometimes use consonance. In addition to adding a soft, subtle musical quality to a poem, consonance can be an effective way to link sound, meaning, and mood.

Check Understanding

Have students read the **Definition** at the bottom of page 426. Then, have students work in pairs to create two or four lines of poetry exemplifying consonance. Ask students to share their work with the whole class. Ask them to discuss the following questions:

- What effect does this repetition of sound create in the reader or hearer?
- Is this element easier or more difficult to use than rhyme?

Figurative Language

Set Goal

Students will learn that figurative language is language that goes beyond its literal meaning.

Teach and Discuss

Read aloud the **Example** on page 427 as students follow along. At the end, ask students what the poem seems to be about. Point out that Anne Bradstreet is expressing her feelings about "blemishes" and "defects" that she sees in her own book.

Then, read the **Description**, emphasizing that Bradstreet is actually talking about her book, not her child. This comparison is an example of figurative language. Figurative language shows a relationship between two essentially unlike things. Emphasize that poets use figurative language to create stronger, fresher images in their work. Simile, metaphor, personification, and hyperbole are figures of speech, or devices for achieving figurative language. Ask students:

- What figure of speech is important in "The Author to Her Book"?
- What human qualities are given to the book?

Check Understanding

Ask students to read the **Definition** at the bottom of the page. Then, have students choose, from books in your classroom or school library, poems that look interesting to them and share them in groups of four. After each student reads his or her selected poem aloud to the group, the group members discuss whether they heard figurative language in it. Examples should be jotted down. Students can discuss these questions:

- What type of figurative language is this?
- Why do you think the poet chose to use this device?
- What effect does it have on the reader?

Free Verse

Set Goal

Students will learn that free verse is poetry without a regular rhyme scheme, meter, or form.

Teach and Discuss

Ask for a volunteer to read aloud the **Example** by Frances Chung on page 428 while the other students follow along. Ask students how they know this is free verse.

Next, read the **Description** with the class. Point out that there is no set pattern of rhyme or stress in free verse, but a poem in free verse may use rhythm and other poetic devices. Emphasize that free verse sounds natural or conversational, as if the author is speaking or thinking. Also point out that, in free verse, poets often ignore the conventions of capitalization and punctuation.

Check Understanding

Then have students read the **Definition** at the bottom of page 428. To demonstrate understanding, have students write their own free verse poems. Give them several days to a week to do this. Then, ask them to share their work in small groups. Ask the groups to discuss:

- Is the use of free verse appropriate to what the author is trying to say?
- What would the poem be like if it were rewritten to conform to a set of rules, such as those of a sonnet?

Hyperbole

Set Goal

Students will learn that hyperbole means exaggeration—an obvious stretching of the truth to emphasize a strong feeling or to create a humorous effect.

Teach and Discuss

Have a student volunteer read aloud the **Example** on page 429 of the handbook. Ask the rest of the students to watch for examples of hyperbole.

Then read the **Description** with the students. Point out that students use hyperbole when they stretch the truth to make a point or cause others to laugh. Emphasize that hyperbole is simply another word for exaggeration and that it is used for a purpose. The effect of hyperbole may be serious or humorous.

Check Understanding

Have students read the **Definition** at the bottom of page 429. Then, give them an assignment to complete over the next week. Students can watch for and listen for examples of hyperbole in books, movies, television shows, and real life. They jot down the examples, including where the examples came from. You might want to make it a contest, awarding a small prize to the person or team who brings in the most examples of hyperbole. The examples may be posted on the bulletin board for discussion of questions such as these:

- Why did this person (or character) use hyperbole?
- Did another person or character miss the speaker's exaggeration?
- What would this example sound like if it were rewritten without hyperbole?

Imagery

Set Goal

Students will learn that imagery appeals to the five senses and creates pictures in the reader's imagination.

Teach and Discuss

Ask students to read the **Example** on page 430, and then have a volunteer read it aloud. Have students identify words and phrases in "Theme in Yellow" that appeal to the sense of sight, the sense of touch, and the sense of hearing.

Now, read the **Description** with students. Help them understand that imagery appeals to the five senses and also to feelings within the reader, such as sadness or joy. Point out that poets use sensory details to make images vivid and lively. The effect of imagery is that readers will experience and feel things in a new way.

Often a poet will attempt to create a single image in a stanza or poem as a whole. "Seeing" the images suggested by the words and phrases is often the most challenging part of reading a poem. As students understand the imagery in poems, they will better understand and enjoy the poems themselves.

Check Understanding

Have students read the **Definition** at the bottom of page 430. Then, ask students to work in pairs or small groups to choose poems that appeal to one or more of the five senses. They can use books in your classroom or school library. Groups can share their poems with the rest of the class and discuss the following questions:

- What does the poet picture in the poem?
- To what sense or senses does each image appeal?
- Do any of the images appeal to senses inside the reader, such as hunger or pain?

Inversion

Set Goal

Students will learn that inversion is the placing of a word or part of a sentence out of its normal position. This is done for emphasis, to create mood, or to alter the rhythm of a line.

Teach and Discuss

Read aloud the **Example** from "Kubla Khan" on page 431 as students listen for words or phrases that seem out of place. Ask volunteers to also read the lines aloud.

Next, read the **Description** with the students. The lines that show normal word order and inverted word order illustrate the poetic effect created when the object is put before the verb. Suggest that students read the two lines aloud so that they can hear the different ways they sound. Emphasize that inversion is a technique used for emphasis, to create a certain mood, or to achieve a certain rhythm in a line.

Check Understanding

Have students read the **Definition** at the bottom of page 431. To demonstrate understanding, have students work in pairs to add inversions to the lines of a poem or poems previously read. Here are some questions they can explore:

- What is the effect of the inversion?
- How does the inversion change the rhythm of the line or lines?
- Does inversion make a poem more difficult to understand? Why or why not?

Lyric

Set Goal

Students will learn that a lyric is a poem that directly expresses the speaker's thoughts and feelings in a musical way.

Teach and Discuss

Have students read the **Example** on page 432 from "When I Heard the Learn'd Astronomer." Call attention to the two annotations. Then ask a volunteer to read the lines aloud. After the reading, ask students what they notice about the lines in this poem. How does the poem make them feel?

Then, read the **Description** with the students. Emphasize that a lyric poem expresses thoughts rather than tells a story. Explain that a lyric attempts to create a single, unified impression. Ask students to say words or phrases that help develop the calm feeling in this lyric. In addition to the words listed on the page, they may suggest *moist night-air, from time to time,* and *stars.* Write the words on the chalkboard as they are mentioned.

Check Understanding

Have students read the **Definition** at the bottom of page 432. Then, ask students to choose a favorite lyric from a collection of lyrics. Students can share their favorite lyric in a small group of peers or display it on the bulletin board. They can explore these questions:

- What mood is created in this lyric?
- What is the speaker saying?
- Why do you like this lyric?

Metaphor

Set Goal

Students will learn that a metaphor is a comparison between two unlike things that does not use the word *like* or *as*.

Teach and Discuss

Ask for a volunteer to read aloud the **Example** on page 433 of the handbook. Then, ask students to say in their own words what a *metaphor* is.

Read the **Description** with the students. Have them use the information to explain the comparison Eve Merriam makes in the poem "Metaphor." How is morning like a clean sheet of paper? The idea in this metaphor is that a new day means new opportunities. This idea is conveyed through the image of a clean sheet of paper. Emphasize that metaphors are used to help readers see something in a new and unusual way.

The way we think about things often depends on our metaphors for them. Are our bodies machines or finely tuned instruments? Is our multicultural society a melting pot or a salad bowl? Poets use metaphors to help shape the ways readers imagine—and thus think—about the things that surround us.

Check Understanding

Have students read the **Definition** at the bottom of page 433. Then, as a whole class, ask students to brainstorm a list of metaphors for a subject of their choice, such as love, parents, school, or the future. Get the students started by giving a few examples of your own: love is a tornado, a river, a flower, and so on. After generating the list, discuss the following questions:

- What does this metaphor add to your understanding of the original subject?
- What does this metaphor tell you about the author's thoughts and feelings?
- How does this metaphor make you, the reader, feel about the subject?

Mood

Set Goal

Students will learn that mood is the feeling created by a poem. Mood is developed through carefully chosen words and phrases.

Teach and Discuss

Have students read silently the **Example** on page 434. Ask them to pay special attention to the highlighted words. Then, ask them how the poem made them feel. What mood was created?

Read the **Description** with the students. Point out that the mood is the atmosphere created by the poet. Caution students not to confuse mood with tone, which is the poet's attitude toward the subject of the poem. Emphasize that authors create an overall feeling, or mood, by the words, phrases, and images they choose. Invite students to suggest other moods that poets may create, such as gloomy, calm, or anxious.

Check Understanding

Have students read the **Definition** at the bottom of the page. Then, ask students to choose a poem they like from the classroom or school library. In small groups, have students share the poem they chose and discuss the following:

- What mood is created in this poem?
- Is the mood a quality that made you like the poem?
- How does the author create the mood in this piece?

Onomatopoeia

Set Goal

Students will learn that onomatopoeia is the use of a word with a sound that imitates the meaning of the word.

Teach and Discuss

Ask a student to volunteer to read the **Example** on page 435 of the handbook. Have the rest of the class listen for words that sound like what they mean.

Then, read the **Description** with the students. Point out that poets use the sounds of words to add meaning when they employ onomatopoeia. Emphasize the examples given to help students better understand this concept. Ask them to say the words aloud. Invite students to suggest additional examples (*sizzle, hiss, splash,* and so on).

Check Understanding

Have students read the **Definition** at the bottom of the page. Then, have them work in small groups to brainstorm as many onomatopoeic words as they can. Each group then shares its list with the whole class, discussing the following questions:

- What does the word make you think of?
- What does the word make you feel?
- Why would poets use these words in their poetry?

Personification

Set Goal

Students will learn that personification is the attribution of human qualities to animals, objects, or ideas.

Teach and Discuss

Ask a student volunteer to read aloud the **Example,** a poem by Langston Hughes, on page 436. Point out that the poet is giving human qualities to the rain.

Then read the **Description** with the students. Go over with them the specific human attributes given to the rain in "April Rain Song." Point out that personification is a kind of figurative language because it involves a comparison. Ask students:

- What specific human qualities does Langston Hughes give the rain?
- How do these qualities relate to the way the poet says he feels about rain?

Check Understanding

Have students read the **Definition** at the bottom of page 436. Then, working in pairs, have students choose an object, animal, or idea and personify it in a few lines of writing. (It doesn't have to be a formal poem.) Ask students to share their work with the class and discuss these questions:

- What effect does the personification create?
- What does the personification tell you about the object, animal, or idea?
- What does the personification tell you about the author's attitude toward the subject?

Repetition

Set Goal

Students will learn that repetition is the use more than once of a sound, word, phrase, or sentence.

Teach and Discuss

Have a volunteer read aloud the **Example** on page 437. Ask students to identify the repeated elements in "Someone" by Walter de la Mare. Point out that phrases, sounds, and words are all vehicles used by poets in repetition.

Then, read the **Description** with the students. Ask students to find in the poem examples of rhyme (*right, night; wall, call, fall, all*), alliteration (*listened, looked, left; busy, beetle; tap-tapping*), and consonance (*door, sure*). Emphasize that repetition is a poetic device that helps establish rhythm, emphasize ideas, and set a mood. Repetition is used often in poetry.

Check Understanding

Have students read the **Definition** at the bottom of page 437. Then, working in pairs, have students look for examples of repetition in poetry books from your classroom or school library. Here are some questions they can discuss:

- What is being repeated?
- What effect does the repetition create?
- Why do you think the author used this (or these) repetition(s)?

Rhyme and Rhyme Scheme

Set Goal

Students will learn that rhyme is the repetition of an ending sound, and that a rhyme scheme is the pattern of rhyme in a poem.

Teach and Discuss

Have students turn to page 438 of the handbook and read the **Example** silently. Then, ask students to identify words in the poem that rhyme. Point out that the rhyme is based on the vowel sound and consonants that follow in accented syllables.

Read the **Description** with the students. Ask students to note that rhyming sounds are not necessarily spelled in the same way, as in *unfurled* and *world.* Go over the difference between end rhyme (at the ends of lines in a poem) and internal rhyme (within the same line). Emphasize that rhyming poetry can have different rhyme schemes, and that rhyme schemes are usually designated with letters, such as *abab, cdcd,* and so on. The effect of the rhyming pattern is to create a sense of order.

Check Understanding

Have students read the **Definition** at the bottom of page 438. Then, have students work in pairs or small groups to write a four-line poem about the school using a rhyme scheme of *abab* or *abba.* Ask volunteers to share their poems. (You may display the poems on the bulletin board.) Discuss the following:

- What is the rhyme scheme?
- What effect does the rhyme scheme create?
- What other rhyme schemes can you imagine?

Rhythm

Set Goal

Students will learn that rhythm is the musical quality of a poem created by a pattern of stressed and unstressed syllables.

Teach and Discuss

Read aloud the **Example** on page 439, exaggerating the stressed syllables so that students can easily hear the rhythm. Invite students to join in and read aloud the last stanza with you.

Now read the **Description** with the students. Point out that the rhythm in "Stopping by Woods on a Snowy Evening" is regular, with an unstressed syllable followed by a stressed syllable. In other patterns, there may be one stressed syllable followed by an unstressed one or a stressed syllable followed by two unstressed syllables. Even free verse will have its own kind of rhythm. Emphasize the connection between rhythm in poetry and rhythm in music.

Check Understanding

Have students read the **Definition** at the bottom of page 439. In small groups, have students choose a different poem by Robert Frost and attempt to mark the stressed and unstressed syllables. Have a volunteer from each group read one or two lines aloud to the whole class, exaggerating the stressed syllables. Here are some good questions for discussion:

- Was it difficult to figure out the rhythm? If so, why?
- Why is rhythm important to the poem?
- What effects do different rhythms create in readers?

Simile

Set Goal

Students will learn that a simile is a comparison between two unlike things using the word *like* or the word *as*.

Teach and Discuss

Have students turn to page 440 of the handbook and read the **Example** silently. Then, ask students to point out the comparisons made in the two poems, "Lost" by Carl Sandburg and "Stars" by Gary Soto. The annotations and highlighted words provide clues.

Read through the **Description** with the students. Point out that a simile is a figure of speech expressing a similarity between two unlike things. Similes are one kind of figurative language. Both an image and an idea are expressed in a simile. Emphasize that identifying similes is fairly easy because the word *like* or *as* is used. Ask students to say how a simile differs from a metaphor.

Check Understanding

Have students read the **Definition** at the bottom of page 440. Then, have students work with partners to come up with their own similes. First, brainstorm a list of prompts, such as, "Her eyes were like ______." "He was as funny as ______." Have students generate as many similes as they can; then ask for volunteers to share their similes with the whole class. Discuss the following:

- How are the two things similar?
- What does the simile say about the original subject?
- Why would writers use similes?

Stanza

Set Goal

Students will learn that a stanza is two or more lines of poetry arranged into regular patterns of length, rhythm, and often rhyme scheme. Usually, stanzas contain different images, ideas, or thoughts.

Teach and Discuss

Have students turn to page 441 of the handbook and silently read the **Example.** Then, ask how the poem is organized. How many stanzas are there, and how many lines in each stanza?

Read through the **Description** with the students. Point out the connection between the meaning "to stand" or "to stay" and the function of a stanza as a single unit. Also help students understand what a stanza is by talking about how it is like a paragraph in prose. Emphasize that a stanza often contains its own idea, thought, or feeling. Go over the names for the different kinds of stanzas.

Check Understanding

Have students read the **Definition** at the bottom of page 441. Then, have students work in pairs to find poems with at least two stanzas. Ask students to discuss:

- What idea, thought, or feeling changes between stanzas?
- What kind of stanza is it (couplet, tercet, quatrain, quintet, sestet, septet, or octet)?
- Why might the poet have organized the poem in this way?

Symbol

Set Goal

Students will learn that a symbol is something concrete that stands for something abstract, such as an idea or feeling.

Teach and Discuss

Read aloud the **Example** on page 442. Ask students what symbol they noticed in this poem by John Crowe Ransom. The highlighted words will help them identify the symbol.

Read the **Description** with the students. Talk about common symbols in everyday life, such as a flag, a traffic sign indicating two lanes are merging into one, or a sign pointing toward a hospital. Emphasize that a symbol is usually something concrete—a thing, a person, or a place—that represents or stands for something abstract—an idea or emotion. Literary symbols can be universal, such as a flying bird for freedom or a scale for justice, or they can be specific to a particular work.

Check Understanding

Have students read the **Definition** at the bottom of page 442. Then, in small groups, have students brainstorm a list of objects, places, or people in their lives that symbolize something abstract. For example, their house or apartment might symbolize safety or a feeling of being trapped. Here are some good questions for small-group discussion:

- What does the object, place, or person symbolize?
- What might it symbolize in someone else's life?
- How might you use that symbol in a poem?

Tone

Set Goal

Students will learn that tone is the attitude that the writer or speaker has toward the subject or audience.

Teach and Discuss

Read aloud the **Example** from "The Weary Blues" on page 443 while the students follow along silently. Then, ask students to say how they think the author or speaker feels about his subject matter.

Read through the **Description** with the students. Point out that common words to describe the tone of a poem include *serious, solemn, joking, spirited*, and *casual.* Emphasize that tone is not the same as mood. Sometimes the tone in a literary work is evident, and sometimes the reader has to hunt for clues to figure it out. Ask students:

- What clues in the lines from "The Weary Blues" point to the poet's tone?
- The tone can be described as respectful, or appreciative and enthusiastic. What other words can you suggest to describe the tone?
- What does understanding the poet's tone add to your understanding of the poem overall?

Check Understanding

Have students read the **Definition** at the bottom of page 443. Then, have students work with partners to identify the tone in other poems by Langston Hughes. Partners can discuss the following:

- What is the poet's attitude toward his subject and audience in this poem?
- How can you tell what his attitude is?
- What effects does the tone have on the reader?

Reading Drama

Introduction to Reading Drama

Ask students to name a few plays they have read for a class or seen performed. Point out that reading a play is different from seeing one performed because readers must picture in their minds what the characters and scenes look like, as well as "hear" the way the lines are spoken by the characters. Direct students to read page 446. Then, talk with them about the important points made, such as the tradition of telling stories that evolved into current-day plays and the things that make reading a play one of the easiest reading assignments.

Reading a Play

Goals

In this lesson, students will read an excerpt from *The Miracle Worker* by William Gibson. Students will learn to:

- ✔ understand and appreciate the genre of drama
- ✔ use the reading strategy of summarizing
- ✔ understand the structure of plays

Background

Help students connect this lesson with their prior knowledge by asking them to:

- define *drama*
- give examples of plays they have seen or read
- discuss what they like and what they dislike about reading plays
- talk about plays they have seen or read that they liked and say why they liked these plays

Opening Activity

Explain to students that plays tell stories through dialogue and action. Reading a play, then, is different from reading a novel or short story and requires different strategies and skills. Tell students that they will learn some helpful strategies for reading drama in the current lesson.

Overview

	Content	Teacher's Guide page	Reader's Handbook page
Selection	from *The Miracle Worker* by William Gibson		449–451, 454–455, 461–462, 463, 465
Reading Strategy	Summarizing	299, 438	452, 730
Rereading Strategy	Visualizing and Thinking Aloud	303, 440	466, 736
Tool	Summary Notes Magnet Summary Character Map Plot Diagram Storyboard	299, 300 300 300 301 303	453, 456, 754 457, 747 459, 460, 740 464, 750 467, 753

Ancillaries

	Grade	Content	Page
Overhead Transparency	9–12	Previewing a Play	Numbers 29 and 30
Lesson Plan Book	9 10 11 12	Reading a Play Reading a Play Reading a Play Reading a Play	155, 160–163 165, 170–173 164, 166–169 164, 166–169
Student Applications Book	9 10 11 12	from *Oedipus the King* by Sophocles from *A Doll's House* by Henrik Ibsen from *Beyond the Horizon* by Eugene O'Neill from *Caesar and Cleopatra* by George Bernard Shaw	166–174 165–174 161–171 163–172
Test Book	9–12	Short-answer Test Multiple-answer Test	
Website		www.greatsource.com/rehand/	

Before Reading

Set a Purpose

First, students need to set a purpose for reading. Direct students to the Setting a Purpose questions on page 448 of the *Reader's Handbook*.

Setting a Purpose

- **What is the setting?**
- **What are the main characters like, and what is the relationship between them?**
- **What motivates the characters?**
- **What is the central conflict, and how is it resolved?**
- **What is the theme?**

B Preview

Remind students of the importance of previewing before reading. Using the Preview Checklist on page 448 of the handbook, have students preview the parts of the play on pages 449–451. Point out that the annotations will help them find what to look for in previewing.

Preview Checklist

✓ *the front and back covers and title page*
✓ *the cast of characters*
✓ *the number of acts and scenes*
✓ *any information about the general setting and staging*

The front and back covers show the title and author. Often they provide information about the action and characters as well as comments from reviewers. The title page repeats the title, shows the number of acts, and includes remarks made by Annie Sullivan. In addition, students can preview the cast of characters and a description of the setting.

Overhead Transparencies

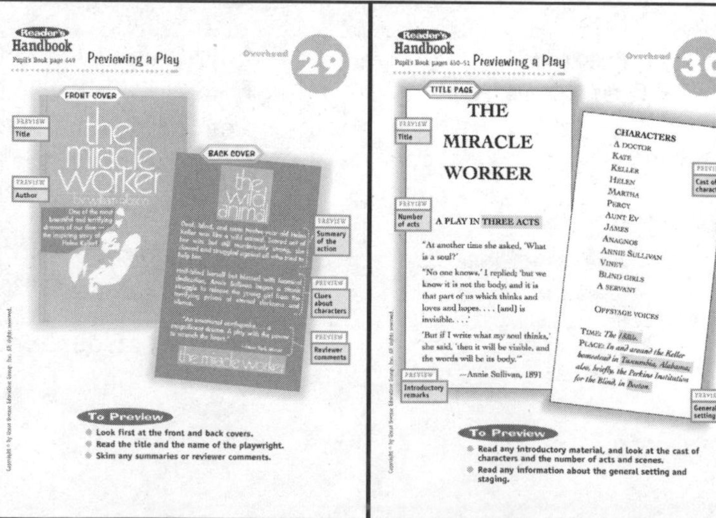

C Plan

Ask students to sum up what they learned about the play during their preview. Invite students to answer the questions at the top of page 452. Emphasize that the information readers learn from previewing the play helps decide on and formulate make a plan for reading.

Reading Strategy: Summarizing

Now introduce the strategy of **summarizing.** Explain that this is a good strategy for reading drama because it helps students keep track of setting changes, character traits and relationships, the sequence of events, and themes.

Emphasize that summarizing means retelling only the main points or most important information in their own words. Explain that knowing what's most important is not always easy. Graphic organizers can help students know what's most important in a play.

Have students look at the Summary Notes on page 453. Emphasize that this is an excellent tool for effective summarizing.

During Reading

D Read with a Purpose

Now students are ready to read. Remind them that they need to read for a purpose. Remind them of the questions, listed on page 453, for which they need answers. Suggest using sticky notes or, if possible, a highlighter to mark the pertinent information.

1. Summary Notes

When students are finished reading the passage on pages 454–455, have them look at and read through the completed Summary Notes on page 456.

2. Magnet Summary

Encourage students to then create a Magnet Summary, as shown on page 457.

MAGNET SUMMARY

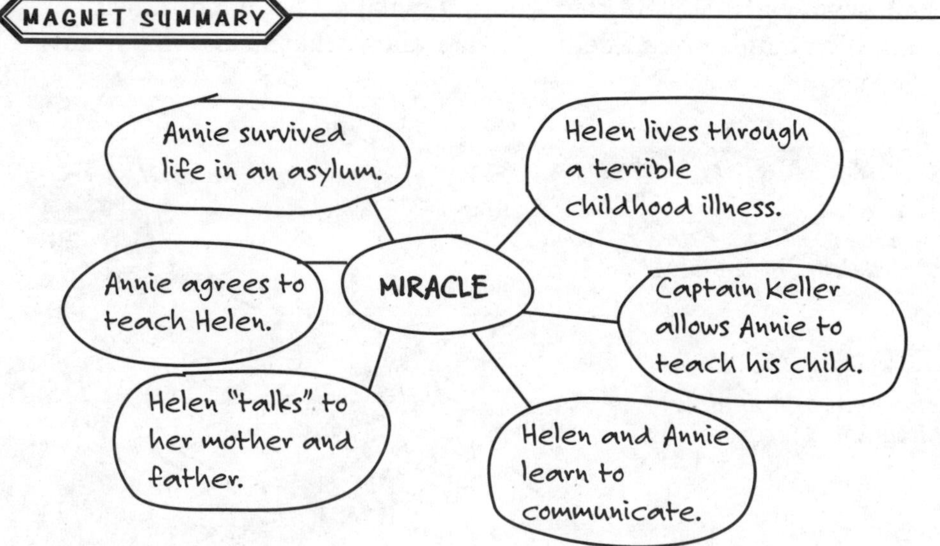

Help students see how completing the graphic organizers enables them to write effective summaries. Read the Summary on page 458. It shows how the details can be collected during reading and used afterward to write the theme statement.

3. Character Map

Another useful tool for reading drama is the Character Map. This graphic organizer is useful for analyzing a character and seeing how others feel about that character. Examples are provided on pages 459 and 460 for Captain Keller, Annie, and Kate Keller.

Have students read the excerpt on pages 461 and 462, taking note of important information about the characters in *The Miracle Worker.* The information on these pages is used in the Character Maps on page 460. Also point out the mention of the garden house on page 461, which helps establish the setting.

How Plays Are Organized

Explain to students that almost all plays are divided into acts and scenes. A scene change often indicates a change in setting—in time, place, or both. Point out that *The Miracle Worker* contains three acts. In this play the scenes are not labeled; instead, a change in lighting signals the start of a new scene.

Like other types of fiction, drama typically consists of five parts: exposition, rising action, climax, falling action, and resolution. Ask students to turn to page 464 in their handbooks and read the actions plotted on the Plot Diagram.

PLOT DIAGRAM

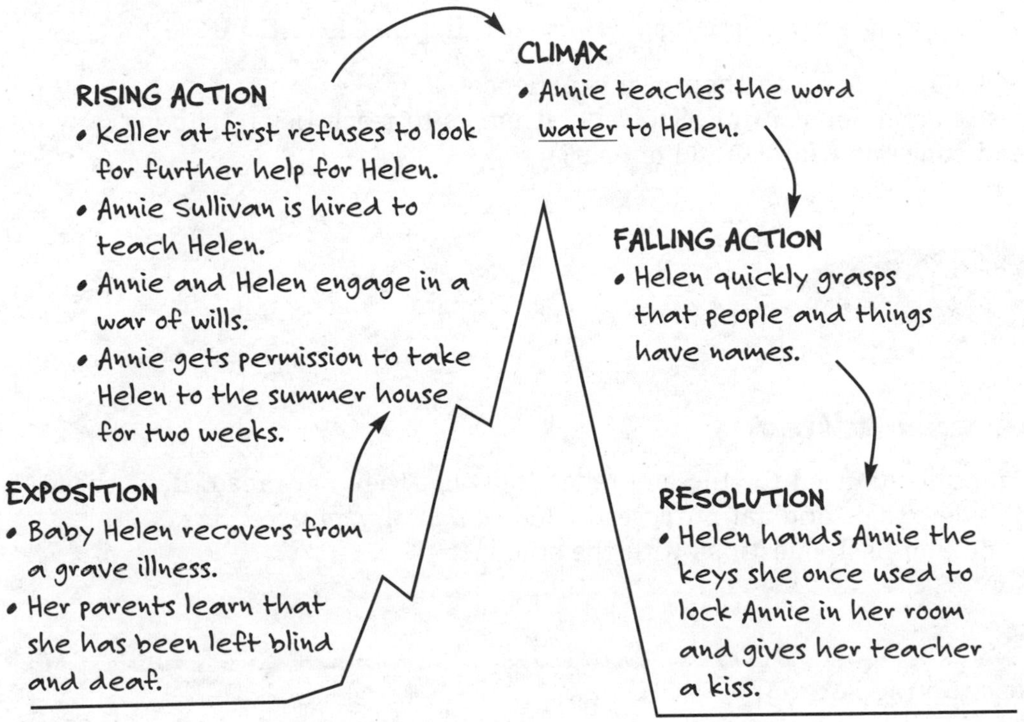

EXPOSITION

- Baby Helen recovers from a grave illness.
- Her parents learn that she has been left blind and deaf.

RISING ACTION

- Keller at first refuses to look for further help for Helen.
- Annie Sullivan is hired to teach Helen.
- Annie and Helen engage in a war of wills.
- Annie gets permission to take Helen to the summer house for two weeks.

CLIMAX

- Annie teaches the word water to Helen.

FALLING ACTION

- Helen quickly grasps that people and things have names.

RESOLUTION

- Helen hands Annie the keys she once used to lock Annie in her room and gives her teacher a kiss.

During Reading

E Connect

Remind students that responding to what they read or making connections as they read is very important. Good readers actively try to relate and respond to what they read. Have students look at the reactions of one reader, illustrated by the sticky notes on page 465.

You can also help students connect by telling them to:

- ask themselves questions
  (How would I feel if I were in Annie's situation?)
- think about the meaning of the play
  (What is the message about sticking with something that is difficult?)
- compare what they learn to their own experience
  (How does reading about Annie Sullivan's attempts to reach Helen help me understand someone who is blind or deaf?)

After Reading

F Pause and Reflect

After reading, students need to stop and reflect on what they have read. Have them go back and review their original purposes in *The Miracle Worker* excerpts. Go over the Looking Back questions with the students.

Looking Back

- **Can I describe the setting?**
- **Can I describe the main characters and their motivations?**
- **Can I retell the central conflict and summarize the plot?**
- **Do I understand the main message, or theme, of the play?**
- **Can I explain what I did and did not like about the reading and support my opinion with evidence?**

Students may still be uncertain of the answers to some of these questions. Therefore, they need to return to the play and reread for clarification and additional information.

G Reread

Encourage students to return to the play with a different strategy or tool so that they can get a fresh look at it. Introduce the strategy of visualizing and thinking aloud.

Rereading Strategy: Visualizing and Thinking Aloud

Explain that the strategy of **visualizing and thinking aloud** is especially good for reading a play because a play is meant to be seen and heard. Have students think about what the setting of *The Miracle Worker* would look like and what the characters would look and sound like.

Show them the example of the Storyboard created by one reader, shown on page 467. This tool, as well as sketching in general, can help students better visualize the action of the play.

H Remember

After rereading, it is time for students to make the play "their own." Have students do one of the activities given on page 468 of the *Reader's Handbook* or the creative assignment below.

Creative Assignment: Have students imagine that they are putting on a production of *The Miracle Worker.* Form small groups based on which job students would like to do: design the set, design the costumes, create posters, or decide which current-day movie or TV star will play which role and create the playbill.

Summing Up

Review the lesson by reading over the Summing Up on page 468 of the handbook. Talk about the tools covered in this lesson: Summary Notes, Magnet Summary, Character Map, Plot Diagram, and Storyboard. Go over the initial goals for the lesson. Discuss which ones students feel they achieved and which ones that they need more work on:

1. **understanding and appreciating the genre of drama**
2. **using the reading strategy of summarizing**
3. **understanding the structure of plays**

Assessment and Application

Use the Quick Assess checklist to evaluate students' ability to read and understand a play. Give students the opportunity to apply what they have learned through one of the two activities below. For students who are comfortable with the reading process and strategy, use the suggestion for independent practice or an activity of your own. For students who need guided help with the strategy, use a *Student Applications Book*.

Quick Assess

Can students

- explain how a play differs from novels and short stories?
- explain why summarizing and visualizing and thinking aloud are good reading and rereading strategies for a play?
- name two or three useful tools for reading a play?

1. Independent Practice

To show that they understand the lesson, students can apply the strategy of **summarizing** or the strategy of **visualizing and thinking aloud** to a play of their choice.

Ask students to:

- Complete Summary Notes while reading the play.
- Apply the strategy of visualizing and thinking aloud, using a Storyboard.
- Complete a Character Map for each major character in the play.

2. Student Applications Books

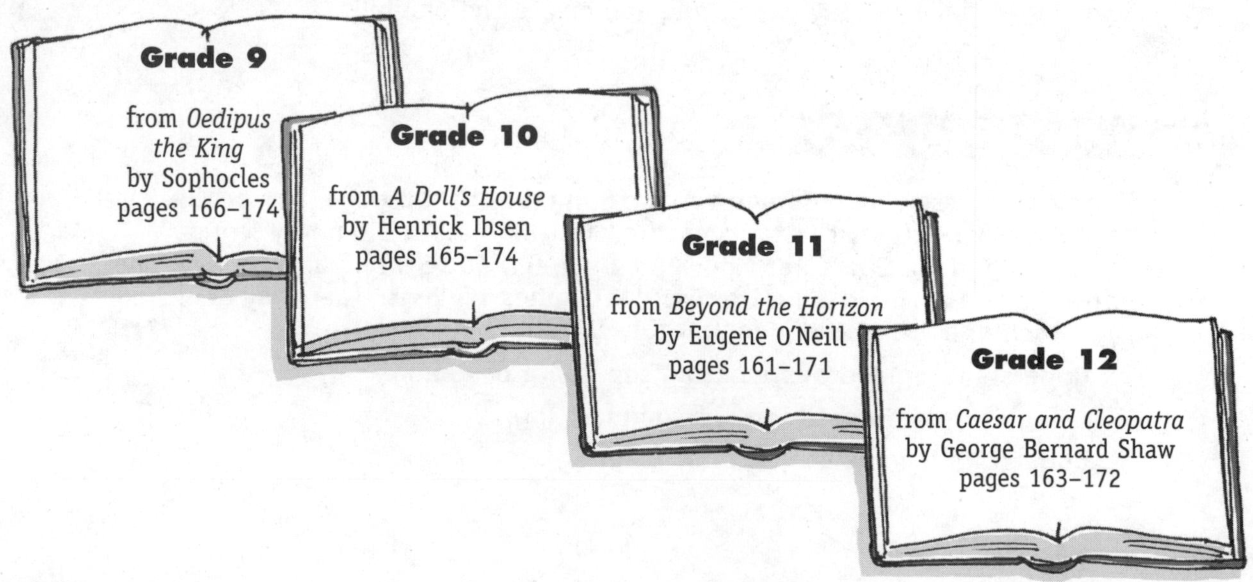

Test Book

See *Test Book* for short-answer and multiple-choice tests.

Focus on Language

Goals

Here students will focus on language in a play. This lesson will help them learn to:

- find the key lines and speeches in a play
- understand how the stage directions contribute to a play
- examine how dialogue reveals characters, plot, and theme

Background

Remind students that in a play the story unfolds primarily through dialogue. Help students connect this lesson with their prior knowledge by asking them to:

- name plays that they have seen or read
- discuss the challenges of reading (as opposed to seeing) a play

Overview

	Content	Teacher's Guide page	Reader's Handbook page
Selection	from *The Miracle Worker* by William Gibson		470, 471, 472, 473, 474, 475
Tool	Inference Chart	307	473, 746
	Paraphrase Chart	308	476, 749

Ancillaries

	Grade	Content	Page
Lesson Plan Book	9	Focus on Language and Theme	164, 166–169
	12	Focus on Language	165, 170–173
Student Applications Book	9	from *Oedipus the King* by Sophocles	175–176
	10	from *A Doll's House* by Henrick Ibsen	175–177
	11	from *Beyond the Horizon* by Eugene O'Neill	172–173
	12	from *Caesar and Cleopatra* by George Bernard Shaw	173–174
Test Book	9–12	Short-answer Test	
		Multiple-answer Test	
Website		www.greatsource.com/rehand/	

Before Reading

Explain to students that focusing on the language in a play means they must go back and reread parts of the dialogue. However, they don't necessarily have to examine every word. Emphasize that students will be focusing on three elements: key lines and speeches; stage directions; and dialogue as a clue to character, plot, and theme.

During Reading

Let students know that on their first reading of a play, they should mark passages of dialogue that seem important, either with a highlighter or with sticky notes. Then, on the second reading, students will be able to find important passages more easily.

1. Key Lines and Speeches

Have students read the excerpt from *The Miracle Worker* on page 470. Emphasize that key lines and speeches often occur during tense moments between characters.

2. Stage Directions

Explain that reading stage directions is more important than students may initially think. Just because this text is in parentheses does not mean that students can skip it. In *The Miracle Worker,* especially, the stage directions provide the only clues to what Helen is thinking and feeling. Have students read the excerpt on page 471 to exemplify this.

3. Dialogue

Emphasize that students need to be sure they understand and think about what is being said. Point out that dialogue serves at least three purposes:

- establishes character
- advances the plot
- reveals the theme(s)

Dialogue and Character

Emphasize that playwrights work hard to get their dialogue to sound right. Characters have to speak as real people would speak and also sound different from one another. Ask students to read the excerpt on the bottom of page 472 and top of page 473, noting clues in the dialogue that characterize James and Annie.

Then, have students look at the completed Inference Chart at the bottom of page 473. Explain that this tool is especially useful for making inferences about characters in a play.

INFERENCE CHART

TEXT	WHAT I CONCLUDE
"James: Sooner or later, we all give up, don't we?"	James is easily defeated. He is really referring to the fact that he feels defeated by his father.
"Annie: Maybe you all do. It's my idea of the original sin."	Annie is determined and focused.
"James: Why can't you let her be? Have some—pity on her, for being what she is—"	James has given up on Helen and thinks she's learned all she'll ever learn.

Dialogue and Plot

Explain that dialogue also advances the plot of a play. Characters' speeches and interactions with one another make things happen. Have students read the excerpt on page 474, noting how this dialogue moves the plot forward.

Dialogue and Themes

Emphasize that dialogue also reveals the themes of the play. Students should pay close attention to dialogue in which a main character makes a strong statement about the world, society, or people in general. In addition, students should take note of moments when a character has a deep insight or recognizes a change in himself or herself. Have students read the excerpt on page 475 to see an example of this.

After Reading

After reading, students need to take a moment to reflect on what they have learned. Students can ask themselves, "What are the most memorable scenes and speeches in the play?"

Have students read through the completed Paraphrase Chart on page 476. Encourage them to use a tool such as this one to better remember what they read.

PARAPHRASE CHART

TEXT	MY PARAPHRASE
"Annie: Let me keep her to what she's learned and she'll go on learning from me. Take her out of my hands, and it all comes apart."	Annie tells the Kellers that they must listen to what she says about Helen. Otherwise, Helen will stay locked in her silent world.
MY THOUGHTS I agree with what Annie says, and I can't understand why the Kellers fight her so much. I think they feel sorry for Helen, but she needs to learn.	

Summing Up

Have students read the points in Summing Up at the bottom of page 476. Ask students to say in their own words what they learned in this lesson.

Assessment and Application

Use the Quick Assess checklist to evaluate students' ability to understand language in plays. Give students the opportunity to apply what they have learned through one of the two activities below. For students who are comfortable with the reading process, use the suggestion for independent practice or an activity of your own. For students who need guided help, use a *Student Applications Book.*

Quick Assess

Can students

- ☑ say why understanding dialogue in a play is so important?
- ☑ explain why readers need to pay attention to the stage directions in a play?
- ☑ name one or two tools that are useful for focusing on language in drama?

1. Independent Practice

To show that students understand the lesson, they can apply an Inference Chart or a Paraphrase Chart to the dialogue of another play.

2. Student Applications Books

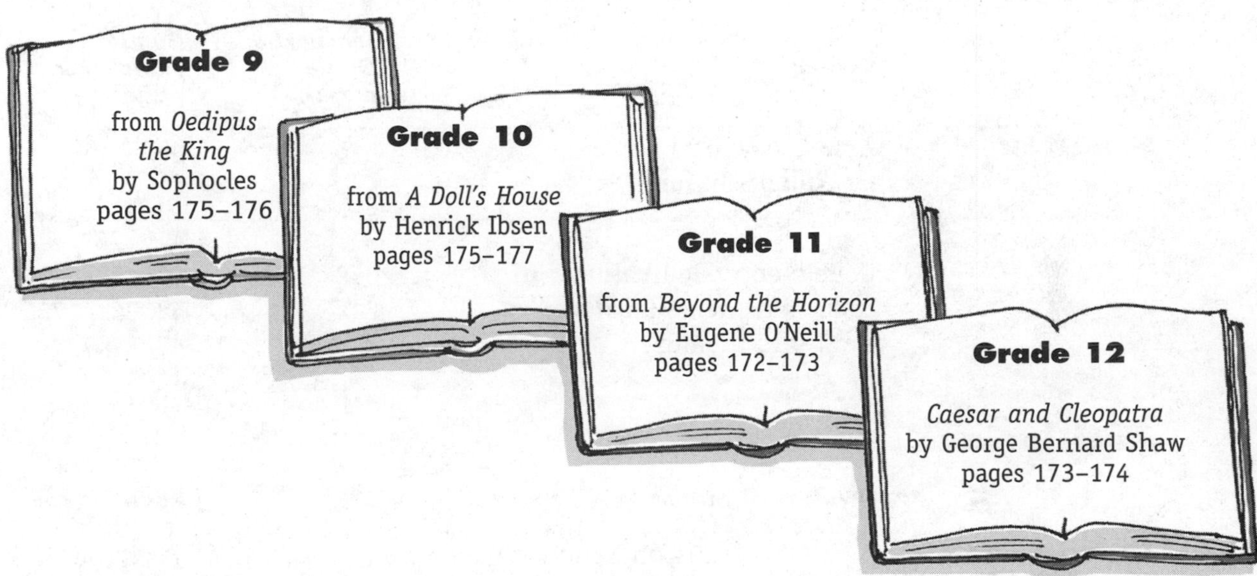

Test Book

See *Test Book* for short-answer and multiple-choice tests.

Focus on Theme

Goals

Now students will focus on understanding theme in a play. This lesson will help students to:

- recognize the themes of a play
- use a three-step plan for understanding the themes
- understand how plot, characters, and dialogue offer clues to theme

Background

Help students connect this lesson with their existing knowledge by asking them to:

- name some common themes found in literature
- discuss what readers can do to figure out the theme

Overview

	Content	Teacher's Guide page	Reader's Handbook page
Selection	from *The Miracle Worker* by William Gibson		480
Tool	Web	311	479, 757
	Double-entry Journal	312	481, 743
	Topic and Theme Organizer	312	481–482, 755
	Main Idea Organizer	313	484, 747

Ancillaries

	Grade	Content	Page
Lesson Plan Book	9	Focus on Language and Theme	164, 166–169
	11	Focus on Theme	165, 170–173
	12	Focus on Theme	174, 176–179
Student Applications Book	9	from *Oedipus the King* by Sophocles	177–179
	10	from *A Doll's House* by Henrick Ibsen	178–179
	11	from *Beyond the Horizon* by Eugene O'Neill	174–175
	12	from *Caesar and Cleopatra* by George Bernard Shaw	175–177
Test Book	9–12	Short-answer Test Multiple-answer Test	
Website		www.greatsource.com/rehand/	

Before Reading

Remind students that the theme of a play is the playwright's message to the audience. In drama, as in other forms of literature, the theme is usually not stated. Readers must piece together clues to discover it. They need to infer the theme from all of the evidence provided. Let students know that identifying theme is made easier by following a three-step plan. The steps are summarized at the bottom of page 477.

Step 1: Find the major ideas, topics, or symbols.

First, students need to determine the topic or big idea of the play. Usually, the topic is clear after a simple preview of the title, first several lines, and any background information or summaries. You may want to refer students to the front and back covers shown on page 449.

Read through the process of determining the topic of *The Miracle Worker* on page 478. Have students note the list of topics written by one reader, appearing at the bottom of the page.

During Reading

Let students know that, during reading, they should look for clues about the playwright's message. One source of clues can be repeated words or symbols.

Read through the section on page 479 with the students to model the process of noting repeated words and symbols. Have students examine the Web created by one reader, which appears on the page.

WEB

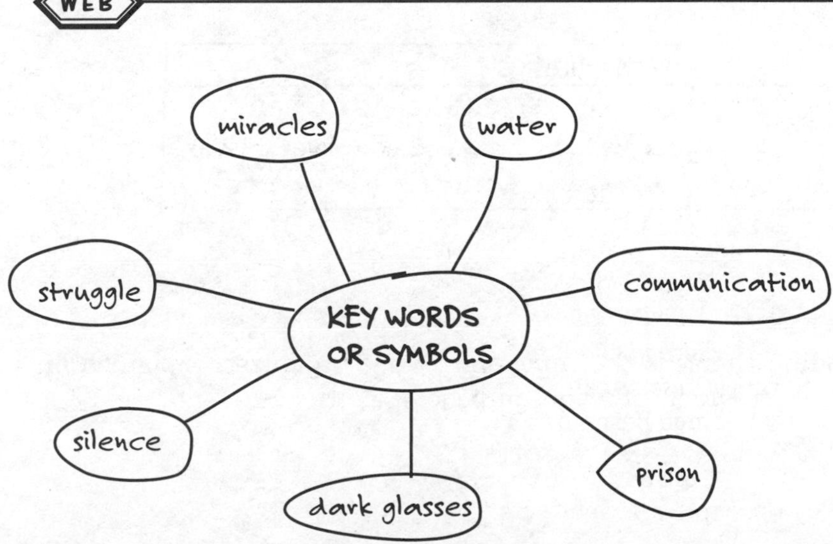

Step 2: Find out what the characters do and say that relates to the general topics or symbols.

Emphasize to the students that they need to pay close attention to what the characters say or do that relates to the general topic of the play. Read through the description of this on page 480.

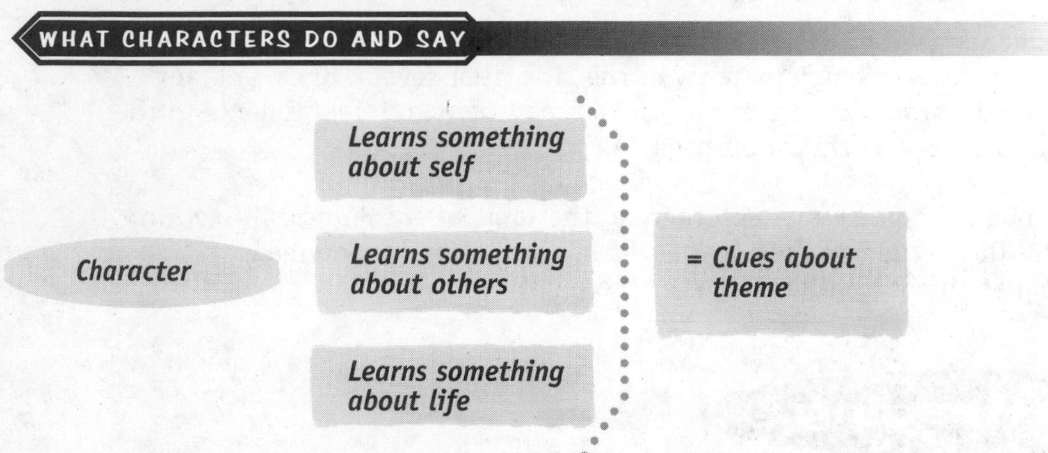

Interpreting Characters

Have students read the excerpt at the bottom of page 480. Then have them read through the Double-entry Journal on page 481 for an example of how to record their thoughts about what characters say.

DOUBLE-ENTRY JOURNAL

QUOTE	MY THOUGHTS
"I'll give you two weeks in this place, and it will be a miracle if you get the child to tolerate you."	Keller wants a miracle, and Annie seems to think she can deliver. I think she might be "The Miracle Worker."

Interpreting the Theme

Another useful tool for finding theme is the Topic and Theme Organizer, explained on page 481. Have students look at the illustration on page 482.

After reading, students should review the clues they've found and decide what they mean. Remind students that the theme is the author's point about the topic of the play.

Step 3: Come up with a statement of the playwright's point or message about the topic.

Have students turn to page 483 in the handbook. At this point they should ask themselves, "What is the playwright telling me about miracles?" Direct their attention to the organizer.

Finally, ask students to look at the Main Idea Organizer on page 484. Explain that this tool is useful for organizing the important details that support the statement of theme. It also ensures that students will find some evidence to support their idea about what the theme is.

MAIN IDEA ORGANIZER

THEME: People can make their own miracles.		
DETAIL #1	DETAIL #2	DETAIL #3
Annie manages to overcome her past and becomes a happy, successful adult.	Annie uses her wits and hard work to give language to Helen.	Helen overcomes challenges and learns how to communicate with the world.

Summing Up

Have students read the points in the Summing Up at the bottom of page 484. Then, ask students to say in their own words what they learned in this lesson.

Assessment and Application

Use the Quick Assess checklist to evaluate students' ability to find the theme of a play. Give students the opportunity to apply what they have learned through one of the two activities below. For students who are comfortable with the reading process, use the suggestion for independent practice or an activity of your own. For students who need guided help with the strategy, use a *Student Applications Book.*

Quick Assess

Can students

- define *theme*?
- explain the different steps readers should follow to identify the theme in a play?
- name two or three tools that are useful for organizing a reader's thoughts on theme?

1. Independent Practice

To practice using the lesson, students can apply the three-step plan to understanding the theme in a play of their choice.

2. Student Applications Books

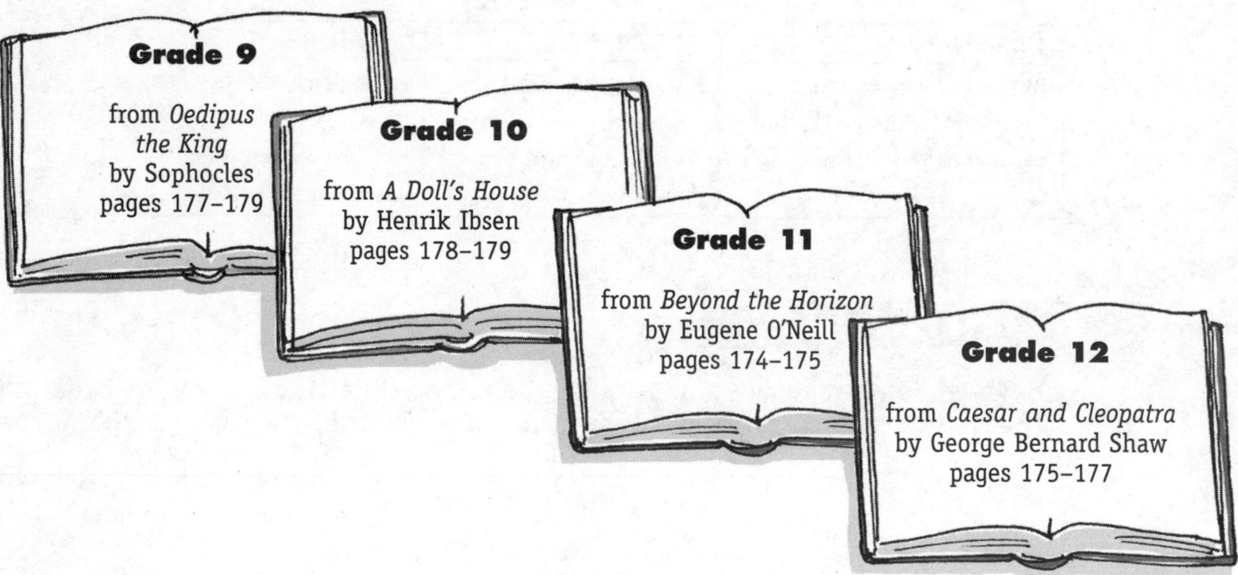

Test Book

See *Test Book* for short-answer and multiple-choice tests.

Focus on Shakespeare

Goals

Here students will focus on reading Shakespeare. This lesson will help them learn to:

- understand Shakespeare's language and style
- practice the reading strategy of using graphic organizers
- focus on some of Shakespeare's topics and themes

Background

Help students connect this lesson with their prior knowledge by asking them to:

- discuss Shakespearean plays they know about
- talk about famous lines they've heard from Shakespeare

Overview

	Content	Teacher's Guide page	Reader's Handbook page
Selection	from *Romeo and Juliet* by William Shakespeare		487–488, 489, 490, 492, 497
Reading Strategy	Using Graphic Organizers	317, 439	491, 734
Tool	Summary Notes	317	492, 754
	Setting Chart	318	494, 752
	Plot Diagram	318	494, 750
	Character Development Chart	318	494, 740
	Web	318	495, 757
	Cause-Effect Organizer	318	496, 739
	Paraphrase Chart	318	497, 749

Ancillaries

	Grade	Content	Page
Lesson Plan Book	9	Focus on Shakespeare	165, 170–173
	10	Focus on Shakespeare	174, 176–179
	11	Focus on Shakespeare	174, 176–179
Student Applications Book	9	from *A Midsummer Night's Dream*	180–181
	10	from *The Merchant of Venice*	180–181
	11	from *Hamlet, Prince of Denmark*	176–177
	12	from *Othello, the Moor of Venice*	178–179
Test Book	9–12	Short-answer Test/Multiple-choice Test	
Website		www.greatsource.com/rehand/	

Before Reading

Remind students that before reading they need to have a plan. Direct students' attention to the reading plan on page 486. Suggest that first they read the entire play for sense and then reread key scenes for specifics.

Read through the Preview Checklist on page 486 with students. Then ask students to preview the excerpt from *Romeo and Juliet* on pages 487 and 488. The annotations will help them find the preview items from the checklist.

Preview Checklist

- ✓ *the title*
- ✓ *any background information, summaries, or illustrations*
- ✓ *the cast of characters (here called the dramatis personae)*
- ✓ *the location and numbering of notes*
- ✓ *the characters in capital letters*
- ✓ *the stage directions in italic type*

During Reading

Remind students that on their first reading they read the entire play for a sense of what's going on, what the characters are like, and what the characters' motivations are. You may want to tell them that making sense of Shakespeare can sometimes be difficult.

Read for Sense

Acknowledge to students that the language of Shakespeare probably sounds odd and confusing to people today. Ask students to read the excerpt on page 489 to get a general sense of what Nurse is saying. Point out the definitions of terms and phrases given at the bottom of the page. Encourage students to read the passage first and then go back to skim, inserting the definitions for the terms and phrases that caused confusion.

Focus on Speeches

Now have students read the passage on page 490. Let students know that this is an important moment in the play. Speeches that are highly emotional, that signal a turning point in the action, or that reveal a character's future plans usually are important in a play. Have students read the passage as they did the previous one. Call students' attention to the footnoted definitions.

Shakespeare's Language

Now take a moment to read through the chart on page 491 of words that were common during Shakespeare's time. Invite students to imagine how our language might sound in another 400 years.

Reading Strategy: Using Graphic Organizers

Suggest the reading strategy of **using graphic organizers** for Shakespearean plays. Begin by showing students the Summary Notes on page 492. Emphasize that this organizer will help students better comprehend what's going on as well as help them keep track of the characters.

SUMMARY NOTES

ACT AND SCENE: Act 1, scene 2
MAIN POINT: Capulet agrees that Paris can marry Juliet if she accepts the match.
1. Capulet invites Paris to a feast. 2. Romeo and Benvolio find out about the feast. 3. Capulet's servant says they can attend if they are not Montagues, but Romeo is a Montague. 4. Benvolio and Romeo decide to attend, Romeo in hopes of seeing Rosaline, his beloved.

Shakespeare's Style

Another reason why Shakespeare's plays are challenging is that most of the dialogue is written in verse. Point this out to students, and explain that servants and commoners speak in prose, while everyone else speaks in verse.

Read the description of Shakespeare's style on page 492. Then have a student volunteer read aloud the sample of verse.

Three tips appear at the top of page 493. Read through these tips with students.

After Reading

After reading, students need to take a moment to reflect. Although at this point they will have a general idea of the play and its characters, they will need to reread for clarification and specifics.

Read for Specifics

On the second read, students will need to use additional graphic organizers. Show students the examples of the Setting Chart, Plot Diagram, and Character Development Chart on page 494.

Shakespeare's Topics

Love

Remind students that they need to understand the theme of the play in order to fully appreciate it. Let them know that Shakespeare's favorite topic was love. He commented on this topic in many different works, some comedic and some tragic.

Point out the example of the Web on the bottom of page 495. This is how one reader worked out what, specifically, Shakespeare was saying about love in *Romeo and Juliet.*

Revenge

Another one of Shakespeare's favorite topics is revenge. Sometimes it is the major plot, and sometimes it is a subplot. Show students the Cause-Effect Organizer used to explore the topic of revenge in *Romeo and Juliet.*

Shakespeare's "Voice"

Point out to students that Shakespeare creates music with words in his plays. Invite students to "listen" to this music by reading the excerpt on the top of page 497. Ask students to read it silently first, and then ask for volunteers to read the passage aloud.

Now have students examine the Paraphrase Chart. Invite students to share their thoughts and feelings about the excerpt they just read.

Summing Up

Have students read the points in the Summing Up on page 498. Ask students to say in their own words what they learned in this lesson.

Assessment and Application

Use the Quick Assess checklist to evaluate students' ability to understand a Shakespearean play. Give students the opportunity to apply what they have learned through one of the two activities below. For students who are comfortable with the reading process and strategy of using graphic organizers, use the suggestion for independent practice or an activity of your own. For students who need guided help with the strategy, use a *Student Applications Book*.

Quick Assess

Can students

- ☑ name a few reasons why reading a Shakespearean play is challenging?
- ☑ describe the plan for reading a Shakespearean play?
- ☑ name two or three graphic organizers that will help them better make sense of a Shakespearean play?

1. Independent Practice

To show that they understand the lesson, students can apply one of the graphic organizers described to a Shakespearean play in your curriculum.

2. Student Applications Books

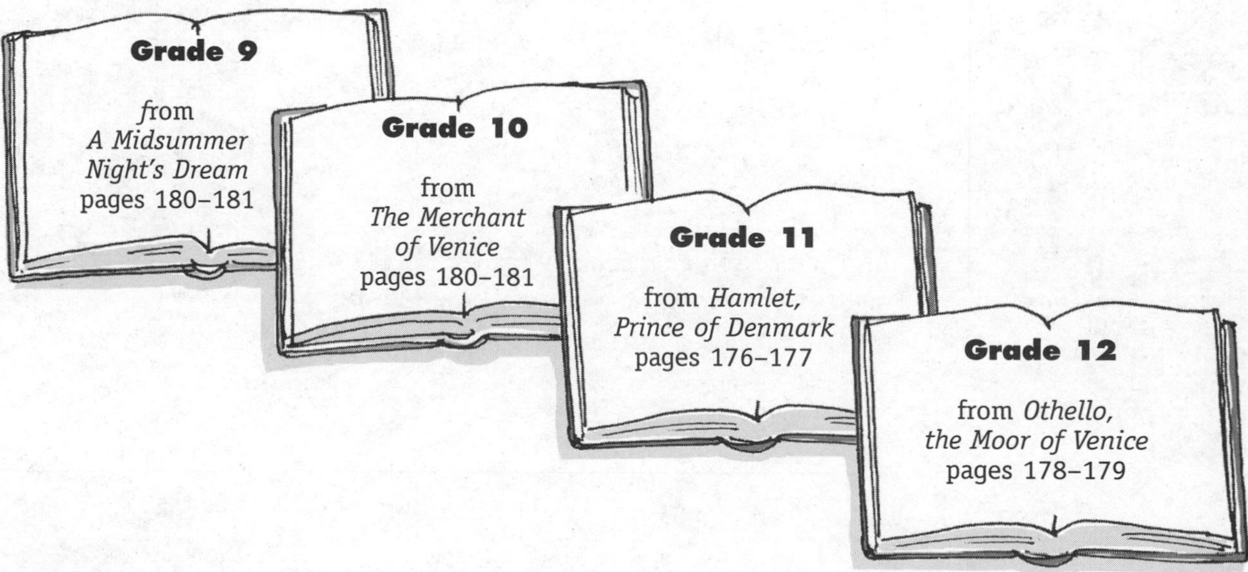

Test Book

See *Test Book* for short-answer and multiple-choice tests.

Elements of Drama

This section introduces and explains common elements in drama. The handbook provides examples, descriptions, and definitions. Use this section to familiarize students with the terms and the overall purposes of these elements.

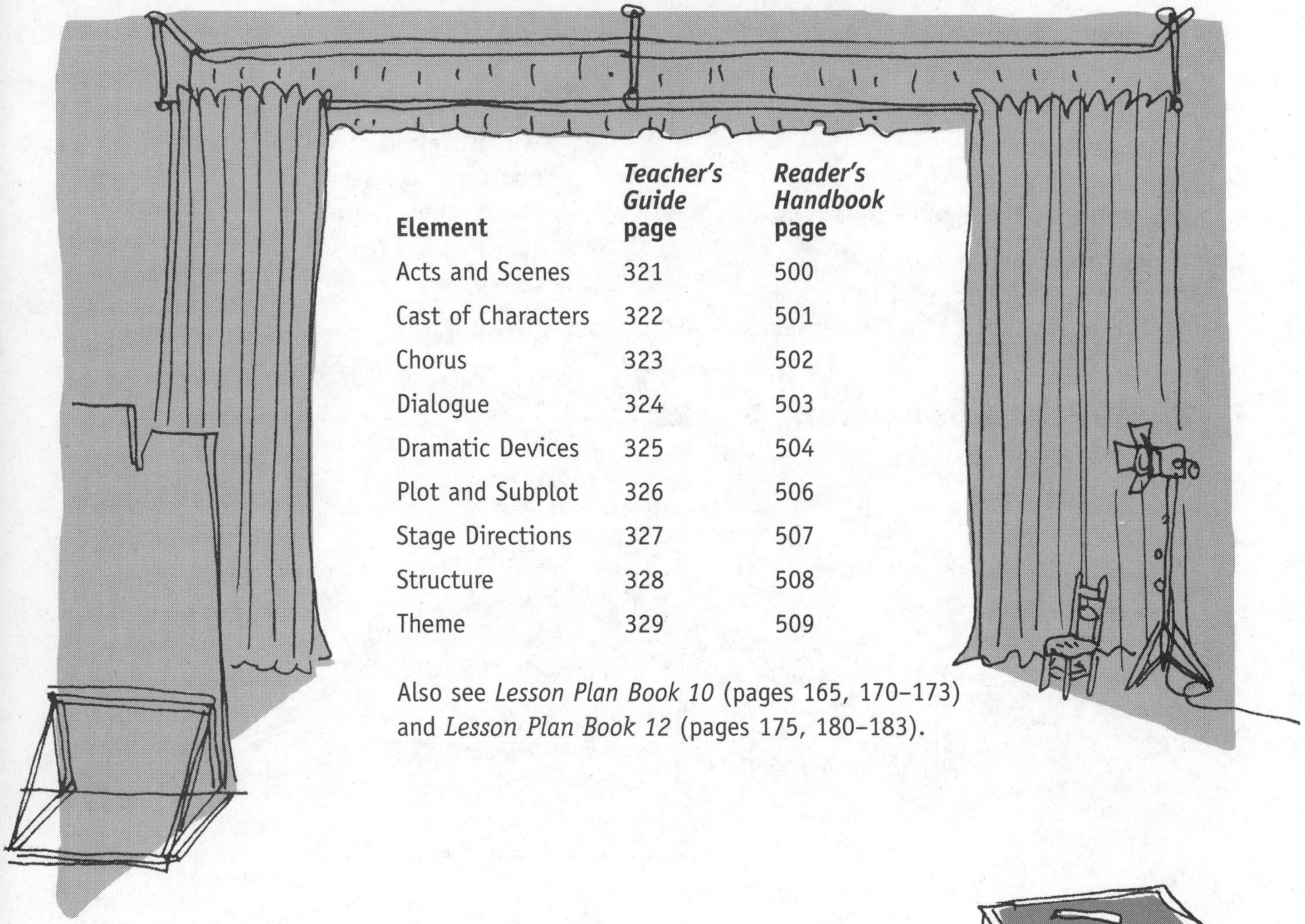

Element	***Teacher's Guide* page**	***Reader's Handbook* page**
Acts and Scenes	321	500
Cast of Characters	322	501
Chorus	323	502
Dialogue	324	503
Dramatic Devices	325	504
Plot and Subplot	326	506
Stage Directions	327	507
Structure	328	508
Theme	329	509

Also see *Lesson Plan Book 10* (pages 165, 170–173) and *Lesson Plan Book 12* (pages 175, 180–183).

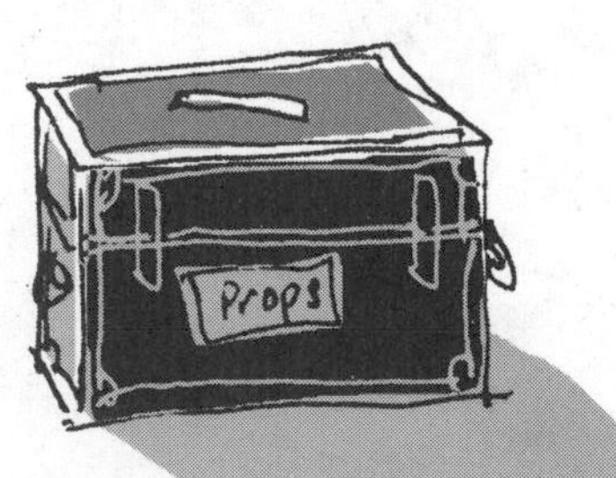

Acts and Scenes

Set Goal

Students will learn that acts are the major divisions in a dramatic work, and scenes are smaller divisions within an act. Time, place, or both may change between scenes and acts.

Teach and Discuss

Read through the **Example** from *The Man Who Came to Dinner* on page 500 with the students. Point out how the acts and scenes are designated. Ask students to describe the place and how changes in time are shown.

Then, read the **Description** with the students. Discuss the difference between acts and scenes. Explain that the acts show the major division of action in a play. Each act may be divided into several scenes. Point out that scenes may be long or short. Sometimes a scene explains something or serves as a transition. Emphasize that a change of act or scene usually means a change in place or time as well.

Check Understanding

Finally, have students read the **Definition** at the bottom of page 500. Then, have the class glance through a play that you plan to study in the future. Ask the students:

- How many acts do you see?
- Approximately how many scenes are in each act?
- What changes in time or place are indicated by the change of scene?

Cast of Characters

Set Goal

Students will learn that the cast of characters is the list appearing at the beginning of the play telling who will be in it.

Teach and Discuss

Have students look at the **Example** from *Langston Hughes: Poet of the People* shown on page 501. Explain that in this play the main character is based on a real person, but in many plays the characters are fictional. Point out that there is a separate list for "Extras," the characters who appear briefly on stage.

Read through the **Description** with the students. Explain that the cast of characters includes both major and minor characters. Emphasize that characters' relationships to each other are often specified in the cast of characters. Although many plays show the characters in order of importance, sometimes the characters are listed by their order of appearance on the stage. Ask students:

- How can a cast of characters help in previewing a play?
- Why would you go back to the cast of characters while reading a play?

Check Understanding

Have students read the **Definition** at the bottom of the page. Then, show the class the cast of characters for a play you plan to read in the future. Questions for discussion include the following:

- Who are the main characters in this play?
- What can you learn about the relationships among the characters from the cast of characters?
- Why do you think playwrights include a cast of characters?

Chorus

Set Goal

Students will learn that a chorus is a group of actors who speak in unison to describe and comment on the main action of the play through song, dance, or recitation.

Teach and Discuss

Ask for volunteers to take parts and read aloud the **Example** from *Oedipus Rex* on page 502. Have several students read the part of the chorus together.

Then read the **Description** with the students. Help them understand the purpose served by the chorus in Greek drama (describing and commenting on the main action). Ask them to tell the different ways the chorus can present information (words, song, dance, and chants). Make sure they know that most modern plays don't have a chorus. Point out that, in some plays, a single character may play the part of the chorus, stepping to the front of the stage to comment on the action.

Check Understanding

Have students read the **Definition** at the bottom of page 502. Then, ask students to form small groups and read the first scene of *Oedipus Rex* or another play that includes a chorus. At least three students should read the part of the chorus in unison. In a whole-group discussion, ask students:

- What does the chorus contribute to the scene?
- What would the scene be like without the chorus?
- Why do you think playwrights include a chorus?

Dialogue

Set Goal

Students will learn that dialogue is the conversation between characters in a play.

Teach and Discuss

Ask for two volunteers to take the parts and read aloud the **Example** from *The Glass Menagerie* on page 503. Invite many students to volunteer, and have different pairs read the excerpt again and again, each pair experimenting and playing with intonations.

Then read the **Description** with the class. Remind them that dialogue in a play can establish character, advance the plot, and reveal theme(s). Clarify the distinction between speech tags, which indicate the character who is talking, and the stage directions, which tell how a line is said. Emphasize that paying attention to the dialogue can help them understand the characters, plot, and theme.

Check Understanding

Have students read the **Definition** at the bottom of page 503. To demonstrate their understanding, students can work in pairs to write short scenes, using the appropriate conventions of drama, such as speech tags and stage directions. You may stipulate the situation, such as a conflict between best friends over a love interest or a conflict between a parent and teenager over using the family car. If time permits, have pairs exchange scripts and perform each other's scenes for the rest of the class. During the scene writing, the pairs should consider these things:

- How will the two characters reveal what they are like through dialogue?
- How will the conflict be revealed through dialogue?
- What stage directions should be included to tell the actors how to speak or what to do?

Dramatic Devices

Set Goal

Students will learn that playwrights use dramatic devices, such as monologues or soliloquies and asides, to add interest to a play.

Teach and Discuss

Ask for a volunteer to read aloud the **Example** from *Abingdon Square* on page 504 as the other students follow along. Explain that this is a monologue or soliloquy—a speech made by a character who is alone on the stage.

Ask another volunteer to read aloud the **Example** of an aside from *Romeo and Juliet.* Point out that an aside is not supposed to be heard by the other characters.

Then read through the **Description** of dramatic devices on pages 504 and 505. Explain that a monologue and a soliloquy are essentially the same device. A monologue may be part of a play, or it may be presented as a work by itself. A soliloquy is a speech by a character in a play that is intended to inform the audience of what the character is thinking or to give the audience important background information.

Further point out that when one character speaks to the audience while other characters are on stage, the device is called an aside.

Check Understanding

Have students read the **Definition** on page 505. Then have students form small groups and brainstorm examples of the dramatic devices discussed. Invite students to think about plays they have read or seen as well as movies and television shows. After students have jotted down their examples, discuss as a whole group:

- What was one example you thought of?
- Why do you think the playwright used that device?
- How did it affect you and the rest of the audience?

Plot and Subplot

Set Goal

Students will learn that plot refers to the main action in the play and that subplot is a smaller story that enhances the audience's understanding of character and theme.

Teach and Discuss

Have students look at the **Example** of plot and subplot in *Romeo and Juliet* depicted on page 506 of the handbook. Ask students to say how the subplots are related to the main plot. Help them understand that the characters or situations in the subplot are related in some way to the main plot.

Now, read the **Description** with the students. Explain that even though a subplot is less important than the main plot, it often clarifies the events of the main plot. Sometimes the action of a subplot affects the action of the main plot, as in *Romeo and Juliet.* Other times the subplot is not essential to understanding the main plot. Playwrights may use subplots to add interest or to provide relief from the events in the plot.

Check Understanding

Have students review the **Definition** at the bottom of page 506. Then, ask them to work in pairs, brainstorming and summarizing the plots and subplots of two or three movies, television shows, or plays they have seen recently. They may create a graphic organizer similar to the one shown on page 506. The pairs should discuss these questions:

- What was the main conflict, and how did it affect the events of the plot?
- What were the subplots?
- How did the subplots affect the main plot?
- What was the resolution of the plot and subplots?

Stage Directions

Set Goal

Students will learn that stage directions are the playwright's instructions to the actors and directors as to how a play is to be performed.

Teach and Discuss

Ask students to read the **Example** from *The Importance of Being Earnest* on page 507 of the handbook. Then ask volunteers to read aloud the parts of Cecily and Gwendolen. Assign a student to read the stage directions as well. Have students pay particular attention to the highlighted words, which show how to say the lines and what to do.

Then, read through the **Description** with the students. Emphasize the importance of reading stage directions. Point out that they give readers a means for imagining the setting, characters, and action. Ask students how stage directions are set apart from the other text of the play.

Check Understanding

Now, have students read the **Definition** at the bottom of page 507. To demonstrate their understanding, have students work in pairs or small groups, reading aloud another scene from *The Importance of Being Earnest.* One student is designated to read the stage directions, and the others must pay close attention in order to know what to do and how to deliver a line. After the small group activity, discuss as a whole group:

- What did the actors learn from the stage directions?
- What did the stage directions tell you about the characters?
- How did the stage directions advance the plot or reveal the conflict?

Structure

Set Goal

Students will learn that the structure of a play is its organization.

Teach and Discuss

Have students examine the Plot Diagram in the **Example** on page 508. Read through it with them. Relate the general descriptions of the five parts of a plot to the sentences about what happens in *Romeo and Juliet*. Point out that this is the same structure found in many novels and short stories.

Then, read through the **Description** with the students. They should be able to remember that the structure of a play is its organization because *structure* and *organization* mean essentially the same thing. Emphasize the five parts of the traditional plot structure.

Check Understanding

Have students read the **Definition** at the bottom of page 508. Then, ask students to draw a Plot Diagram, including the labels "Exposition," "Rising Action," "Climax," "Falling Action," and "Resolution." Instruct students to take the diagram home and over the next few days complete it for a movie or television show. Here are some questions for them to consider:

- Did the structure of the show follow the diagram exactly?
- Were any elements missing? If so, which ones?
- Did you sense that the climax was coming? If so, how did you know it was coming?

Theme

Set Goal

Students will learn that a theme is a playwright's statement about people, the world, or life.

Teach and Discuss

Ask students to volunteer to read parts in the **Example** from *Romeo and Juliet* on page 509, or read the excerpt aloud as the class follows along. Ask them to pay special attention to the highlighted lines that are a clue to the theme.

Read the **Description** with the students. Emphasize that a theme is what the author is saying about the topic of the play. Point out the difference between a major theme and minor themes. Go through the process of finding the big idea, looking for what characters say and do that relates to the big idea, and making a theme statement that explains the author's message. Conclude by explaining that finding the theme of a play is very much like finding the theme of a short story or novel. The theme is inferred from statements and actions within the play.

Check Understanding

Have students review the **Definition** at the bottom of page 509. Then, have students look back at a familiar play. In a whole-group discussion, ask students:

- What topics are presented in this play?
- What does the playwright have to say about the topic?
- What do you think is the theme and why?

Reading on the Internet

- Introduction to Reading on the Internet
- Reading a Website
- Elements of the Internet

Introduction to Reading on the Internet

Talk with students about using the Internet, asking them to share their experiences and describing your own experiences as well. Then, direct students to page 512 in the handbook and have them read the page silently. Follow up by asking a volunteer to read aloud the first paragraph on the page. Make sure students understand that the Internet is a very large network connecting computers around the world and that it was originally developed by the U.S. Department of Defense. Ask students to tell what they expect to find in the chapter.

Reading a Website

Goals

Here students will read a site sponsored by the National Gallery of Art. They will learn to:

- ✔ use the reading process for websites and evaluate them
- ✔ use the strategy of reading critically to examine a website
- ✔ understand the organization of websites

Background

Help students connect this lesson with their prior knowledge by asking them to:

- define *website*
- describe the characteristics of a website
- compare reading websites to reading other types of text
- discuss why reading websites might be difficult

Opening Activity

Invite students to talk about their favorite websites. Point out that website reading is very different from reading more traditional types of texts because a website reader can move around freely; he or she is not restricted to page-by-page reading.

Overview

	Content	Teacher's Guide page	Reader's Handbook page
Selection	Websites		516, 518, 519, 521
Reading Strategy	Reading Critically	334, 437	520, 726
Rereading Strategy	Skimming	337, 437	525, 728
Tool	Website Profiler Web Timeline	334, 336 335 338	520, 524, 757 522, 757 527, 755

Ancillaries

	Grade	Content	Page
Overhead Transparency	9–12	Previewing a Website	Number 31
Lesson Plan Book	9 10 11 12	Reading a Website Reading a Website Reading a Website Reading a Website	174, 176–179 175, 180–183 184, 186–189 184, 186–189
Student Applications Book	9 10 11 12	www.sportsfans.com www.moviemania.movies.com www.petscape.com www.gardengenius.com	182–188 182–189 178–186 180–187
Test Book	9–12	Short-answer Test Multiple-answer Test	
Website		www.greatsource.com/rehand/	

Before Reading

Set a Purpose

First, students need to set a purpose for reading the website. Direct their attention to the Setting a Purpose questions on page 515.

Setting a Purpose

- **When and where did Johannes Vermeer live?**
- **What kind of life did he have?**
- **What kind of pictures did he paint?**
- **What are some of his most important paintings?**

Remind students to write down additional questions that come up as they look for answers to the first ones.

See What's Out There

Explain that students now need to "see what's out there"—they need to use a search engine to help them find information. Remind students to keep notepaper at hand to jot down various addresses on the Internet (called URLs, for *U*niform *R*esource *L*ocators).

Stay Focused

Then have students look at the results of the Google search on page 516. Discuss how difficult it may be to stay focused on a screen like this with so many possible links. However, if students don't stay focused, they can lose a lot of time clicking on links.

Preview

Explain that students can preview a website just as they preview a textbook chapter. Follow the Preview Checklist on page 517. The annotations on page 518 point out the things to preview on the home page of the National Gallery of Art.

Preview Checklist

✓ *the name and overall appearance*
✓ *the main menu or table of contents*
✓ *the source or sponsor*
✓ *any description of what it contains*
✓ *any images or graphics that create a feeling*
✓ *the purpose of the site*

Before Reading

After previewing the National Gallery of Art home page, ask students what they learned about the site. Point out that this site has several potentially useful categories. Have students imagine they have clicked on "The Collection" to see if Vermeer's name appears.

C Plan

The results of the search have shown that this is a useful site. It contains the information that students will need. Remind students that they now need a plan for obtaining that information.

Reading Strategy: Reading Critically

Emphasize to students that one of the most important questions to ask as they begin to read a website is, "How much can I trust the information on this site?" This is why **reading critically** is an essential reading strategy for website reading.

Walk through the steps for reading Internet sites given on page 520 of the handbook. Ask students to take turns reading aloud.

Have students imagine they have gone to the National Gallery of Art site. Direct their attention to the Website Profiler at the bottom of page 520.

WEBSITE PROFILER

URL:	
SPONSOR	DATE
POINT OF VIEW	EXPERTISE
REACTION/EVALUATION	

During Reading

Have students imagine they have clicked on "Biography" from the National Gallery's "The Collection" page. Ask students to examine the screen on page 521. Since this appears to be a good source of information, students may want to print out the pages or take notes on them. (Remind students to paraphrase—not copy—when they take notes.)

D Read with a Purpose

Tell students to keep their research questions in mind during reading. Suggest that they take notes on each major research question.

Take Notes

Explain to students that using graphic organizers can make note-taking easier. Have students examine the Web on page 522 to see how one reader did this.

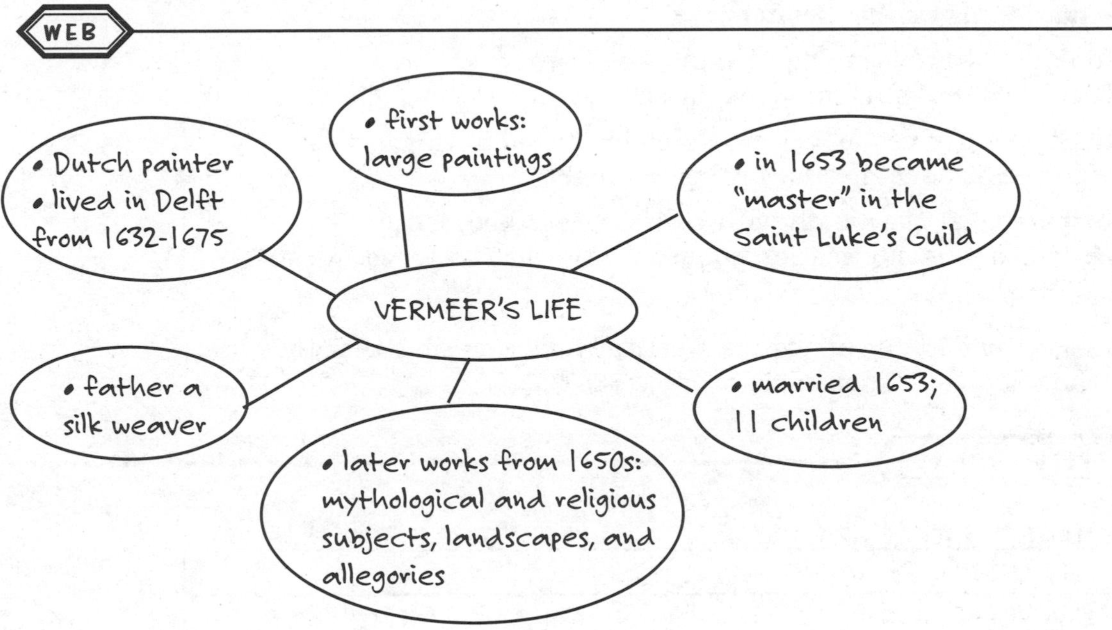

Don't Plagiarize

Caution students against copying and pasting website information. Explain that this is plagiarizing, which will get students into serious trouble. Remind students that information taken from the Internet, like information in book, must be paraphrased.

How Websites Are Organized

Explain to students that knowing how websites are organized will help them read faster and with better comprehension. Have students look at the organizational structures of a website and a book on page 523. Point out that a website is almost like a solar system, with each "planet" providing additional information through its link.

E Connect

Remind students that an important part of the reading process is to respond to or make connections with the text as they read. This is true of website reading as well. Suggest the following ways in which students can make connections:

- ask themselves questions (What is this website saying?)
- think about the meaning of what they learn (Is this website stretching the facts?)
- think about someone who would be interested in this material (Who might be interested in this website?)
- compare what they learn with their previous knowledge (How does this information compare with what I learned in class?)

Encourage students to complete a Website Profiler on sites that they use. Have them look at the example on page 524.

WEBSITE PROFILER

NATIONAL GALLERY OF ART

URL: http://www.nga.gov	
SPONSOR United States	**DATE** has a 2002 copyright date
POINT OF VIEW The gallery promotes the work of classical and modern artists. Masters such as Vermeer have a featured place within the museum and on the website.	**EXPERTISE** The museum is run by experts in the field.
REACTION/EVALUATION Site was excellent. Very nicely designed; you can move around quickly. Includes quality information and images. Like the viewing, interactive options for the images. Would come back just to take more of the virtual exhibit tours.	

After Reading

F Pause and Reflect

After reading and gathering information, students should take a moment to ask themselves a few questions. Review the Looking Back questions with the students.

Looking Back

- **Did I find the information I was looking for?**
- **Was I confused or puzzled by anything I read?**
- **What else would I like to know about this subject?**

G Reread

Students will need to do some rereading to increase their understanding and obtain more information. Suggest they use a different reading strategy—skimming—for rereading.

Rereading Strategy: Skimming

Let students know that **skimming** is an excellent rereading tool. Explain that they can skim for general ideas, such as the source and purpose of the site. Because skimming involves quickly glancing back at the material to get specific information, they can skip information that doesn't meet their purpose or seems to be incorrect.

Have students turn to page 526 and read through the tips for skimming a website. Students may take turns reading aloud, or you may read aloud while they follow along.

After Reading

Remember

To remember the new information they have learned, students need to do something with it. Have them do one of the suggested activities described on page 526–527. Students may choose to email a friend or organize what they have learned using a Timeline. Call their attention to the Timeline on page 527.

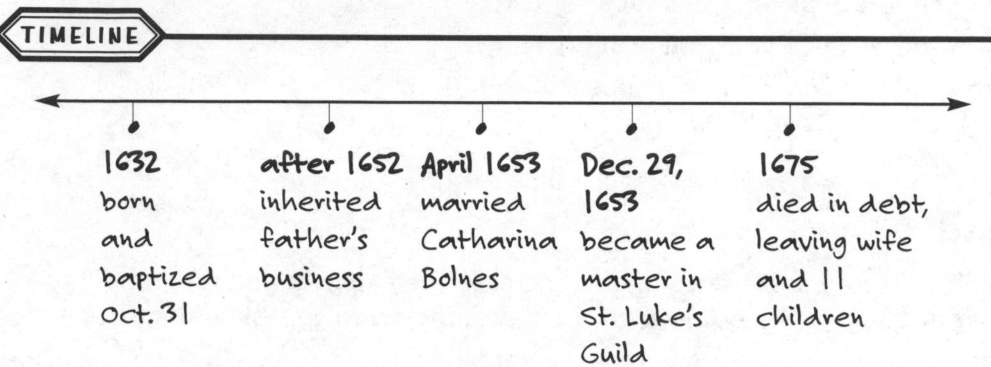

Some students may want to try the creative assignment below.

Creative Assignment: Have students use the Google search engine to find information on an artist, musician, writer, sports figure, or entertainer of their choice. Have students show the websites to a friend or partner and discuss the information contained there.

Summing Up

Review the lesson by reading the Summing Up on page 527 of the handbook. Talk about the tools in this lesson: Website Profiler, Web, and Timeline. Go over the initial goals for the lesson. Discuss which ones students feel that they achieved and which ones that they need more work on:

1. **using the reading process for websites and evaluating them**
2. **using the strategy of reading critically to examine a website**
3. **understanding the organization of websites**

Assessment and Application

Use the Quick Assess checklist to evaluate students' ability to read and understand websites. Give students the opportunity to apply what they have learned through one of the two activities below. For students who are comfortable with reading websites, use the suggestion for independent practice or an activity of your own. For students who need guided help with the strategy, use a *Student Applications Book*.

Quick Assess

Can students

- ☑ say why reading critically is an important strategy when reading a website?
- ☑ explain what skimming is and say why it's a useful rereading strategy?
- ☑ name one or two tools useful for website reading?

1. Independent Practice

To show that they understand the lesson, ask students to apply the strategies they have learned to another website.

Ask students to:

- Complete a Website Profiler while reading a new website of their choice.
- Apply the strategy of critical reading to a new website of their choice.
- Apply the strategy of skimming in order to obtain key information from a new website of their choice.

2. Student Applications Books

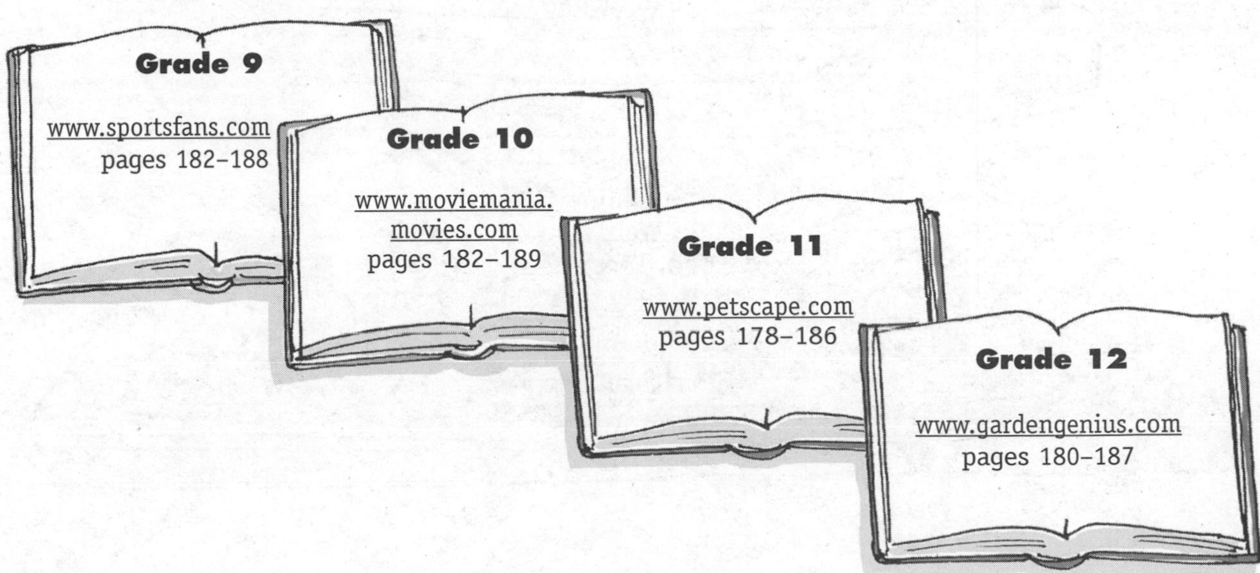

Test Book

See *Test Book* for short-answer and multiple-choice tests.

Elements of the Internet

This section introduces and explains the common elements of the Internet. The handbook provides examples, descriptions, and definitions. Use this section to familiarize students with the terms and the overall purposes of these elements.

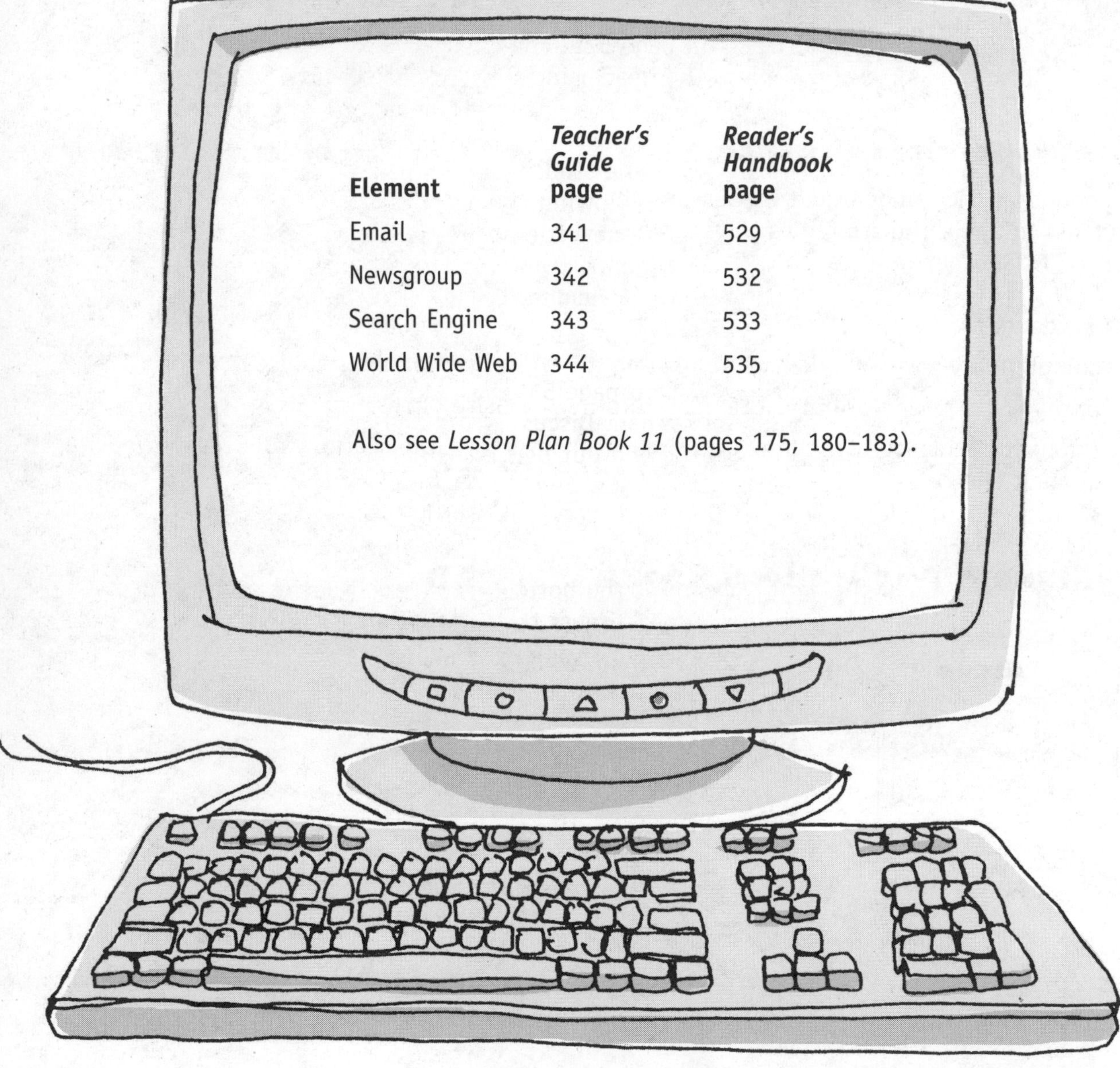

Element	***Teacher's Guide* page**	***Reader's Handbook* page**
Email	341	529
Newsgroup	342	532
Search Engine	343	533
World Wide Web	344	535

Also see *Lesson Plan Book 11* (pages 175, 180–183).

Email

Set Goal

Students will learn that email is an electronic message sent from one computer to another.

Teach and Discuss

Have students look at the **Example** on page 529. Point out the two basic parts of the email: the header and the body. The header includes the email addresses of the sender and the recipient.

Then, read through the **Description** with the students on pages 530 and 531. Point out that email has changed people's lives, allowing them to keep in touch with old friends who have moved away and to make new friends by using "chat rooms." Go over the four lines in the header with students. Point out the additional elements: the abbreviation for *forward*, the use of attachments, and the signature at the bottom of an email.

Emphasize the items in the bulleted list on page 531, sharing your own stories, if appropriate, about email troubles you've had. Discuss with students how to use email wisely. Stress the importance of never giving out personal information.

Check Understanding

Then have students read the **Definition** at the bottom of page 531. Give students the opportunity to send an email to someone. Discuss the following:

- Do you exchange email with anyone? If so, whom?
- What are the advantages of email?
- Why should you always protect your identity in a chat room?

Newsgroup

Set Goal

Students will learn that a newsgroup is an online discussion area created for people with a common, particular interest.

Teach and Discuss

Have students look at the **Example** on page 532. Ask them to comment on what they notice about it. Bring out the common interests of people who belong to this newsgroup.

Then, read through the **Description** with the students. Go over the use of the abbreviation *soc* for *society* and the focus on African culture. Emphasize that participants in the newsgroup can respond directly to each other, or they can post their comments for the group.

Check Understanding

Have students read the **Definition** at the bottom of the page. Then, have students participate in a newsgroup discussion of their choice. Here are some good questions to follow the activity:

- What newsgroup did you participate in?
- What did you learn?
- What are the advantages of participating in a newsgroup discussion?

Search Engine

Set Goal

Students will learn that a search engine is an online tool to help Internet users find information and resources.

Teach and Discuss

Have students look at the **Example** on page 533. Ask them to comment on the features they see on the "screen." Call their attention to the annotations that point to the name of the search engine, the place to type key words, and where to click to start the search.

Then read through the **Description** with the students. Point out that search engines have different rules. Ask students:

- Does your favorite search engine work best by typing questions or by typing key words?
- Why is it important to choose specific key words?

Emphasize that students need to evaluate the quality and reliability of the results of the search engine. Have students analyze the **Example** on page 534. Discuss the search terms used (*physics, roller coasters*) and the results of the search. Students may note that "AND" is not necessary in using this search engine.

Check Understanding

Ask students to read the **Definition** at the bottom of page 534. Students can demonstrate their understanding by finding and analyzing two or three different search engines. Ask students to answer the following questions:

- What features do these search engines have?
- Which search engine did you like best? Why?
- How did you decide which link or links were most likely to be useful?

World Wide Web

Set Goal

Students will learn that the World Wide Web is the system of computers around the world that are joined and can share information.

Teach and Discuss

Have students examine the **Example** on page 535. Ask them to identify the features they see. Make sure they know they are looking at a home page. Call special attention to the pop-up menu and the links.

Then read through the **Description** on pages 536 and 537. Students may take turns reading aloud. Discuss the information given about browsers, the special features of different sites, links, plug-in applications, and URLs. Have students find the browser, box for entering search terms, featured resources, information about museum events and activities, links, and website address on the example home page. Invite students to share their experiences with the Web as you progress through this section.

Be sure also to spend some time discussing the concept of the World Wide Web. It is a system of computers around the world that share files and allow users to access the files on them. Help students appreciate the enormous access they now have to all kinds of information that's now only a few clicks away.

Check Understanding

Have students read the **Definition** on page 537. To demonstrate their comprehension, students can find a website and answer the following:

- What is this site's URL?
- Who publishes the site?
- What information did you find on the site?

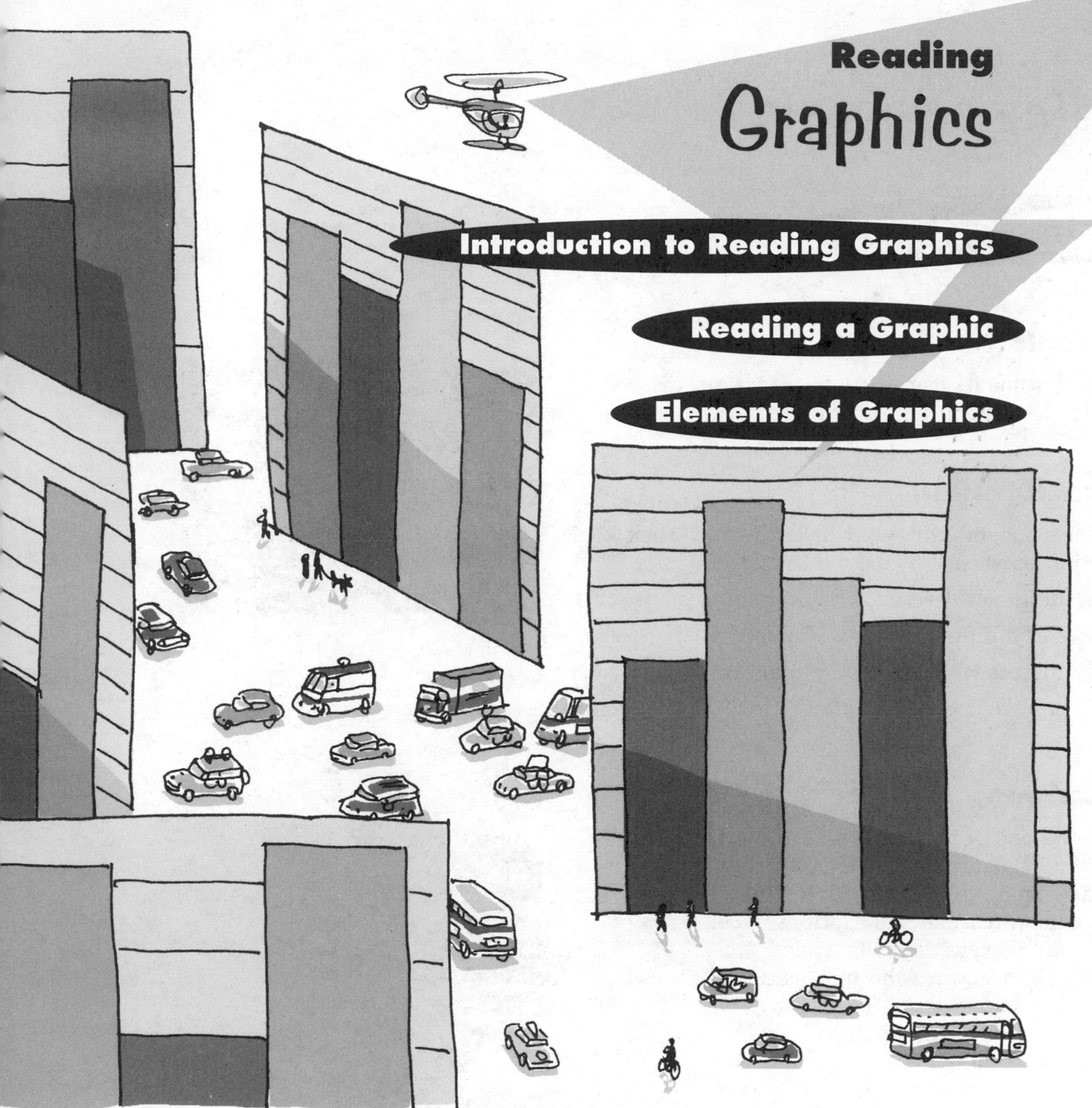

Introduction to Reading Graphics

Sketch the outline of a simple pie chart or table on the chalkboard and ask students where they sometimes see such a graphic. They probably will mention textbooks, newspapers, or magazines. Direct students to read page 540 in the handbook. Discuss with them favorite graphic organizers they have used in working through the *Reader's Handbook*. Point out that, even though they see graphics every day, this chapter will help them use visuals more effectively.

Reading a Graphic

Goals

Here students learn how to read a graphic. This lesson will help them learn to:

- recognize different kinds and elements of graphics
- use the reading strategy of paraphrasing
- see how a graphic is organized

Background

Help students connect this lesson with their prior knowledge by asking them to:

- define or describe what a graphic is
- name different types of graphics
- discuss why writers use graphics
- say what types of information might be found in a graphic

Opening Activity

Using one of the students' current textbooks, show students an example of a graphic (any type) and discuss its features. Common features are captions, labels, headings, keys, legends, scales, units of measure, and information on the source. Ask students to be aware of these features as they read.

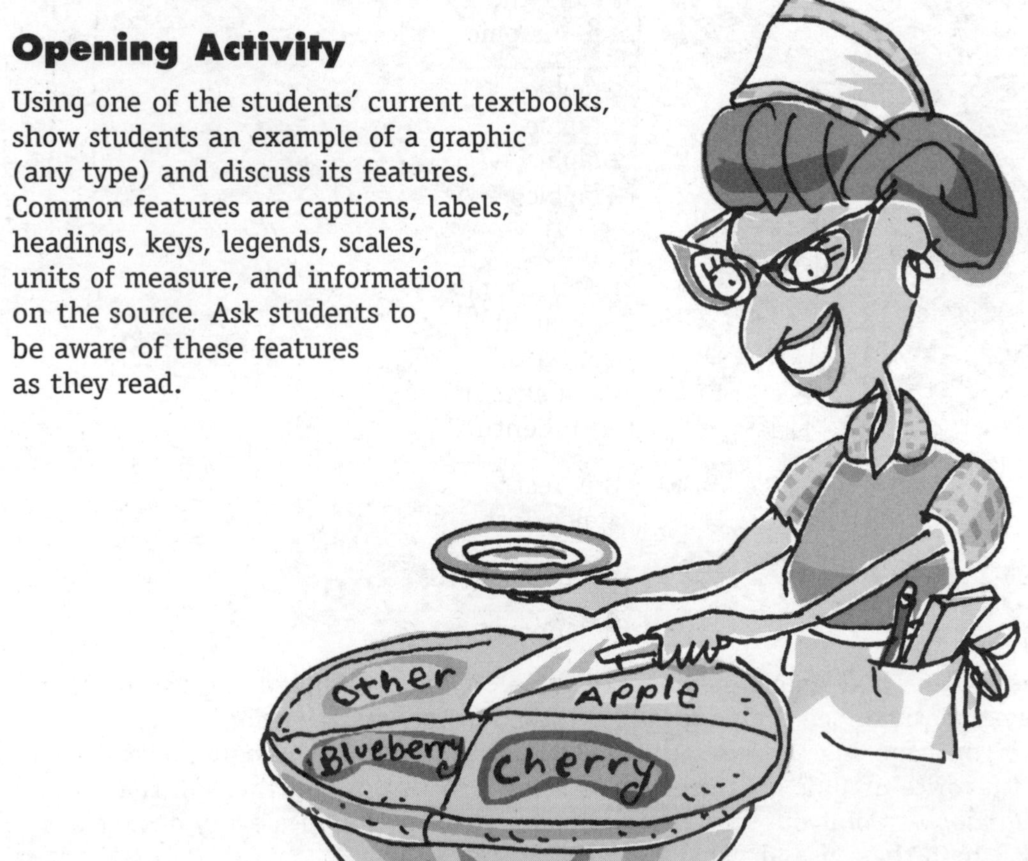

Overview

	Content	Teacher's Guide page	Reader's Handbook page
Selection	"Digital Kids"		543, 547
Reading Strategy	Paraphrasing	349, 435	545, 722
Rereading Strategy	Reading Critically	352, 437	551, 726
Tool	Paraphrase Chart	349	545, 546, 549, 749
	Critical Reading Chart	352	551, 743
	Summary Notes	353	553, 754

Ancillaries

	Grade	Content	Page
Overhead Transparency	9–12	Previewing a Graphic	Number 32
		How to Read a Graphic	Number 33
Lesson Plan Book	9	Reading a Graphic	175, 180–183
	10	Reading a Graphic	184, 186–189
	11	Reading a Graphic	185, 190–193
	12	Reading a Graphic	185, 190–193
Student Applications Book	9	"Kilowatt Climb"	189–196
	10	"Transportation Trends: Vehicles per U.S. Household"	190–197
	11	"Stock Price: SARA"	187–192
	12	"Major Earthquakes of the Twentieth Century"	188–193
Test Book	9–12	Short-answer Test	
		Multiple-choice Test	
Website		www.greatsource.com/rehand/	
Content Area Guide		See also the *Content Area Guides* for Math, Science and Social Studies.	

Before Reading

A Set a Purpose

Just as with other types of reading, students need to set a purpose for reading a graphic. Direct them to the Setting a Purpose questions on page 542 of the *Reader's Handbook.*

Setting a Purpose

- **What is the graphic about?**
- **What does it say about the subject?**

B Preview

Remind students of the importance of previewing before reading. Using the Preview Checklist on page 542, have students preview "Digital Kids" on page 543. The annotations will help them find the items on the checklist. Have them comment on the numbers and what they mean.

Preview Checklist

- ✓ *the title or heading*
- ✓ *any captions or background text*
- ✓ *any labels and column and row headings*
- ✓ *any colors, patterns, icons, or other symbols*
- ✓ *any keys or legends*
- ✓ *the scale or unit of measurement*
- ✓ *the source of both the graphic and its data*

Overhead Transparency

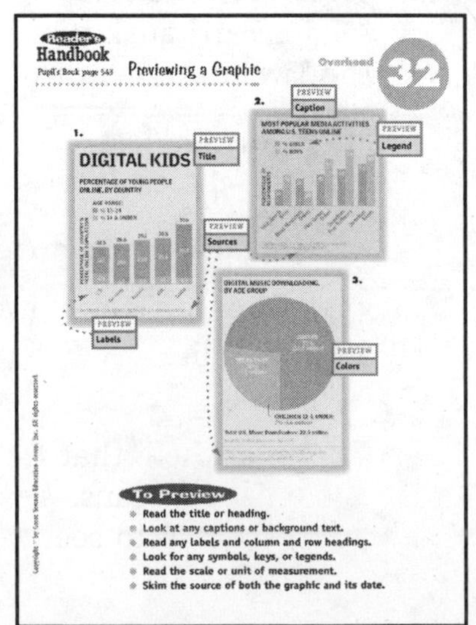

Before Reading

C Plan

Ask students to sum up what they learned about the graphic during their preview. Read the list at the top of page 544. Then remind students that they always need a plan for reading.

Have students take turns reading aloud the steps of the plan for reading a graphic on page 544. Explain that a good reading strategy for graphics is paraphrasing.

Reading Strategy: Paraphrasing

Remind students that **paraphrasing** means restating the information given in their own words. Emphasize to students that the strategy of paraphrasing will help them process and understand the information as well as remember it better.

Have students look at the Paraphrase Chart on page 545. Explain that this chart is useful for reading graphics. They can use a Paraphrase Chart to record their paraphrases and thoughts.

PARAPHRASE CHART

TITLE	MY PARAPHRASE
MY THOUGHTS	

During Reading

D Read with a Purpose

Now students are ready to read. Remind them that their purpose in reading is to find out what the graphic is about and what it means. Ask them to look at the completed Paraphrase Chart on the bottom of page 546 to see how their Paraphrase Chart should look when finished.

How Graphics Are Organized

Explain that knowing the different parts of graphics is crucial to understanding them. Also emphasize that different types of graphics—charts, graphs, or timelines, for example—are used depending on what point the writer wants to make.

Have students turn to page 547 and look at the different parts of the graphic shown. Point out the title, legend, and text in the captions. Then read the paragraphs on page 548.

Finding the Axes

Make sure students know that the horizontal axis is referred to as the *x* axis and the vertical axis is referred to as the *y* axis. It's important to figure out what the *x* and *y* axes are measuring in order to understand the comparison being made in the graphic. Have students find the axes in the graphic at the bottom of the page.

Finding the Legend

The legend is called the key because it provides the key to what the colors, abbreviations, symbols, and so on in the graphic mean. Have students note the position of the legend in the graphic on page 548, but point out that the position can vary depending on the particular graphic.

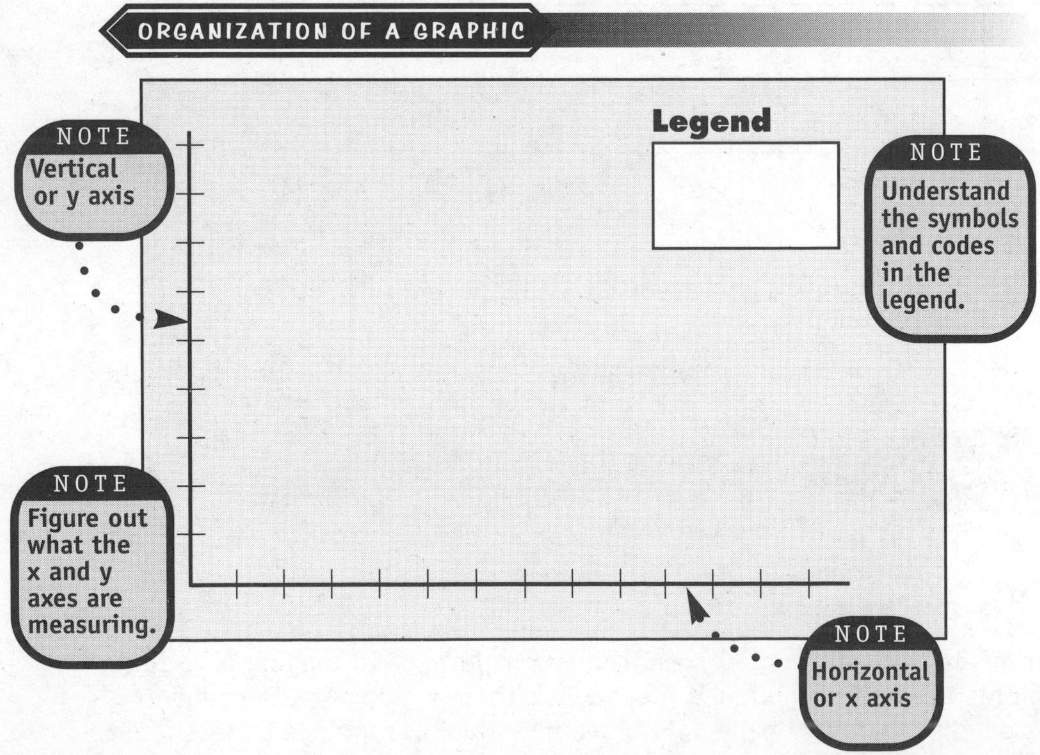

During Reading

E Connect

Let students know that, even when reading graphics, connecting is an important part of effective reading. Have students read through the completed Paraphrase Chart on page 549 to see an example of how one reader connected to the information in the graphics.

Help students connect with the text in the graphics by having them:

- ask themselves questions
  (Where would I have fallen if I'd been surveyed for this study?)
- think about the meaning or importance of the information in the graphic
  (Is this information surprising? What does it tell me that I hadn't realized before?)
- make judgments about the results of the graphic
  (Why would there be more young people online in these other countries than in the United States?)
- evaluate the results by comparing them to their prior knowledge
  (Do these results seem accurate to me?)

After Reading

Pause and Reflect

After reading, students need to stop and reflect on what they have learned. Go over the Looking Back on page 550.

Looking Back

- **Do I understand what the graphic is about?**
- **Can I explain in my own words what I learned?**
- **Is there anything about the graphic that confuses me?**

Students may still be uncertain of the answers to some of these questions. Therefore, they will need to do some rereading in order to clarify their understandings.

After Reading

G Reread

Explain that students should return to the graphics with a different strategy or tool so that they can get a fresh look at the information.

Rereading Strategy: Reading Critically

Introduce the strategy of **reading critically.** Emphasize to students that they should always critically evaluate the information in a graphic. This means they need to question the accuracy of the information and think about its implications. Of course, this does not mean that readers should conclude new information is wrong simply because it contradicts what they thought before. However, data presented visually is easily distorted, and readers must be careful not to be misled.

Read through the Critical Reading Chart, which shows an example of one reader's critical thinking, on page 551. Then read through the sections on page 552.

Reading a Graphic Critically

Students should take note that the information presented in "Digital Kids" came from different sources: the U.S. Census Bureau and three companies. Different methods were used to collect the data.

Evaluating the Sources

Ask the students if they think the sources of information in "Digital Kids" are good sources. Would the agency or companies collecting the data have any reasons for collecting false information or presenting it in a biased way? When a survey has been conducted, readers need to know how the survey "sample" was selected and how many of the persons surveyed responded to it. If the sample was not selected randomly or the response rate was low, then the answers do not necessarily represent the answers of people in general.

After Reading

H Remember

After rereading, students need to do something with the information to remember it. Have students do one of the assignments on page 552. They can either conduct a survey or make a list. Call attention to the Summary Notes on page 553. As an alternative, suggest the creative assignment below.

Creative Assignment: Have students brainstorm questions or issues that they would like to explore in a simple survey of the class, such as how many students' parents speak a different language at home, how many watch a certain television program, and so on. In small groups, students can incorporate the data gathered into graphics to display and compare.

Summing Up

Review the lesson by reading the Summing Up on page 553 of the handbook. Go over the initial goals for the lesson. Discuss which ones students feel they achieved and which ones that they need more work on:

1. **recognizing different kinds and elements of graphics**
2. **using the reading strategy of paraphrasing**
3. **seeing how a graphic is organized**

Then quickly review the tools covered in this lesson: Paraphrase Chart, Critical Reading Chart, and Summary Notes.

Assessment and Application

Use the Quick Assess checklist to evaluate students' ability to read and understand graphics. Give students the opportunity to apply what they have learned through one of the two activities below. For students who are comfortable with the reading process and strategy, use one of the suggestions for independent practice or an activity of your own. For students who need guided help with the strategy, use a *Student Applications Book.*

Quick Assess

Can students

- ✓ summarize the plan for reading a graphic?
- ✓ explain why paraphrasing and reading critically are good reading and rereading strategies for graphics?
- ✓ identify and understand the legend, axes, and captions in a graphic?

1. Independent Practice

To show that they understand the lesson, students can apply the strategy of **paraphrasing** or **reading critically** to a graphic in one of their current textbooks.

Ask students to do one of the following:

- Complete a Paraphrase Chart on the graphic.
- Complete a Critical Reading Chart.
- Write a set of Summary Notes.

2. Student Applications Books

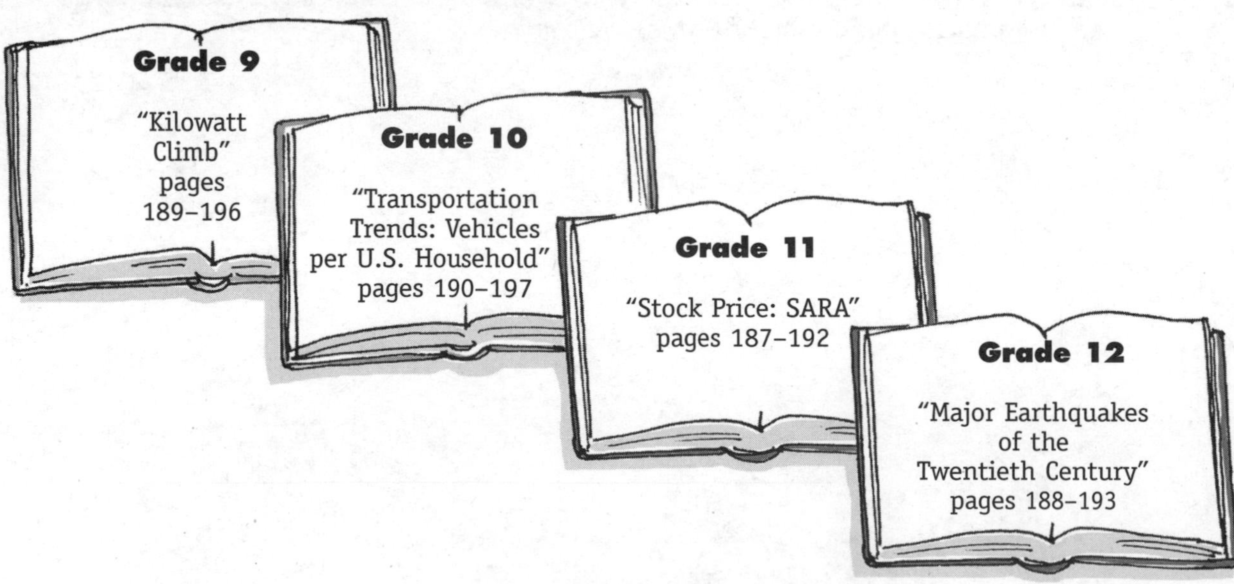

Test Book

See *Test Book* for short-answer and multiple-choice tests.

Elements of Graphics

This section introduces and explains common elements of graphics. The *Reader's Handbook* provides examples, descriptions, and definitions. Use this section to familiarize students with the terminology and the overall purposes of these elements of graphics.

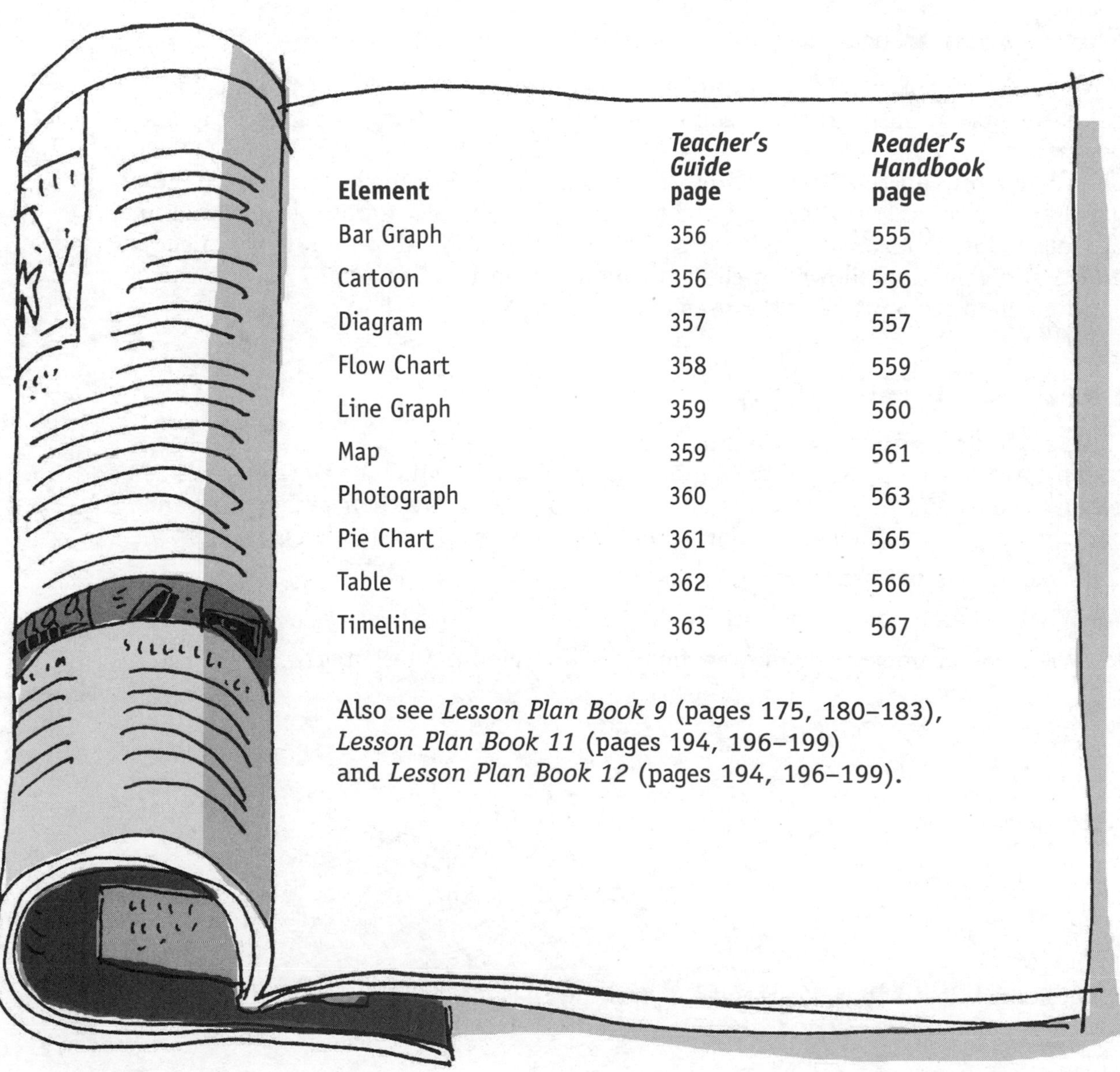

Element	***Teacher's Guide* page**	***Reader's Handbook* page**
Bar Graph	356	555
Cartoon	356	556
Diagram	357	557
Flow Chart	358	559
Line Graph	359	560
Map	359	561
Photograph	360	563
Pie Chart	361	565
Table	362	566
Timeline	363	567

Also see *Lesson Plan Book 9* (pages 175, 180–183), *Lesson Plan Book 11* (pages 194, 196–199) and *Lesson Plan Book 12* (pages 194, 196–199).

Bar Graph

Set Goal

Students will learn that a bar graph is a graphic that uses vertical or horizontal bars to show or compare information.

Teach and Discuss

Have students look at the **Example** of the bar graph on page 555 of the handbook. Ask students to tell what they learned by reading and thinking about this graphic.

Then read through the **Description** with students. Emphasize that to understand a bar graph, students need to read and understand the title, captions, labels, and units of measurement. Ask students to describe the information shown on the vertical axis and the information shown on the horizontal axis in this bar graph. How do the captions help students read the graph?

Check Understanding

Have students read the **Definition** at the bottom of page 555. Then, using a bar graph from one of the students' current textbooks, have students work in pairs to paraphrase what the bar graph is about. Students can write their paraphrases and compare them with those of other pairs. Here are some good questions to consider:

- What is this bar graph about?
- What is being compared or shown?
- What conclusions can you draw from the information presented?

Cartoon

Set Goal

Students will learn that a cartoon is a drawing that makes humorous but meaningful comments about society and life.

Teach and Discuss

Have students look at the **Example** cartoon on page 556 of the handbook. Ask them to say why this cartoon is funny and what comment it makes on contemporary American life.

Then read through the **Description** with students. Emphasize that a cartoon is supposed to make its point quickly. If a reader has to look at a cartoon for a long time, it is probably not a very good cartoon. Ask students what details in this cartoon help them understand its point.

Check Understanding

Have students read the **Definition** at the bottom of page 556. Then supply students with copies of cartoons from *The New Yorker,* a newspaper, or another source. Ask students to form small groups and have them read and discuss several cartoons. They can consider these questions:

- Is the cartoonist's point clear? Why or why not?
- What comment is the cartoonist making about life or society?

Diagram

Set Goal

Students will learn that a diagram is a drawing with labels that shows or explains something.

Teach and Discuss

Have students look at the **Example** on page 557. Read the labels with the students, asking volunteers to take turns reading aloud. Then ask students to sum up what they learned from the diagram.

Read the **Description** on page 558 with students. Emphasize the steps that they should follow when examining a diagram. Ask students to tell where they should begin when reading a diagram. Why is it difficult to know where to begin? How do the arrows help in reading this diagram? What could students do to remember and better understand this diagram?

Check Understanding

Have students read the **Definition** at the bottom of page 558. Then have them work in pairs to study diagrams in one of their current textbooks. Ask students to discuss:

- What is the purpose of the diagram?
- Is it easy to understand? Why or why not?
- What are the key parts or terms of the diagram?

Flow Chart

Set Goal

Students will learn that a flow chart shows a sequence of steps to create a product, make a decision, or complete a process.

Teach and Discuss

Have students examine the **Example** on page 559 of the handbook. Discuss with them the purpose of this graphic and what they learned from it.

Then read the **Description** with students. Emphasize the importance of following the arrows in a flow chart to fully understand what is being depicted. Ask students why a flow chart is sometimes called a decision-making tree.

Check Understanding

Now have students read the **Definition** at the bottom of the page. To demonstrate their understanding, have students look at a flow chart in one of their current textbooks. In a whole-group discussion, ask students:

- What is being described?
- How would you progress through the flow chart?
- Is any part of this flow chart confusing? If so, what?

Line Graph

Set Goal

Students will learn that a line graph shows points, representing times or places, that are plotted and connected by one or more lines to show change.

Teach and Discuss

Have students look at the **Example** on page 560. Model how to read the axes as well as the line that shows the change in annual trips on U.S. mass transportation systems. Ask students to sum up what this line graph is saying.

Then read the **Description** with the class. Emphasize that a line graph displays the relationship between different data over time. Ask students to identify the years covered in the graph and the years during which there was the greatest growth in trips on U.S. mass transportation systems.

Check Understanding

Now have students read the **Definition** at the bottom of page 560. To demonstrate understanding, have students look at a line graph in one of their current textbooks. Ask questions such as these:

- What is the line graph about?
- What information do the axes contain?
- What can you conclude from this line graph?

Map

Set Goal

Students will learn that a map is a reduced drawing of the world or part of the world showing places, boundaries of countries, bodies of water, cities, or geographic regions.

Teach and Discuss

Have students examine the **Example** on page 561. Have them think aloud about what they see on this map. Go over the title, labels, colors in the key, and scale. Ask volunteers to tell different things shown on the map.

Then read the **Description** with the students. Go over the kinds of maps listed at the top of page 562. Ask students what kind of map they would use to find land elevations. What kind of map would they use to locate the boundary of a congressional district? What kind of map would they use to find how many people between the ages of 21 and 30 live in a particular area? Remind students that to interpret maps correctly they need to look at the symbols, the key or legend, and the scale.

Check Understanding

Go over the **Definition** at the bottom of page 562. Then have students find maps in their current history book. Working in pairs, students can find the legend or key, scale, labels, and other features that help them understand the map. Students can discuss these questions:

- What is the purpose of this map? (What kind of map is it?)
- What parts of the map help readers understand it better?
- Where is _______ on the map?

Photograph

Set Goal

Students will learn that a photograph is a picture from real life that captures a moment and tells a story with the image.

Teach and Discuss

Have students look at the **Example** on page 563. Ask them to describe what they see in this photograph and say what the situation might be.

Then read the **Description** with students. Emphasize that photographs are used not only for visual interest but also to highlight important information. Invite students to ask themselves the questions on page 564 when looking at a photograph. What makes this image so powerful? Why might the photographer have chosen to take the photo from a particular angle or perspective? What did students notice first when looking at this photograph? Point out that with digital technology photographs can now be enhanced or even changed, in essence creating a visual lie.

Check Understanding

Now have students read the **Definition** at the bottom of page 564. Ask students to work in pairs looking at the photographs in their science, history, or other class textbook or in newspapers or magazines. Have students present the most interesting photograph they find to the whole class, discussing these points:

- What makes this photograph interesting?
- How much information can you learn about the chapter or article by looking at this photograph?
- What is the purpose of this photograph?

Pie Chart

Set Goal

Students will learn that a pie chart is a circular graph showing the parts of a whole.

Teach and Discuss

Have students look at the **Example** of pie charts on page 565 of the handbook. Have students tell what they learn from each one in turn.

Then read the **Description** with the students. Discuss the three steps they should follow in reading a pie chart: (1) pay attention first to the title, captions, and any related text; (2) identify what the pieces represent; (3) compare the sizes of the pieces. Emphasize that the "pieces" of the pie show the relative sizes of the pieces compared with each other. Each piece is given as a percentage of the whole. For example, what percentage of the '89 class is married? What percentage attended a four-year college? What percentage consider themselves to be middle class?

Check Understanding

Go over the **Definition** at the bottom of page 565. Then have students work in pairs examining and discussing pie charts from their current textbooks. In a whole-class discussion, ask students:

- What did you learn from the pie chart that you examined?
- Why do you think the writer chose to use a pie chart to depict that data?

Table

Set Goal

Students will learn that a table is a list of information or statistics arranged in columns and rows.

Teach and Discuss

Have students turn to page 566 of the handbook. Show them how you would read this table to find specific information. Challenge students to a contest in finding the answers to specific questions, such as "What year was Hal Greer elected to the Basketball Hall of Fame?"

Then read the **Description** with students. Explain that tables are not just lists in columns and rows. The information is related in some way, and the purpose is usually for reference and to make a comparison. Ask students to describe the procedure they would follow to read the table on Hall of Fame players.

Help break down each step for students. Begin with a question, such as, "What player has the most assists?" Explain how you move your eye first over to the heading "Assists" and then down, comparing numbers until you find the largest one. Then, you need to read over to the left to find the name of the player (John Havlichek).

Check Understanding

Have students read the **Definition** at the bottom of page 566. Then have students look at tables in their current textbooks. Working in pairs, students can discuss:

- What is the purpose of this table?
- What type of information is in the columns and rows?
- Why did the writer decide to include a table in this chapter?

Timeline

Set Goal

Students will learn that a timeline is a type of chart that shows a series of events organized in chronological order.

Teach and Discuss

Ask students to turn to page 567 of the handbook and look at the **Example.** Point out that this timeline has a title, dates, and key events. Ask students to name a few interesting facts they can learn from it.

Read the **Description** with students. Emphasize that timelines provide an excellent review of important material that can be useful when studying for tests or writing papers. Go over the hints for using timelines. Ask students why it is a good idea to read the title first. What are the beginning and end dates on the timeline in the example? Why are the beginning and end dates important?

Check Understanding

Have students read the **Definition** at the bottom of page 567. Then ask students to find an example of a timeline in their current history textbook. Discuss the following questions in a whole-group session:

- What time span is represented in this timeline?
- What interesting facts can you learn from this timeline?
- Why do you think the author included a timeline?
- How might one event have caused others?

Reading for the

Everyday World

Introduction to Everyday Reading

Ask students to tell about some of the things that they read outside of their school reading. You may need to get them started thinking about everyday reading by giving a few suggestions, such as TV guides, posters for upcoming events, and recipes. Direct them to read page 570 in the handbook and then discuss with them the examples given of real-world writing. Point out that there are strategies to help them with this kind of reading. Ask them why this kind of reading can be just as important as the reading they do for school assignments.

Reading a Driver's Handbook

Goals

Here students read excerpts from a driver's handbook. In this lesson they will learn to:

- ✓ set a purpose for reading a driver's handbook
- ✓ use the reading strategy of skimming to get information
- ✓ understand the organization of a driver's handbook

Background

Help students connect this lesson with their prior knowledge by asking them to:

- say what types of information they would expect to find in a driver's handbook
- discuss how reading a driver's handbook might be different from reading other types of texts
- talk about any experiences they've had reading or looking at a driver's manual

Opening Activity

Bring in a copy of your state driver's manual and show it to the students. Have them identify the different parts or elements of the manual. Ask students to be aware of the different parts or elements of a driver's manual during the upcoming lesson.

Overview

	Content	Teacher's Guide page	Reader's Handbook page
Selection	from *Rules of the Road*		573, 574, 578
Reading Strategy	Skimming	368, 437	575, 728
Rereading Strategy	Visualizing and Thinking Aloud	370, 440	579, 736
Tool	Key Word or Topic Notes Web Summary Notes	368 369 370	575, 576, 746 577, 757 579–580, 754

Ancillaries

	Grade	Content	Page
Overhead Transparency	9–12	Previewing a Driver's Handbook	Number 34
Lesson Plan Book	9 10	Reading for the Everyday World Reading a Graphic	184, 186–189 185, 190–193
Student Applications Book	9 10 11 12	Right-of-Way Rules Passing Another Vehicle California Voter Pamphlet: Proposition 40 Auto Insurance Policy	197–204 198–204 193–203 194–201
Test Book	9–12	Short-answer Test Multiple-choice Test	
Website		www.greatsource.com/rehand/	

Before Reading

Set a Purpose

Students need to set a purpose even for their "everyday" reading. Direct students to the Setting a Purpose question on page 572 of the *Reader's Handbook*.

Setting a Purpose

- **What do I need to know to pass the written examination for a driver's license?**

Preview

Remind students of the importance of previewing before reading. Read through the Preview Checklist on page 572.

Now have students preview the table of contents on page 573 and the excerpt on page 574.

Preview Checklist

✓ *the table of contents*
✓ *any headings*
✓ *any words in large type, boldface type, or all capital letters*
✓ *any numbered or bulleted lists*
✓ *any graphic elements, such as illustrations and diagrams*

Overhead Transparency

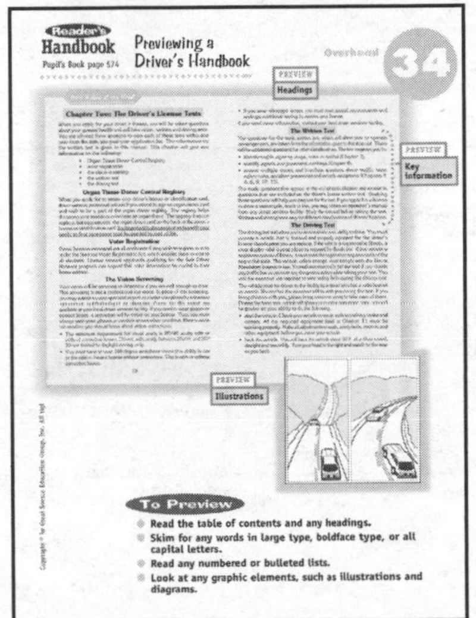

Before Reading

C Plan

Ask students to say in their own words what they learned during their preview. Direct their attention to the bulleted items at the top of page 575. Then remind students that they always need a plan for reading and suggest the strategy of skimming.

Reading Strategy: Skimming

Remind students that **skimming** means running their eyes quickly over a page to find the information they need. Skimming enables students to know the key topics in the driver's manual and where to look for important information about those topics.

If students are not allowed to mark in their driver's manual, Key Word or Topic Notes will serve as a useful tool for recording important information. Have students look at the example at the bottom of page 575.

During Reading

D Read with a Purpose

Now students are ready to read. Remind them that their purpose is to find the information likely to be on the driver's license examination. Have students look at the completed Key Word or Topic Notes on page 576 so that they know what their completed organizers are supposed to look like.

KEY WORD OR TOPIC NOTES

KEY WORDS OR TOPICS	NOTES
traffic signs	• Key signs include: Stop, Yield, Wrong Way, and Do Not Enter. • Note U-sign for "No U-Turn" and the arrow sign that means "No Right Turn."
signals	Signals are like the red, green, and yellow lights.
pavement markings	These are the marks in the middle of a road. • Two solid lines mean "no passing." • Broken yellow lines mean "passing allowed." • Two-way turn lanes are like the lanes we have in front of school.

During Reading

Read with a Purpose continued

If students prefer, they could also take notes in a Web. Show them the example of the completed Web on page 577.

WEB

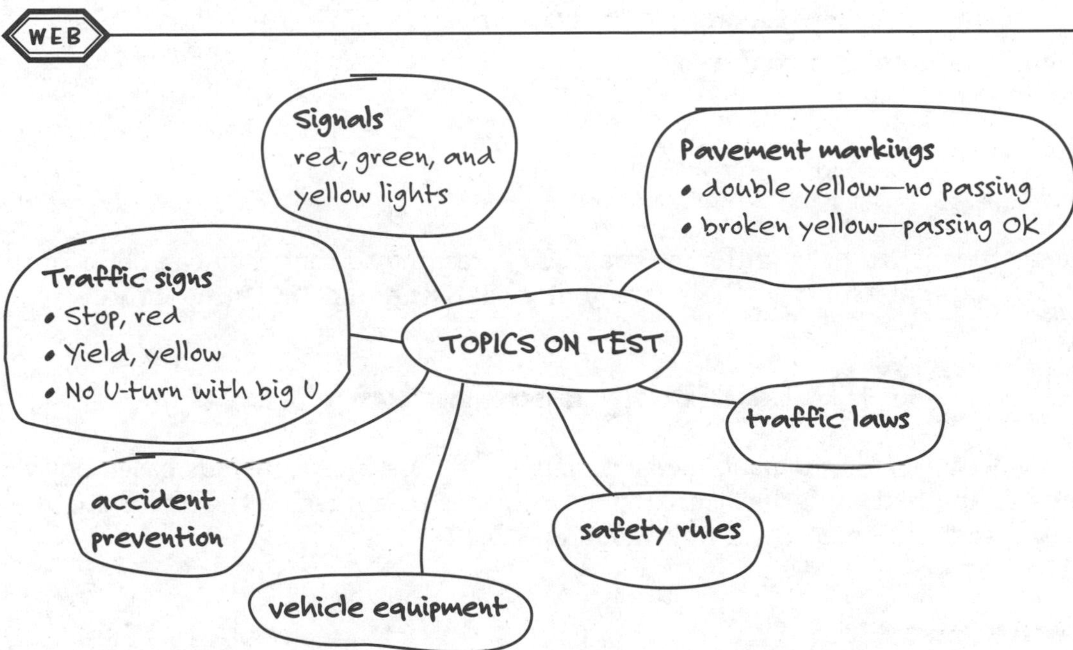

E Connect

Making connections to everyday reading will help students better remember the information they need to know. Have students look at the sticky notes in the example on page 578. Help students by directing them to:

- ask themselves questions
  (What are five places where I should not make a U-turn?)
- evaluate the information
  (Why shouldn't I make a U-turn on a one-way street?)
- share the reaction they might write on sticky notes
  (Have I ever seen a driver make an illegal U-turn and thought it was dangerous?)

After Reading

F Pause and Reflect

After reading, students need to stop and think about what they have learned. Go over the Looking Back questions on page 578.

Looking Back

- **Do I know what I need to know to pass the driver's exam?**
- **Is there anything that confuses me?**

G Reread

Encourage students to use a different strategy for reading so that they can get a fresh look at the materials. Suggest the strategy of **visualizing and thinking aloud**.

Rereading Strategy: Visualizing and Thinking Aloud

Remind students that visualizing means forming a picture in their minds based on the words in the text, and that thinking aloud means paraphrasing the material out loud. Ask students to read the Think Aloud on page 579.

H Remember

After rereading, students need to do something with the information to remember it. Have students follow one of the suggestions in the handbook. They can ask and answer questions or write Summary Notes. As an alternative, ask them to try the creative assignment below.

Creative Assignment: Working with your own state driver's manual, have pairs or small groups of students choose a section and dramatize the rule or instruction. Students in the audience identify which rule or instruction is being enacted.

Summing Up

Review the lesson by reading the Summing Up on page 580 of the handbook. Go over the initial goals for the lesson. Discuss which ones students feel they achieved and which ones that they need more work on:

1. **setting a purpose for reading a driver's handbook**
2. **using the reading strategy of skimming to get information**
3. **understanding the organization of a driver's handbook**

Assessment and Application

Use the Quick Assess checklist to evaluate students' ability to read and understand a driver's manual. Give students the opportunity to apply what they have learned through one of the two activities below. For students who are comfortable with the reading process and strategy, use one of the suggestions for independent practice or an activity of your own. For students who need guided help with the strategy, use a *Student Applications Book*.

Quick Assess

Can students

- say why skimming is a good reading strategy for a driver's manual?
- explain why visualizing and thinking aloud is a good rereading strategy?
- name one or two tools that can be useful for everyday reading?

1. Independent Practice

To show that they understand the lesson, students can apply either the strategy of **skimming** or the strategy of **visualizing and thinking aloud** to their state driver's manual.

Ask students to do one of the following:

- Complete a Key Word or Topic Notes organizer.
- Take notes using a Web.
- Write a set of Summary Notes.

2. Student Applications Books

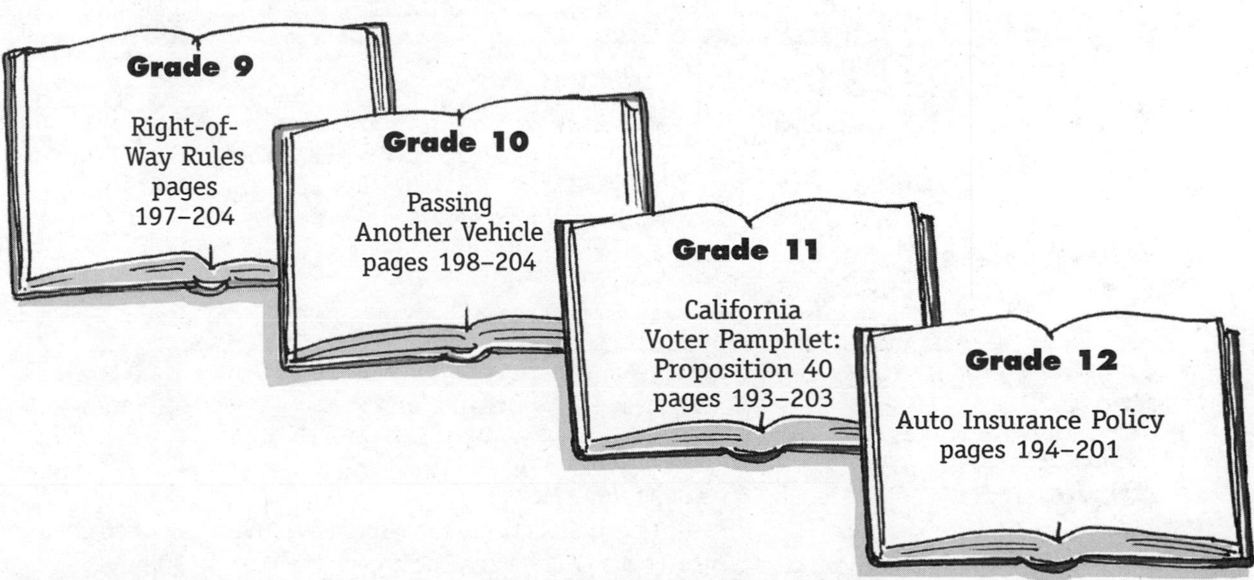

Test Book

See *Test Book* for short-answer and multiple-choice tests.

Focus on Reading Instructions

Goals

Here students focus on how to read instructions. This lesson will help them to learn to:

- identify a purpose for reading instructions
- use the strategy of close reading to learn what the instructions explain
- understand the organization of instructions

Background

Remind students that everyday reading includes reading instructions. Help students connect this lesson with their prior knowledge by asking them to:

- talk about the last time they had to read instructions for something
- say why reading instructions is sometimes frustrating
- discuss strategies they have used to read and comprehend instructions

Overview

	Content	Teacher's Guide page	Reader's Handbook page
Selection	Cell Phone Instructions DVD Player Instructions		583 584
Reading Strategy	Close Reading	373, 433	585, 714

Ancillaries

	Grade	Content	Page
Lesson Plan Book	9 11	Reading for the Everyday World Focus on Reading Instructions	184, 186–189 195, 200–203
Student Applications Book	9 10 11 12	"Memory Dialing: Storing Numbers" "Starting Your Mower" "Operating Instructions for Microwave Oven" "Auto Focus Camera Instructions"	205–206 205–206 204–205 202–203
Test Book	9–12	Short-answer Test Multiple-choice Test	
Website		www.greatsource.com/rehand/	

Before Reading

Explain to students that most instructions involve:

- one or more diagrams
- a process or series of steps

Preview Checklist

- ✓ *the title and headings*
- ✓ *the steps in the process*
- ✓ *any diagrams or graphics*
- ✓ *any key words in boldface or capital letters*
- ✓ *any bulleted lists*

Emphasize that previewing instructions will help students get an idea of how they should read. Go over the Preview Checklist.

Remind students that, before they read, they should have a specific purpose in mind. Have students look at the purposes for reading cell phone and DVD instructions shown at the bottom of page 582. Then have students preview the examples on pages 583 and 584.

Ask students to say in their own words what they learned from the preview. Then suggest the strategy of close reading for reading the instructions.

Reading Strategy: Close Reading

Explain that **close reading** means carefully reading every word and sentence. Emphasize that this is an effective strategy for reading instructions because it ensures that no step will be missed.

Six steps to help students read instructions are described on pages 585 and 586. Go over these with students.

1. Highlight or Mark

Encourage students to use a highlighter or pen to mark the most important words and phrases in the instructions. If students are not allowed to mark in their books, have them use sticky notes.

2. Think Aloud

Encourage students to think aloud while reading to aid comprehension. Remind students that thinking aloud involves putting the instructions in their own words. Read the example at the bottom of page 585.

THINK ALOUD

So, as a first step, I turn everything off and unplug the phone. Then I need to get the cover off. Don't use the antenna. I should use a coin or something like that to get the cover off.

3. Reread

Let students know that hardly anyone understands instructions completely by reading them once. Some rereading will be needed.

4. Go Step by Step

Mention to students that many people read one step at a time and then follow that step. This is often the most efficient procedure.

5. Read the Diagram

Remind students that most instructions include diagrams. It is helpful to look back and forth, from the diagram to the real object, while performing the tasks.

6. Ask Yourself Questions

Let students know that asking questions while reading is also a good way to clarify the text. Students may ask questions such as, "Does this mean do that before that?" or "Did this work?"

Sometimes, even after reading and rereading, the instructions don't make sense. If this happens, students can ask a friend for help or go back to the instructions and check off the steps as they go.

1. Ask a Friend for Help

Remind students that often "two heads are better than one." The student may ask a friend to read the instructions aloud as he or she performs the tasks.

2. Check Off the Steps

If no one is available to help out, students may try going back and checking off the steps, one at a time. This ensures that steps are not skipped accidentally.

Students may also try the creative assignment below.

Creative Assignment: Provide a small appliance, such as a transistor radio, a cellular phone, or a blender. With students, go over the instructions for using or putting together the appliance, and ask volunteers to help with the various steps. Afterward, discuss what students probably would not have discovered on their own if they hadn't read the instructions.

Summing Up

Have students read the points in the Summing Up at the bottom of page 587. Ask students to say in their own words what they learned in this lesson.

Assessment and Application

Use the Quick Assess checklist to evaluate students' ability to read and follow instructions. Give students the opportunity to apply what they have learned through one of the two activities below. For students who are comfortable with the reading process and strategy, use the suggestion for independent practice or an activity of your own. For students who need guided help with the strategy, use a *Student Applications Book*.

Quick Assess

Can students

- set a purpose before reading instructions?
- explain why close reading is a good strategy for reading instructions?
- name one or two practices that are useful for reading or rereading instructions?

1. Independent Practice

To show that they understand the lesson, students can apply the strategy of **close reading** to another set of instructions.

2. Student Applications Books

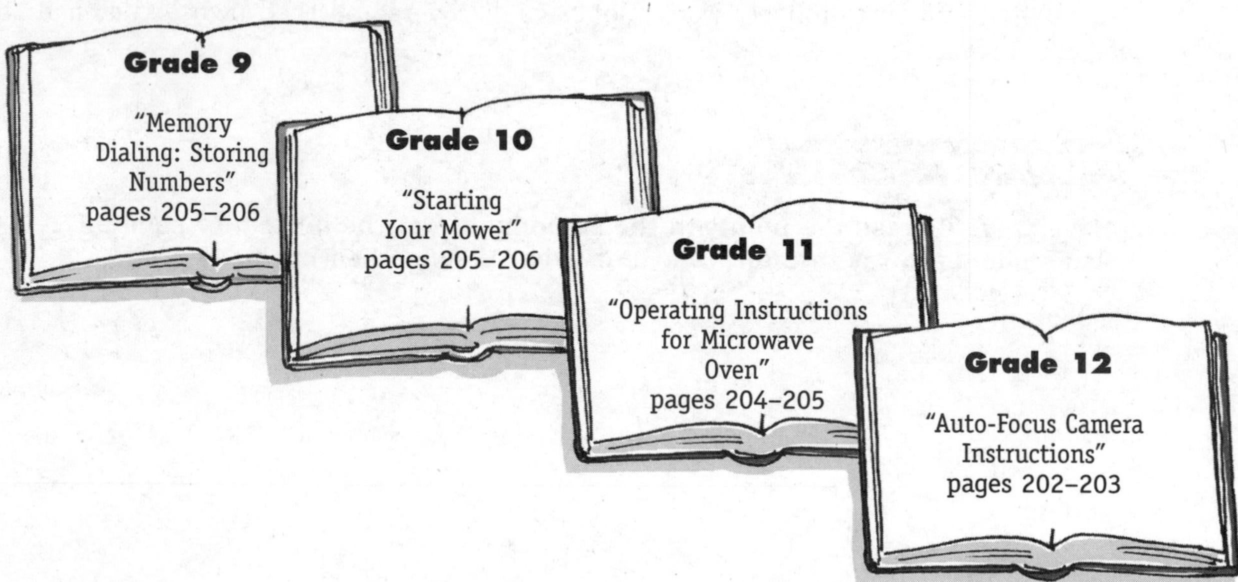

Test Book

See *Test Book* for short-answer and multiple-choice tests.

Focus on Reading for Work

Goals

Now students will focus on workplace reading. This lesson will help students to:

- ☑ set a purpose for a number of different kinds of work-related reading
- ☑ use the strategy of skimming to get the information they need
- ☑ understand the organization of different types of work-related writing

Background

Help students connect this lesson with their existing knowledge by asking them to:

- talk about the jobs they have held
- say what types of reading they had to do on the job or during their job training
- discuss the purposes of different types of workplace reading

Overview

	Content	Teacher's Guide page	Reader's Handbook page
Selection	Memo on Workplace Safety Job Description Work Schedule		590 591 592
Reading Strategy	Skimming	378	593, 728

Ancillaries

	Grade	Content	Page
Lesson Plan Book	9	Reading for the Everyday World	184, 186–189
Student Applications Book	9 10 11 12	"Dress Code Policy" "Sick Leave Policy" "Employee Handbook: Handling Complaints" "Company Picnic Memo"	207–209 207–209 206–207 204–205
Test Book	9–12	Short-answer Test Multiple-choice Test	
Website		www.greatsource.com/rehand/	

Before Reading

Explain to students that any type of job requires quite a bit of reading. By following four easy steps, students will be able to get this reading done efficiently—quickly and with good comprehension. Read the four steps on the bottom of page 588 with students.

Identifying a Reading Purpose

Emphasize the importance of thinking about what students need to know before beginning to read. Call their attention to the purposes for the three kinds of workplace reading on page 589. Then ask students to preview the three examples of everyday writing. Remind them that the annotations can help them find things to look for while previewing.

Reading Strategy: Skimming

When students are looking for specific information, **skimming** is the best reading strategy. To skim, students run their eyes quickly over the material for key words and important parts.

During Reading

Now ask students to go back and read the memo, job description, and work schedule. Have students note how key words and features have been highlighted in the examples. Share the tips with students.

Tip #1: Read Titles or Headings

Have students pay attention to the headings as they skim, thinking about how the titles or headings relate to their purpose for reading.

Tip #2: Highlight

Remind students that, if they are allowed to do so, using a highlighter to mark key words and key sections of a text is helpful. Emphasize that marking the text makes it easier to go back and find the information when they need it again.

Tip #3: Connect the Information to Yourself

Let students know that work-related reading is often dull. Making connections to the text will help students become more engaged with the reading, which will improve their comprehension.

After Reading

Workplace reading is usually done to get specific information. Let students know that once they find what they're looking for, they're done reading. If they don't find it, however, they must keep looking.

1. Reread

Let students know that sometimes readers simply skim too quickly. If this was the problem, students need to return to the material and read a bit more slowly. Students may also need to look in different places in the text for the information they need.

2. Ask for Help

Sometimes even after rereading students haven't found what they need. Encourage them to ask a friend for clarification, if necessary.

Students may also try the creative assignment below.

Creative Assignment: Ask students to work in pairs or small groups to brainstorm a list of other kinds of workplace reading that may be needed to do a job. Some possibilities include a list of recycling procedures, an evacuation route in case of fire, a memo regarding a change in company policy, an employee manual, a list of menu specials to recommend to customers, and the agenda for an employee meeting.

Summing Up

Read through the Summing Up on page 595 with the students. Ask students to say in their own words what they learned in this lesson.

Assessment and Application

Use the Quick Assess checklist to evaluate students' ability to read for work. Give students the opportunity to apply what they have learned through one of the two activities below. For students who are comfortable with the reading process and strategy, use the suggestion for independent practice or an activity of your own. For students who need guided help with the strategy, use a *Student Applications Book.*

Quick Assess

Can students

- ☑ set a purpose for reading work-related materials?
- ☑ say why skimming is a good skill to use for reading at work?
- ☑ say what to do if they can't find the information they need in the reading material?

1. Independent Practice

To show that they understand the lesson, students can apply the strategy of **skimming** to materials they received from their own workplace or from a parent's workplace.

2. Student Applications Books

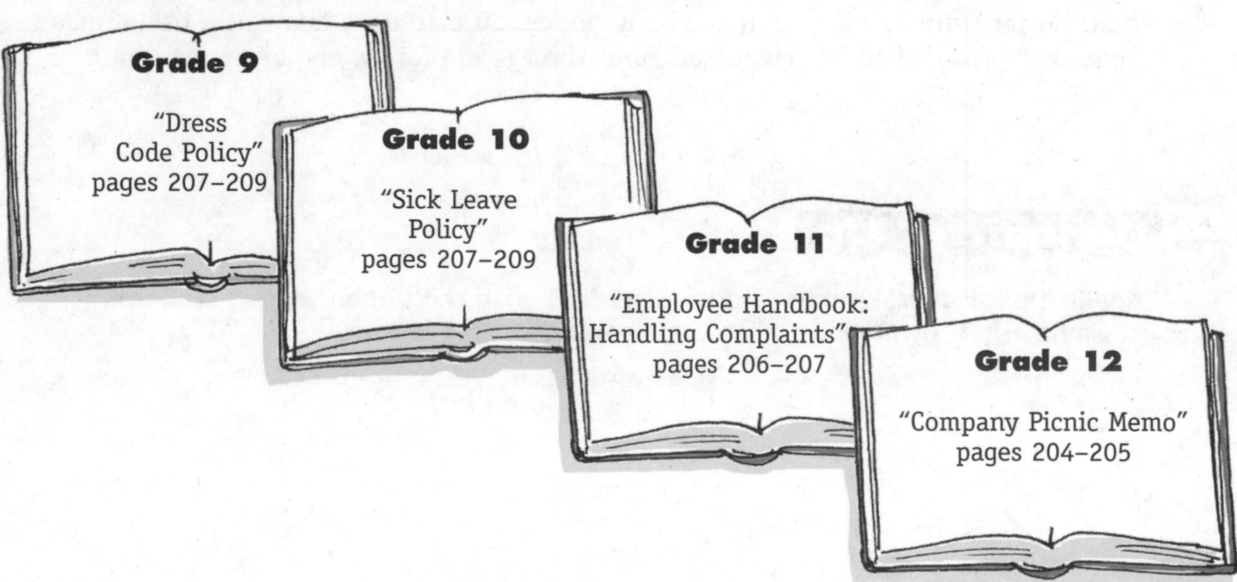

Test Book

See *Test Book* for short-answer and multiple-choice tests.

Reading for Tests

Introduction to Reading for Tests

Ask students why it is important to know how to take tests. Have them describe some of the things that give them trouble when taking a test, such as misunderstanding a question or running out of time before finishing the last questions. Direct students to page 598 in their handbooks and ask them to read the first two paragraphs silently. Then have a volunteer read aloud the third paragraph. Follow up with a discussion of standardized tests or exit exams students have taken. Ask them to finish by reading the last paragraph.

Reading Tests and Test Questions

Goals

Here students read an excerpt from a multiple-choice reading test. This lesson will help them learn to:

- ✓ prepare for various kinds of tests
- ✓ use the reading strategy of skimming
- ✓ understand how tests are organized and what kinds of questions they include

Background

Help students connect this lesson with their prior knowledge by asking them to:

- talk about how taking tests makes them feel
- describe different kinds of tests they are expected to take
- discuss how they usually prepare for and take a test
- talk about the problems they may encounter while taking tests

Opening Activity

Discuss the common elements of tests and test questions, such as time limits, instructions, information on scoring, readings, and different question types. Ask students to be aware of these elements while working through the sample test in this lesson.

Overview

	Content	Teacher's Guide page	Reader's Handbook page
Selection	Midyear English Test "The Laugher" by Heinrich Böll		601–604, 607, 608, 609, 610, 611, 613, 614, 615
Reading Strategy	Skimming	385, 437	605, 728
Rereading Strategy	Visualizing and Thinking Aloud	388, 440	614–616, 736
Tool	Main Idea Organizer	386	611, 747

Ancillaries

	Grade	Content	Page
Overhead Transparency	9–12	Previewing a Test Reading Fact or Recall Questions Reading Inference Questions Reading Essay Questions	Number 35 Number 36 Number 37 Number 38
Lesson Plan Book	9	Reading Tests and Test Questions	185, 190–193
	10	Reading Tests and Test Questions	194, 196–199
	11	Reading Tests and Test Questions	204, 206–209
	12	Reading Tests and Test Questions	195, 200–203
Student Applications Book	9	from *Thirteen Senses: A Memoir* by Victor Villaseñor	210–216
	10	from *Krik? Krak!* by Edwidge Danticat	210–216
	11	from *Here at The New Yorker* by Brendan Gill	208–215
	12	from "Walking Tours" by R. L. Stevenson	206–212
Test Book	9–12	Short-answer Test Multiple-choice Test	
Website		www.greatsource.com/rehand/	

Before Reading

Set a Purpose

Emphasize to students that they must first determine what the test questions are asking. Then they must decide question-by-question what information is needed for the answer. Direct students to the Setting a Purpose questions on page 600 of the *Reader's Handbook*.

Setting a Purpose

- **What is the test question asking?**
- **What information is needed to answer it?**

Preview

Let students know that, on the morning of the test, they should review their notes quickly before school, focusing on areas that gave them the most trouble while studying. Then students should gather any materials they need to take the test, such as pens, pencils, and so on.

When the teacher distributes the exam, students should preview the entire test before starting, if possible. Emphasize how important previewing tests is. Read through the checklist on page 600 with students.

Preview Checklist

- ✓ *the amount of time you have to take the test*
- ✓ *the instructions about how to mark answers*
- ✓ *whether or not there is a penalty for wrong answers*
- ✓ *the types of questions, such as multiple-choice, true-false, short answer, or essay*
- ✓ *any test passages, maps, diagrams, or other graphics*

Now have students preview the sample test on pages 601–604.

Overhead Transparency

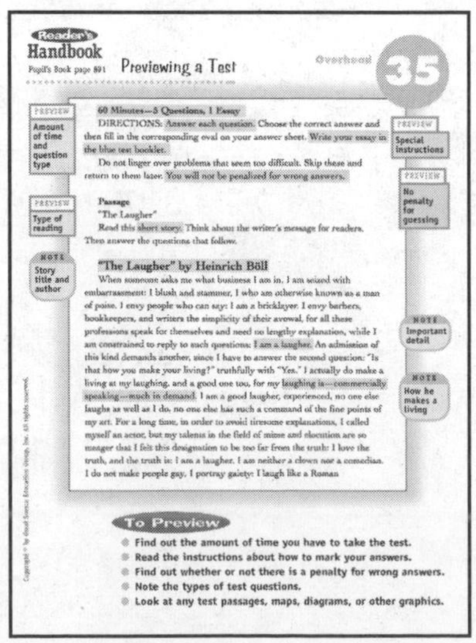

Reader's Handbook
Pupil's Book page 601
Previewing a Test
Overhead 35

PREVIEW: Amount of time and question type

60 Minutes—5 Questions, 1 Essay

DIRECTIONS: Answer each question. Choose the correct answer and then fill in the corresponding oval on your answer sheet. Write your essay in the blue test booklet.

PREVIEW: Special instructions

Do not linger over problems that seem too difficult. Skip these and return to them later. You will not be penalized for wrong answers.

PREVIEW: No penalty for guessing

PREVIEW: Type of reading

Passage
"The Laugher"
Read this short story. Think about the writer's message for readers. Then answer the questions that follow.

NOTE: Story title and author

"The Laugher" by Heinrich Böll

When someone asks me what business I am in, I am seized with embarrassment: I blush and stammer, I who am otherwise known as a man of poise. I envy people who can say: I am a bricklayer. I envy barbers, bookkeepers, and writers the simplicity of their avowal, for all these professions speak for themselves and need no lengthy explanation, while I am constrained to reply to such questions: I am a laugher. An admission of this kind demands another, since I have to answer the second question: "Is that how you make your living?" truthfully with "Yes." I actually do make a living at my laughing, and a good one too, for my laughing is—commercially speaking—much in demand. I am a good laugher, experienced, no one else laughs as well as I do, no one else has such a command of the fine points of my art. For a long time, in order to avoid tiresome explanations, I called myself an actor, but my talents in the field of mime and elocution are so meager that I felt this designation to be too far from the truth: I love the truth, and the truth is: I am a laugher. I am neither a clown nor a comedian. I do not make people gay, I portray gaiety: I laugh like a Roman

NOTE: Important detail

NOTE: How he makes a living

To Preview

- Find out the amount of time you have to take the test.
- Read the instructions about how to mark your answers.
- Find out whether or not there is a penalty for wrong answers.
- Note the types of test questions.
- Look at any test passages, maps, diagrams, or other graphics.

Before Reading

C Plan

Ask students to say in their own words what they learned during their preview. Instruct students to put a check mark or star next to the questions they think they know how to answer and to answer these questions first when taking the test.

Reading Strategy: Skimming

Remind students that **skimming** means running their eyes quickly over a page to find the information they need. In a test, such as the sample in this lesson, students may be required to return to the passage again and again to find the answers to the questions. Emphasize that skimming serves this purpose well.

Also emphasize that in taking tests students should skim only after doing a careful first reading. Ask students to turn to page 605 of their handbooks and read the steps for answering test questions. Call attention to the tips for different ways to skim at the bottom of the page.

During Reading

D Read with a Purpose

Instruct students to follow certain steps when reading a test.

TEST PLAN

✔ Read the Passage
✔ Read the Questions
✔ Skim for Answers

1. Read the Passage
Tell students to use a highlighter or pen to mark key words or passages, if permitted, while reading the test. Taking notes in the margins or on sticky notes is also a good idea.

2. Read the Questions
Emphasize that the easiest way for students to raise their test scores is by reading each question and the possible answers *very carefully*. This way, they will understand what information the questions are asking them to find. Students should be sure to read every answer before deciding on the best one.

3. Skim for Answers
Sometimes students will find the exact words of an answer in the passage. Other times they will have to look for answers that paraphrase the passage.

During Reading

Understanding the type of question being asked will also help improve students' test scores. Read the question types on the bottom of page 607 with students. Factual recall questions, critical thinking questions, and essay questions are elaborated on in the next four pages in the handbook.

FACTUAL RECALL QUESTIONS
Remind students that the answer in a factual recall question is "right there" in the passage. Have students look at the example on page 608.

CRITICAL THINKING QUESTIONS
Explain that this type of question requires students to make an inference based on the passage. Remind students that an inference requires combining information from the passage with their prior knowledge. Read the inference questions chart and the examples on pages 609–610.

INFERENCE QUESTIONS

WHAT I LEARNED	+ WHAT I ALREADY KNOW	= ANSWER
"my own laughter I have never heard"	doesn't sound happy	Probably "C. somber and serious"

ESSAY QUESTIONS
Emphasize to students that essay questions require careful reading, planning, and checking. Read through the example on page 611. Point out that the first step is to analyze carefully what the question is asking. Next, focus students on how to respond to the essay question—first, take a moment to plan, and only then begin to write. Direct students' attention to the Main Idea Organizer at the bottom of the page to see how one reader planned an essay.

MAIN IDEA ORGANIZER

MAIN IDEA		
It's possible to laugh and still be serious.		
DETAIL #1	DETAIL #2	DETAIL #3
He bemoans his fate.	Although the narrator is a laugher by profession, he says he is a "very solemn person."	His brothers and sisters "have always known" him to be "serious."
CONCLUSION A person who seems happy may actually be quite serious on the inside.		

How Tests Are Organized

Now have students look at the visual of how tests are usually organized on page 612. Stress that questions usually progress from easiest to hardest. Also point out that on tests with reading passages, the questions will often follow the order of the information in the passage.

ORDER OF QUESTIONS

E Connect

Making connections to test questions will help students access their prior knowledge, which will in turn help raise their test scores. Point this out while emphasizing the importance of making connections, even to test questions. Suggest the following ways to connect with text:

- ask themselves questions
  (What do I think about Böll's profession of being a "laugher"?)
- think about the meaning of the passage and questions
  (What is the contrast between Böll's profession and the life he leads when not at work?)
- compare the passage and questions to what they already know
  (How is Böll's reaction to his work like the reactions of people I know to their work?)
- evaluate the quality of the reading passage and questions
  (What do I think about this reading passage and what it is saying about laughter?)

After Reading

Tell students to always leave three to five minutes at the end of a test to check their answers.

F Pause and Reflect

When checking their answers, students need to double-check their understanding of what the test questions were asking. Have students consider the Looking Back questions on page 614.

Looking Back

- **Have I answered every question to the best of my ability?**
- **Are there answers that I need to rethink or spend more time on?**
- **Is my writing in the essay answer neat and free of spelling and grammatical errors?**

Students may need to return to some of the more difficult questions, rethink their answers, and reread some of the passage. Emphasize that rereading can help clarify what the question is asking or what the passage is saying.

G Reread

Suggest the strategy of **visualizing and thinking aloud** for rereading. Remind students that this strategy helps clarify the material.

Rereading Strategy: Visualizing and Thinking Aloud

Tell students that visualizing means forming a picture in their minds based on the words in the text and that thinking aloud means paraphrasing the material out loud. Ask students to read the Think Aloud on page 615. Talk about how thinking aloud can help eliminate answers that are wrong. Have students next read the Think Aloud at the top of page 616 and discuss how this reader decided answer D is correct.

THINK ALOUD

It's possible that C. is the correct answer, but the word afraid bothers me. This doesn't seem like a guy who is scared. He seems like a guy who is depressed. So I'm going to say D. is correct.

After Reading

Remember

Though most students feel like just forgetting about a test once it's over, they should try to resist this urge. Let students know that after taking a test, there is an opportunity to learn more about the subject in preparation for a future test or to learn how to take a test. Some good activities include talking about the test with a classmate and testing themselves, described on page 616.

1. Ask a Classmate

As students discuss test questions, they learn which ones were difficult for others and answers to the ones that gave them trouble. Emphasize the benefits of knowing answers in preparation for future tests. Point out too that talking with other students can help their confidence, because they will probably have classmates who struggled through parts of the test too.

2. Test Yourself

Students can question themselves. By doing this, students can help themselves learn how they learn.

What helped me most to answer the test questions?

What would I do differently for the next test?

How well prepared was I?

You may also ask students to do the creative assignment below.

Creative Assignment: Have students work in groups of three to write a different set of multiple-choice questions for "The Laugher." Have students include different question types. Groups can then share their questions with one another to see the similarities and differences.

Summing Up

Review the lesson by reading the Summing Up on page 616 of the handbook. Talk about the three basic types of questions covered: factual recall, critical thinking, and essay. Go over the initial goals for the lesson. Discuss which ones students feel they achieved and which ones that they need more work on:

1. **preparing for various kinds of tests**
2. **using the reading strategy of skimming**
3. **understanding how tests are organized and what kinds of questions they include**

Assessment and Application

Use the Quick Assess checklist to evaluate students' ability to read tests. Give students the opportunity to apply what they have learned through one of the two activities below. For students who are comfortable with the reading process and strategy, use one of the suggestions for independent practice or an activity of your own. For students who need guided help with the strategy, use a *Student Applications Book*.

Quick Assess

Can students

- ☑ name the steps in the process for reading tests?
- ☑ say why skimming is a good strategy for taking tests?
- ☑ name the three basic question types explained?

1. Independent Practice

To show that students understand the lesson, ask them to apply the strategy of **skimming** or **visualizing and thinking aloud** to a test they have taken previously or to a practice test.

Ask students to do one of the following:

- Do a Think Aloud for a passage from the test.
- Complete a chart for inference questions.
- Complete a Main Idea Organizer in preparation for writing an essay question.

2. Student Applications Books

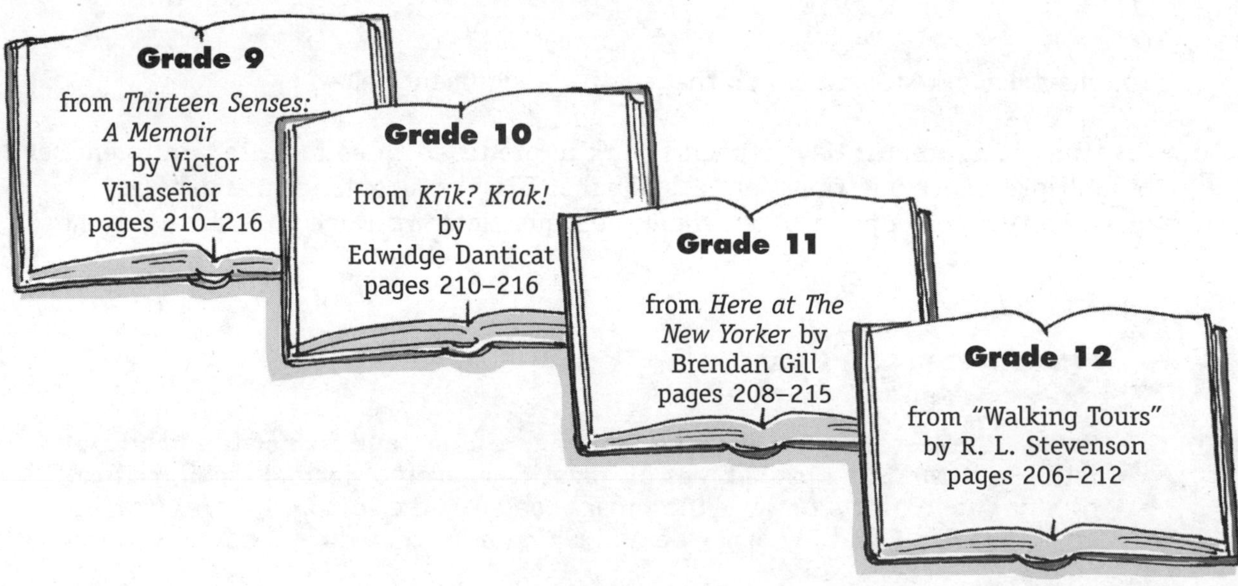

Test Book

See *Test Book* for short-answer and multiple-choice tests.

Focus on English Tests

Goals

Here students focus on how to take an English test. This lesson will help them to learn to:

- use critical thinking skills and the strategy of skimming to answer questions about a reading passage
- prepare for tests by strengthening their knowledge of grammar, usage, and mechanics
- use context clues and other methods to help with vocabulary questions

Background

Help students connect this lesson with their prior knowledge by asking them to:

- discuss English tests they have taken in the past
- say why English tests can be hard for students
- talk about how they usually prepare for English tests and what strategies they use while taking them

Overview

	Content	Teacher's Guide page	Reader's Handbook page
Selection	Sample Questions		620, 621, 622, 623
Reading Strategy	Skimming Thinking Aloud	393, 437 393, 440	619, 728 620, 736

Ancillaries

	Grade	Content	Page
Lesson Plan Book	11	Focus on English Tests	205, 210–213
Student Applications Book	9 10 11 12	Sample English Test Questions Sample English Test Questions Sample English Test Questions Sample English Test Questions	217–218 217–219 216–217 213–214
Test Book	9–12	Short-answer Test Multiple-choice Test	
Website		www.greatsource.com/rehand/	

Explain that most English exams will test students' knowledge of reading; grammar, usage, and mechanics; and vocabulary. Read through the four tips on page 618.

Tip #1: Make Note Cards

Encourage students to make note cards to help them study for English tests. A term (such as *appositive*) may be written on one side of the card and the definition on the other.

Tip #2: Take a Practice Test

Encourage students to ask their teachers what will be covered on the test, and then create a practice test. Students may exchange practice tests with classmates.

Tip #3: Build Your Vocabulary

Tell students that good ways to improve their vocabularies are to increase the amount and type of reading they do, keep a vocabulary notebook or note cards, and try to learn the meanings of some new words before each test. Emphasize to students that building their vocabularies will help them on standardized tests as well.

Tip #4: Learn Key Rules

Encourage students to study the rules for grammar, usage, and the mechanics of writing before taking an English test. For example, students should be clear on sentence fragments and run-on sentences, subject-verb agreement, and the basic comma rules and rules for capitalization.

Remind students to preview a test before starting work on it. Students should take note of what kinds of questions are on the test. Encourage students to make check marks or stars by the questions they feel they can answer and begin with those.

During Reading

After preparing for and previewing the test, students are ready to start work on it. Remind students to answer the easiest questions first.

Reading Passage Questions

Remind students to read the passage carefully first, and then go back and skim for information to answer the questions. Emphasize that some questions will require them to make inferences.

Have students read the passage and sample question on page 620. Then have them read the Think Aloud.

Grammar, Usage, and Mechanics Questions

Some English tests include questions on grammar, usage, and mechanics. Such questions require that students know the rules for capitalization, punctuation, verb and pronoun usage, and subject-verb agreement. They must also be able to apply the rules. Have students read through the sample question on page 621.

Vocabulary Questions

Explain to students that vocabulary questions may be about word definitions, parts of speech, and word analogies or about how words relate to one another. Have students read through the sample question on page 622.

Review the common kinds of word analogies displayed at the bottom of page 622. Invite students to explain each analogy type in their own words to reinforce their understanding. Then have students look at the sample analogy question on page 623.

After Reading

Remind students to leave a few minutes at the end of the test to check and double-check their answers. This includes proofreading any writing done to make sure it is free of obvious errors. Encourage students to look back at the questions that seemed hardest and check those answers again.

Summing Up

Have students read over the points in the Summing Up section at the bottom of page 623. Ask students to say in their own words what they learned in this lesson.

Assessment and Application

Use the Quick Assess checklist to evaluate students' ability to take an English test. Give students the opportunity to apply what they have learned through one of the two activities below. For students who are comfortable with taking English tests, use the suggestion below for independent practice or an activity of your own. For students who need guided help with the strategy, use a *Student Applications Book*.

Quick Assess

Can students

- ☑ name two or three ways to prepare for an English test?
- ☑ name two or three ways to improve their vocabularies?
- ☑ explain how to preview and take an English test?

1. Independent Practice

To show that they understand the lesson, have students apply **skimming** or **thinking aloud** to a previous or practice English test.

2. Student Applications Books

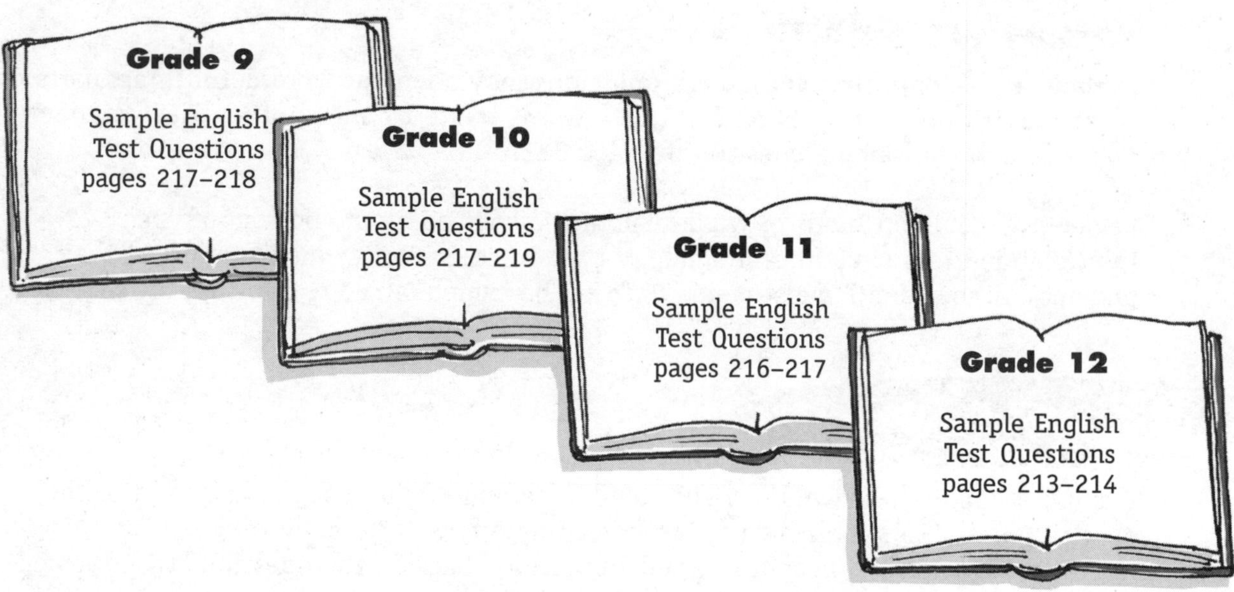

Test Book

See *Test Book* for short-answer and multiple-choice tests.

Focus on Writing Tests

Goals

Now students will focus on writing tests. This lesson will help students to:

- read and understand the kinds of questions that appear on writing tests and essay questions
- revise effectively
- use graphic organizers to plan and write

Background

Help students connect this lesson with their existing knowledge by asking them to:

- describe essay tests they've taken in the past
- discuss how they have prepared for writing tests and what strategies they have used while taking these tests
- say why writing tests are important

Overview

	Content	*Teacher's Guide* page	*Reader's Handbook* page
Selection	Sample Test and Question		628, 629
Tool	Main Idea Organizer	397	629, 630, 747

Ancillaries

	Grade	Content	Page
Lesson Plan Book	9 12	Focus on Writing Tests Focus on Writing Tests	194, 196–199 204, 206–209
Student Applications Book	9 10 11 12	"The Need for a New School Holiday" "New School Gym or Library?" "School Uniforms" "Morality of Zoos"	219–221 220–221 218–219 215–216
Test Book	9–12	Short-answer Test Multiple-choice Test	
Website		www.greatsource.com/rehand/	

Before Reading

Encourage students to find out as much about the test as they can before the day of the test. Emphasize that the more they know about the test in advance, the more confident they will feel.

Explain that writing tests often involve correcting sentence errors, improving sentences and paragraphs, and responding to essay questions in a certain time frame. By following certain tips, students can improve their performance on writing tests.

Tip #1: Prepare for a Writing Test

Read through the four steps to prepare for a writing test at the top of page 625. Encourage students to review the basic rules for grammar, usage, and mechanics; complete a practice test; talk to students who have taken the test previously; and formulate a plan for how to attack the test.

Tip #2: Preview a Writing Test

Emphasize the need to preview any test before starting work on it. Students need to know what types of questions are included and how much time they have for each test section. Students should keep in mind that test writers generally put the easiest questions first.

During Reading

In the first few minutes of starting work on the test, students need to pause to collect their thoughts and feel confident. Encourage students to breathe deeply and relax before starting work.

Read through Tips 3 to 5 on page 626 with the students.

Tip #3: Read the Directions

Emphasize the need to read the directions carefully. Making sure they understand the directions and the questions is the easiest way for students to improve their test scores.

Tip #4: Read the Possible Answers Carefully

When answering multiple-choice questions, students need to read all the possible answers carefully. Discourage students from simply marking the first choice that seems plausible. Test writers often include one or more answers that are partially true. If students aren't careful, they may seize on that one before seeing that part of the answer is false or that another answer is completely true.

Tip #5: Read the Writing Prompt

Read through the common types of writing prompts, explained at the bottom of page 626. Invite students to recall and discuss other prompts they have had to respond to in the past.

COMMON KINDS OF PROMPTS

Prompt #1: Personal *You are asked to write about a personal experience or belief. For example:*
Write about an experience that changed your life.

Prompt #2: Social *You are asked to give your opinion about a social problem or issue. For example:*
Discuss illiteracy in America and what you can do to help.

Prompt #3: Academic *You are asked to write about a piece of literature, an event in history, or something else you've learned about in school. For example:*
Discuss the topics of remorse and revenge in Charles Dickens's *A Tale of Two Cities*.

Tip #6: Use a Writing Plan

Now emphasize the need for a writing plan when responding to prompts. Read through the plan on page 627 with the students.

1. Writing the Topic Sentence

Discuss the importance of getting a plan for writing a topic sentence.

2. Supporting Your Topic Sentence

Stress the need to use examples from the reading, preferably three or four.

3. Concluding the Essay

One effective way to conclude an essay is to give a reason for what is stated in the topic sentence. Review the model essay response with students.

Then ask students to read through the sample test on page 628 to see how they may use this plan to respond to a prompt.

Now have students examine the sample writing directions at the top of page 629, taking note of the key words. These key terms let students know what type of essay is expected of them (descriptive), what the subject is (a building), and that students need to form and state their opinion, give supporting details, and check for errors.

Direct students' attention to the Main Idea Organizer on page 629. Point out that this tool can help them sort out and organize their thoughts, especially under the pressure of a test. Then have them read through the example on page 630.

After Reading

After writing their essays, students need to go back and proofread. Some useful revision questions are shown on page 631.

REVISION QUESTIONS

Simply by reading through their essays and correcting spelling errors, adding a comma or capital letter where needed, or inserting a clarifying word or phrase, students can greatly improve their essays.

Summing Up

Have students read over the points in the Summing Up section at the bottom of page 631. Then ask students to say in their own words what they learned in this lesson.

Assessment and Application

Use the Quick Assess checklist to evaluate students' ability to take a writing test. Give students the opportunity to apply what they have learned through one of the two activities below. For students who are comfortable with writing tests, use the suggestion below for independent practice or an activity of your own. For students who need guided help with the strategy, use a *Student Applications Book*.

Quick Assess

Can students

- ☑ say what basic areas are covered on a writing test?
- ☑ describe the writing plan for responding to prompts?
- ☑ name a useful tool for organizing their thoughts before writing?

1. Independent Practice

To show that they understand the lesson, students can use the Main Idea Organizer to organize their thoughts and compose an essay on a different writing prompt.

2. Student Applications Books

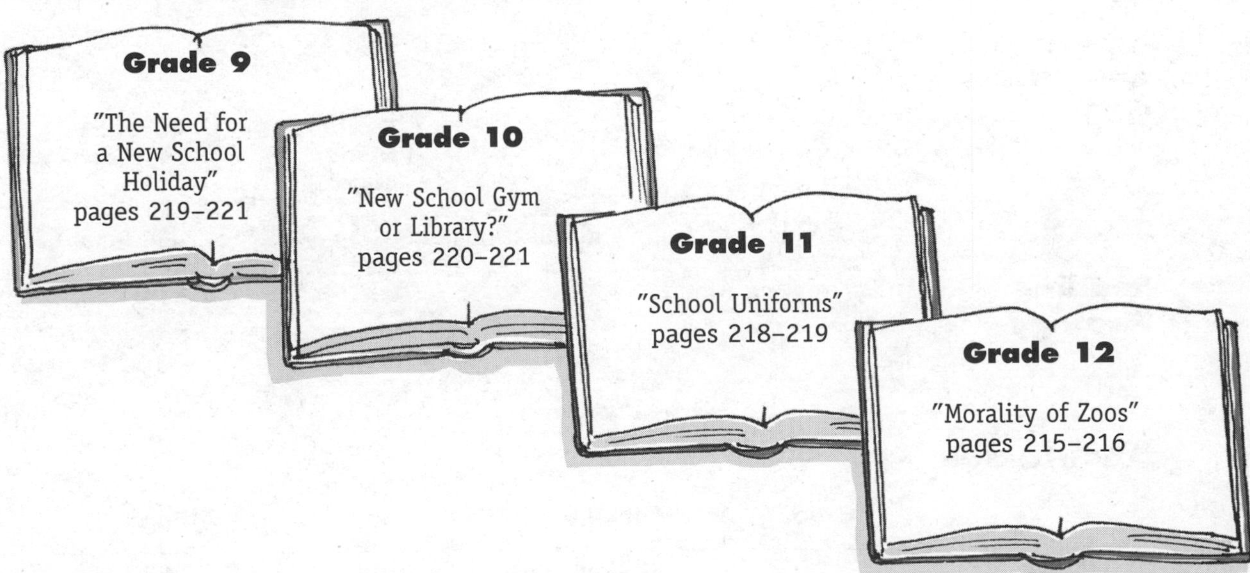

Test Book

See *Test Book* for short-answer and multiple-choice tests.

Focus on Standardized Tests

Goals

Here students focus on taking a standardized test. This lesson will help them to learn to:

- get ready for a standardized test
- read the directions, questions, and answers on all types of tests

Background

Help students connect this lesson with their prior knowledge by asking them to:

- talk about standardized tests they have taken in the past
- discuss how they feel about taking standardized tests
- say why standardized tests can be difficult for students
- discuss ways students can prepare to take standardized tests

Overview

	Content	Teacher's Guide page	Reader's Handbook page
Selection	Sample Directions and Questions		634, 635, 636
Reading Strategy	Thinking Aloud	402, 440	635, 636, 736

Ancillaries

	Grade	Content	Page
Student Applications Book	9	Shakespeare Question	222–223
	10	Food and Drug Administration Question	222–223
	11	Grammar Questions	220–221
	12	Grammar Questions	217–218
Lesson Plan Book	9	Focus on History and Standardized Tests	195, 200–203
Test Book	9–12	Short-answer Test Multiple-choice Test	
Website		www.greatsource.com/rehand	

Before Reading

Explain that standardized tests basically follow the same format. Standardized tests are divided into parts (two or three), and almost all contain a verbal or writing part. Let students know that the following tips can help them increase their scores.

Tip #1: Visit the Test Website

Most states have a test website that includes information about upcoming standardized tests. Encourage students to visit this website, or allow class time to access the site together.

Tip #2: Take a Practice Test

Sometimes practice tests are available on the state or district websites. Also, practice tests are available in test preparation books available in bookstores. Encourage students to obtain and take one of these practice tests. Alternatively, you may provide the class with practice tests and allow class time for the students to take them. Taking practice tests does help students perform better on the actual test.

Tip #3: Prepare Yourself Mentally and Physically

Emphasize the importance of eating well and getting enough sleep before taking the test. These simple steps can help students maintain their endurance through the long test.

Tip #4: Relax

Also emphasize the importance of relaxing before beginning work on the test. Demonstrate strategies for relaxing, such as deep breathing and positive thinking. Let students know that being well prepared will help them feel confident and relaxed.

During Reading

After preparing for and previewing the test, students are ready to start work on it. Remind students to try to relax before beginning.

Tip #5: Preview the Test

Remind students to preview the test, if permitted, before starting work on it. Students should take note of what kinds of questions are on the test. Encourage students to make check marks or stars by the questions they feel they can answer and begin with those.

Tip #6: Listen to the Instructions

Emphasize the importance of listening very carefully to all verbal instructions. Students should take note of time limits and penalties for guessing.

Tip #7: Read the Directions and Questions

Stress the importance of reading the directions carefully. If marking up the test booklet is permitted, students should use a highlighter or pen to mark key words and phrases in the directions.

Now have students silently read the sample test directions on page 634. Instruct them to focus on key words or phrases. After the whole class has read the directions, ask students to summarize them.

Tip #8: Read Every Answer

Tell students to read every answer possibility before making a choice. Remind them that some answers may be only half true, and not to stop there but to read all answer choices. Emphasize that this will only take a few seconds and will help students avoid careless mistakes.

Have students read the sample question on page 635. Encourage them to use the strategy of **thinking aloud** to work through the answer. Read over the Think Aloud example at the bottom of the page.

Tip #9: Eliminate Wrong Answers

Instruct students to eliminate answer possibilities that are obviously wrong. If students can narrow down the possibilities to two but are unsure of the one correct answer, they should guess because the directions on this test say there is no penalty for guessing.

Tip #10: Make Educated Guesses

Reinforce the concept of *educated* guessing. Stress that this does not mean randomly filling in ovals. Instead, students need to gather all the information they can before marking an answer. Read through the sample question and Think Aloud sections on page 636 with the students to demonstrate this process. Point out that this reader kept thinking about the choices until it was possible to make an educated guess.

Remind students to leave a few minutes at the end of the test to check and double-check their answers. Encourage students to look back at the questions that seemed hardest and rethink those answers carefully.

Summing Up

Have students read the points in Summing Up at the bottom of page 637. Ask students to tell in their own words what they learned in this lesson.

Assessment and Application

Use the Quick Assess checklist to evaluate students' ability to take a standardized test. Give students the opportunity to apply what they have learned through one of the two activities below. For students who are comfortable with taking standardized tests, use the suggestion below for independent practice or an activity of your own. For students who need guided help with the strategy, use a *Student Applications Book.*

Quick Assess

Can students

- ☑ describe ways to prepare for standardized tests?
- ☑ name a strategy that will help them work through the answers to questions?
- ☑ explain what to do once they are finished taking the test?

1. Independent Practice

To show that they understand the lesson, students can apply the strategy of **thinking aloud** to a practice standardized test.

2. Student Applications Books

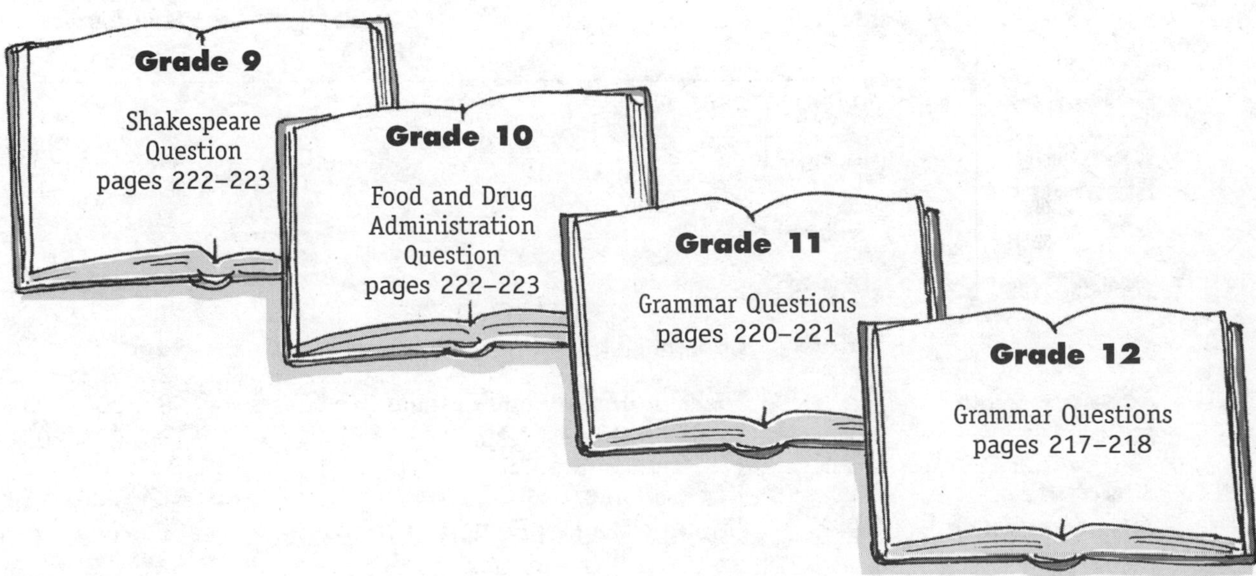

Test Book

See *Test Book* for short-answer and multiple-choice tests.

Focus on History Tests

Goals

Now students will focus on taking a history test. This lesson will help students to:

- prepare for a history test
- preview common elements on a history test
- use test-taking tips that can help raise their test scores

Background

Help students connect this lesson with their existing knowledge by asking them to:

- describe history tests they've taken in the past
- discuss how they have prepared for history tests

Overview

	Content	Teacher's Guide page	Reader's Handbook page
Selection	Sample Questions		640, 641
Reading Strategy	Thinking Aloud	406, 440	640, 642, 736

Ancillaries

	Grade	Content	Page
Lesson Plan Book	9	Focus on History and Standardized Tests	195, 200–203
	10	Focus on History Tests	195, 200–203
Student Applications Book	9	Fall of Rome/Caste System	224–225
	10	Bubonic Plague/French Revolution	224–226
	11	Pre-Civil War America	222–223
	12	Industrial Revolution	219–220
Test Book	9–12	Short-answer Test Multiple-choice Test	
Website		www.greatsource.com/rehand/	
Content Area Guide		This lesson appears in the *Content Area Guide: Social Studies.*	

Before Reading

To prepare for a history test, students need to return to the chapters covered on the test. Instruct students to pay close attention to study guides and material before or after the chapters that summarize the content. Also instruct students to memorize key definitions and important details about time and place.

Direct students' attention to the list of items to study on page 638. Emphasize the importance of memorizing names, dates, people, and places; answering end-of-chapter questions; and studying maps, timelines, graphs, primary sources, and political cartoons. Then go through the additional test-taking tips beginning on page 639.

Tip #1: Create a Top Ten List

Encourage students to create a "top ten" list of the most important topics to study. Emphasize that they should find out as much as they can about the test from their history teacher. Then tell students to learn a few things about each item on their list.

TOP TEN LIST

1. African-American slavery
2. Abolitionism
3. Abraham Lincoln
4. Secession
5. Confederate Army
6. Union Army
7. Battle of Bull Run
8. Gettysburg
9. Emancipation Proclamation
10. Reconstruction

Tip #2: Learn How to Read Graphics

Encourage students to review the section on Reading a Graphic in the handbook. Emphasize that graphics usually contain a great deal of important information.

Tip #3: Use Graphic Organizers

Stress that graphic organizers make excellent study aids. Suggest that students create Main Idea Organizers and Sequence Notes.

Tip #4: Preview

Remind students to preview the test before they begin working on it. Emphasize the importance of reading directions, noting time limits, and seeing what types of questions the test includes.

During Reading

Remind students to begin by answering the questions they are most sure of. However, emphasize that even questions that seem ridiculously easy need to be read carefully. Ask students to read the sample question on page 640.

Tip #5: Eliminate Incorrect Answers

Tell students that when they come to a question they're unsure of, they should eliminate the possibilities that are clearly incorrect. Then students can make an educated guess.

Tip #6: Beware of Partially True Answers

Remind students that some answers look right but are in fact only half true. Suggest that they use the strategy of **thinking aloud** and then read through the Think Aloud example on the bottom of page 640.

Tip #7: Look at the Big Picture

Tell students that when they come to a graphic on a test, they need to pause and try to see "the big picture." Have students examine the graphic and read the question and possible answers on page 641. Then read through the Think Aloud on page 642 with the students to show them how one reader thought through this answer.

After Reading

Emphasize the importance of leaving a few minutes at the end of the test period to check over answers. Encourage students to return to the questions that were most difficult for them and rethink their answers.

Summing Up

Have students read over the points in the Summing Up section at the bottom of page 642. Then ask students to say in their own words what they learned in this lesson.

Assessment and Application

Use the Quick Assess checklist to evaluate students' ability to take a history test. Give students the opportunity to apply what they have learned through one of the two activities below. For students who are comfortable with history tests, use the suggestion below for independent practice or an activity of your own. For students who need guided help with the strategy, use a *Student Applications Book.*

Quick Assess

Can students

- describe good ways to prepare for a history test?
- explain what to do when answering questions they are uncertain of?
- describe how to read and interpret a graphic on a history test?

1. Independent Practice

Ask students to show that they understand the lesson by working through a practice history test.

2. Student Applications Books

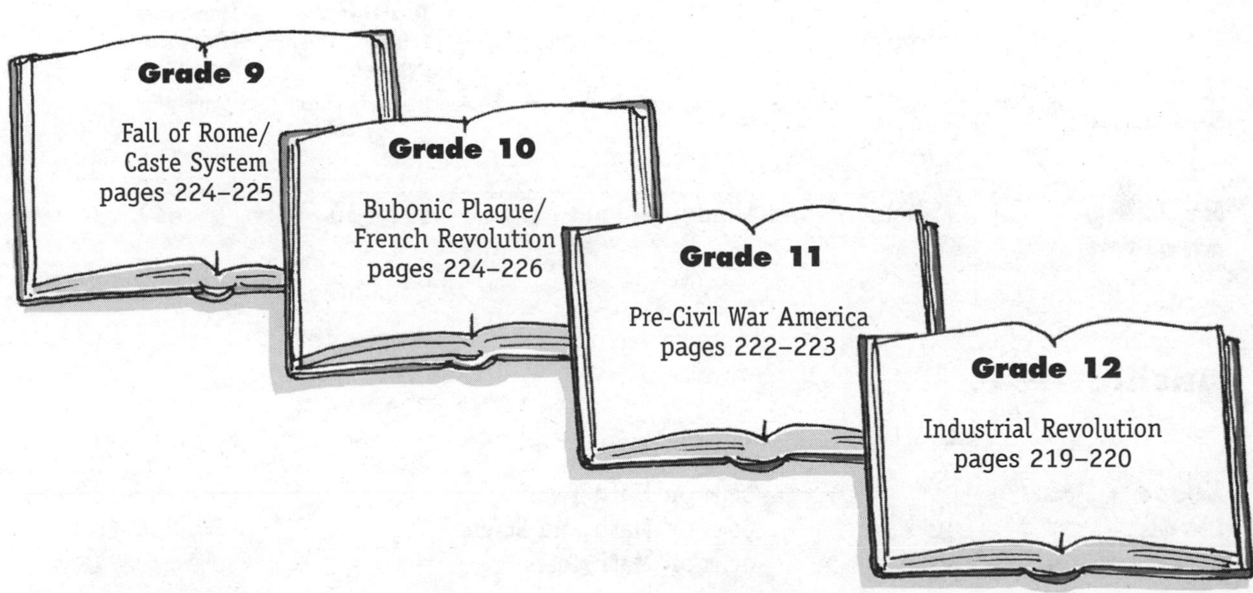

Test Book

See *Test Book* for short-answer and multiple-choice tests.

Focus on Math Tests

Goals

Now students will focus on taking a math test. This lesson will help students to:

- prepare for a math test
- plan how to use their time during a test
- understand word problems, equations, and graphics

Background

Help students connect this lesson with their existing knowledge by asking them to:

- discuss how they usually prepare for math tests and what strategies they use while taking these tests
- say why math tests can be difficult for students

Overview

	Content	Teacher's Guide page	Reader's Handbook page
Selection	Sample Questions		644, 645, 646, 647, 648, 649
Reading Strategy	Visualizing and Thinking Aloud	409–410, 440	645–649, 736

Ancillaries

	Grade	Content	Page
Lesson Plan Book	9 10 12	Focus on Math Tests Focus on Math and Science Tests Focus on Math Tests	204, 206–209 204, 206–209 205, 210–213
Student Applications Book	9 10 11 12	Calculating Averages Calculating Averages Calculating Area Calculating Percentages	226–227 227–228 224–225 221–222
Test Book	9–12	Short-answer Test Multiple-choice Test	
Website		www.greatsource.com/rehand/	
Content Area Guide		This lesson appears in the *Content Area Guide: Math.*	

Getting Ready

To prepare for a math test, students should review previous homework assignments and quizzes. Students should then review the chapters covered on the test. Students also need to memorize any of the terms, rules, and formulas they will probably need to know for the test.

Previewing

Remind students to preview the test before they start to work on it. This will let them know what types of questions are on the test, which questions they should begin with, and how to plan their time.

During Reading

Remind students to begin by answering the easiest questions and that even easy questions need to be read carefully.

Solving the Easy Problems

Ask students to read the sample question on page 644. Point out the problem notes at the side of the page.

Solving the Challenging Problems

Now have students examine a more challenging problem. They can begin with the sample question on page 645.

Tip #1: Eliminate Wrong Answers

Have students go through the process of eliminating wrong answers using the strategy of **thinking aloud**. The problem notes on the side of the page model this process.

Tip #2: Plug in Answers

Now have students try plugging in the possible answers. Have them read through the sample question and Think Aloud on page 646 to see how this is done.

Tip #3: Visualize the Answer

Another good strategy for taking math tests is **visualizing** the answer. Ask students to read through the sample question and the Visualize and Think Aloud example on page 647.

Tip #4: Try Easier Numbers First

Trying to plug in the easier answer choices first is helpful for eliminating incorrect options. Have students read through the sample question and Think Aloud on page 648.

After Reading

Most students leave problems involving geometric shapes, graphs, charts, and diagrams for the end of the test because these problems seem the hardest. Remind them that they need to use formulas they have learned in class to solve these kinds of problems.

Now read through the sample question and Think Aloud on page 649 with the students. Let students know that often problems that seem hard at first may not actually be that hard. Remind students not to lose their composure but to step back and think through the problem step by step.

Summing Up

Have students read over the points in the Summing Up section at the bottom of page 649. Then ask students to say in their own words what they learned in this lesson.

Assessment and Application

Use the Quick Assess checklist to evaluate students' ability to take a math test. Give students the opportunity to apply what they have learned through one of the two activities below. For students who are comfortable with math tests, use the suggestion below for independent practice or an activity of your own. For students who need guided help with the strategy, use a *Student Applications Book*.

Quick Assess

Can students

- describe good ways to prepare for a math test?
- explain what to do when working through math problems?
- name a reading strategy that will help them work through math problems?

1. Independent Practice

To show that they understand the lesson, students can work through a practice math test.

2. Student Applications Books

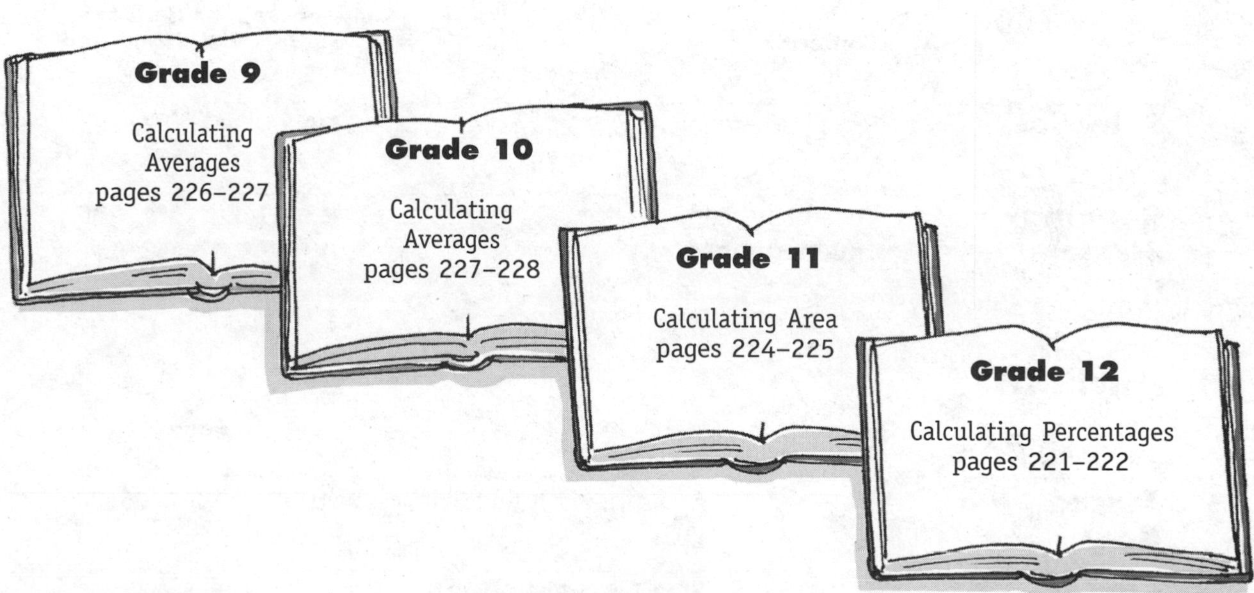

Test Book

See *Test Book* for short-answer and multiple-choice tests.

Focus on Science Tests

Goals

Now students will focus on taking a science test. This lesson will help students to:

- ☑ prepare for science tests
- ☑ preview and work through test solutions
- ☑ read science tables, charts, diagrams, and graphs

Background

Help students connect this lesson with their existing knowledge by asking them to:

- describe science tests they've taken in the past
- discuss how they usually prepare for science tests and what strategies they use while taking these tests

Overview

	Content	*Teacher's Guide* page	*Reader's Handbook* page
Selection	Sample Questions		652, 653, 654
Reading Strategy	Visualizing and Thinking Aloud	413, 414, 440	651, 736 652–654, 736

Ancillaries

	Grade	Content	Page
Lesson Plan Book	10	Focus on Math and Science Tests	204, 206–209
Student Applications Book	9 10 11 12	Star Apparent Magnitude The Five Brightest Stars/Food Web Velocity The Human Eye	228–229 229–230 226–227 223–224
Test Book	9–12	Short-answer Test Multiple-choice Test	
Website		www.greatsource.com/rehand/	
Content Area Guide		This lesson appears in the *Content Area Guide: Science.*	

Before Reading

Read through the tips for preparing for science tests, beginning on page 650, with the students.

Tip #1: Learn Science Terms

Point out that science vocabulary is very different from our everyday vocabulary. Encourage students to acquire science terms over time rather than waiting until the night before the test to try to learn them. Suggest learning a few new science terms each week, writing the words in a designated section in their science notebooks.

Tip #2: Read and Review

Emphasize the importance of reading and reviewing their science books. Tell students to especially attend to the study guide or any summary material. These need not be long study sessions. "Refresher" courses on key points can help a lot.

Tip #3: Make Yourself Diagrams

Encourage students to use the strategy of **visualizing.** They can draw pictures or diagrams to represent processes and concepts in their science books. Visualizing aids in comprehension as well as recall.

VISUALIZE

NOTES

At the core of an atom is a nucleus. The nucleus is made up of particles called protons and neutrons.

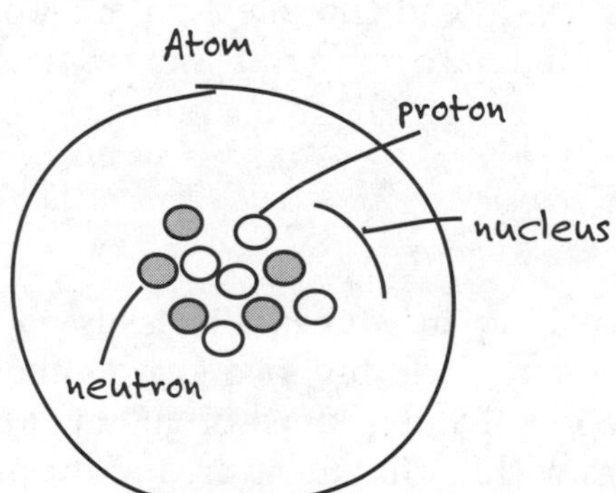

Tip #4: Learn How to Read Graphics

Encourage students to learn how to understand graphics before taking a science test. Have students review the section on Reading a Graphic in the handbook if necessary.

Tip #5: Preview

Remind students to always begin with a preview. They can mark the easy questions to answer first and budget their time for the different parts of the test.

During Reading

Explain that science tests can contain many types of questions, including multiple-choice, true-false, short answer, and essay.

Science Knowledge

Students' knowledge of scientific terms, facts, and formulas is tested on the "science knowledge" part of science exams. Have students use the strategy of **thinking aloud** as they read through the sample question and Think Aloud on page 652.

Science Reasoning

"Science reasoning" refers to drawing conclusions from a set of data. With the students, read through the section on answering this type of question, along with the sample question and Think Aloud, on page 653 of the handbook. Then have students read and interpret a graphic. A sample is shown on page 654.

After Reading

After completing the easier questions on the test, students will need to return to answer the harder ones. Tell students to use the same strategies to answer the more challenging questions: Read the question and answer choices carefully, visualize, think aloud, and eliminate wrong answers. Sometimes students will need to make an educated guess.

Make a Guess

Emphasize that making an *educated* guess is not the same as making a *random* guess. If students can eliminate all but two answer choices, then it is a good idea to guess. They will have a 50 percent chance of guessing correctly. Caution students to read carefully for clues within the question and for partly true answer choices.

Check Your Work

Remind students to leave a few minutes at the end of the test to check their work. Encourage them to spend time rereading and rethinking the more difficult questions.

Summing Up

Have students read over the points in the Summing Up section at the bottom of page 655. Then ask students to say in their own words what they learned in this lesson.

Assessment and Application

Use the Quick Assess checklist to evaluate students' ability to take a science test. Give students the opportunity to apply what they have learned through one of the two activities below. For students who are comfortable with science tests, use the suggestion below for independent practice or an activity of your own. For students who need guided help with the strategy, use a *Student Applications Book*.

Quick Assess

Can students

- ☑ describe good ways to prepare for a science test?
- ☑ name a strategy that will help them answer the questions on science tests?
- ☑ describe how to make an "educated" guess?

1. Independent Practice

To show that they understand the lesson, students can work through a practice science test.

2. Student Applications Books

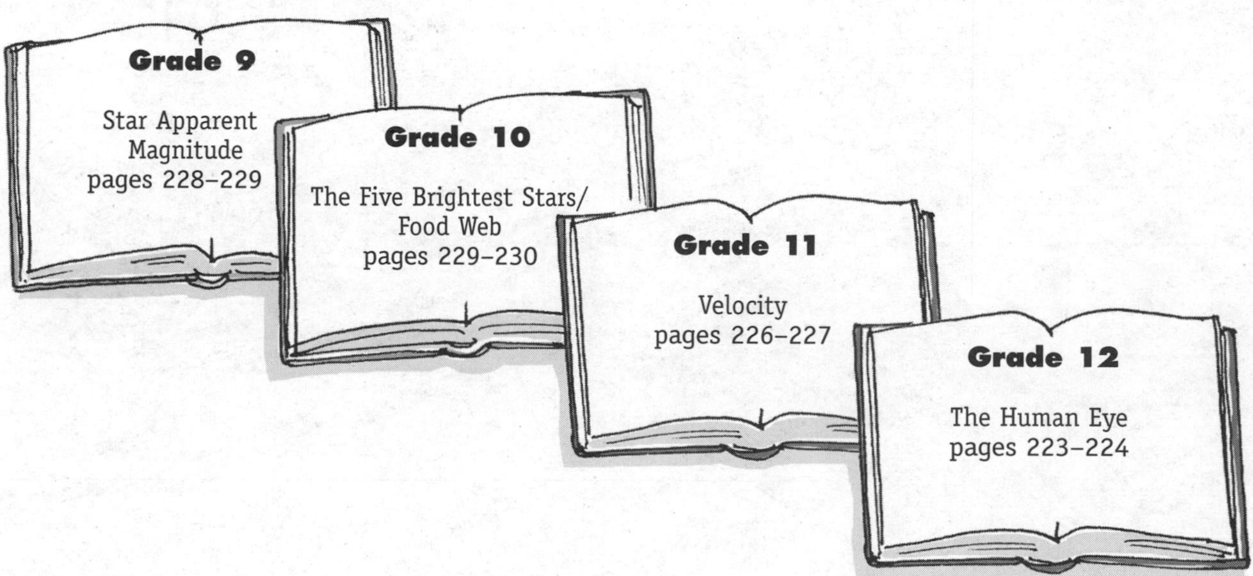

Test Book

See *Test Book* for short-answer and multiple-choice tests.

Improving Vocabulary

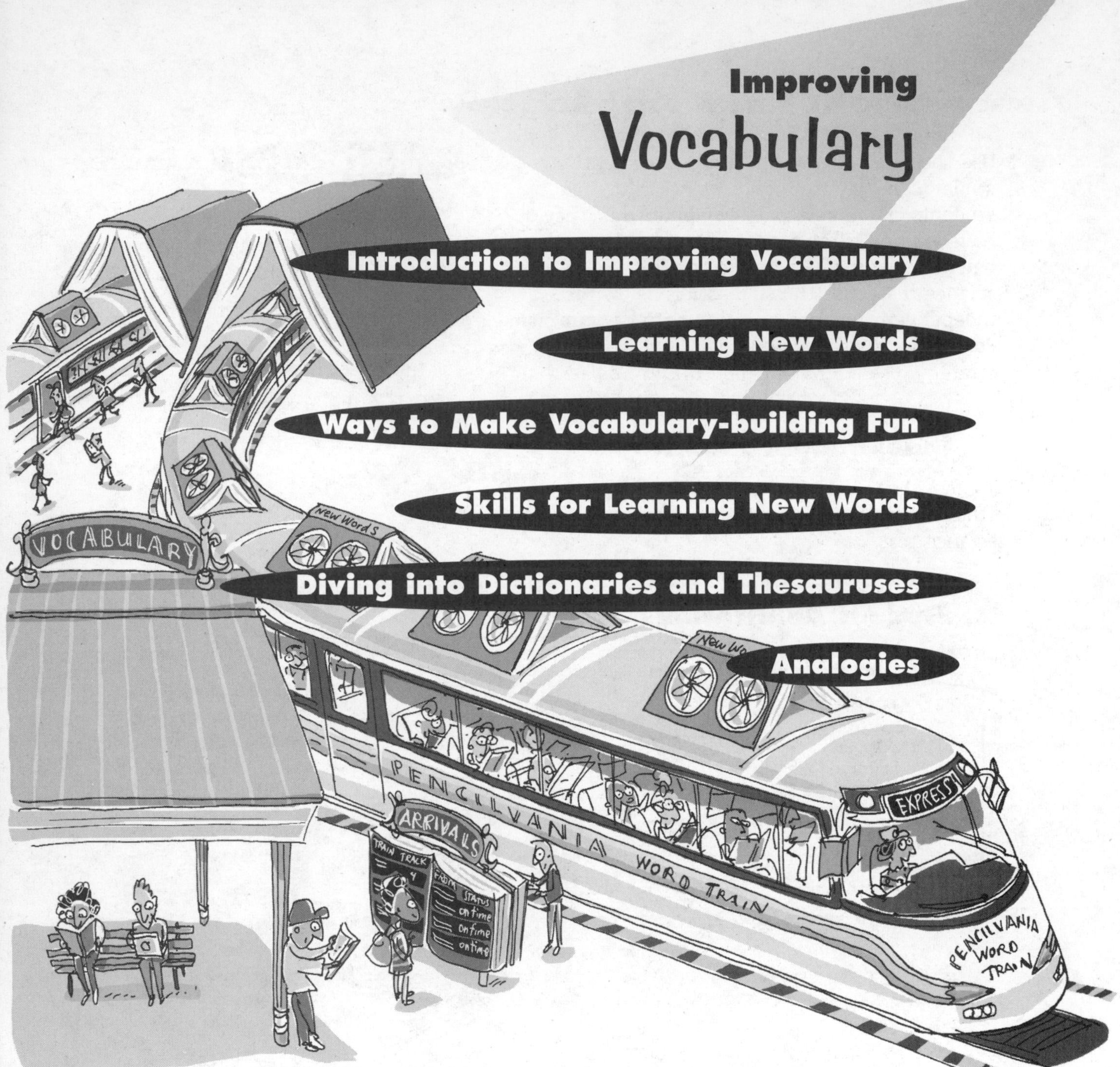

Introduction to Improving Vocabulary

Talk with students about why it is a good idea to improve their vocabularies. Discuss how words help people express their ideas and learn about the world around them. Emphasize that working with words can be fun, and point out that many people enjoy playing word games or doing crossword puzzles. From a practical point of view, a large vocabulary will help them do well on school assignments and standardized tests. Direct students to page 658, and have volunteers read the paragraphs aloud.

Improving Vocabulary

Here students will learn new words, ways to build vocabulary and vocabulary skills, uses of dictionaries and thesauruses, and how to read analogies.

Learning New Words

Emphasize the importance of learning new words. Compare building a vocabulary to building up muscles—with just a little bit of work every day, the result is impressive. Also stress that learning new words is not that difficult.

Why Build a Strong Vocabulary?

Let students know that building a strong vocabulary will improve their reading ability and academic performance. Point out that a good vocabulary will help students think clearly and communicate their thoughts to others.

Collecting New Words

One way to build vocabulary strength is by collecting words. Suggest to students that they collect words, just as they collect CDs. Go over the seven ways to make words their own.

1. Keep a Vocabulary Journal
Encourage students to keep a special notebook for new vocabulary. Different parts of the notebook should be designated for different categories of words. Have students look at the sample vocabulary journal entries on page 661.

2. Look Up Words
Point out that students can look up words from their textbooks in the textbook glossary. Other words can be looked up in a dictionary. Go over the sample dictionary entry for *vulnerable* on page 662. Show how one reader incorporated that definition in the vocabulary notebook example.

3. Pronounce Words
Explain that saying words out loud can help students fix the new words in their minds. Remind students that the dictionary gives information on how to pronounce words.

4. Keep Study or Note Cards
Tell students that another way to collect words is with a file card box. In this system, students write a word on one side of the card and its definition on the other. Show students the example on page 663.

5. Learn Words Every Day
Encourage students to add new words to their long-term memory by following the steps on page 664. Have students take turns reading each of the points aloud.

6. Use New Words

Emphasize that students need to use new words in speech and in their writing. Suggest that they make a point of using their new words when talking to friends and family and when doing a writing assignment for school.

7. Create Concept Maps

Suggest that students create concept maps for the important terms learned in school. Walk through the description and example given on pages 664 and 665.

Ways to Make Vocabulary-building Fun

Let students know that building a vocabulary can be fun. Suggest the following three ways to make it fun.

1. Read in Your Leisure Time

Emphasize that the best way to acquire a large vocabulary is by doing a lot of reading just for fun. Magazines, newspapers, and novels are all good sources of new words. Encourage students to spend about half an hour a day reading anything they like.

2. Be an Active Listener

Encourage students to ask for the meanings of unfamiliar words when talking with people, especially older people. If students are afraid of appearing stupid, point out that *looking* smart is not nearly as good as *being* smart.

3. Play Word Games

Suggest that students play word games to help build their vocabularies. Bring a few word games to class so that students can become familiar with them. If possible, allow class time for students to play the games together.

Skills for Learning New Words

Explain that students need to acquire certain skills for learning new words. Once students have these skills, they will find it easier to build a vocabulary.

Context Clues

Emphasize the importance of being able to infer the meanings of words from context. Remind students that *context clues* are the words, phrases, and sentences around the unfamiliar word. Often, readers will be able to tell in general what a word means by looking at the surrounding text.

Recognizing Context Clues

Have students read the excerpt from Edgar Allan Poe's "The Masque of the Red Death" on page 667. Ask them to try to infer the meaning of *pestilence* from this passage. Then have students read the excerpt from Nathaniel Hawthorne's "Dr. Heidegger's Experiment" at the bottom of that page to infer the meaning of *mendicant*. Finally, have them try to infer the meaning of *incumbent* in the excerpt from *An American Tragedy* by Theodore Dreiser on page 668.

Kinds of Context Clues

Review the different types of context clues with the students. These include definitions or synonyms, concrete examples, contrast clues, description clues, words or phrases that modify, conjunctions that show relationships, and unstated or implied meanings.

1. DEFINITIONS OR SYNONYMS

Explain to students that, especially in textbooks, writers will give synonyms for or definitions of a difficult word. Show students the examples on page 669.

2. CONCRETE EXAMPLES

Another type of context clue is a concrete example. These are examples that illustrate and clarify a difficult concept. Have students read the example on page 669.

3. CONTRAST CLUES

Explain that sometimes the text contains opposite meanings that give clues to the meaning of a challenging word. Read through the example in the excerpt from John Berendt's *Midnight in the Garden of Good and Evil* on page 670. Another example is provided in the excerpt from *The Sea Wolf* at the bottom of that page.

4. DESCRIPTION CLUES

Tell students that sometimes an author's description reveals the definition of a word. Have students read through the example at the top of page 671.

5. WORDS OR PHRASES THAT MODIFY

Explain that modifiers are adjectives, adverbs, or phrases and clauses that often provide clues to the meaning of a word. Read the excerpt from *House Made of Dawn* by N. Scott Momaday at the bottom of page 671.

6. CONJUNCTIONS SHOWING RELATIONSHIPS

Often writers provide context clues with conjunctions that show relationships among words. Read through the example on page 672.

7. UNSTATED OR IMPLIED MEANINGS

Emphasize to students that sometimes they will be able to infer word meanings by drawing on their own prior knowledge. Have students read the excerpt from "Zlateh the Goat" on the bottom of page 672 to infer the meaning of *chaos*.

Beyond Context Clues

Acknowledge that word meanings cannot always be inferred from context. When this happens, students need other strategies for finding the meaning of a word. Suggest that they check a dictionary immediately, pause to ask someone else for the meaning, or jot the word down to find its meaning later.

Understanding Roots, Prefixes, and Suffixes

Emphasize that using word parts to figure out unknown words is very effective. Word roots, prefixes, and suffixes all give important clues to word meaning.

Word Roots

Explain that a *word root,* sometimes called a *base word,* is the part of the word that carries the word's meaning. Walk through the list of words on page 673 that can be understood at least partially by knowing that *ped* and *pod* refer to "foot."

Prefixes

Remind students that prefixes are the word parts at the beginning of some words that change their meaning. Read through the lists on page 674 to show how the prefixes *pre-* and *dis-* affect the meanings of these words. A more complete list of prefixes is given in the Reader's Almanac.

Suffixes

Remind students that suffixes are word parts added to the ends of words. Explain that when a suffix is added to a word, the part of speech as well as the meaning may change. Read through the list of words with suffixes, along with their parts of speech and meanings, on page 674.

Putting Word Parts Together

Again, emphasize that one of the best ways to build vocabulary is to learn the meanings of word parts. Read the list of general tips on page 675 with students. Explain that knowing word parts helps you know part of many different words, even if you don't know the whole meaning. Make this point by telling students that *pre-* means "before," and knowing this prefix helps you understand what the words *preamble*, *prelude*, and *predetermine* mean.

Word Families

Knowing word families is also helpful for understanding words. Explain to students that a word family is a collection of words that are built on the same root. Read through the examples of word families on page 676.

Diving into Dictionaries and Thesauruses

Emphasize to students the importance of becoming comfortable with dictionaries and thesauruses. Dictionaries are very useful for readers.

Using Different Dictionaries

Explain that there are different kinds of dictionaries; students do not need to carry around a 12-pound unabridged dictionary. Show students examples of smaller, more convenient dictionaries. Point out that such dictionaries also tend to have simpler definitions, which are easier to understand.

Why Use a Dictionary?

Have students read through and discuss the list of what they can find in a dictionary. Ask students to talk about why they do or do not use a dictionary. Ask why they think so many students resist using dictionaries.

Focus on Using a Dictionary

Explain that dictionaries are not all alike. Some are simpler and easier to use. Some are a bit intimidating. Walk students through the sample dictionary entries on pages 678 and 679 to show the differences that exist among dictionaries.

Parts of a Dictionary

Let students know that becoming more familiar with the parts of a dictionary will help them feel more comfortable using a dictionary. Have students look at the examples on page 680 and the explanations on page 681.

Focus on Using a Thesaurus

Emphasize that a thesaurus is also an extremely useful tool for building vocabulary. Remind students that a thesaurus is simply a collection of synonyms—words that have the same or almost the same meaning. Show students the example on page 682. Have students take note of the important parts of the thesaurus entry, such as the way the entry word is shown, the part of speech label, the word meanings, and the synonyms for each meaning.

Connotation and Denotation

Review the definitions of *connotation* and *denotation* with the students. Then read the thesaurus example on page 683 to show how a thesaurus can help writers choose words with the connotations they wish to convey. Go over with students the Think Aloud on the top of page 684.

Analogies

Remind students that an analogy is an expression that shows similarities between two things. Explain that analogies are commonly included on standardized tests.

How to Read Analogies

Read the sample analogies on page 685 and discuss the different ways that analogies are written. Explain that analogies on tests may appear in one of these forms.

Sample Analogy Questions

Now have students examine the sample analogies on the top of page 686. Suggest that students use the **thinking aloud** strategy to work through analogy questions on tests. Read through the example of one reader's Think Aloud on the bottom of the page.

Types of Analogies

1. Analogies in Which Word Order Is Not Important

Remind students that analogies represent different kinds of relationships between words, such as synonyms, antonyms, rhyming words, homophones, parts of the same thing, or two examples from the same class. Each type is illustrated on page 687 of the handbook. Read the examples of these types of analogies with your students. Emphasize that in these examples the order in which the words are presented is not important.

2. Analogies in Which Word Order Is Important

Explain to students that word order is important in some cases. Read through the examples of the analogies on pages 688 and 689. Ask students to use the thinking aloud strategy to work through the analogies that are not immediately clear to them.

Summing Up

Now read through the Summing Up on page 689 with the students. Ask them to say in their own words what they learned about building a vocabulary.

Assessment and Application

Use the Quick Assess checklist to evaluate what students have learned about improving vocabulary. Give students the opportunity to apply what they have learned through one of the two activities below. For students who are able to work independently, use one of the suggestions for independent practice or an activity of your own. For students who need guided help with the strategy, use a *Student Applications Book*.

Quick Assess

Can students

- name two or three ways to increase their vocabulary?
- name two or three different types of context clues?
- give an example of a prefix, root word, and suffix?
- explain what kinds of information can be found in a dictionary?
- name two or three examples of types of analogies?

1. Independent Practice

To show that they understand the lesson, students may do one of the following activities:

- Begin a vocabulary notebook, as described in this lesson.
- Jot down unknown words while reading for enjoyment and find the definitions, either by asking someone or using a dictionary.
- With a partner, skim textbooks, magazine articles, novels, and other reading materials for words that can be understood by examining prefixes, roots, or suffixes.
- With a partner, create a list of examples of analogies in which word order is not important and a list of examples of analogies in which word order is important.

2. Student Applications Books

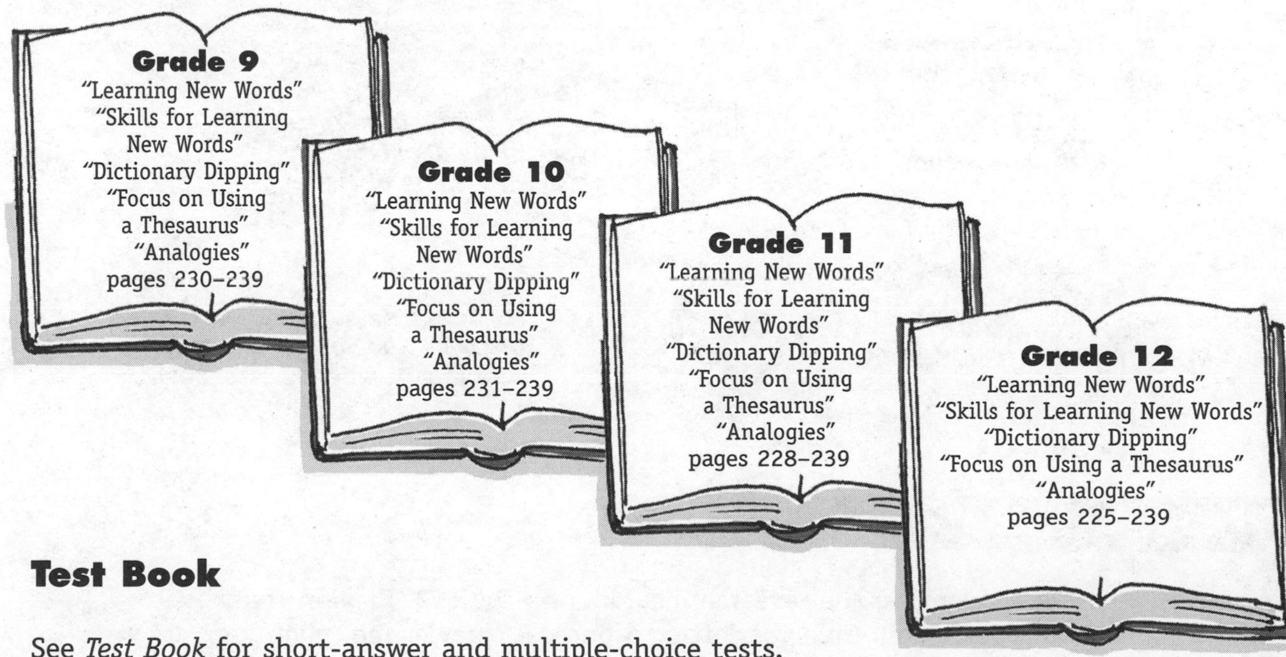

Test Book

See *Test Book* for short-answer and multiple-choice tests.

Doing Research

Goals

Here students learn the basics of doing research. This lesson will help them learn how to find useful information, keep track of information, and evaluate and document sources.

Opening Activity

Emphasize that effective researchers find the most and best information in the least amount of time. Read the list of eight reasons for doing research on page 691.

REASONS FOR RESEARCH

1. To find answers or information you need
Let's say you're going to buy a stereo and want to know which one is the best deal.

2. To write a paper or essay for class
How else will you learn the causes for the French Revolution?

3. To prepare a talk or presentation
Perhaps you want to give a talk on hiking the Appalachian Trail.

4. To give yourself that extra edge on an upcoming test
Find out about Sigmund Freud before you take a test about his theories.

5. To write a news story or editorial for the school paper
Imagine your assignment: to find out how a school board member voted at the last three board meetings.

6. To take part in a debate
Gather the facts to argue your point about the scientific value of cloning.

7. To take part in a class discussion
Researching Kate Chopin's life can help you understand the settings, characters, plots, and themes in her book The Awakening.

8. To satisfy your curiosity
Discover what other people have said about your favorite movie.

The Basics of Research

Have students examine the research diagram on page 692. Explain that, like reading, doing research involves setting a purpose, previewing, planning, reading with a purpose, connecting, pausing and reflecting, rereading, and remembering.

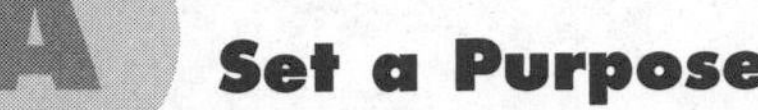

A Set a Purpose

Emphasize the need for students to be clear and specific in their purpose for doing research. Students need to be able to say exactly what they are looking for.

B Preview

In researching, previewing means getting a sense of what materials are available and which ones to look at first. Explain that students need to first gather their materials for research and then make a plan.

C Plan

Emphasize that students need to choose a strategy that will help them meet their purpose in doing research. Read through the list of strategies given at the top of page 693.

D Read with a Purpose

Explain to students that they can avoid getting buried in a pile of sources by reminding themselves of their purpose. Suggest that students write their purpose on an index card and keep it in front of them.

E Connect

Remind students that making connections to what they are reading will help them maintain interest and comprehension. Asking questions during reading and relating the material to their own lives will help students make connections.

F Pause and Reflect

Let students know that after they've completed their research, they need to take a moment to reflect on the information they have found. Students need to ask themselves if they have found enough information or if they need to look for more.

G Reread

Tell students that rereading is an important part of researching. Rereading involves double-checking facts, evaluating sources, and preparing themselves to write about or present what they have found.

H Remember

Emphasize that students must find a way to remember what they have found, especially if they are doing research over several days. Note-taking, especially on index cards, is a good way to record the important information.

Finding Sources

Explain that students will use primary and secondary sources. Read through the chart of examples of sources on page 694.

Primary Sources

Tell students that a primary source is an original source. It informs directly rather than through another person's interpretation. Read the list of primary sources on page 695 with students.

TYPES OF PRIMARY SOURCES

autobiographies	*memoirs*	*diaries*
journals	*logs*	*experiments*
observations	*surveys*	*polls*
interviews	*panels*	*letters*
shows		*speeches*

Secondary Sources

Explain that a secondary source is a text containing information that other people have gathered and interpreted. A textbook is a good example of a secondary source. Other secondary sources include a newspaper, an encyclopedia, a TV documentary, and a website. Go over with students the various secondary sources listed on page 696.

The Internet and the Library

The library and the Internet are the two main places where students can find information.

Using the Internet

Remind students that although the Internet is a good source of information, there are problems in using it for research. Point out that it is easy to get lost on the Internet because so much information is available. In addition, emphasize that students must determine whether information they find on the Internet is reliable. Students may wish to review "Reading on the Internet" on pages 511–537 in the handbook.

Using the Library

Emphasize that the library offers information in easy-to-understand formats. In many ways, the library is a more efficient place than the Internet for doing research because the information is reliable and clearly organized.

THE COMPUTER CATALOG

Remind students that their first stop in the library will be the computer catalog. If possible, take the students on a field trip to your school or local library and walk them through the steps of accessing databases on the computer catalog. If a field trip is not possible, have students examine the sample screens on pages 698 and 699 of the handbook.

KEY WORD SEARCHES

Explain that a computer catalog search begins by typing in a key word. These words serve as links to pertinent items.

SEARCHES FOR TITLES

Remind students that they can locate a specific book by typing in the title. Typing the major words in the title will also access the book of interest.

SEARCHES FOR AUTHORS

Remind students that they can find books by typing in the author's last name. If they don't know exactly how to spell the last name, they can try typing in the first few letters.

SEARCHES FOR SUBJECTS

When students don't have particular books in mind, a key word search can access books pertinent to a topic. Emphasize the importance of being as specific as possible.

REFINING A SEARCH

Explain that refining a search can save students a great deal of time. Searches can be refined by using Boolean operators, as shown on page 700. With students, read the list of example key words entered and what the computer would show during a Boolean search.

BOOLEAN OPERATORS

Key words you enter	The computer will show you
fiction	*listings that contain the word* fiction
fiction and *wild*	*listings that contain the words* fiction *and* wild
wild or *call*	*listings that contain either* wild *or* call
wild not *animal*	*listings that contain the word* wild, *but not the word* animal
wild with *London*	*listings that contain the word* wild *and the name* London

Using Call Numbers

Students need to know how to interpret call numbers to locate their sources in a library. Read through the Dewey Decimal System chart on page 701 with the students. Point out that there are 10 major subject classes, which are then broken down into divisions, sections, and subsections.

DEWEY DECIMAL SYSTEM

Call numbers	What you'll find there
000–099	***General Works:*** encyclopedias, atlases, handbooks, and other books that cover many subjects
100–199	***Philosophy***
200–299	***Religion***
300–399	***Social Sciences:*** books on education, government, law, economics, and other social sciences
400–499	***Languages:*** dictionaries and books about grammar
500–599	***Sciences:*** books about biology, chemistry, all other sciences, and math
600–699	***Technology:*** books about computers, engineering, inventions, medicine, and cooking
700–799	***Arts and Recreation:*** books about painting, music, and other arts, plus sports and games
800–899	***Literature:*** poetry, plays, essays, famous speeches, and literary criticism
900–999	***History, Travel, and Geography***

IN THE STACKS

Explain that the call numbers tell students where the books are located in the stacks, which means on the bookshelves. Tell students to look at the directional signs posted on the ends of the bookshelves to find the correct shelf.

FICTION AND BIOGRAPHIES/AUTOBIOGRAPHIES

Explain that fiction, biographies, and autobiographies are usually located in their own sections. Fiction is shelved alphabetically by the author's last name, and biographies and autobiographies are alphabetized by the last name of the person about whom the book was written.

Using Reference Works

Discuss the general reference section of the library, and point out that it contains dictionaries, encyclopedias, atlases, and other reference works. Read through the useful types of books available, described on pages 702 and 703.

Finding Articles in Periodicals

Make sure students know that periodicals are newspapers, magazines, and journals. Emphasize that articles can be found using the periodical database or the periodical index.

PERIODICAL DATABASES IN THE LIBRARY

Explain that a periodical database is obtained online in the library. Often the entire article of interest is available online and can be printed out, sometimes for a fee.

PERIODICAL DATABASES ON THE INTERNET

Many newspaper and magazine websites allow users to search their archives. Remind students to use a search engine to find a particular website that lists Web periodicals.

USING THE *READER'S GUIDE TO PERIODICAL LITERATURE*

Explain that the *Reader's Guide to Periodical Literature* is a print index to articles published in more than 200 magazines, journals, and newspapers. Students can search this reference by topic or by an author's last name.

LOCATING ARTICLES FROM THE *READER'S GUIDE*

Read the section on how to use the *Reader's Guide* on page 705. Emphasize that students will need to make notes on the name of the periodical, its date, and the title and page number of the article. Have students examine the sample from the *Reader's Guide to Periodical Literature*.

OTHER PERIODICAL INDEXES

Explain that other indexes are available also. The *General Periodical Index* is similar to the *Reader's Guide* but is published on CD-ROM.

Evaluating Sources

Remind students that they need to evaluate the reliability of the sources they plan to use for research. With students, read the checklist on page 706.

Encourage students to use an organizer, such as the Source Evaluator, to synthesize their notes about a source.

Checklist for Evaluating a Source

- ❑ **Is the information current and up-to-date?**
- ❑ **Does the information seem complete and reasonable?**
- ❑ **Is the source an expert?**
- ❑ **Can you check the accuracy of the information?**
- ❑ **What is the point of view of the source?**
- ❑ **How objective does the information seem?**
- ❑ **Are there obvious errors, questionable facts, or sloppy writing?**

Keeping Track of Information

Emphasize to students that they need a method for keeping track of the information they gather. Have students read the section on pages 707–709.

Reading Sources

Students should first remind themselves of their research purpose and then preview the sources they have collected or accessed. Emphasize the need for students to work systematically through each source and discard any materials that won't help them meet their purpose for doing the research.

Taking Notes

Now emphasize the importance of note-taking. Encourage students to find a note-taking system that works best for them. Have students examine the example of index cards on page 708. Ask students to volunteer to read aloud each type of card shown.

Paraphrasing

Go over the example author's words and discuss the differences between the poor paraphrase and the good paraphrase of the words. Make sure students know when to use question marks and ellipses. Caution them not to plagiarize another writer's words.

Documentation

Read the section beginning on page 710. Stress the purpose of documentation, which is to let readers know the original source for the idea or information. Explain that there are two types of documentation: informal and formal.

Informal Documentation

Have students look at the example of informal documentation on page 710. Point out the references to two books within the text of the report.

Formal Documentation

Emphasize that formal documentation is more involved. Read through the examples on page 711. Contrast the MLA and APA styles. Point out the list of sources for documentation that is on page 712.

Assessment and Application

Use the Quick Assess checklist to evaluate students' understanding of how to do research. Give students the opportunity to apply what they have learned through one of the two activities below. For students who are able to work independently, use the suggestion for independent practice or an activity of your own. For students who need guided help with the strategy, use the suggestion for guided practice.

Quick Assess

Can students

- ☑ describe the process for doing research?
- ☑ discuss where they can find sources and how to evaluate them?
- ☑ describe a good way to keep track of the information they find?
- ☑ explain the difference between informal and formal documentation?

Independent Practice

To show that they understand the lesson, students can apply what they have learned to their next research project.

Ask students to do one or more of the following:

- Complete a Source Evaluator.
- Take notes on index cards.
- Prepare their documentation according to APA or MLA style.

For guided practice, have students choose a research topic. Then ask them to answer the following questions:

- How did you apply the process for doing research?
- Where did you find your sources?
- How did you evaluate your sources?
- What methods did you use to keep track of information?
- How did you document your sources?

Test Book

See *Test Book* for short-answer and multiple-choice tests.

Strategy Handbook

Explain to students that the Strategy Handbook contains a collection of key reading strategies they can use to read more efficiently. Students should understand each strategy, including its purpose, how it is used, and when it is used.

This *Teacher's Guide* includes goals, teaching and discussion tips on how to introduce the strategies and model their use, and ideas for checking understanding by having students apply the strategies.

Key Strategies	***Teacher's Guide* page**	***Reader's Handbook* page**
Close Reading	433	714
Looking for Cause and Effect	433	716
Note-taking	434	718
Outlining	435	720
Paraphrasing	435	722
Questioning the Author	436	724
Reading Critically	437	726
Skimming	437	728
Summarizing	438	730
Synthesizing	439	732
Using Graphic Organizers	439	734
Visualizing and Thinking Aloud	440	736

Also see *Lesson Plan Book 9* (pages 214, 216–219), *Lesson Plan Book 10* (pages 214, 216–219), *Lesson Plan Book 11* (pages 214, 216–219), and *Lesson Plan Book 12* (pages 214, 216–219).

Close Reading

Set Goal

Students will learn that close reading means reading word for word, sentence by sentence, line by line. Students will learn that they should read closely when they come to an important paragraph or section or when it is important to understand and think about the meaning of each word, as in poetry.

Teach and Discuss

Read the **Description** on page 714. Discuss when and why this strategy should be used. Have students examine the Double-entry Journal on page 715, and explain why this is a good tool to use while reading closely.

Then distribute a short poem to the students, and walk the class step-by-step through the process, referring to the **Using the Strategy** section. Draw a Double-entry Journal on the board, and fill it out during the discussion.

Check Understanding

Now have students read the **Definition** at the bottom of page 715. Ask students to explain the strategy in their own words. Students can apply the strategy to the next poem, short story, or other difficult text that they are assigned to read.

Looking for Cause and Effect

Set Goal

Students will learn that looking for cause and effect means understanding the process by which one event brings about another.

Teach and Discuss

Read the **Description** on page 716. Discuss when and why this strategy should be used. Have students examine the three graphic organizers for cause and effect on pages 716 and 717.

Use a brief section in the students' current science or history textbook, and walk the class step-by-step through the process described in the **Using the Strategy** section. Draw the appropriate graphic organizer on the board, and fill it out during the discussion.

Check Understanding

Now have students read the **Definition** at the bottom of page 717. Ask students to explain the strategy in their own words. Then have students apply the strategy to another section in their science or history book.

Note-taking

Set Goal

Students will learn that note-taking is a method for remembering key events and details from a reading or lecture.

Teach and Discuss

Read and discuss the **Description** on page 718. Emphasize that taking notes is especially important in preparing for a test.

Point out that the note-taking tools in **Using the Strategy**—the 5 W's and H Organizer, Key Word or Topic Notes, Summary Notes, and Timeline—are to be used for different purposes. Ask students to brainstorm situations in which they would use each note-taking technique.

Ask students to choose one of the note-taking tools to use with a current assignment in history, science, or literature. After they have worked through a short section or chapter, have them form small groups and compare their notes, explaining to each other why they chose the tool they did.

Check Understanding

Now have students read the **Definition** at the bottom of page 719. Ask students to explain the strategy in their own words. Then have students apply one of the note-taking tools to another section in their science or history book or a literary work.

Outlining

Set Goal

Students will learn that outlining helps organize the most important topics and details in their reading, especially in textbooks and reference works.

Teach and Discuss

Read and discuss the **Description** on page 720. Make sure students understand that the chapter headings in their textbooks can provide the structure for an outline. These chapter headings can often be used as the main headings in the outline.

Explain the differences between Topic Outlines and Sentence Outlines as described under **Using the Strategy.** Have students brainstorm kinds of reading for which outlining would be useful.

Ask students to apply this strategy to their current history textbook reading. Students may work in pairs or individually, while you circulate to answer questions and check their work.

Check Understanding

Now have students read the **Definition** at the bottom of page 721. Ask students to explain the strategy in their own words. Then have students create a Topic or a Sentence Outline for a chapter in their science or history book.

Paraphrasing

Set Goal

Students will learn that paraphrasing means using their own words to summarize or retell what they have read.

Teach and Discuss

Read and discuss the **Description** on page 722. Emphasize that paraphrasing is a strategy for better comprehension and recall because it requires students to more deeply process what they have read. Paraphrasing will also help them do better on tests.

Distribute copies of a short magazine or newspaper article of interest to your students. Go through the steps in **Using the Strategy** with the students, creating your own Paraphrase Chart on the board.

Check Understanding

Now have students read the **Definition** at the bottom of page 723. Ask them to explain the strategy in their own words. Then have students apply the strategy to one of their current reading assignments in any subject.

Questioning the Author

Set Goal

Students will learn that questioning the author is the strategy of asking questions, as they read, about why an author chose a certain subject, used a particular word, made a character do or say something, or selected a particular setting.

Teach and Discuss

Read and discuss the **Description** on page 724. Emphasize that this strategy helps students become more engaged and interested in a reading that may otherwise seem uninteresting. It also improves comprehension.

Distribute copies of a short newspaper or magazine article that will be interesting to your students. Then walk through the steps in **Using the Strategy** with students. Invite students to discuss each question for evaluating author's purpose on page 725.

Check Understanding

Now have students read the **Definition** at the bottom of page 725. Ask students to explain the strategy in their own words. Then have students apply the strategy to another reading of their choice, either from their textbooks or a magazine or newspaper.

Reading Critically

Set Goal

Students will learn that reading critically means finding and evaluating a writer's main idea.

Teach and Discuss

Read and discuss the **Description** on page 726. Emphasize that reading critically does not mean mistrusting everything authors say, but it does involve thinking about and judging whether the author is reliable.

Distribute copies of an editorial from the local newspaper. The topic of the editorial should be somewhat familiar to the students, so they will have enough prior knowledge to make judgments. Then, with the Critical Reading Chart displayed by an overhead projector, walk through the critical reading questions in the first step under **Using the Strategy**. Invite students to contribute their ideas to complete the Critical Reading Chart.

Check Understanding

Now have students read the **Definition** at the bottom of page 727. Ask them to explain the strategy in their own words. Then, working in pairs or small groups, have students apply the strategy to a news story or magazine article of their choice.

Skimming

Set Goal

Students will learn that skimming means glancing quickly through a reading selection, either to get a general idea of what it is about or to find specific information.

Teach and Discuss

Read and discuss the **Description** on page 728. Emphasize the different purposes for skimming.

Distribute copies of a reading passage and copies of questions from an older test. Then walk students through the procedure for skimming the reading passage as described in **Using the Strategy.** Also demonstrate how information needed to answer test questions can be found using the strategy of skimming.

Check Understanding

Now have students read the **Definition** at the bottom of page 729. Ask them to explain the strategy in their own words. Then have students work in their current science or history textbooks, skimming sections or chapters for the answers to end-of-section or end-of-chapter questions.

Summarizing

Set Goal

Students will learn that summarizing is telling the main events or main points in a selection as briefly as possible and in their own words.

Teach and Discuss

Read and discuss the **Description** on page 730. Emphasize that summarizing is valuable for improving both comprehension and recall of reading material.

Distribute copies of a short story, or choose a brief short story from the students' current anthology. Draw a Fiction Organizer on the board. Then read through the story with the students, modeling the application described in the **Using the Strategy** section and filling in the graphic organizer as you progress. Invite students to read sections of the story aloud and provide their own summaries as you fill in the Fiction Organizer.

You may also want to work through summarizing a piece of nonfiction using a Nonfiction Organizer. If so, distribute a short essay, editorial, news story, or other selection and discuss with students the subject, the writer's viewpoint, the supporting details, and definitions or explanations.

Check Understanding

Now have students read the **Definition** at the bottom of page 731. Ask students to explain the strategy in their own words. Then, working in pairs, have students choose something they would like to read, either fiction or nonfiction, from a textbook or other source. Have them apply the strategy of summarizing, completing either a Fiction Organizer or a Nonfiction Organizer.

Synthesizing

Set Goal

Students will learn that synthesizing is the process of considering all the different parts of a text and combining them to see the "big picture."

Teach and Discuss

Read and discuss the **Description** on page 732. Emphasize that this strategy can be used with both fiction and nonfiction.

In **Using the Strategy**, students are reminded that synthesizing involves looking at many different elements closely to see how they work together. Distribute a brief work of fiction or nonfiction and demonstrate how to apply the strategy of synthesizing. Have students volunteer to read sections aloud. Using a Fiction Organizer or Main Idea Organizer on the overhead or chalkboard, demonstrate how readers can identify the important information in the reading and gather the different details together in a graphic organizer.

Check Understanding

Have students read the **Definition** at the bottom of page 733. Then ask students to explain the strategy in their own words. Working in pairs, students can apply the strategy of synthesizing to fiction or nonfiction of their choice.

Using Graphic Organizers

Set Goal

Students will learn that a graphic organizer is a visual picture of the ideas in a reading and that such organizers help improve comprehension and recall.

Teach and Discuss

Read and discuss the **Description** on page 734. Emphasize that graphic organizers are helpful for improving reading comprehension and recall. In addition, they are very useful in studying for tests.

Go over with students the reading tools shown under **Using the Strategy**. Distribute copies of a short reading passage. Ask students to determine which of the organizers shown would be appropriate to use. Then draw the organizer on the board and read the selection with the students, demonstrating how to apply the strategy.

Check Understanding

Now have students read the **Definition** at the bottom of page 735. Ask them to explain the strategy in their own words. Then have students select something they would like to read from your class library, choose an appropriate graphic organizer, and begin reading. You may circulate to answer questions and check understanding.

Visualizing and Thinking Aloud

Set Goal

Students will learn that visualizing and thinking aloud means making a mental picture of what they read and talking through their thoughts about what they are reading or drawing.

Teach and Discuss

Read and discuss the **Description** on page 736. Emphasize that this strategy is especially helpful for working through math problems. Point out that visualizing involves mental pictures and sketching while thinking aloud involves talking through the ideas in the reading. Visualizing and thinking aloud often go together.

Distribute copies of word problems from a previous math exam. Demonstrate how to apply the strategy of visualizing and thinking aloud to the problems, as described in the steps under **Using the Strategy.** Ask for student input as you progress through the work.

Check Understanding

Now have students read the **Definition** at the bottom of page 737. Ask students to explain the strategy in their own words. Then have students apply the strategy to a concept or process in their current science reading. Students may work in pairs, discussing the process as they go.

Reading Tools

Blackline Masters

Each of the thirty-eight reading tools in the Reader's Almanac of the *Reader's Handbook* is included in this *Teacher's Guide* in a format suitable for copying. Use the blackline masters that follow to reinforce and supplement the lessons in the handbook.

- Argument Chart
- Cause-Effect Organizer
- Character Development Chart
- Character Map
- Character Web
- Classification Notes
- Close Reading Organizer
- Concept Map
- Critical Reading Chart
- Double-entry Journal
- Evidence Organizer
- Fiction Organizer
- 5 W's and H Organizer
- Flow Chart
- Inference Chart
- Key Word or Topic Notes
- Magnet Summary
- Main Idea Organizer
- Making Connections Chart
- Nonfiction Organizer
- Outline
- Paraphrase or Retelling Chart
- Plot Diagram
- Preview Chart
- Problem-Solution Organizer
- Sequence Notes
- Setting Chart
- Source Evaluator
- Storyboard
- Story String
- Study or Note Cards
- Summary Notes
- Timeline
- Topic and Theme Organizer
- Two-novel Map
- Venn Diagram
- Web
- Website Profiler

ARGUMENT CHART

NAME ....

An Argument Chart helps you examine and analyze persuasive writing, such as a speech, magazine article, or editorial.

Viewpoint	Support	Opposing Viewpoint

Cause-Effect Organizer

NAME ....

A Cause-Effect Organizer helps you sort out what are causes and what are the effects coming from them. It shows the relationship between the causes and effects.

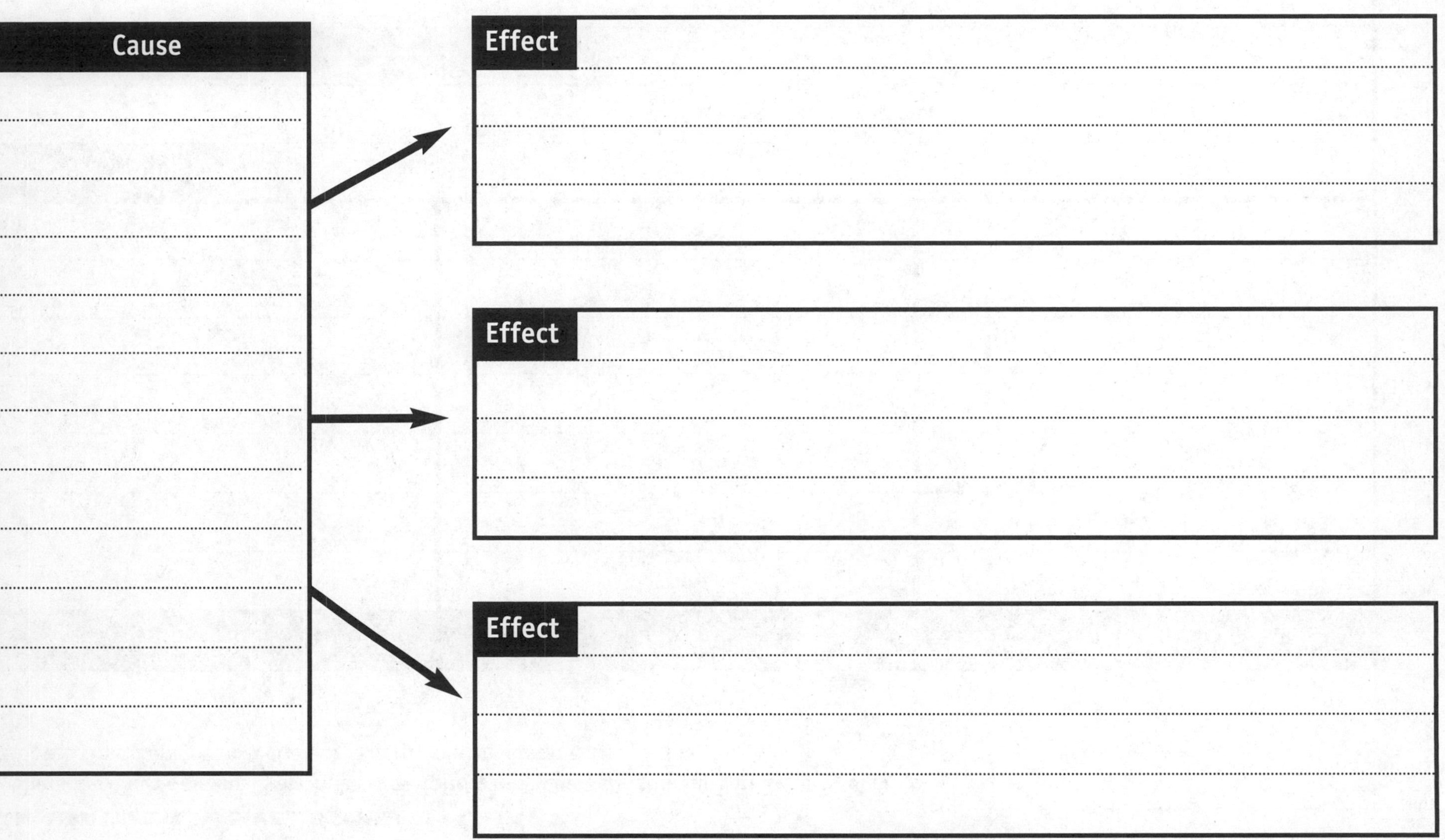

Character Development Chart

NAME ______________________________

A Character Development Chart helps you follow how characters change in a story, play, or novel. The changes in a character help you understand the theme.

Beginning	Middle	End

Possible Themes:

Character Map

NAME ....

A Character Map helps you understand and analyze a character in a story, play, or novel. This tool helps you see how you—and other characters—feel about the character.

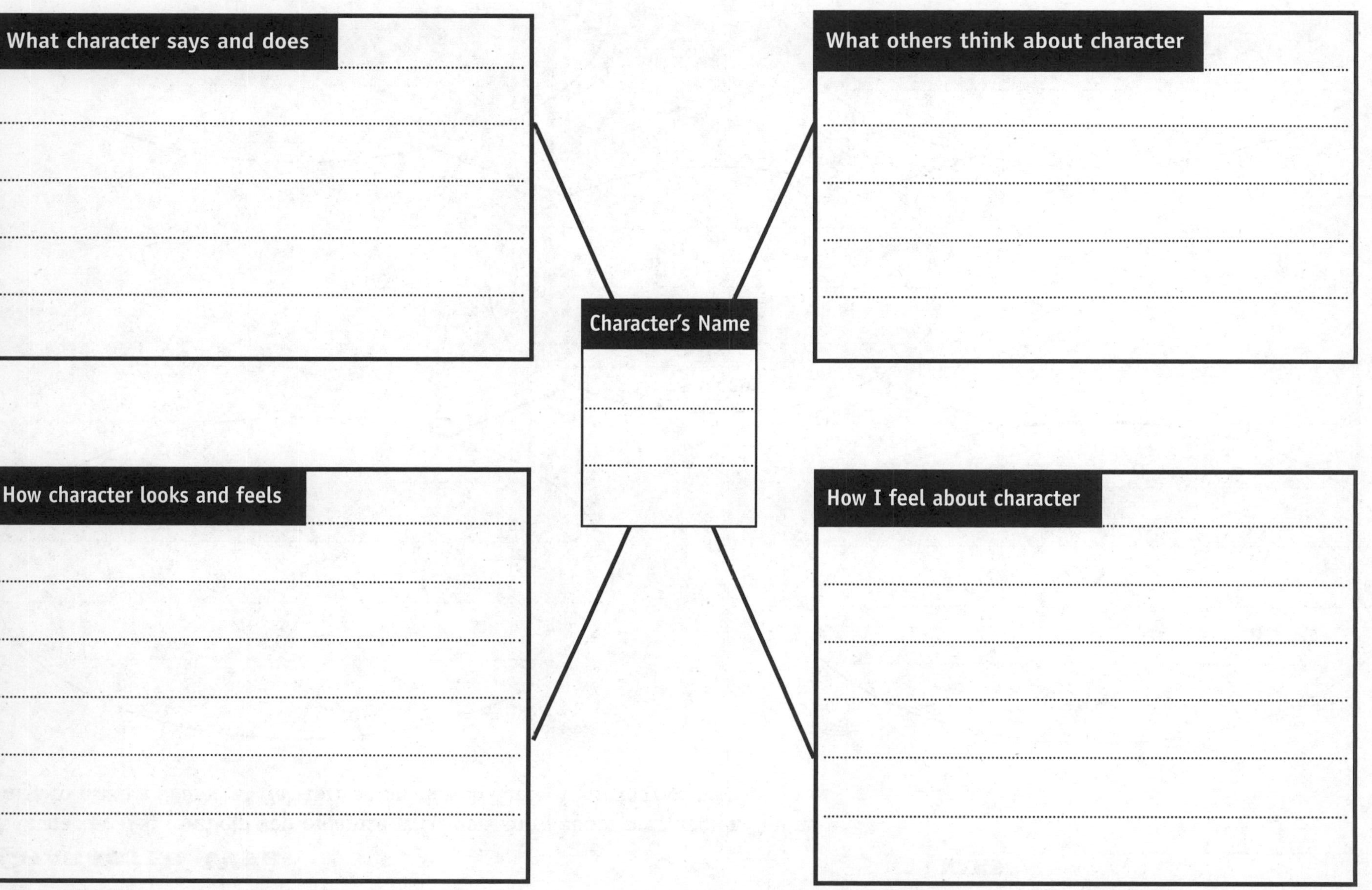

Character Web

NAME ____________________

A Character Web can help you organize what you know about a character. You may want to make a Character Web for each major character in a story or novel.

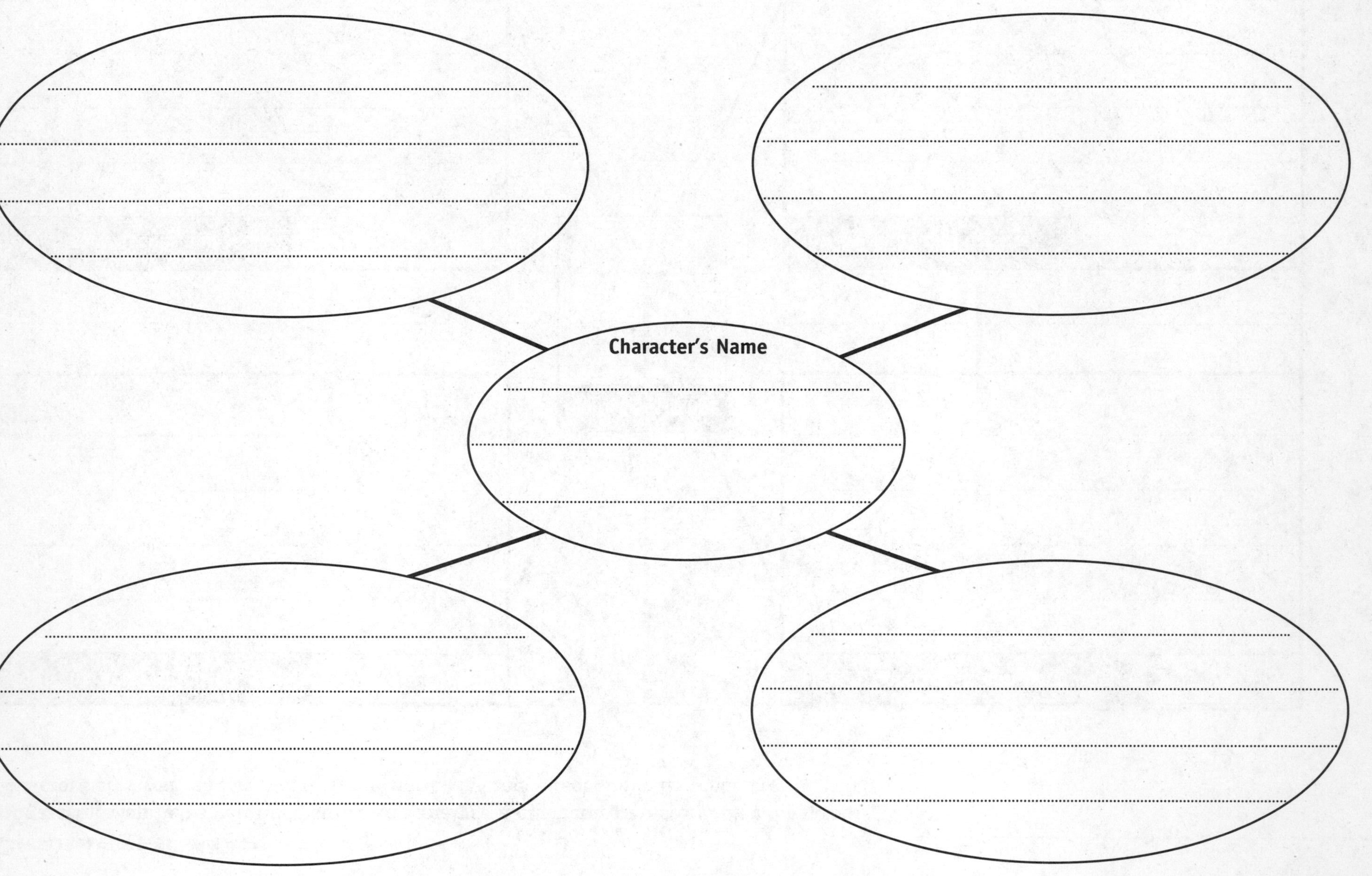

CLASSIFICATION NOTES

NAME ______________________

Use Classification Notes to help you organize separate types or groups and sort out characteristics about them.

Close Reading Organizer

NAME ____________________

A Close Reading Organizer is a good tool to use when you want to focus on the meaning of words, phrases, and sentences.

Text	What I Think About It

Concept Map

NAME ....

A Concept Map helps you organize everything you know about a concept or idea.

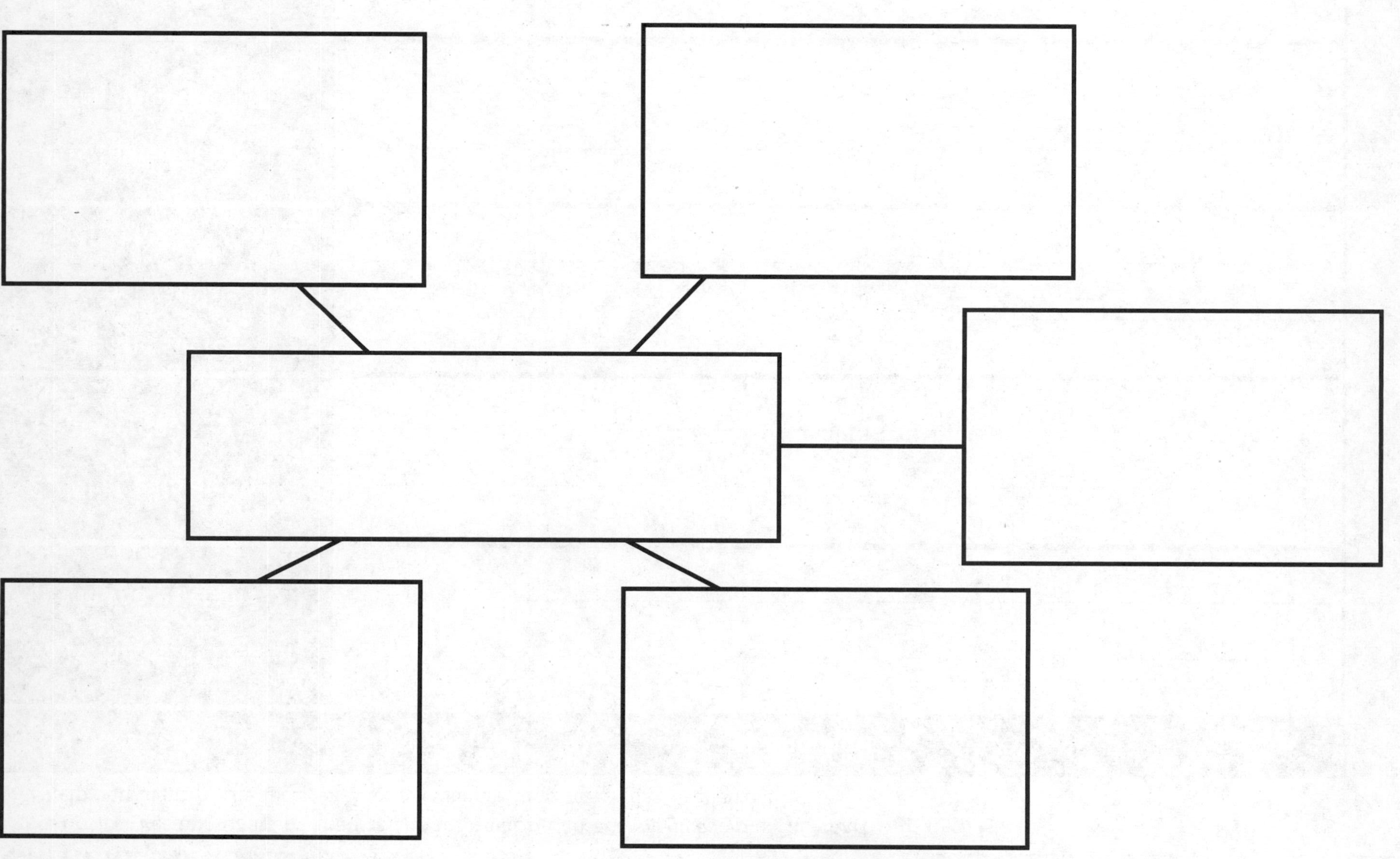

Critical Reading Chart

NAME ______________________

Use a Critical Reading Chart to analyze the information an author gives you. The chart will help you identify the facts, opinions, evidence, and main idea or viewpoint.

My Questions	My Thoughts
1. Is the main idea or viewpoint clear?	
2. What evidence is presented?	
3. Are the sources authoritative and reliable?	
4. Is the evidence convincing?	
5. Is there another side of the story?	

Double-entry Journal

NAME ______________________

A Double-entry Journal helps you interpret a text.

Quotes	My Thoughts

Evidence Organizer

NAME ____________________

You can use an Evidence Organizer to record the evidence or support for a viewpoint or assertion in persuasive writing. This chart helps you analyze whether the supporting details are convincing.

Viewpoint		
Supporting Detail	**Supporting Detail**	**Supporting Detail**

Fiction Organizer

NAME ....

Use a Fiction Organizer to collect all of the key information about a story, novel, or play.

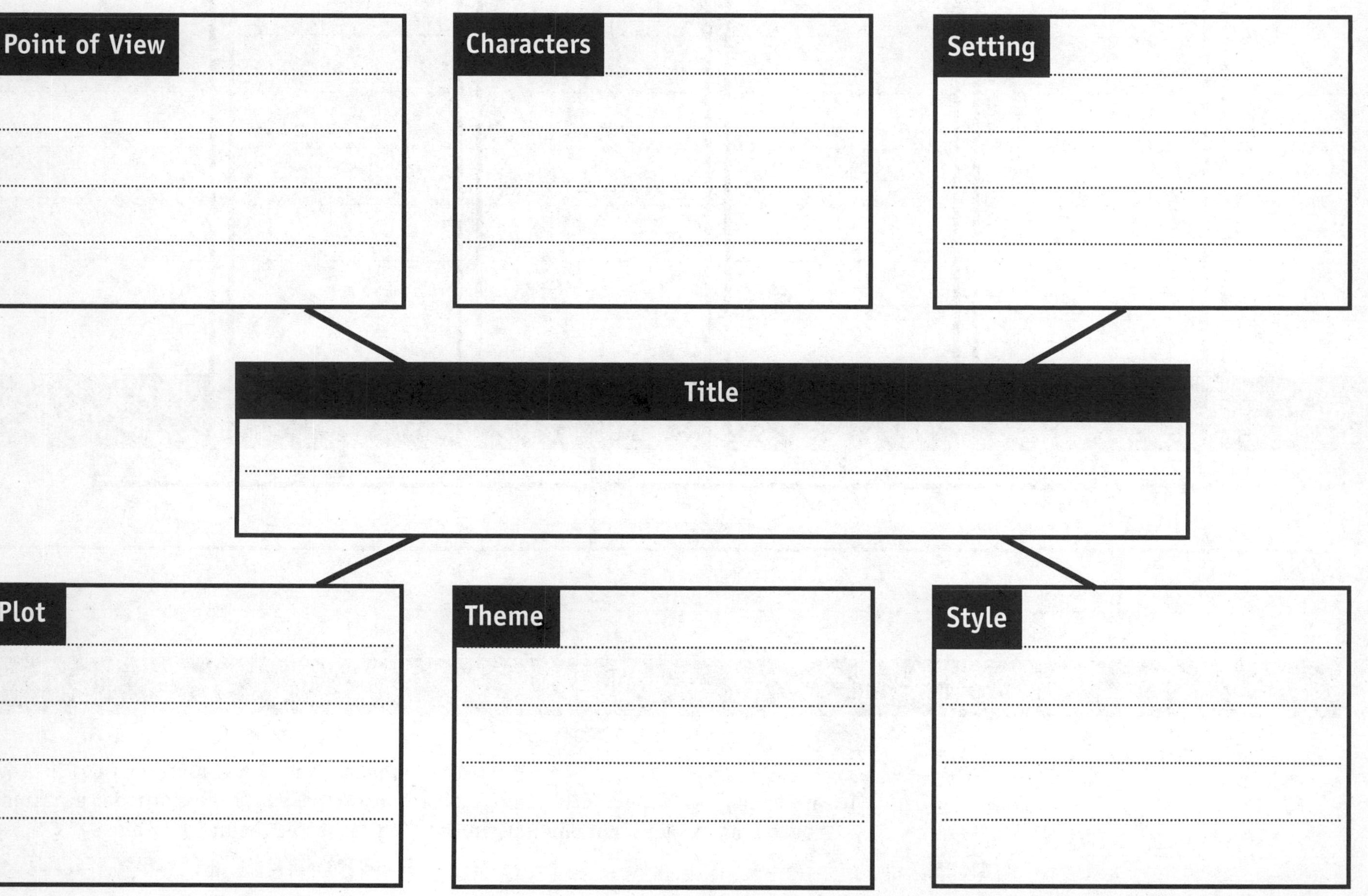

5 W's and H Organizer

NAME ....

Use a 5 W's and H Organizer to gather key information about a subject. By asking yourself a reporter's questions (*who, what, where, when, why,* and *how*), you can learn most of the important information about a subject.

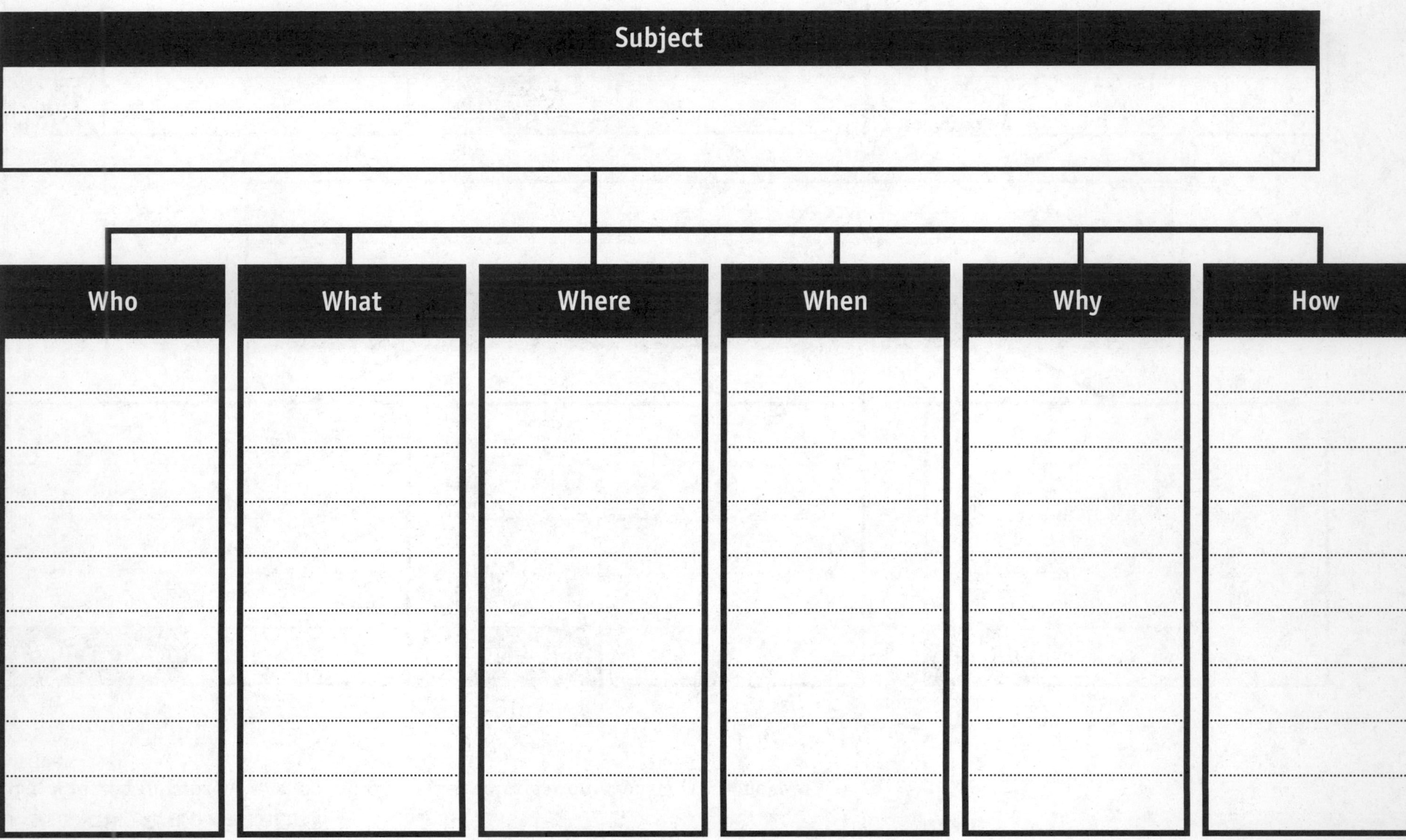

Flow Chart

NAME ....

A Flow Chart shows a sequence of operations. It is useful for helping you remember the steps in an experiment or the stages of a process.

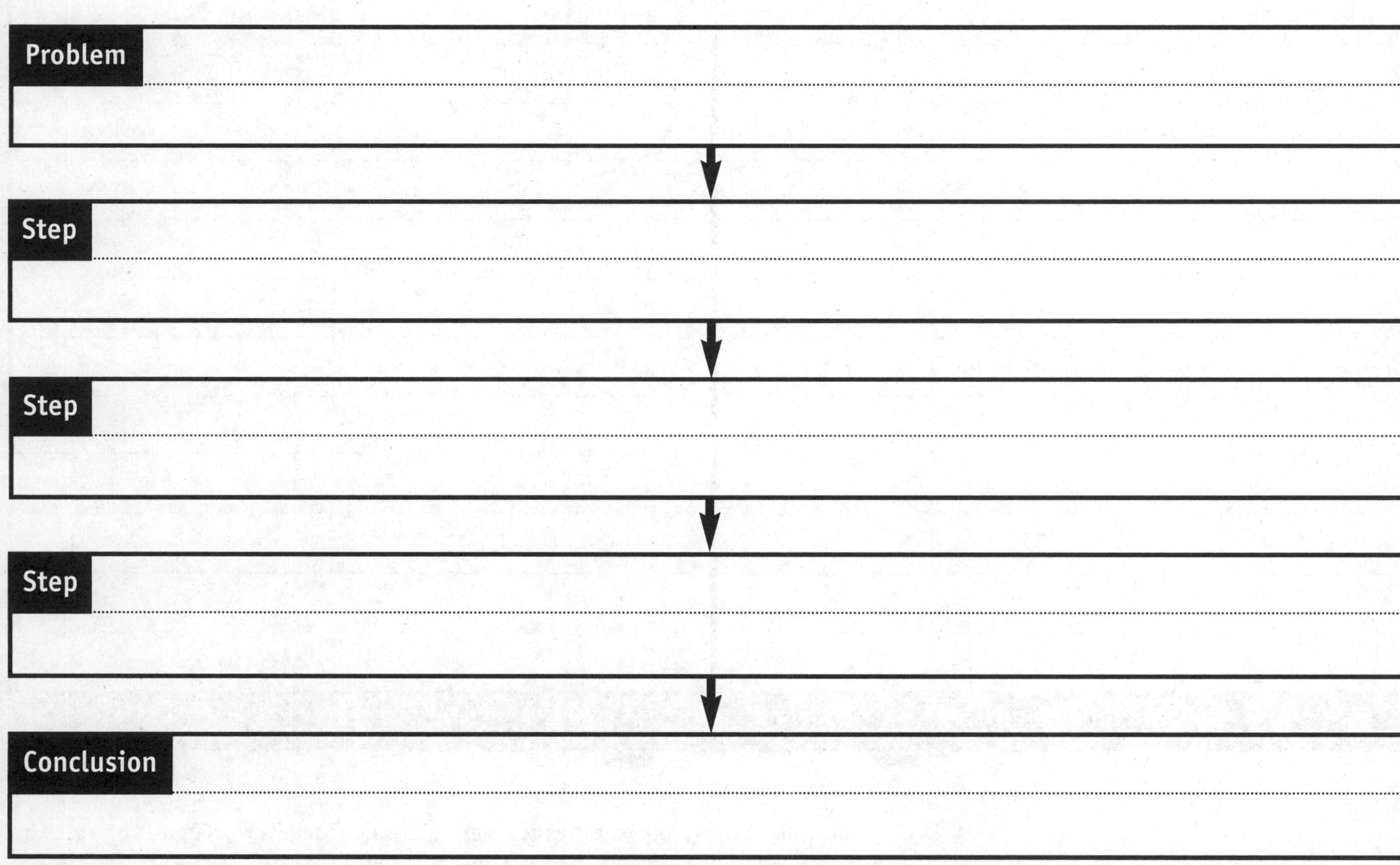

Inference Chart

NAME ______________________

Use an Inference Chart when you have to read between the lines and look a little closer at part of a reading. This chart helps you draw conclusions about what you read.

Text	What I Conclude

NAME ______________________

Key Word or Topic Notes

Use Key Word or Topic Notes to help you stay organized and pull out the main ideas from your reading. Key Word or Topic Notes work well for taking notes on textbooks and other nonfiction.

Key Words or Topics	Notes

Magnet Summary

NAME ....

Use a Magnet Summary to help you organize your thoughts after reading. Choose one word that is important to what you have read. Then, collect all of the other words, ideas, and details you can think of around it and summarize your ideas about the "magnet word."

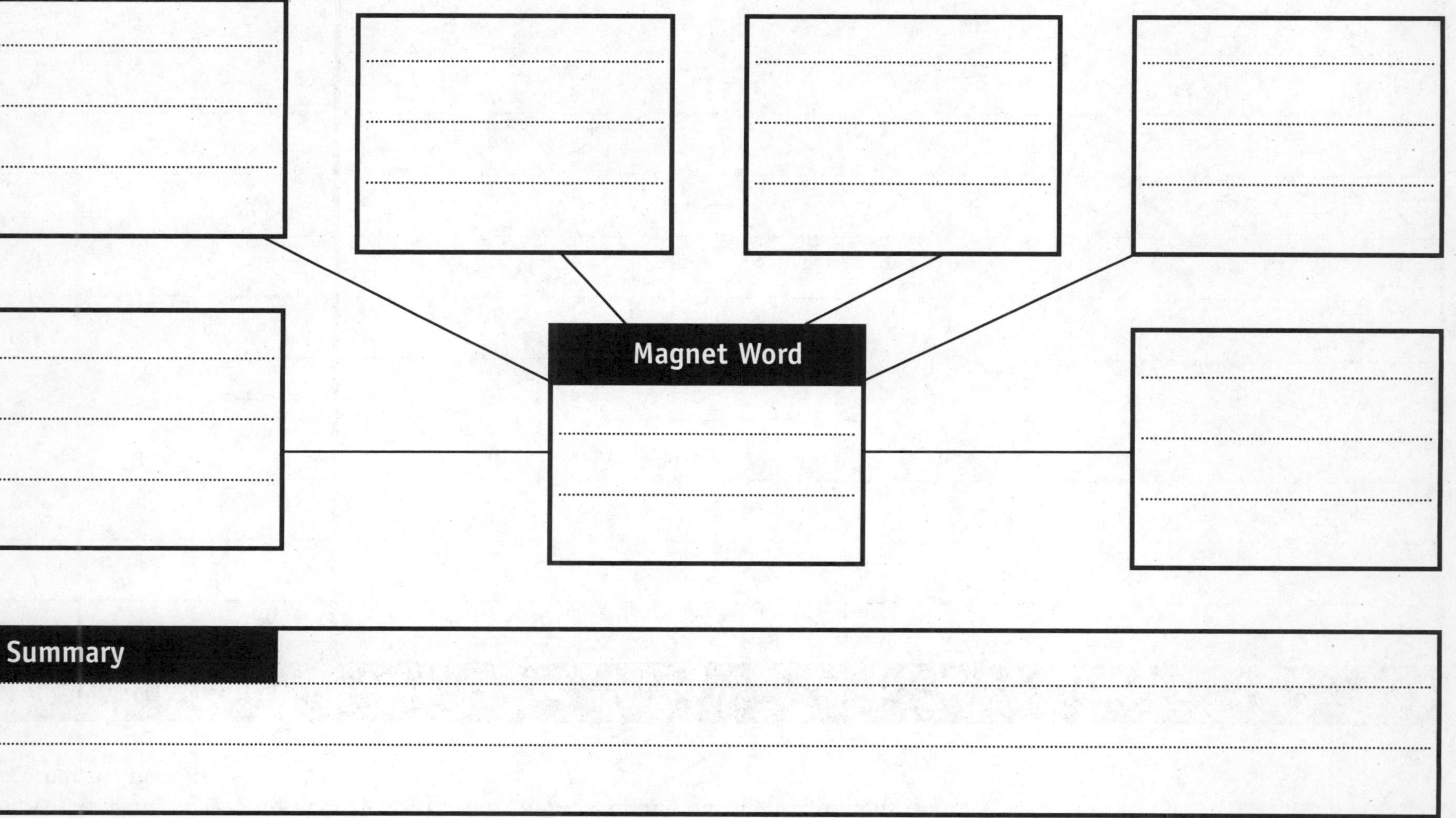

Main Idea Organizer

NAME ....

A Main Idea Organizer helps you sort out the big ideas and the smaller details. This tool works best with nonfiction, such as biography, magazine articles, persuasive writing, and textbooks.

Main Idea		
Detail	**Detail**	**Detail**
Conclusion		

Making Connections Chart

NAME ______________________

A Making Connections Chart can help you relate to a written work and increase your understanding. It works best with fiction, but it can be used with nonfiction too.

I wonder why . . .	
I think . . .	
I can relate to this because . . .	
This is similar to . . .	
This reminds me of . . .	

Nonfiction Organizer

NAME ______________________

A Nonfiction Organizer helps you sort out what you learn in essays, articles, speeches, editorials, and so on. It divides these nonfiction works into three parts: introduction, body, and conclusion.

Subject	
Introduction	
Body	
Conclusion	

OUTLINE

NAME ____________________

An Outline helps you understand the organization of what you're reading. Use words or phrases (Topic Outline) or full sentences (Sentence Outline) to sort out main ideas, topics, and subtopics.

I. Main Topic 1 ____________________

A. subtopic ____________________

B. subtopic ____________________

C. subtopic ____________________

II. Main Topic 2 ____________________

A. subtopic ____________________

B. subtopic ____________________

C. subtopic ____________________

III. Main Topic 3 ____________________

A. subtopic ____________________

B. subtopic ____________________

C. subtopic ____________________

Paraphrase or Retelling Chart

NAME ....

A Paraphrase or Retelling Chart helps you do two things at once. It helps you understand parts of a text or graphic by putting them in your own words and helps you collect your own thoughts about the work.

Lines	My Paraphrase

My Thoughts

Plot Diagram

NAME ....

A Plot Diagram shows you how a story is organized. It highlights the five main parts of a story.

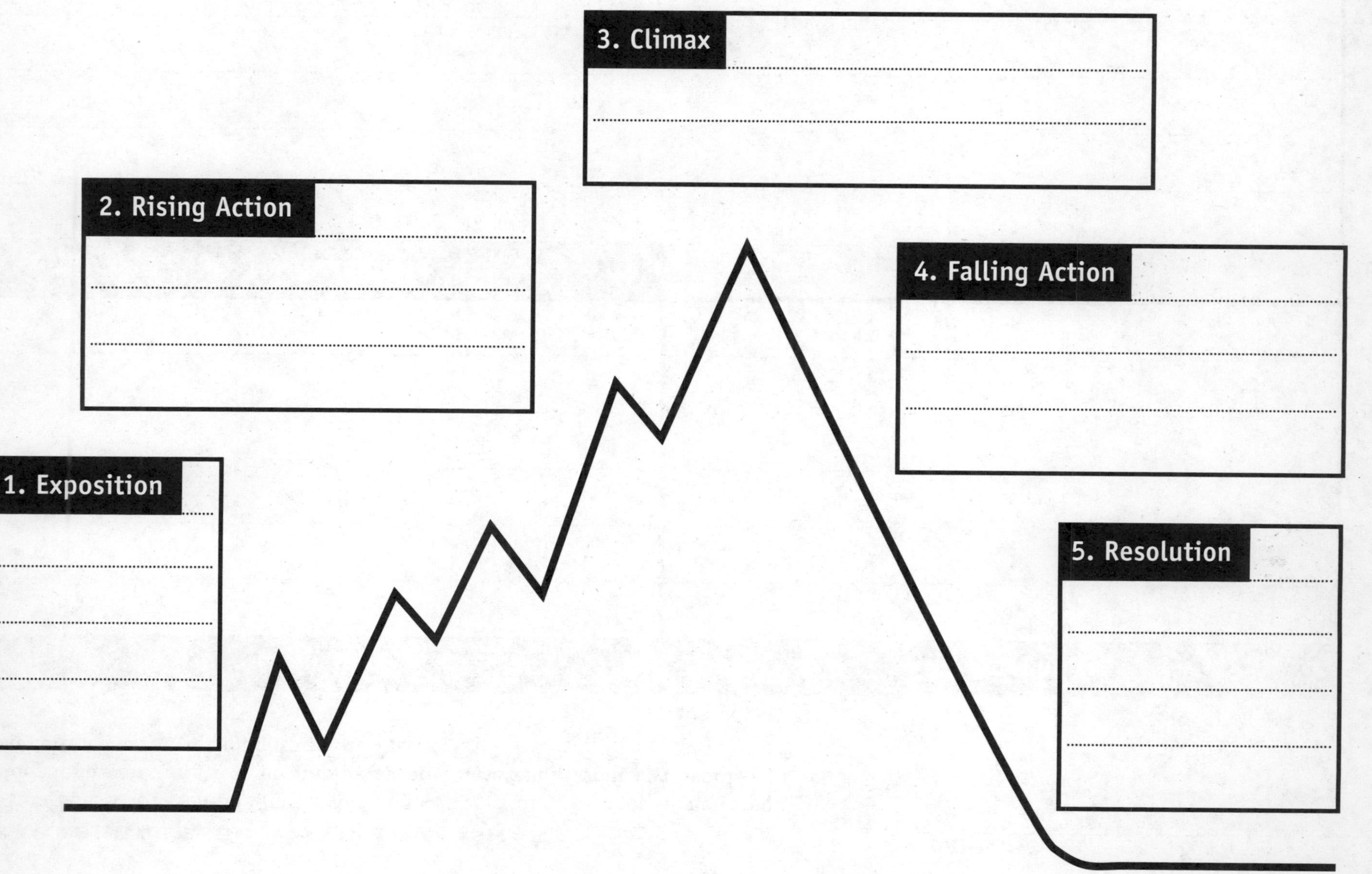

NAME

Preview Chart

A Preview Chart can give you a head start on what a reading might be about. Use it to jot down notes as you skim a persuasive essay, a speech, or an editorial.

Title

Clues about the Topic	Clues about the Assertion

Problem-Solution Organizer

NAME ____________________

A Problem-Solution Organizer is a practical tool for recording information from a textbook. It helps you see how problems were or could be solved in history, math, or science. This organizer is also useful for recording information from an editorial or article.

Problem	Solution

Sequence Notes

NAME ....

Sequence Notes are a lot like Timelines, but they don't always contain dates. They are useful for recording the events in a long work or in a process and are especially helpful when you want to review for a test.

Setting Chart

NAME ______________________

To help you understand fiction and keep track of details about when and where a story took place, create a Setting Chart. Make a chart for each major scene or setting.

Clues about First Time	Clues about First Place

Clues about Second Time	Clues about Second Place

Source Evaluator

NAME ....

A Source Evaluator is a practical tool for doing research. Use it to record information, dates you found the information, and your opinions.

Research Purpose	
Source Type	
Title or Location	
Date	
Expertise	
Bias, if any	
Reactions	

Storyboard

NAME ....

A Storyboard can help you keep track of events in a story, novel, or play. It works best for longer works that have a lot of events. A Storyboard helps you remember what happened and in what order things happened.

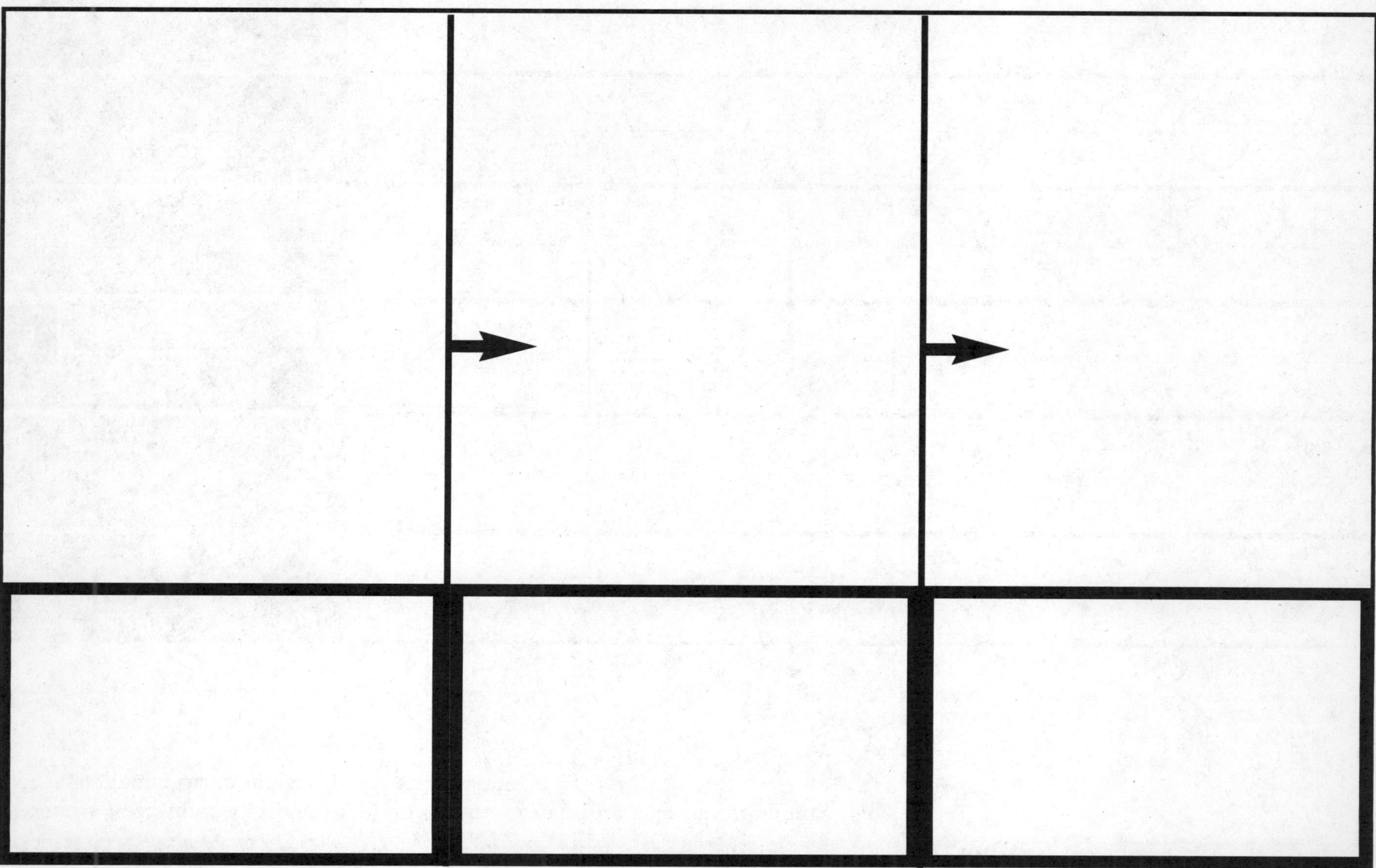

Story String

NAME ....

To keep track of a series of events in a story, novel, or play, use a Story String. It helps you see a chain of events and keep the time order straight, so you can remember what caused what in the story.

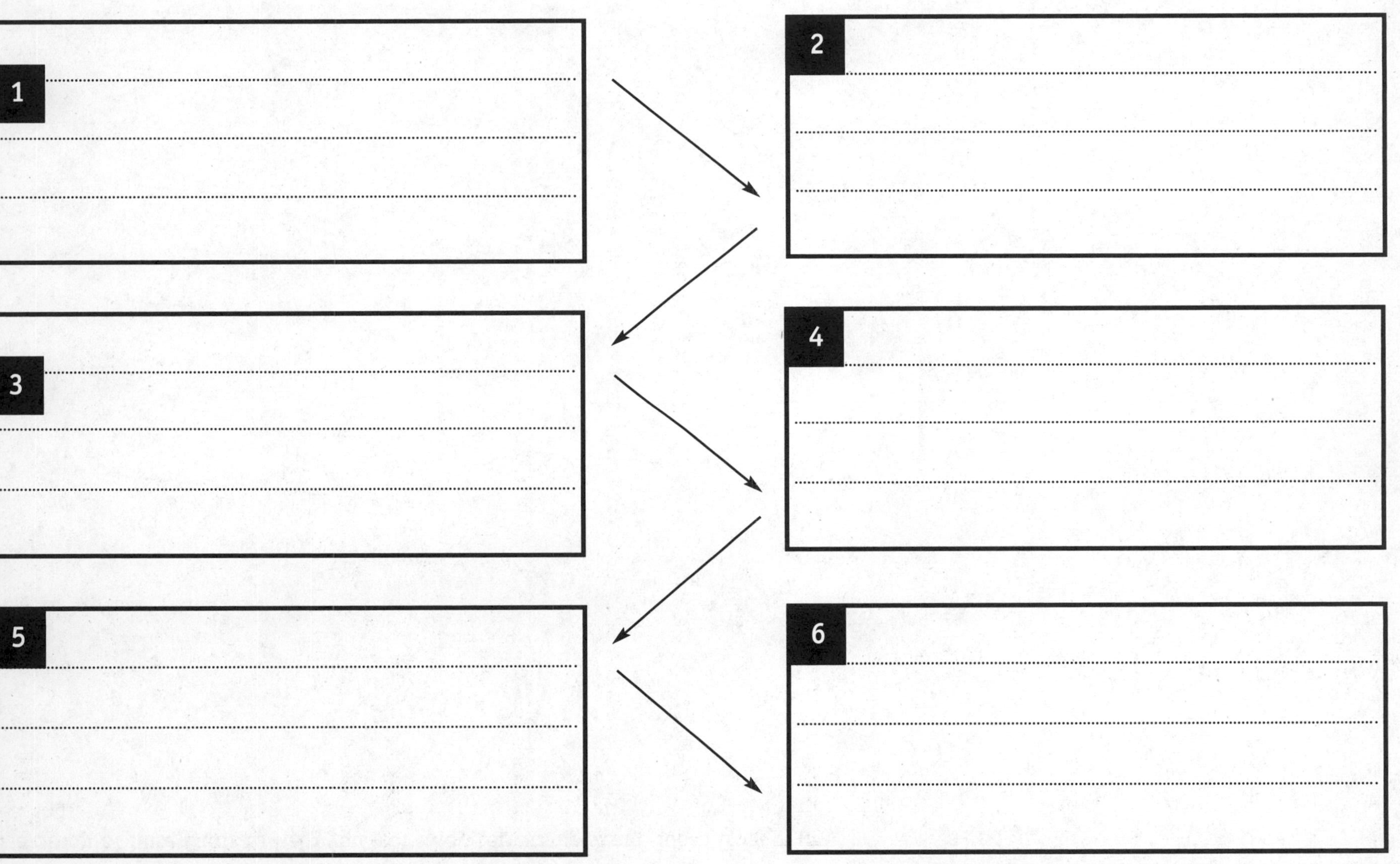

Study or Note Cards

NAME ______________________

Use Study or Note Cards to help you learn key terms, facts, and ideas from your reading.

Summary Notes

NAME

Summary Notes help you focus on the most important parts of what you're reading. You can create a summary for each page in your textbook, each scene in a play, or each chapter in a book.

Title or Topic

Main Point

1.

2.

3.

4.

TIMELINE

NAME ....

Use a Timeline to keep track of a series of dates or events.
It works best when you need to put events in order.

Topic and Theme Organizer

NAME ....

A Topic and Theme Organizer helps you find the theme. First, write the big idea or main topic. Then, tell what the characters say or do related to the topic. Finally, come up with a theme statement that says what's important to learn based on those details.

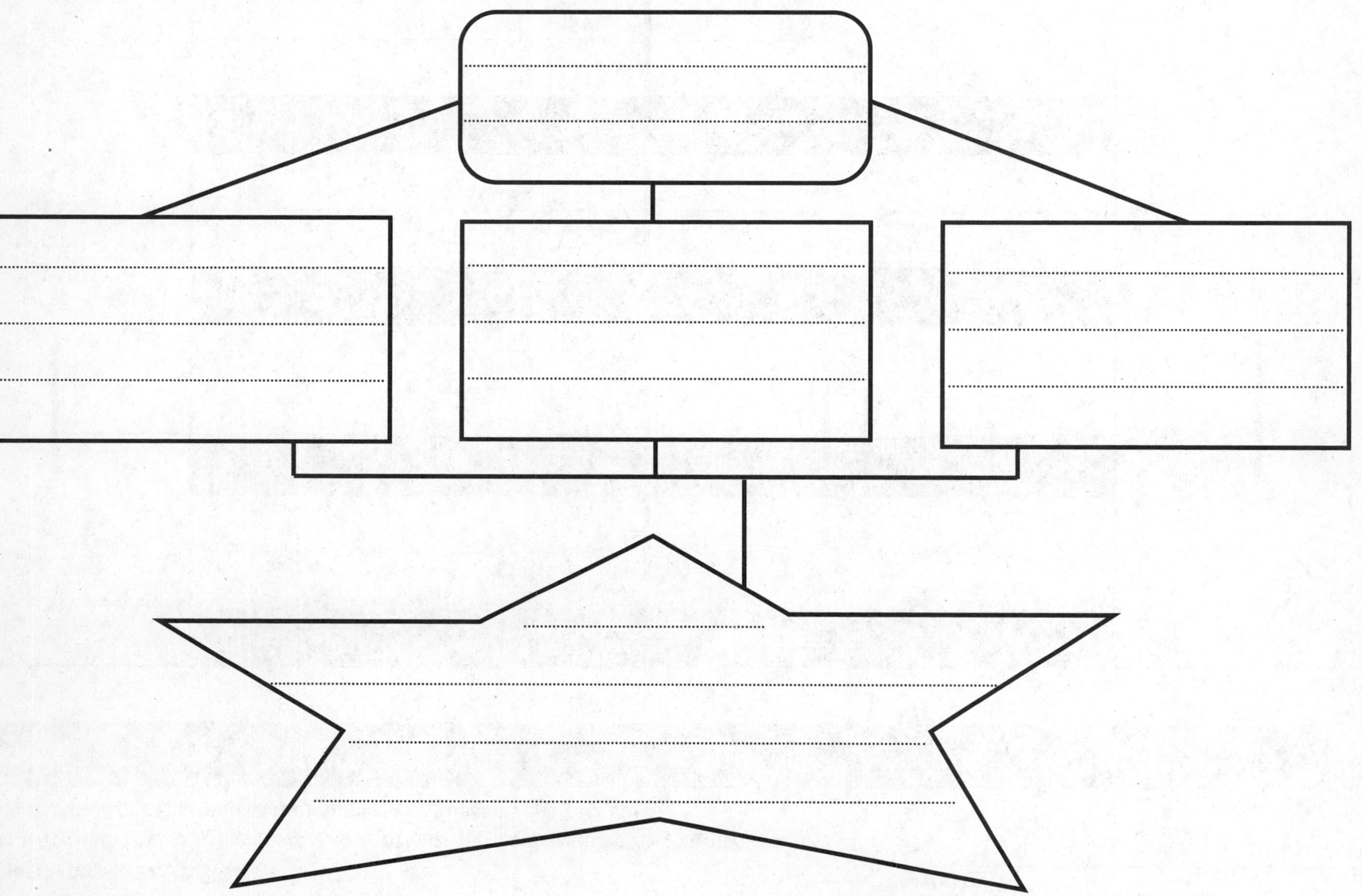

Two-novel Map

NAME ____________________

Use a Two-novel Map to compare and contrast the major elements of two works. This reading tool will help you organize your ideas about the works.

Title	Title
Characters	**Characters**
Setting	**Setting**
Plot	**Plot**
Theme	**Theme**

Conclusions

Venn Diagram

NAME ....

To compare two characters, stories, poems, settings, essays, and so on, use a Venn Diagram. This tool will help you see what's different and what's the same when you compare two things.

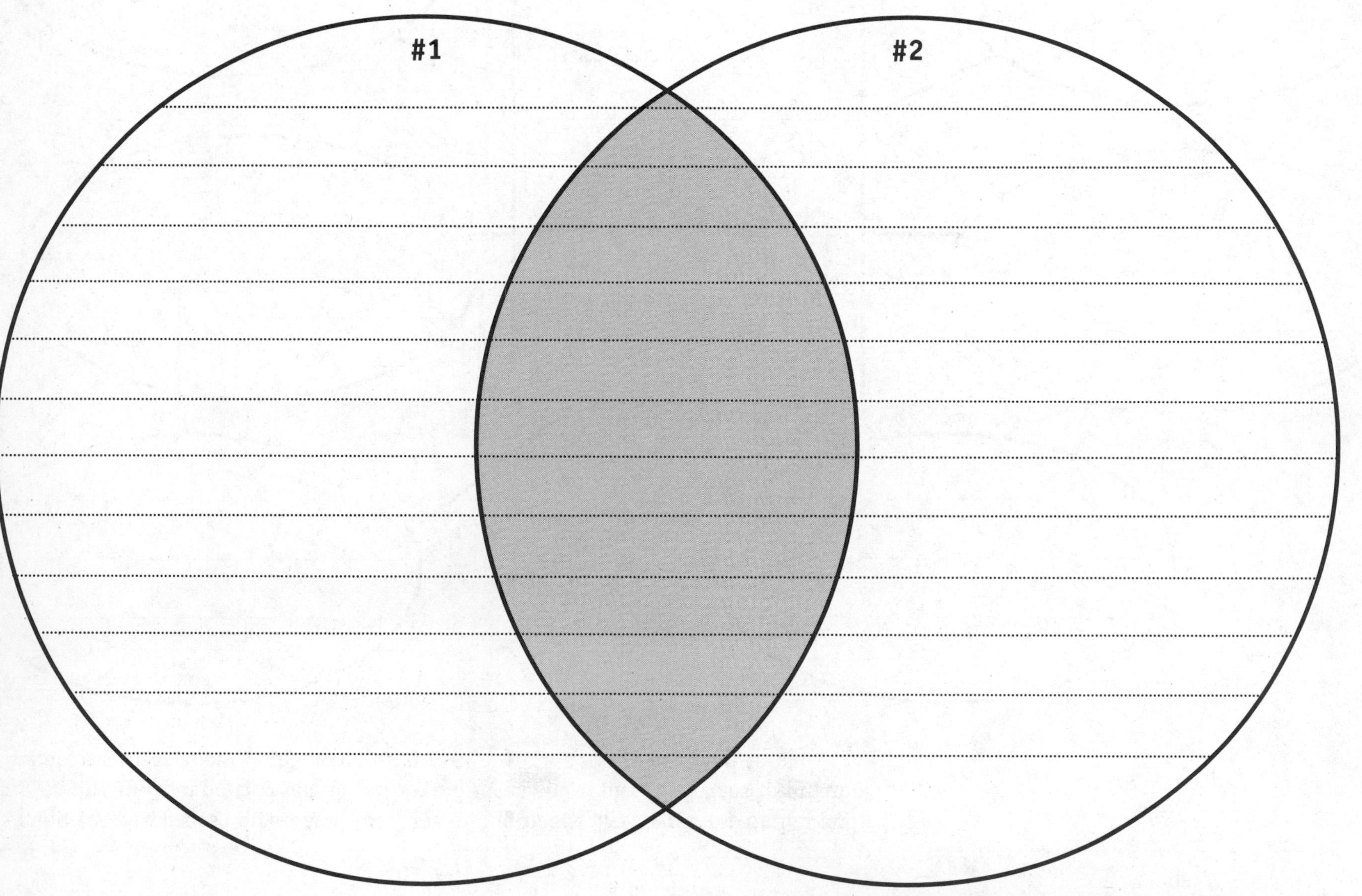

WEB

NAME ....

Webs are great all-purpose organizing tools for taking notes. They work for fiction and nonfiction and link supporting details with main ideas and topics. Use Webs to organize and brainstorm ideas about a character, an event, a word, a viewpoint, and so on.

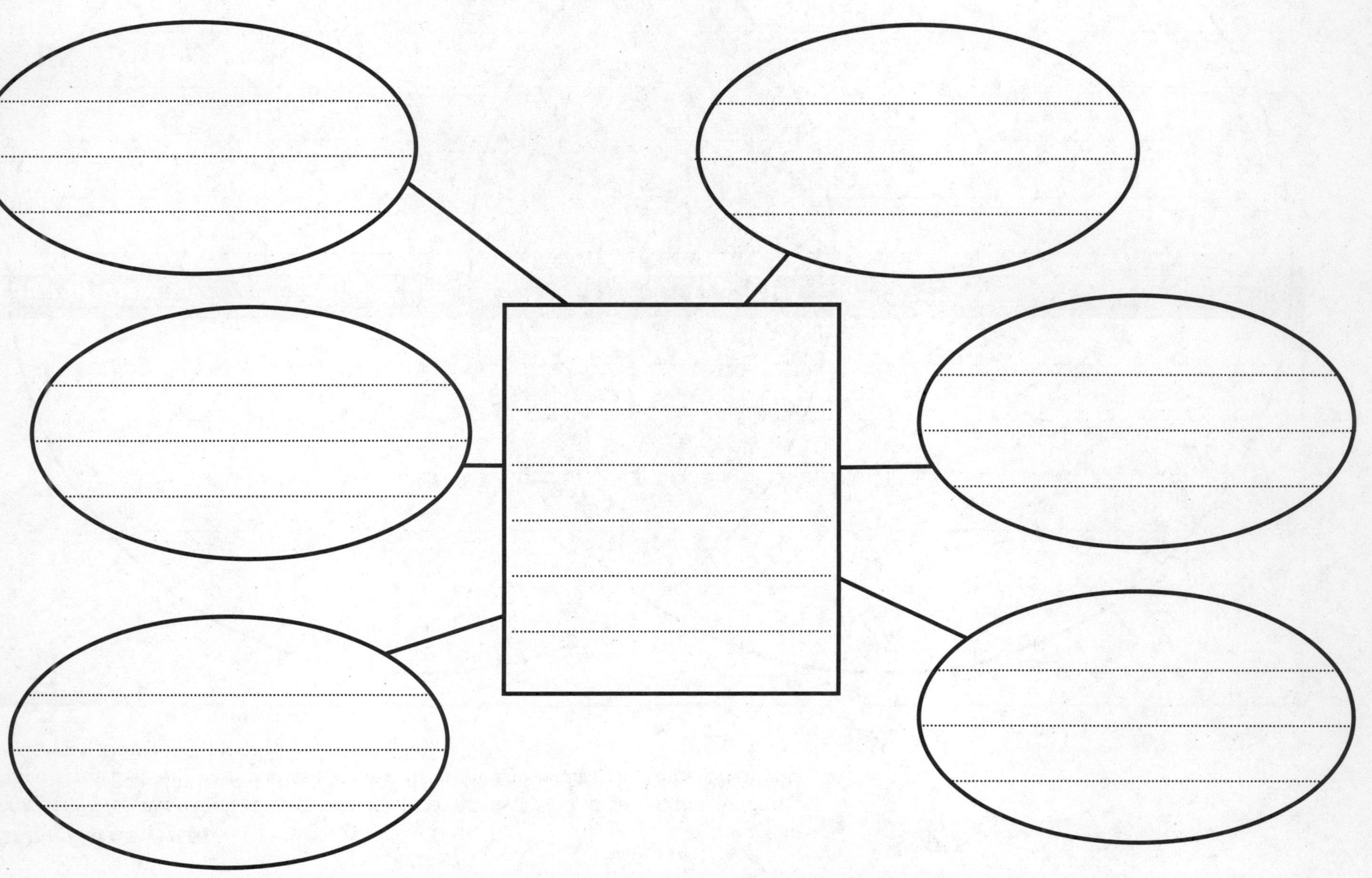

Website Profiler

NAME ____________________

To check out how trustworthy a website is, use a Website Profiler. It looks at who made the site, when it was updated, its point of view, and how good its information is. A Website Profiler helps you judge how reliable a site is.

Name (URL)	
Sponsor	**Date**
Point of View	**Expertise**
Reaction	

Lesson Index